Landscaping

2nd Edition

**by Teri Dunn Chace,
Editors at the National
Gardening Association, Philip Giroux,
Bob Beckstrom, Lance Walheim
Contributions by Michael MacCaskey,
Bill Marken, Sally Roth**

A Wiley Brand

Landscaping For Dummies®, 2nd Edition

Published by: **John Wiley & Sons, Inc.,** 111 River Street, Hoboken, NJ 07030-5774, www.wiley.com

Copyright © 2022 by John Wiley & Sons, Inc., Hoboken, New Jersey

Published simultaneously in Canada

For general information on our other products and services, please contact our Customer Care Department within the U.S. at 877-762-2974, outside the U.S. at 317-572-3993, or fax 317-572-4002. For technical support, please visit https://hub.wiley.com/community/support/dummies.

Wiley publishes in a variety of print and electronic formats and by print-on-demand. Some material included with standard print versions of this book may not be included in e-books or in print-on-demand. If this book refers to media such as a CD or DVD that is not included in the version you purchased, you may download this material at http://booksupport.wiley.com. For more information about Wiley products, visit www.wiley.com.

Library of Congress Control Number: 2021953439

ISBN: 978-1-119-85348-0; ISBN: 978-1-119-85349-7 (ebk); ISBN: 978-1-119-85350-3 (ebk)

SKY10033320_021522

Contents at a Glance

Table of Contents

Introduction

We figure that you can find two kinds of people in the world — those who have waited and waited until they have a home or some property that they can landscape and those who never gave landscaping a second thought and suddenly find themselves having to do just that. Whichever camp you belong to, welcome — this book is for you.

Good landscaping can do many things for you and your home. A well-planned landscape beautifies your house, wedding it with the surroundings and making it a part of a neighborhood or native terrain. And doing so increases the home's value. Landscaping also makes your house and yard more useful and better able to complement your family's lifestyle, whether you hardly ever step foot in your backyard or want to spend every possible moment outdoors.

Appropriate landscaping can also be functional. Trees can shade your home to increase your comfort and reduce energy use. Thorny shrubs can create an impenetrable barrier against possible intruders. Groundcovers and lawns reduce dust from bare ground and can be a play area. Entertain or eat outdoors on a patio or deck. And if you leave room for a garden, you can have fresh salads, veggies, and herbs to enjoy on that patio or deck.

A good landscape also solves problems, providing privacy from nearby neighbors, preventing erosion on steep ground, or channeling water out of soggy, low spots.

Last but not least, a yard you landscape yourself (or with a little help) roots you in place and becomes a place of beauty and sanctuary.

About This Book

Landscaping For Dummies provides you a mixture of ideas, step-by-step instructions, and answers to practical questions like:

>> "Do I have enough space for this?"

>> "Will this look right with the style of my house?"

>> "How much time will I need to spend taking care of this?"

>> "Can I really afford this?"

>> "What is the best choice for this spot?"

If all you really want is a shady, secluded spot to hang a hammock, this book can help you. If your plans are more ambitious and include a large brick patio, sweeping flowerbeds, and a potting shed, we can get you there, too.

You see, the steps to designing any landscape, whether simple or sophisticated, are the same. And there are no shortcuts here. This book takes you from the beginning to the end of the landscaping process — from dreaming up ideas, putting them on paper, and estimating costs to choosing plants and installing substantial structures like patios, decks, and walls. We also know you may not be able to do all the work yourself, so we also tell you when to get help and how to make sure the job is getting done properly.

The only thing we can't do is come over next weekend and help.

This book is organized so that you can pick it up and start anywhere to get at the information you need — just thumb through or browse the Table of Contents in the front or the index in the back.

This is the second, revised, updated edition. A couple of decades have gone by since the first edition. The world has changed, and so have we. Although many of the basic landscaping and gardening principles and techniques remain about the same, we've made some key changes and updates, including the following:

>> New ideas to kick-start your landscape planning.

>> Useful advice and tips for taming your site so the nonplant additions or renovations, such as fences, walls, gates, paths, decks, patios, and so on, are not only long-lasting and attractive, but also sensitive to the way your landscape is already.

>> Tons of updated information and ideas for planting everything from trees to shrubs and vines to flowers, in sun or shade. We separate out and beef up the chapters on annuals, perennials and bulbs, succulents and container gardening, and groundcovers to help you access the information more easily.

>> Insight into lawns and the reality that they take space from actual gardens and consume a lot of resources and time, so you may consider alternative groundcovers.

>> New information about the current trends toward native plants and matching your plant choices more closely to your climate and soil.

>> Straight talk about dealing with critters, from deer to insect pests, and some sensible information and advice about weeds and weed control.

>> Revisions to how you can deal with and prepare for extreme weather and understand climate and climate change.

Foolish Assumptions

When writing this book, we've made a few assumptions about you, our dear reader. We assume the following:

>> You're bored with or disappointed in the way your yard looks, but you need inspiration — and advice — on how to make it better.

>> Although you've greatly admired beautiful plantings or backyard designs, you haven't a clue how to make something like that happen in your own yard.

>> You really want to spend more enjoyable time in your yard but need help figuring out how to block out neighboring properties or views and make yours into a true sanctuary.

>> Buying trips you've made to the garden center have left you overwhelmed and confused. Plants you chose in the past just haven't lasted or done well.

>> Landscaping in an ecologically wise way is important to you, but you don't know how or where to begin.

>> You've experienced success with DIY indoor projects and feel ready, willing, and able to tackle your outdoor spaces, but need guidance and information.

Icons Used in This Book

Throughout this book, you can find icons — small pictures next to the text that point out extra-important information. Here's what they all mean:

TIP

For gems of accumulated wisdom — quite often the kind learned by painful experience! — follow this icon.

WARNING

Consider this icon like a stop sign — when you see it, stop and pay extra attention, because we only use it to help you avoid serious mistakes or bodily harm.

REMEMBER

You're trying to work correctly and efficiently *and* to be sensitive to the environment. Problem is, you may not always know what's right and what isn't. When you see this icon, we're pretty certain that we're steering you in the proper direction.

TECHNICAL STUFF

This icon highlights the jargon and concepts that you need to know, either to communicate with your contractor or to understand and buy materials and plants for yourself.

Beyond This Book

This book is chock-full of tips and other pieces of helpful advice you can use as you landscape your yard. If you want some additional tidbits of wisdom, check out the book's Cheat Sheet at www.dummies.com. Just search for "Landscaping For Dummies Cheat Sheet."

Where to Go from Here

We hope you're starting to feel excited about your new landscape and the creative juices are starting to flow. So, now what? You can flip through the index or Table of Contents to find a subject that interests you.

Or you can turn to whatever section looks to have the answers and information you're wanting most, whether it's Part 2's chapter on paths, Part 3's chapter on using containers in your landscape, or Part 5's "theme" gardens. You can backtrack to drawing a plan or taming a slope later; it's all here.

When you're ready, roll up your sleeves and let us empower and guide into making the home landscape you've always wanted. It's easier than you think and more fun than you can imagine.

1

Getting Started with Landscaping

Chapter **1**

Designing Your Landscape: The Birth of Your Design

Just envision it: You walk out your back door to a beautiful, comfortable oasis. Transforming your yard isn't only totally doable, but the process is also rewarding and yes, fun. The new look begins with new thinking: figuring out what you want most, finding inspiring ideas, and dovetailing those dreams with practical considerations.

Your new, improved landscape should be a place you and those you live with genuinely enjoy and use. The *hardscape* (the parts of your landscape that are physically hard, like a deck or fence) can create an outdoor room for relaxing as well as for entertaining from time to time. The plants can provide bright color, privacy, sunblock, or minimal maintenance — whatever you're looking for. The idea is to make it *yours*, personalized the way *you* like it. It will become your outdoor home, practical *and* pretty.

Here we encourage you to think what's possible. You can cross the bridge between dreaming and reality. We show you how in this chapter.

Starting with Dreams — Create Your Wish List

A landscape can be whatever suits you. Experienced landscape designers often say something like "Form follows function," which simply means that a landscape should meet the needs of the people who use it. In other words, you can design the most elaborate landscape with thousands of dollars' worth of beautiful plants and expensive paving, but if you can't find a comfortable place to set up the barbeque and you *love* to grill, what good is such a yard to you?

The place to start, really, is with a wish list. Here are some possibilities to jog your thinking. Do make your own list and tinker with it. This process is your time to be creative, so have fun:

>> Create a sanctuary for pollinators, butterflies, and/or birds.

>> Grow and harvest fresh herbs for cooking.

>> Create low-maintenance flowerbeds.

>> Raise food for your family.

>> Make a space that's private and shielded from noise and distractions.

>> Work with color ideas to make some really beautiful displays.

>> Play catch (or fetch) on the lawn (with your kids or dog).

>> Cut fresh flower bouquets.

>> Reduce water bills and maintenance costs.

>> Entertain guests in comfort and style.

>> Sip adult beverages while lounging around a firepit.

>> Create a shady retreat.

>> Garden in harmony with nature.

>> Enclose your yard in living plants rather than fencing.

>> Grow vegetables and fruit for canning.

>> Swing in a hammock with a good book (or take a nap).

>> Replace dull foundation plantings.

>> Play sports such as volleyball, badminton, croquet, or flag football.

>> Add a lot more color, especially in nonpeak times.

- » Enjoy the garden after the sun goes down.
- » Erect a buffer between you and neighboring properties.
- » Swim in a pool or soak in a spa.
- » Admire fish and waterlilies in a small pond.
- » Supervise kids in a sand box, play structure, or fort.
- » Make a small garden seem bigger or more interesting.
- » Compost lawn clippings, raked leaves, and kitchen scraps.
- » View colorful flowers or container plants.
- » Grow gorgeous roses.
- » Grow scented flowers and fragrant herbs.
- » Make an attractive yard that stands out in your neighborhood.
- » Create a meadow of wildflowers.
- » Cook and serve meals outdoors.
- » Relax in the shade created by a vine-covered pergola.
- » Install a gazebo and make a path out to it.
- » Make a resilient landscape, one that can tolerate challenging weather.
- » Hold barbecue parties or potluck dinners.

After the brainstorming and wish-listing, an important part of this process is looking at what you have with new eyes. Sure, you may have some limitations and parameters, but even you can rethink or work them to your advantage. New possibilities will emerge. As you proceed, your dreams and goals will come into clearer focus.

Gathering good ideas

Collecting new-to-you and fresh, inspirational ideas for your landscape design is in many ways a treasure hunt. The following sections can spur your inspiration.

Plan weekend outings to nurseries

Plants are often displayed at nurseries according to their needs for sun or shade. For example, ferns are displayed in a shade house, whereas daylilies are displayed in full sun. After a visit or two, you can figure out which plants you like and start imagining where to plant them.

Some nurseries offer lectures or demos on weekends, which are usually free and are valuable for gathering information on plants and gardening.

Visit local botanical gardens and arboretums

Check out the labels and interpretative signage. Some of the plants may be unusual, but more than likely they're proven in your climate. Find out, too, if the venue is hosting speakers or holding workshops. If so, sign up and attend. Such events are often free or inexpensive, giving you the opportunity to learn while meeting other gardeners.

Join a garden club or plant society

These groups frequently have informative speakers at their meetings and periodically offer garden tours. Garden tours are great because they offer you the opportunity to observe the use of various landscape elements, both hardscape and plants. Your local nursery should be able to hook you up with garden clubs or societies dedicated to specific plants, like the Rose Society or Rhododendron Society.

Tour your neighbors' yards

Ask people how they did what they did. You may find that even normally reserved or private people love to talk about their yard. Also, seeing the level of landscaping in your neighborhood gives you a benchmark on the level and quality of landscaping that the neighborhood warrants.

Go online

Start with social media, such as Pinterest, Instagram, and Facebook. Search for "landscaping design ideas" and specific wishes to find many sites, blogs, and images.

TIP

In particular, pause at the websites of landscape designers, which tend to tout dreamy completed jobs, often with before-and-after images or progress shots. They can give you clues as to how planning and building can proceed. You'll also pick up on philosophies and techniques you can use.

Subscribe to garden magazines or trawl their websites

They can increase your warehouse of knowledge on plants and their uses.

Of course, after you subscribe or provide your email address, you soon receive every mail-order plant catalog in the country or are added to those email lists, which is great for you.

Create idea caches on your computer's desktop, or manually clip articles or images that interest you and make idea-board collages. Or make folders organized by plant type. Here are labels on some of the folders we keep: bulbs, perennials, annuals, evergreen trees and shrubs, deciduous trees and shrubs, vines, tools, lawns and groundcovers, bugs (both good and bad), plant diseases, decks and patios, garden paths, and garden furniture.

Magazines and catalogs can also alert you to problems in the care and maintenance of plants in the landscape. Magazines including *Garden Design*, *The English Garden*, *Gardens Illustrated*, and *Gardenista* are sources of inspiration geared more to design ideas, whereas *Fine Gardening*, *Horticulture*, *Garden Gate*, *Birds & Blooms*, *Better Homes & Gardens*, and *Sunset* offer lots of practical information on plants and planting.

Chat with a Master Gardener

Your closest Cooperative Extension office can put you in touch with a Master Gardener, or alert you to any event or gathering a group of them may be planning. Master Gardeners are knowledgeable about plants and gardening. They can answer your questions and point you to good resources, including their favorite suppliers in your area.

THINKING LONG TERM

How long you plan to live in your house influences your landscape planning. If you're only planning to live in your house a couple of years, concentrate on fast-growing trees and shrubs to give you a more powerful effect sooner. Expensive projects like a deck or gazebo may add to the value of your home, but you may not recoup those costs before you're ready to move.

In general, the shorter your stay, the less complex your landscape plans should be. If you plan to stay in your house for a long time, go ahead and tackle more difficult projects, such as adding a deck, fence, pool, or patio (see Part 2).

Are you or someone else in your home aging, or planning to stay and garden at this address until older? Is anyone, of any age, handicapped or mobility-challenged (regular visitors or residents)? Sooner or later, you and your landscape design may need to accommodate these specialized needs. Among the design ideas that facilitate such folks are: wider, flatter smoother paths providing access to different spots, elevated gardening beds, comfortable (shady) places to sit, and specialized maintenance tools. Among many great resources for ideas and advice is www.accessiblegardens.com.

Use this book

Flip to Part 2 of this book for information on building hardscape and Part 3 for ideas on plants. You can also check out the latest edition of *Gardening Basics For Dummies* by Steven Frowine and the Editors of the National Gardening Association (John Wiley & Sons, Inc.).

Drawing within the Lines: Living with Practical Issues

Some parts — only a few, don't fret — of working with your landscape are non-negotiable. Here we discuss them in greater detail, in case one or more applies to your situation. Although they may be necessary considerations, they don't need to derail your dreams. Just find ways to address them.

Making sure you know where your property lines are

Our advice here is quite blunt: Don't work near or on the bounds unless you know where the bounds are. By that, we mean, don't plan a change, or don't start up a new fence, hedge, or any landscaping project close to the edges of your property unless you know for certain where the legal lines are.

REMEMBER

You won't find your property lines drawn on the ground. If you're lucky, though, you may find *monuments,* or markers, at one or more property corners. These markers may be conspicuous posts driven into the ground, but more likely, they're small pipes, rebar, or brass medallions, often buried over time under soil. Property corners at the street are usually marked by small crosses inscribed in the concrete curb or gutter. If you can't find your markers easily, ask your immediate neighbors or long-time residents living nearby. As a good-neighbor policy, you may want to conduct the search with your immediate neighbors anyway, especially to clarify the ownership of fences.

Keep in mind that your actual property line may be set back several feet/a meter or so from its markers. Also check your deed to see whether the street occupies an easement along the front of your property (an *easement* essentially means that your city, county, or neighbors may use the space if ever needed).

When you can't verify your property lines, you need to hire a professional land surveyor (PLS); they can also provide seasoned advice about any disputes or ambiguities.

REMEMBER

Tax maps, sorry to report, are estimations and won't hold up in a legal dispute. Deeds have written descriptions, not so useful to you in this situation. If your deed references a recent survey map, that can be useful . . . you can trace it.

Verifying whether you need permits

If you're contemplating some new and substantial features or dramatic changes (a grade change or rerouting where water flows, for example), make sure you call your municipality permitting office to find out if a permit is required. New decks, patios, and water features are among the items that some municipalities regulate.

WARNING

Don't find out the hard way that you've planned, or worse, completed something that isn't allowed or doesn't meet codes. The penalty can be anything from a citation and fine, to an order to dismantle what you installed, or both.

Lawns remain popular in front yards, at least, in some areas. You may have read about homeowners who turned their front yard into a food garden or a wildflower meadow, only to get in trouble. (This stance is changing in some areas, though. For more on lawns and lawn alternatives, see Chapter 16.)

REMEMBER

If you live in a development, make sure to check the covenants of your HOA (homeowner's association) to see if there are any restrictions on hardscapes and plantings.

Considering children and pets' safety

If you have children or pets living with you or visiting now and then, their safety isn't just a matter of showing you care. Their safety can be or become a legal issue. When you have concerns or questions, check with your local municipality or homeowners association.

Here are a few basic principles to bear in mind:

>> **Incorporate raised beds or elevated planter boxes (for flowers as well as vegetables or herbs).** Kids and pets tend to prefer flat, easily accessible areas.

>> **Take out, and don't plant, any plants known to have poisonous leaves or berries.** Look them up; the information is readily available online. Cross-check with the American Association of Poison Control Centers. When in doubt, err on the side of caution and remove/avoid.

>> **Avoid planting thorny bushes or trees, especially in high-traffic areas.** These obstruct sightlines and access and also can snag or scratch skin and clothing.

>> **Monitor children and pets when they are in the yard**. Doing so is especially important if you lack fences or have a water feature.

>> **Never leave your tools, supplies, or sprays lying about . . . or even accessible.** Kids are curious, and these items are often hazards. Better safe than sorry — put stuff away, up high, out of reach. If you've decanted garden chemicals or sprays into other containers (jugs, jars, sprayers), be sure they're both clearly labeled *and* stored out of reach.

>> **Don't set up a play structure or swing set close to trees, fences, or the property line/neighbor's yards.** You don't want to risk injury or damage, to people *or* property.

Consider creating areas especially for children and pets, so the rest of the landscape is (ideally) freed up for your many other ideas and plans. Kids need places to play, relax, hide, or make forts. Get them involved in designing their areas and helping you around the yard. (How about a bean-pole teepee? Or a sunflower house?) Perhaps have a storage area or bench for their toys (see the section, "Designating storage areas," later in this chapter for ideas).

Dogs are creatures of habit and will mark, and lounge, in the same spots, especially if you train them that way. If you create a run or outdoor play yard for a dog, make sure it's big enough for the breed, has shade/shelter from the hot sun, and is easy to clean. As for sandboxes, if cats are in the area, keep the box covered when not in use (because cats think they're litter boxes)!

Addressing water issues

Whether you have too much or too little, anticipating water issues is a big part of landscape design. We're not just talking about make sure you have a faucet for a hose hookup not too far from the flowerbed. There are two major areas of concern here, both related to climate/weather and both within your ability to exercise at least some measure of control:

>> **Flood control:** Your property may need a retention area to hold runoff during a major storm event. This tends to be more likely and urgent if your property slopes. Some municipal codes require residential properties to be ready for a 6- to 8-inch (15.2 to 20.3 cm) rain event. Check with City Hall and your codes officer and/or call a professional landscaper in your area to clarify and get advice.

>> **Collecting water:** In dry climates or areas with very long, hot summers, homeowners look for ways to gather and use what water they can for their yards and gardens. This can be anything from installing a so-called *rain garden* (a garden set up to deliberately receive and benefit from water running from your house's gutters) to setting up a rain-collection barrel to using *gray water* (basically, used household water from sinks and drains). You may get necessary information and guidance from your municipality and/or a local professional. For more discussions on all these avenues, check Chapter 5.

Designating storage areas

Inevitably, you need designated areas in your home landscape for storing things when you aren't using them and to avoid clutter. Vehicles may or may not go in the garage along with your gardening equipment, tools, and supplies.

When creating your landscape design, make sure you don't forget your storage needs. Here are some ideas:

>> **Storage shed:** You may need a shed dedicated to yard and garden maintenance if you don't already have one. Having one for your tools and garden supplies can help alleviate any crowding in your garage. (Or if you don't have a garage, a shed is a great place to keep all your yard gadgets and tools.) Think about how big it needs to be and where you want it. Don't forget to figure out if will block access or sun. Last but not least, for security and safety, be sure it has a latching or locking door.

>> **Potting shed:** These often look like playhouses, complete with shuttered windows and windowboxes, but they can be as practical as they are cute. Install shelves and hooks, a utility or dry sink, a potting bench, and hanging nesting wire baskets for storing gardening tools and supplies. You can also use a shed as a cool, dry place to dry freshly harvested bundles of herbs and to store stacked unused pots. (A *she-shed* is similar but may be less practical. It may look the same on the outside, but inside, harbors a comfy snoozing or reading nook, or art supplies.)

>> **Storage bins:** These can be anything from weather-tough plastic bins with fitted lids that get stashed somewhere until needed to the outdoor equivalent of a parson's bench — that is, a bench on your deck or patio whose seat lifts up to allow storage within.

>> **Outdoor closet:** This can be tall and skinny and perhaps fit into a corner. It's a place to store or hang long-handled tools such as rakes and shovels as well as perhaps a coiled hose and other useful items.

TIP

Make a list of items you expect to be storing; doing so helps clarify what you have and where you plan to put it. If you're good with numbers, you can go ahead and calculate the amount of space (volume) your stored tool collection would require and then you'll really know the size you need.

Site Analysis — Understanding What You Have

Here we come to grips with your property the way it is now:

>> What are its strengths and weaknesses?

>> What do you like or dislike about your yard?

>> What kind of problems does your landscape have that you need to find solutions for?

This process of assessing your yard is called *site analysis.* This is the time to make a rough drawing. To do some serious drawing — with dimensions — check out Chapter 3.

Figure 1-1 is a sample of what your initial site analysis can look like when you're finished. You identify what you have to work with and imagine what improvements will be there soon.

The following sections help you analyze your site and include some common approaches to help you think fresh and creative thoughts about your landscape. The object here is to bring your unique landscape and its possibilities into sharper focus.

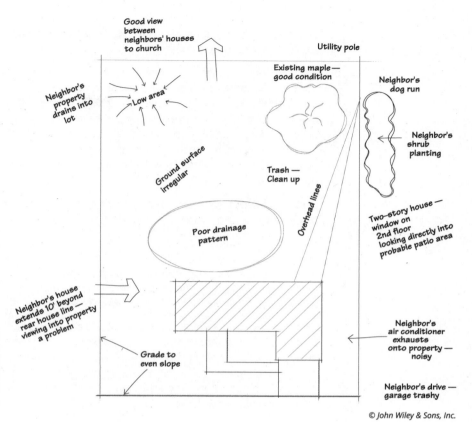

Good view between neighbors' houses to church

Utility pole

Existing maple— good condition

Neighbor's dog run

Neighbor's property drains into lot

Low area

Neighbor's shrub planting

Ground surface irregular

Trash — Clean up

Overhead lines

Two-story house — window on 2nd floor looking directly into probable patio area

Poor drainage pattern

Neighbor's house extends 10' beyond rear house line — viewing into property a problem

Neighbor's air conditioner exhausts onto property — noisy

Grade to even slope

Neighbor's drive — garage trashy

© John Wiley & Sons, Inc.

FIGURE 1-1: A completed site analysis notes significant features of the property.

Drawing your site analysis

Stick to these steps as you draw your site analysis:

1. **Get a sheet of paper and a pencil and sketch your existing property.**

    Include your house with windows and doors, existing plants, and general north/south directions. Although you should try to draw to scale, your rough drawing doesn't have to be very precise.

2. **Go outside and put the drawing on a clipboard and walk around your yard, making notations of the following:**

    -   **Sun and shade:** Mark areas that are sunny or shady, and at what times of the day.

    -   **Views:** Note good and bad views — ones that you may want to preserve and ones you may want to block.

Good views — surrounding hills, the coast, maybe just the nearby skyline — are easy to recognize.

Bad views, on the other hand, take a little more eyeballing. For instance, determine whether the neighbors can see in your yard or you can see in theirs, or whether you feel the need to block your view of their garage or old-car collection. Determine whether you have things on your own property, like a utility or storage area, that you'd rather not see. Figure out what you'll see if you put in a raised deck. Look to see whether utility poles are visible. Check how the view changes when deciduous trees lose their leaves.

- **Prevailing winds:** Note if you regularly feel winds that you may be able to block with fencing or plants.

- **Slope and drainage:** Put in some arrows that give you a rough idea of the contours of your yard. Sloping ground or uneven terrain can be an interesting part of a landscape, especially if you accentuate it with walls or plants combined with stone to simulate a dry streambed. High points may also provide some views that you want to take advantage of.

On the other hand, sloping ground can also mean erosion or drainage problems that can threaten your house or yard. Be sure that water drains away from all the walls of your house. Mark down any areas that seem overly wet or where moss or algae is growing. If you can stand getting wet, go outside in a rainstorm and watch where excess water flows. Just don't take your clipboard with you!

WARNING

Chances are, your landscape isn't isolated, which means that changes you make can adversely affect a neighbor's property. Routing your drainage off your land and onto theirs isn't the answer (and of course, not a recipe for neighborhood harmony — no holiday card!). So, too, can your alterations lead to erosion beyond your property lines. Therefore, you must work to avoid such scenarios and find solutions that work within your own property. If the situation is daunting, seek advice/help from a professional.

- **Existing plants:** Draw in large trees, shrubs, vines, and perennials that you may want to preserve. (Leave out or cross off ones that you mean to get rid of.)

- **Interesting natural features:** A small stream or handsome rocks protruding from the ground can become special landscape features.

- **Noise, smells, and lights:** Let your senses go and write down anything else that you notice — lights at night, noise from next door, and even unpleasant odors. You may be able to do something about them.

- **Winter sights and sounds:** Look to see whether your plants are getting crushed by snow under the eaves. Determine where you put the snow when shoveling or snowblowing, or where a snowplow shoves piles. Be sure to avoid planting or installing seating in those areas.

Do this over a period of several days, at different times of the day. Doing so will give you an opportunity to observe your landscape better or more completely than you perhaps ever have before. In particular, notice when the sun shines (or doesn't) in different areas and for how long.

TECHNICAL STUFF

Does your yard have *microclimates*? Many do! This term refers to a spot that has different and unique conditions, compared to the rest of your landscape. Instead of struggling to alter its natural inclinations, we suggest you capitalize on them. To do so, for example, find moisture-loving plants for a soggy spot. Place a comfy chair in the perpetually shady corner, and put in ferns and other shade-loving plants around it.

3. **Make notations of what you see from *inside* the house including:**

- **Views:** Note the good views and the bad. Look out your windows; what do you see? A nice view of the yard or the neighbors' back porch? Determine who can see in the windows from the street or next door.

- **Sunlight:** Note whether the sun blazes through your windows, heating the house in the afternoon. Or perhaps you get a pleasant light that's cast on the kitchen table as you drink coffee in the morning.

- **Lights:** Observe whether car lights or signs shine through your window at night. (Ask yourself if a tree or even a vine-covered trellis could block that problem.)

4. **Where applicable, consider the needs outlined in the section, "Drawing within the Lines: Living with Practical Issues," earlier in this chapter.**

Note whether you're already accommodating these needs. Are you satisfied/happy? Can you reserve or even add space?

Knowing how much of your yard you can use

Most houses are plunked somewhere in the middle of the lot. Though the surrounding areas may vary in size, you almost always have a front yard, a backyard, and often two side yards — that's called a *four-sided landscape*.

At first, you may have a tough time overcoming the tradition that backyards are where you actually live, front yards are for show, and side yards (if any) are mostly ignored. We suggest you think outside the box and break some of those old rules.

A DAY IN THE LIFE

An accurate sense of where light falls and when in your landscape is so important. Even if you're not home when the sun is full-on a flowerbed, the plants will know — and you'll have planted sun-lovers. So, observe at morning, noon, and evening, and make note. When you're ready to purchase plants for your landscape (flip to Part 3), this information helps you match plants with appropriate light conditions.

Noting sunny and shady areas can also give you ideas about creating more comfortable outdoor living space. In midsummer, the south and western sides of the house are the sunniest and warmest. If you live in areas with cooler summers, place outdoor furniture in those same locations. If, however, you live in an area with hot summers, look into adding shade trees (see Chapter 11) or perhaps installing an arbor or pergola (see Chapter 10).

REMEMBER

Multitask and be flexible. Using your entire yard allows you to take advantage of different times of the day when one part or another of your landscape is at its best. If your backyard is baked on summer afternoons, you can retreat to the cool respite out front. If the under-eight crowd swarms over the play structure, perhaps you can move around to a side yard where you can discreetly keep an eye on the goings-on. A shady nook way in the back of the backyard can allow you to tune out the drone of a weed-whacker a few houses away. These sections break down the parts of your entire yard and give you some ideas to utilize them as potential living spaces.

Your front yard

Shield the front yard with walls of greenery or a privacy fence (flip to Chapter 6), and on weekend afternoons when the rest of the neighborhood is carousing in their backyards, you'll have the front all to yourself.

If you think that's too bold of a step (and it may well be for your neighborhood — or, as we keep cautioning, if you have an HOA), at least you can move some of your ornamental garden beds to the front instead of having a resource-gobbling, boring lawn. Give your home more curb appeal.

You may be surprised at how quickly a beautification copycat campaign can start up after the neighbors see you puttering among the flowers and butterflies.

TIP

Be aware that you may need to keep your front yard neat to avoid neighborhood resentment — in fact, your local municipality may even have a word with you about the state of your yard. If you're inspired to plant a prairie or a naturalistic woodland out front, talk to your neighbors first (and check with your local municipality) so that they know what you have in mind. Keep well-groomed paths so that the landscape looks guided instead of frighteningly wild. (The reaction that you're trying to avoid is "Oh no! What if those weeds come into my yard?")

Your backyard

Backyards are usually best for children's play areas because you don't want them to career out or chase balls into the street. If you're a veggie grower with kids, put your patch near the play area so you can keep one eye on them while you weed the zukes.

REMEMBER

Vegetable patches don't have to be relegated to the backyard — put them wherever the light and soil and convenience are best. Who could kvetch about a well-tended patch, planted in an interesting design of diagonals or squares with vegetables that are interspersed with flowers and herbs? Call it a "kitchen garden" if that helps elevate its reputation. (Keep in mind, though, that food gardens definitely have an off-season that is less attractive.)

Your side yard

Some properties, particularly in housing tracts, have side yards. They're often narrow, sometimes shady, and they're usually overlooked as nothing more than a way to get from the front yard to the back or a place to stash the trash and recycling bins. Give yourself reason to linger by setting up a hammock or moving a bistro table and chair to the area.

If it's sunny, your side yard can be the perfect place for a strawberry patch or a row of raspberry bushes. It can host a whimsical garden ornament of some kind or another (here's the place for your pink flamingo or garden gnome), a small garden pool or fountain, a little herb garden, maybe — and it will become a destination and a sanctuary of its own instead of a waystation.

Walking through the space

You may already have thought about what friends and family intend to do in the yard — picnicking, socializing, growing tomatoes, playing, and so on — but you may also want to think about how you and your family move through your yard.

Your list of outdoor wants and needs — eating, playing, sitting — is a lot simpler to divvy up when spaces are already separate, thanks to the geography of the yard and house. Chances are, you already know where the best patch of lawn is for that pitch-and-catch area you need. You also know the most discreet place to stash the compost pile. You know which neighbor will hate having to see your dog's kennel or run from their bedroom window and which one will sneak your pup a treat when they're outside. You know where the sun beats down on late summer afternoons — perfect for an herb garden — and where the neighbor's oak tree casts a cool pool of shade for those patio cookouts that you can't wait to indulge in.

As you begin to get an idea of where the best places are for all the things on your wish list, stroll around and figure out the routes that will get you and others from one area to the next. As you begin fiddling with potential pathways, you may discover that they can make your garden seem bigger. Obscured by shrubs, ornamental grasses, or other tall plants, paths can double back, twist and turn, and run along for much longer than you may think in a limited space. (Chapter 7 is chockfull of information on designing and building pathways.)

TIP

If you're having trouble visualizing your paths, try this quick trick: sprinkle a biodegradable path of flour or oatmeal through your yard. You can see in a minute whether your path design works.

Focusing on privacy

Even if your neighbors aren't the busybody type, you may still find relief in building in privacy as you create your landscape plan. (Chapters 12 and 20 have ideas, including plant suggestions, for creating privacy.)

Here are some good ways to enclose and protect your yard or parts of it:

>> Tall hedges (see Chapter 12), and arbors (flip to Chapter 10) work wonders at making your yard your own space.

>> Trees are a natural for providing privacy, though if you install new ones, you'll either have to invest in bigger, more expensive specimens or be patient. See Chapter 11 for all sorts of options and ideas.

>> Walls, fences, and even privacy screens help to keep your noise in and other noise out — so that you don't have to keep shushing your kids or resenting the neighbor's kid with his noisy car. (Turn to Chapter 6.)

>> Privacy structures define the boundaries of your landscape. Imagine decorating your living room if it had no walls. A little tricky to make it feel cozy, isn't it? Outdoor living rooms work the same way. Walls make the furnishings — in this case, the plants and ornaments — look better by providing a backdrop. Put that dream fountain you invested in against a wall of lush greenery, and it becomes much more appealing than if the sidewalk, street, or a neighbor's yard forms the backdrop.

Knowing when you'll use your landscape

When dreaming up your ideal landscape, take into account the times of day *and* the times of year in which you plan to use your yard. For example:

>> If you plan to be outdoors in the late afternoon, figure out where you'll be most comfortable at that time of day. Maybe the shady spot under the big tree out back. If the sun shines hot where a patio is or may be, consider installing an overhead structure for shade or planting shade trees.

>> If you want to use the garden (or view the garden) at night, investigate and install well-chosen lighting (see Chapter 10).

>> If you still want to be outdoors during the rainy season, investigate creating a covered patio.

>> If bugs populate the yard at the same time that you do (summer evenings), a screened-in porch or patio will keep them at bay.

>> If you want to get outdoors early in the spring or well into autumn, keep or plant trees and structures that don't block the sun.

>> If you enjoy every minute of summer outdoors, choose trees, shrubs, and flowers that bloom throughout the season (refer to Part 3).

MULTIPURPOSE LANDSCAPING

You have tons of ideas but limited space. No worries. Design some parts of your home landscape to play more than one role or serve multiple purposes. Think functional as well as beautiful. You can find a wide array of good ideas online or by browsing at a garden center. Here are a few examples:

- Terrace a steep site so there are beds of plants alternating with flat, open spaces and stairs connecting them.

- Devote half of a backyard to soft grass for the kids to tumble in, and the other half to a patio or deck with outdoor furniture so they can be easily supervised by lounging adults.

- Replace a lawn with planter boxes flanking wide paths that lead to a destination dining/grilling area.

- Attach decorative containers to a privacy wall or fence, and fill with various colorful and cascading plants.

- Choose food plants that are also beautiful, such as blueberry bushes, Swiss chard, scarlet runner beans, even certain grain plants.

Designing a Low-Maintenance Landscape

Planning your landscape, installing the structures and plants, and admiring your efforts of the finished project are the most gratifying parts of the landscape process. They're also the most time-consuming (whether you do it all yourself, or hire help).

REMEMBER

Maintaining your landscape is just as important, so make sure you include upkeep in your vision and efforts. It's not realistic to ask living plants to thrive on neglect, plus they look so much better and stay in bounds when you tend them. Show you care, and your landscape will repay your attention by being a beautiful, fun, relaxing place to be.

If you want less maintenance, here are some good, sensible ideas:

>> If you're often away, traveling for business or pleasure, you may want a yard with hardscape and very few plants. (See Part 2 for more on hardscape.)

>> Avoid overplanting or using fast-growing plants that get too large for their space. They'll need to be pruned or even, in time, removed.

>> Having cut flowers in annual beds adds lots of color to your yard, but you'll need to replant when you harvest for bouquets. Use lower-maintenance perennials or flowering shrubs instead.

   An *annual* is a plant that completes its life in a single season, and they're generally planted once a year; find out more in Chapter 13. *Perennials,* on the other hand, return year after year and tend to be more full and floriferous as they mature. Chapter 14 explains perennials in more detail.

>> Lawns are a lot of work and consume a lot of resources. Determine whether you want one. Consider having a much smaller one, or instead plant an easy-going groundcover. Check out Chapter 16 for ideas.

>> If you plan to build wooden landscape elements like decks (refer to Chapter 8) and fences (see Chapter 6), plan on painting or applying preservatives every two to three years. Masonry (brick and concrete) needs less maintenance.

>> If you install your landscape without an irrigation system, you end up having to water everything yourself . . . even if you live in a climate where rainfall helps. For a practical discussion on watering and various options, flip to Chapter 5.

Chapter **2**

Thinking like a Designer

M aking an attractive, useful home landscape is both an art and a science. If you're reading this book, you're willing to giving it a go, right?

Designing your property makes it a good and appealing place to be, just like designing the indoors. Take into account your available space, and discover tricks that can make your outside seem either more open or cozier. Color, texture, size, and shape options are endless; the look just depends on your taste. You may well want to include accessories, from the practical to the purely decorative (or items that are actually both). You have lots of choices to ponder, lots of decisions to make, and lots of exciting possibilities to consider.

The object is to create a place that reflects your lifestyle, plant passions, and personality. No need to struggle or stress out with the myriad of choices you have, though. This chapter is here to provide a helpful tour of design principles, tailored to DIY landscapers. That's you. You can do this.

REMEMBER

Landscape is a living canvas. Over time, change is expected and inevitable — as in other areas in your life, nothing is permanent. Watch for opportunities in the future to return to this chapter (and this book) and cook up revisions, improvements, and new ideas.

You get to spend your time, creativity, money, and effort while you can. You'll be maintaining and replacing both plants and hardscape elements while at this address. Live in and love your landscape. You take care of it, and it will take care of you. As the great poet William Blake once remarked, wisely, "Kiss the joy as it flies."

Achieving Unity, Blessed Unity, in Your Landscaping Design

Unity is what keeps all those separate parts of your landscape tied together, so that the eyes and feet of visitors flow from one part of the yard to another. To achieve unity in your landscape, do the following:

» **Clearly define pathways.** Pathways are a first step (no pun intended!) to unifying your landscape. Chapter 7 gives more details how you can add paths and walkways to your design.

» **Link greenery.** A couple of shade trees and a flowering shrub stuck here and there in your lawn *don't* create a unified landscape design. Plant a bed of pachysandra, lirope, or other groundcover or even lay down a thick layer of wood chips at the feet of these to visually link them together, continue the same groundcover along the fence and around the corner to the patio, stick in a couple more of the same sort of flowering shrub at the corner, and presto! Unity.

» **Have a style.** Be clear about what you want the garden to say about you. Consider the following:

- If your tastes run to formal precision, for instance, you probably want clipped hedges, classic statuary, brick or stone pathways, and symmetrical plantings that provide calming mirror images.

- A cottage garden jumble of exuberant flowers with a rustic fence, bent-twig benches, and a concrete frog along the path tells visitors that you're more of a free-spirit type.

A combination of the two styles looks disjointed and has a disquieting effect on your landscape. But having unity in your landscape doesn't mean that you can't have your formal rose garden *and* your wildflower meadow — just don't put them side-by-side. Separated by a hedge, on opposite sides of the house, or linked by a transition zone that gradually makes the shift from control to wilder, your gardens can be as fickle as your little heart desires. Look at the color insert for a way to add unity to your yard.

Focusing on Repetition in Your Design

Repetition of hardscape materials — including brick, wood, stone, concrete, wood chips, and fencing — is a simple way to make your garden look like it's all one piece, even if the areas are distinctly different. The following can make your land-scaping design cohesive:

>> **Select your hardscape materials to match your garden style and repeat them throughout the landscape.** Manmade materials — basically, anything other than plants — carry great weight in the landscape, because they draw viewers' eyes like a magnet.

For example, you can use a single section of diagonal, framed lattice to support a climbing rose along the wall of your house; an L-shaped couple of sections to shield the compost pile from view; or three or four linked sections to serve as a privacy screen along the patio. Depending on how large your yard is, you can repeat the lattice theme in variation by installing solid, vertical-board privacy fence topped by a narrow strip of lattice. (Want a rustic look? Substitute bent-wood or plain lumber. Want a more formal look? Use cast iron and similar-looking materials. You get the idea . . . .)

>> **Stick in the same plants here and there.** (Think, "Here a shrub, there a shrub.") Repeat backbone plants that perform well most of the year, like evergreens (see Chapter 11), groundcovers (refer to Chapter 16), and shrubs (check out Chapter 12), to tie your garden areas to each other.

>> **Repeat shapes to pull things together.** Consider curved outlines of beds, undulating paths, shapely urns, and mounds of plants. At the other end of the spectrum, try no-nonsense point A to point B paths, yardstick-straight bed edges, spiky plant forms, clipped hedges, and vertical board fences.

>> **Use colors again and again.** By repeating colors throughout the landscape, you make it look like it's all one piece — the unity thing again. For example, put in clumps of yellow flowers here and there in various beds, pots, or plantings across your back yard, and you'll find your eye travels from one patch of yellow to the next in a seamless, satisfying way. But if the most eye-catching plant in one bed is red, the next one yellow, the next one white, your poor eyes get confused.

Combine colors of plants with colors of your house or hardscape, too, for unity's sake. For instance, paint a lattice cobalt blue and match it with big folk-art blue-and-yellow flower pots, and you can use that two-tone color scheme to run through the garden.

WARNING

Don't overdo or become overzealous with repetition, however. A little goes a long way!

Playing with Color

Color in your home landscape, just like color indoors, creates moods and impressions. Because your canvas is a living canvas, you can experiment, make discoveries, change your mind, tweak and tinker, and . . . honestly . . . have fun. Refer to the color insert to spark your imagination on how you can use color in your design.

TIP

Hot colors — bright pink, yellow, orange, and orange-red — jump out at you, making distances seem shorter. Cool colors — blues, purples, deep reds, and pastels — recede, making spaces seem longer. If you want to make a small yard seem bigger, plant hot colors at the entryway and cool colors across the garden at the far end where they'll look like a misty watercolor painting.

To make wide-open spaces seem smaller, plant bright, hot colors across the way, where they'll seem to jump forward. Just be sure to choose colors in the same palette. You can use vivid orange and golden yellow dahlias at a gate, for instance, and then soften the hue into apricot and pale lemon yellow as the plantings recede.

This principle also applies to nonplant items, of course. We discuss garden decor and accessories in the section "Adding Décor to Your Design: How Many Pink Flamingos Are Enough?" later in this chapter, but we want to mention that if you want something like a compost pile, tool closet, or storage shed to recede from attention, choose or paint it a darker color.

Here's a garden-color overview with a few brief notes on combinations to jump-start some ideas for you:

>> **Purple:** Majestic and dramatic, purple has a lot of power. What you may not realize is that it can play the role of garden peacemaker; it has the ability to marry colors that otherwise don't get along. However, purple can get lost in shade, unless you pair it with a light-color companion.

>> **Blue:** In any hue, blue looks great with its opposite, orange. It also mixes well with yellow and pink. Blue brings a cooling, calming influence to garden displays.

>> **Yellow:** Radiant yellow is wonderful for brightening dim areas, and it's always so cheerful in the sunshine, on its own, or mixed with other bright colors. Don't overlook pale creamy yellow, which is lovely and calming among pastels.

>> **Orange:** Often fiery and fun, orange also gains sophistication in the company of purple. Combining it with lime green brings out the yellow values in both hues. Orange and white together is also refreshing. Paler versions of orange are beautiful with silver-leaved plants.

>> **Red:** Energizing red is amazingly versatile. Partner it with silver or white, and the result is rich and calming. Use it as an accent in a sea of green, and the whole display wins. Or create a bed of red variations from russet to maroon to burgundy, and the result is sultry.

>> **Pink:** Because pink is so variable, you have lots of possibilities when you use it. It's a favorite in pastel displays and is especially nice with any shade of blue. It doesn't, however, look great next to yellow (you can get a clichéd grocery-store bouquet look) or red (both look a bit flat). Silver and green, though, are great companions.

>> **White:** Okay, we know, white isn't literally a color, but white in your landscaping is often welcome in complex or larger landscapes, giving a spirit of simplicity or purity. (An all-white garden bed can be pretty awesome.) It's especially suited to gardens that are enjoyed in the evening hours, when it glows. Place white at the end of a path or the back of your yard to add depth.

>> **Silver:** Like white, silver stands out in the evening hours. But it's also a wonderful daytime team player, often used as a light-catching foil to other colors, and with good reason, because it both highlights and unifies. We find it has the ability to bind together complex displays. It looks pretty with blue and purple. It does, however, look leaden on rainy days.

>> **Green:** Yes, green is a color in a landscaping design. From pale green to lime green to blue-green to rich, forest green, you have so many variations. If you deploy green with imagination and care, the effects can be downright fabulous, which is true everywhere from small potted displays to elaborate shrub borders and foundation plantings. Green is the great garden unifier and often the dominant color, so we urge you to explore and appreciate it.

Getting Some Rhythm

Repeating elements — whether color, leaf shape, plant forms, lines, hedges, or groundcover — create a rhythm in your landscape, a pacing that you can control by your plant choices just like . . . scrolling through your playlists. If you want slow, smooth-flowing music, choose quiet colors and wide stretches of greenery. To jazz it up, look to bright hues and vertical forms, such as sword-leaved irises, vertical clumps of ornamental grasses, and decorative posts and columns.

The rhythm of your landscape can be as energetic as "Rocky Top" or as elegant as "The Blue Danube." Any eye-catchers in the garden, if accompanied by neighboring plants of lower voltage, work to create a lively rhythm. Clipped shrubs, grasses, vertical plants, big-leafed plants, and anything bigger, brighter, taller, or otherwise strikingly different than its neighbors are all showoffs that grab attention. Use them to make your garden dance with a lively beat.

Restful rhythm makers include stretches of greenery, such as fern beds, shrub plantings, groundcovers, and cool-colored flowers in shades of blue, purple, or pastels.

REMEMBER

Rhythm in a landscape design is partly psychological. You should feel *comfortable.*

Adding Décor to Your Design: How Many Pink Flamingos Are Enough?

Manmade objects carry much more weight in the garden than plants — people's eyes are instantly drawn to them. That's why a single urn or birdbath draws the eye like a magnet, even in the midst of the most beautiful garden (see the color insert for examples).

REMEMBER

Sometimes you must choose what you want to get more attention — the manmade object or the plants. That's particularly true with plants in containers. A very ornate container may detract or outshine the plants in it, and vice versa.

Consider these reminders when adding décor to your landscape:

>> **Exercise some restraint or your landscape will look cluttered.** You can still have your gazing globe, your collection of birdhouses, your gnomes, and your angel fountain, but keep them separate visually with intervening shrubbery or bends in the path so they don't all burst on the scene at once. Your eye should know exactly where to look.

>> **Use décor to highlight their color in your design.** Accessories and garden décor usually have color that generally holds up better and for longer than most plants. Review our color ideas in the section, "Playing with Color," earlier in this chapter and plan accordingly.

TIP

Peruse social media with just décor in mind to find inspiration. You can find scads of ideas on Pinterest, Instagram, Facebook, and beyond.

>> **Place your décor items and then leave the garden.** Go do something else for a while and then return as if you're seeing it for the first time. If your gaze hops around from one outrageous, err, wonderful piece of yard art to another, you have too much stuff.

Paying Attention to Hardscape

The patio, deck, walkways, fences, trellises, and other hardscape elements of your landscape are just as important as the plants. Whether you're shopping for store-bought or creating your own, make your hardscape elements as attractive as your planting beds. Part 2 spells out what you need to know to incorporate hardscape into your landscaping plan.

Here we discuss a few general points for you to remember when you're looking to add hardscape to your plan:

>> **Think how the hardscape looks through the different seasons.** If you live in a cooler climate, you'll be looking at these items unadorned in the off season, when leaves have fallen and plants are dormant. You can soften them in all seasons by planting woody shrubs, vines, ornamental grasses, and trees nearby. A deck or patio without plants may look fine in summer surrounded by lawn grass, but in winter, it can look pretty bleak without a few natural plant forms to anchor it to the earth.

If you live in a milder climate, winter is still a more subdued time of year. Inject color where you can, whether with cushions or pillows on your outdoor seating or on your the deck, patio, or front porch with pots of annuals (calendulas, pansies, primroses, and snapdragons are a few bright and cheery options).

>> **Be prepared for sticker shock when you're shopping for hardscape and the related materials.** Bricks, arbors, benches, fences, and all those other extras can be a much bigger investment than the plants. Considering how valuable they are in transforming an average garden into a great one, though, hardscape is well worth the investment.

Search out the most beautiful arbor in the world, and you'll love your garden forever. Skimp on the deck, and you'll rue your miserly impulse for years.

REMEMBER

>> **Make sure you maintain your hardscape.** You've been thinking about caring for all the plants, but hardscape also requires regular attention. Sweep and yank out encroaching weeds in season. Paint or stain, perhaps annually. Invest in quality materials and build well.

Keeping an Eye on the Details

You may have some favorite plants that you want to include in your new landscape. Acquire an appreciation of the subtler details of those plants before you plant, including the following:

>> **Look at the leaves with an eye toward design attributes.** After all, unless you're growing only annuals, your plants will be mostly leaves much of the time.

>> **Begin to notice the texture of foliage.** Examples include broad and strappy, flat and wide, ferny and delicate, fuzzy, velvety, or shiny.

>> **Consider the form of the flower.** For instance, is it simple and flat like a daisy, emphatically spiky like gayfeather, or soft and wide like yarrow? Also, consider that most perennials bloom for just a few short weeks. What will they add to your garden the rest of the time?

>> **Consider the form and habit of the full plant.** That young plant at the garden center will grow into a garden member of distinct height and shape. Cast a critical eye toward the mature form, which may end up being upright, mounded, arching, single-stemmed, branching, or swordlike. Find out if the plant stays in a clump or expands over time to form a colony.

>> **When you make your choices, contrast and combine plants so they make the most of one another.** Put frilly ferns next to plain-leaved hostas, so they can both show off without competing with each other. Partner upright growers like iris or yucca with mound-forming plants and sprawlers so that they can stand like punctuation points. Echo colors, leaf shapes, and forms to create beds of delicious texture.

In other words, play with your plants. Don't worry if you don't get it picture-perfect on the first try. The best part of gardening is that if you decide you don't like a combination, hey, there's the shovel. Part 3 gives you the ins and outs on different plants you can include.

The Goldilocks Theory: Choosing Plants That Fit

Not too big, not too small — just right. That's the strategy behind selecting plants that are the right scale for your yard and the right proportions to each other. Fill a small yard with great big plants, and you create a feeling of being overwhelmed.

Instead, use small-leafed plants of small stature to stay in scale and make the most of your limited space. If you must have that large plant or tree, make it a focal point by partnering it with low-key plants that don't compete in size and stature.

Choosing the right trees for your yard is where the Goldilocks rule must be obeyed. Judging by the number of mismatched, butchered, hacked-off trees that you see in some places, and the number of houses swamped in blue spruces or hemlocks planted too close to the dwelling, many folks apparently think the cute little tree they're planting stays that size forever. Alas, no.

TIP

When you're looking to select plants (trees, bushes, and so on) that are the right scale and proportion, keep the following in mind:

» **Read the nursery tag to find the ultimate size of the plant.** Remember what happened to the Three Bears and choose trees that fit your yard. Big yard, big tree. Small yard, small tree.

» **Avoid flawed plants.** Stay away from invasive and weak-wooded plants that tend to split like Callery pears and silver maples and ones that produce nuisance seed balls or pods like sweetgums and locusts.

» **Think about the role the plants will play and choose plants to fill a spot.** Need shade? Plant a tree or trees that will provide dense overhead foliage, or erect a structure (trellis, arch, pergola) and plan for vines blanket it. Want a living fence? That's a good job for a hedge (do you want it to have flowers? Thorns to deter unwanted visitors?). Wishing to nurture butterflies? Seek out plants that also support their caterpillars.

» **Create a spot in your landscaping with a certain plant in mind.** You've always wanted a white-flowered clematis. Or a yellow rose. Or a weeping evergreen tree. Discover what conditions (light, space, soil, especially) it will need and clear out or create its perfect home.

Layering Plants to Add Interest

Layering your landscape with plants of different heights definitely improves its look and, indeed, makes it a more comfortable place to be. Groundcovers and grass form the lowest layer, followed by flowering perennials and annuals, then shrubs, then small trees, then medium trees, and then venerable tall trees.

You can also substitute structures for any of the plants: a pedestal birdbath for a mid-height shrub, for instance, or a vine-covered wall or fence for a small tree. A side benefit of this technique is that it leaves room for filtered sunlight and walking paths. (Refer to the section, "Adding Décor to Your Design: How Many Pink Flamingos Are Enough?," earlier in this chapter if you do add décor.)

TIP

Think of layers as you plan the general look of your landscape. Your pencil plan shows only a flat oval for a flowerbed, but in your mind, that flat shape should be three-dimensional, with roses or other flowering shrubs rising above the perennials, and small trees or trellises adding even more height to the bed. Layering not only adds height to your landscape, which instantly makes it more interesting, but it also lets you wedge in more plants than a design that calls for side-by-side planting.

When layering plants in your landscape, keep these suggestions in mind:

>> **Anchor large, old shade trees to your garden.** Big, old shade trees are a great asset, but they can be frustrating to work into a landscape plan because their size makes them stick out. An easy solution is to set up some nonplant items underneath, such as a bench, bistro table and chairs, or a hammock to help integrate it into its surroundings.

>> **Plant smaller trees beside your giant tree and shrubs beside the shorter trees.** This is a little trick called *stepping down,* effectively connecting your big tree to the rest of the garden so your gaze makes a transition to the tops of the trees in graduated steps instead of one giant leap. For instance, consider planting redbuds beneath a big maple tree. You can also use horizontal visual weight to balance height.

REMEMBER

When you add smaller plants, they tend to adjust better to transplanting and grow faster. We know you're bearing their projected mature size in mind, and you're willing to be patient. An added bonus: Smaller plants are less expensive.

Layered planting has another important side benefit: It's good for the birds. Birds like to ladder their way down into a yard, checking their surroundings for safety as they go, heading for their next meal or your birdbath for a dip. (For about making a bird-friendly landscape, see Chapters 12 and 20.)

Chapter **3**

Forming a Working Plan: Getting Serious about Your Design

One reality about landscaping is that you need a plan — on paper. That's easy if you're artistic, a little tougher if you're not. (Also difficult for the non-*artistes* is visualizing what the plan will actually look like. That's why we tell you to take things like chairs and stepladders into the yard to create the semblance of your planned landscape.) This chapter shows you the ropes.

We highly recommend an *assessment drawing* (a sketch of what you have and what you need; flip to Chapter 1). Keep it handy because you're going to refer to it to make sure you don't forget anything. Now you're ready to roll up your sleeves and tackle a more serious process, a *site design drawing*, which can show you how your finished yard will look. Exciting, yes?

We start with *what is* and move to *what will be*. Measure and make the base map first. Then the fun part begins — plotting your dreams. Some people like to sketch first and visualize second. On the other hand, you may work better doing a live mock-up first and then transferring what you come up with to paper. Either way, this chapter can help you get where you're going.

Other realities that this chapter helps you know how to deal with are neighbors and public agencies and their codes, how to estimate and order materials, and who is going to do the work.

Knowing What's Already There — Making a Base Map

Before you can start adding your wonderful new landscape features to your yard, you have to have a map of what's already there. You measure everything and put what you discover onto a drawing, called a *base map*.

TIP

If you have a current surveyor's map of your property, skip this work and trace that. No need to reinvent the wheel.

If you don't have a surveyor's map, you need to draw your own. The following sections list what supplies you need and explains how you can draw your own base map.

Ensuring you have the supplies to draw

In order to do so, pick up a few of the drawing supplies in Figure 3-1, at least graph paper, tracing paper, a good ruler, a pencil, and an eraser. More complicated drawing tools help you keep your lines straight and maintain consistent sizes for the elements of your landscape, but they aren't essential to drawing a useful map.

We recommend that you use graph paper for making this base plan, which has a printed grid of squares that makes transferring real-life elements to a flat piece of paper much easier. You can, for example, use a 1-foot to ¼-inch ratio — a 1-foot-long line in real life covers ¼ inch on graph paper; a 4-foot-line is an inch on graph paper, a 20-foot-long line in real life extends 5 inches on graph paper (for those of you who use metric graph paper and measurements, you can use similar ratios) and so on. If you need to, tape sheets of graph paper together to get everything in.

With all your supplies in hand, you're ready to draw.

Drawing your own base map

You don't have to be a professional surveyor or landscape architect to draw a base map. Just follow these steps and voilà — your very own base map:

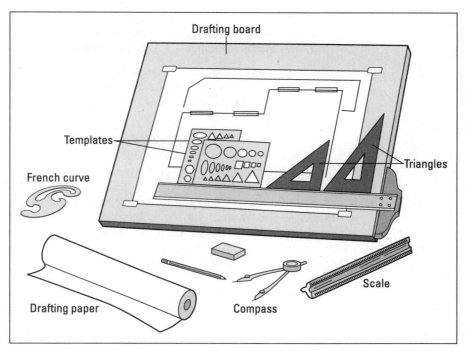

FIGURE 3-1:
Basic drafting
tools help you
draw your plan.

(Labels in figure: Drafting board, Templates, French curve, Triangles, Drafting paper, Compass, Scale)

1. **Measure the lengths of all edges of your property and draw the outline of your yard on the graph paper.**

   Don't guess. Refer to Chapter 1 about discovering where the boundaries actually are.

2. **Measure and draw in the outline of your house.**

   Be sure to place the house exactly where it sits on your lot.

3. **Measure and add the garage, barn, tool shed, chicken coop, and whatever other outbuildings currently exist.**

   Some of the measurements are easy to take, such as the length of building walls, so start there. Then draw in other elements and show their locations in relation to known measurements.

4. **Measure and draw in whatever paving is already in place and that you want to keep, such as the driveway, front walk, basketball court, and so on.**

REMEMBER

   Don't assume that right angles and parallel lines that are formed by walls, fences, driveways, and property lines are always perfect — often they aren't. Verify the distance between objects with as many measurements as you can.

5. **Measure and draw existing elements that you want to keep right where they are, with no changes.**

This may include fences, big trees, hedges, perennials, a vegetable garden, and so forth. For example, indicate the precise location of a tree trunk or plant by measuring the distance from it to two known points, such as two corners of the house.

TIP

Make note of approximate heights of taller elements. To do so, try this: position a 6-foot (1.8 m) tall person under a tall tree. Back away and estimate: how many of that person will it take to measure to the top?

That's a lot of measurements, right? Taking measurements may sound like a pain in the neck — and we won't lie, it is — but you're far ahead of the game when you get estimates for what this new design is actually going to cost. Without measurements, you'll have no idea how much concrete, wood chips, topsoil, bricks or paving stones, groundcover plants, or other materials that you'll need.

Measurements are also vital when adding new elements to your yard. Sure, you can eyeball your yard and make your drawing fit, but when you try to execute the plan, you may find out how fallible that casual method really is. Measurements eliminate guesswork and give you the confidence of knowing that your plan will work.

TIP

Invest in a rolling tape measure (100-foot, 30.5 m) to avoid the frustration of marking off 10-foot (3 m), lengths and adding them up to get a reading on your 400-foot (122 m) side boundary. Enlist a helper when you're ready to measure to make the job go quicker.

Overlaying Your Ideas

Time to get out the tracing paper. Lay it over the graph-paper base map. Sharpen your pencil, stock up on erasers. If you want to start over, change your mind, rethink something, or make a neater drawing, just erase or get another sheet of tracing paper. Yes, there are other, more high-tech ways to accomplish this part of the process, but honestly, this method is easy and it works quite well.

No Leonardo da Vinci drawing skills needed here — just make circular or oval balloons or *goose eggs* and label the circles ("shed," "play area," "vegetable garden" — you get the idea). Include everything, whether things already exist and you want to keep them, or you want them to exist before you're done. If you've made a rough assessment sketch (see Chapter 1), refer to it again to make sure you don't forget anything.

Figure 3-2 shows an example of what your drawing will look like when you're finished.

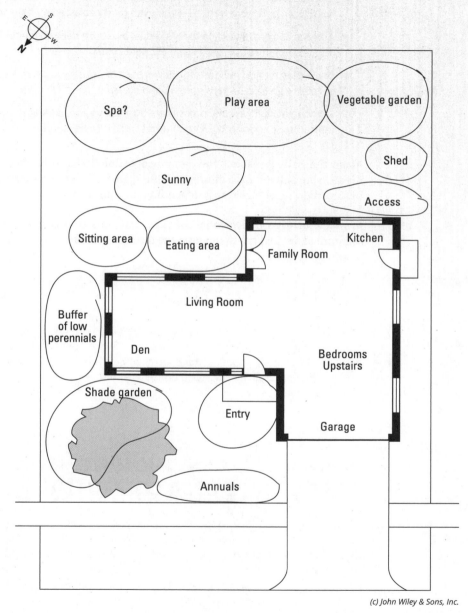

FIGURE 3-2:
Using tracing paper over your base plan, draw shapes to identify what you have and what you want.

Include the following in your sketch:

- >> **Plan activities.** Add balloons for all the special activities that you eventually want to enjoy in your yard — if you ever get this blasted plan finished.

- >> **Add hardscape.** Sketch in fences, a spa, a patio, a deck, front porch improvements, and any other hardscape elements you've chosen.

- >> **Draw plants.** Add balloons for flowerbeds, shrubs, vines, new trees, a vegetable garden or herb garden, and so on.

- >> **Sketch paths.** Draw any paths that you want to add, adding lines to indicate their shapes and widths. *Note:* Paths tend to change as you define use areas.

Make the balloons about the same proportional size that they are in real life. Create a big balloon for a dining or grilling area, say, versus a small balloon for the herb garden — or vice-versa depending on your priorities.

It's okay or even unavoidable for these balloons to occasionally overlap, Venn-diagram style. Just try to imagine the sizes as accurately as possible.

THE PHOTO METHOD

Another way to help visualize how your yard could look is simply to take some photographs, and then upload them to your computer. Sketch features on the photos with any basic drawing software or, if that's too clunky for you, try a landscaping app such as Home Outside, Morpholio Trace, and Concepts App. You can also print out the photos and draw right on them.

PLANNING OR ENVISIONING A LANDSCAPE ON A COMPUTER

Did you think professional landscape designers only use computer technology? Not so! Many start with penciled drawings. True, they do have special software programs at their disposal (such as Autocad, Vectorworks, and Dynascape) as projects advance. But these programs are pricey and, frankly, figuring out how to use them is a rather steep learning curve. Of course, using them is an investment in their business and something they'll use again and again, whereas you're a one-time user. In other words, you don't need to go out and buy those programs to draw your own landscape plan.

The phone or tablet landscape-planning apps are more accessible and affordable, but they do have their limitations. Some restrict you to built-in elements, and they can be time-consuming to master to your satisfaction. Deciding to use them really depends on how tech-savvy you are.

To find options, search online for "best landscape design software," and you'll find up-to-date reviews pretty easily. Here are a few popular ones you can try:

- **Home Outside** (https://homeoutside.com/mobile-app/) is an iOS app developed by celebrated landscape architect Julie Moir Messervy's studio. It offers simple and attractive graphics, an easy interface, the ability to draw elements, a photo import, and even layers so you can try different design ideas on the same base plan.

- **Morpholio Trace** (www.morpholioapps.com) is an elegant app developed for iOS that is great for any level of user. You can start with a sketch of your own, or import a photo or a base plan and then add layers of virtual trace paper to experiment with different ideas. It can be as sophisticated as you want it to be, with tutorials to help you learn how to use its many features. Although it's not specifically for landscape design, it's perfectly suited to that use and includes a gallery of tree and plant graphic icons.

- **Concepts App** (https://concepts.app/en/) is the next level of technical drawing for people who really want to develop accurate plans. Concepts enables its users to progress from rough sketches to measured details in one app. It's available for multiple operating systems.

Putting Your Ideas on the Ground

When you're satisfied with what you've drawn, you need to test-drive your design. Now you get to play with a bunch of objects to make your landscape look alive. Grab stakes (of various heights) and string. Pull your garden hoses out of their perpetual nest-of-snakes tangle, collect wire cages, get rope from the garage, drag out the plastic lawn chairs and buckets, pull along a stepladder or two, and prepare a wheelbarrow load of leaves or a bale (or two) of straw . . . and get ready to play make-believe.

TIP

A cool way to make a straight line easily is to invest in a *chalkline*, a device that looks like a tape measure, but is filled with chalk. The chalk powders a string that you pull out. Tie the chalked string between two uprights, clip the end, and — this is the fun part — lift the taut string in the center with your thumb and forefinger and let it ping hard toward the ground. It snaps against the grass or soil, leaving a perfect straightedge. Use the chalkline to mark potential beds and paths when you're drawing your design, then use it again later when you start digging.

Start with placing and perhaps tweaking (adjusting the positioning) the bigger elements of your scheme first. After that, you can move on to the rest.

Big deals: Designating space for large elements

When we mention "large elements," we mean larger plants, but also bigger hardscape ambitions such as new deck or an arbor. Keep the following in mind when place items:

>> Put lawn chairs where you plan to add shrubs or young trees.

>> Use a regular ladder to represent a substantial arbor.

>> Mark the corners of a proposed new deck, patio, porch extension, or pergola with stakes and string lines between them. (Don't forget these items often require *footings,* that is, take up more real estate than just the part you will use/sit upon/walk upon.)

Filling in the rest

Now you get to make all sorts of messes. Well, your yard may look that way to somebody else. To you, it's a vision taking shape. Do the following when adding the remaining items:

>> Outline curving paths with hose or rope, or sprinkle a path of oatmeal, flour, or white play sand (this last option is sold in bags and has the advantage of not dissolving if it rains), so that you can see the direction it takes. No need to use a lot by making a solid line — a dotted line works.

>> Pound in stakes or use buckets to show the future homes of rosebushes or large perennials in your flowerbeds.

>> Rake the leaves, grass clippings, or straw and fill in the outlines so you can easily get a feel for your new beds.

>> Visualize a fence, long planter box, terraces, or raised beds by putting in stakes at the projected height and running string between them.

By this time your property will no doubt be ringed with throngs of curious neighbors who will be sure that this time you've totally lost your mind. Fill them in, if you feel inclined, or let them wonder as you walk around your new landscape.

Squint your eyes, throw your imagination into full gear, and check the position of the elements you've placed from every vantage point you can think of. Remember, that's not a plastic chair: It's a graceful evergreen. Five-gallon bucket? No, a beautiful flowering shrub.

Shift around any of the parts of your portable garden until you like the way it looks. When you have this part of your yard arranged to your satisfaction, mark your rough plan with revised lines to show bed edges, plant placement, and any other niceties that you want to note. Then move on to the next section of your yard and do it again. Repeat until your landscape plan is finished.

Creating a Final Plan

After you're comfortable with each section of your proposed landscape, transfer your ideas to paper in real form — not just balloons (like we discuss in the section, "Putting Your Ideas on the Ground," earlier in this chapter). Your final plan needs to include the following:

>> **Hardscape:** Be sure to include deck, patio, benches, fences and gates, paths, spa, tool shed, arbor, and so on.

>> **Plantings:** Add flowerbeds, vegetable or herb gardens, trees, shrubs, vines, lawn, and groundcover areas.

>> **Dimensions:** Add dimensions for the house, for each element, and for the entire yard.

Although the example in Figure 3-3 may look a little more professional than your drawing, it gives you an idea of what to shoot for (you can see why you need a pencil and erasers handy). Make a few copies.

REMEMBER

Keep in mind that some hardscape features may require *construction drawings.* For more complex projects (decks, pergolas, and the like), you probably want to have these professionally drawn so you can get construction bids, obtain permits, and order materials.

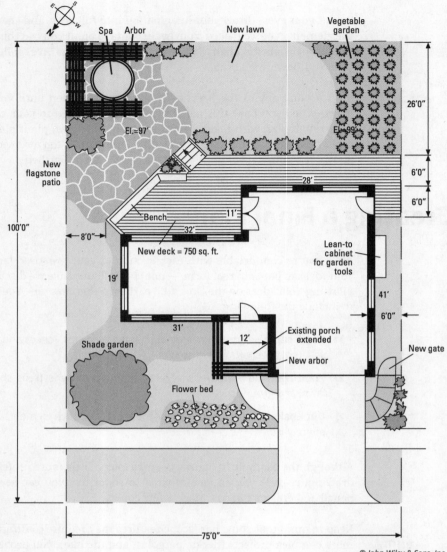

FIGURE 3-3:
The final site plan incorporates needs and features into a functional landscape.

Spa Arbor

New lawn

Vegetable garden

26'0"

El.=97'

El.=99'

New flagstone patio

6'0"

6'0"

28'

11'

Bench

32'

100'0"

8'0"

New deck = 750 sq. ft.

Lean-to cabinet for garden tools

19'

41'

6'0"

31'

12'

Existing porch extended

New arbor

Shade garden

New gate

Flower bed

75'0"

© John Wiley & Sons, Inc.

Making a Shopping List

When you're ready to project spending, this section can help. The easiest way to proceed is to make a spreadsheet (see Table 3-1; you can use it to create your own spreadsheet). You first divide your landscaping project into logical sections (specific types of plants, supplies, building materials, décor, and so forth), and then start filling information and numbers as you can. Lead with your priorities (for example, plants and mulch). Edit, add, subtract, as you progress and refine.

TABLE 3-1: **Your Shopping List**

Element	Type	Quantity	Price Per Unit	Total $	Delivery Charge	Installation Charge	Source/ Supplier
Perennials							
Annuals							
Shrubs							
Trees							
Topsoil/loam							
Mulch							
Bark chips							
Concrete							
Concrete blocks							
Lumber							
Lumber substitute							
Hardware supplies							
Bricks							
Gravel							
Stone							
Sand							
Pavers							
Fencing							
Lattice							
Trellis							
Arbor							
Outdoor furniture							
Composter							
Lighting							
Pots/other containers							
Watering gear							
Irrigation system							
Tools							

Stick to the steps in the following sections as you create your shopping list.

Step 1: List plants and determine their cost

Identify the plants you want to use in each section of the project, and then determine how much they'll cost. Collect prices by shopping nurseries and garden centers or ask a nursery to give you a quote on the whole shebang. Doing it in person is more fun but obviously much more time-consuming. Online shopping, or perhaps making a couple phone calls, may do the trick.

REMEMBER

Check size; little plants are always cheaper than the same one in a larger size.

Step 2: List and calculate the supplies

List the supplies you want to use in each section of the project and calculate how much you need, making sure you're as specific as possible.

You may be in the market for anything from landscape fabric to mulch and topsoil to gravel, but you have to know a bit more about your needs or wishes. Refer to the measurements you took.

TIP

To calculate, start by making a rough sketch of the dimensions of a specific project, such as a flowerbed. Length and width are definitely always required. How deep do you want to lay down mulch and topsoil, 4 inches? 6 inches? (10.1 cm? 15.2 cm?) Multiply these three numbers together to get the desired volume. You'll want to convert the resulting number to cubic yards because that's how these materials are typically sold.

As for other supplies, more simple math may be needed. Take landscape fabric, for example. Will you buy one large piece, or (perhaps unwieldy) roll and then cut it into sections? Consider also how thick you want that landscape fabric to be. It comes in different weights; heavier ones are, of course, more expensive.

Don't stop at "I need gravel." After you determine the volume needed, realize that gravel comes in different-size stones (the grades are numbered), which can affect how much you ultimately purchase. You may need a reconnaissance visit to the supplier to view the various options and help you make up your mind.

TIP

Order a bit more than you think you'll need (you can save or store any excess). Your salesperson can assist you. Most suppliers and contractors recommend +10 percent extra.

Step 3: Get hardscape estimates

This includes brick, pavers, concrete, and other hardscape materials. Don't walk into a home-supply, hardware store, or lumber yard unprepared. When they ask, how big your proposed patio is, don't just offer a sketch. Come prepared with its dimensions. You can do the calculations or go online for help.

Make your own calculations

If you're fortunate, a staffer will be able to help you with a materials cost estimate using that information. If not, you have more math to do:

Hardscape materials are expensive, bulky, and heavy — there's no point in over-calculating and overspending (certainly not past the +10 percent cushion). On the other hand, underbuying is, at least, an annoyance because you'll have to go back and get more.

For example, you want to include flagstone for a new patio. To calculate, take the surface area, divided by 100 equals tons needed so 20 feet (6.1 m) × 10 feet (3 m) = 200 ÷100 (6.1 ÷ 3) = 2 tons.

Use an online calculator

But you don't have to estimate the materials you need manually or with a calculator. The Internet can help. You can find an online resource that makes it easy at www.omnicalculator.com/construction#s-104.

Consider this example of a more complex scenario, paver bricks:

1. **Plug in the surface-area dimensions of the project area.**

   Say, 10 × 20 feet; 3 × 6.1 m

2. **Insert the size of the pavers.**

   Say, 4 × 8 inches; 10.1 cm × 20.3 cm

3. **The calculator tells you how many you need.**

   In this case, you need 900.

   You can insert the price per brick to get the total cost in U.S. dollars.

REMEMBER

The more you do yourself, the less you'll have to prevail upon or pay someone else to do for you. Refer to Part 2 for more information and tips about specific hardscape projects.

Step 4: Make an itemized checklist

Create an itemized checklist of the costs of each section of the project.

Use Figure 3-1 for each section of your landscape and then tally up a grand total.

REMEMBER

Don't neglect to find out delivery charges. You may also get an estimate on installation. Although you may decide starting out that you want to do it all yourself, it's good to know what the installed price is, in case you run out of steam.

Step 5: Consider tools you may need to buy

Every job has its tools, and landscaping is no different. Here are some of the general tools you'll probably need to buy (or borrow):

>> **For planting perennials, annuals, and bulbs:** Square-nosed shovel, long handle pointed shovel, garden spade, stiff-tined rake, hand trowel, hand pruner, and a hose and spray attachment. Optional equipment includes garden gloves, knee pads, plant labels, soaker hose or other irrigation system, bucket, and a bulb planter.

>> **For planting trees, shrubs, and vines:** Square-nosed shovel or garden spade, hoe, stiff-tined rake, and a garden cart or wheelbarrow.

>> **For hardscape:** Posthole digger, pick, digging bar, hammer, handsaw, square, nail set, chisel, plane, circular saw, power drill, power sander, power screwdriver, caulking gun, sawhorse, and stepladder. Also get a level (traditional carpenter's level or one of those spiffy, efficient, but more expensive laser levels).

>> **For planting lawn seed or sod:** Sharp knife, roller, broadcast spreader, and soil preparation equipment, including a rotary tiller and heavy rake.

>> **For maintenance:** Lawn mower/riding mower, weed whacker, hedge clippers, hand pruner, loppers, pruning saw, hoe, lawn rake, and stiff-tined rake.

REMEMBER

The advantage to having separate price tags attached to the various sections of your plan is that you then have an idea of how big a bite each new step will take out of your budget. Keep in mind, though, that the estimates you start with may change — go up, that is — by the time you actually begin the next phase.

Step 6: Take a breath

After creating your spreadsheet, sit with it — that is, don't rush into action. The spreadsheet represents your best-case scenario: all the things you hope and plan to with to your landscape. Take time to think about it. Talk it over with others (those you live with as well as contractors, other DIY landscapers, and the staff of places where you shop or plan to shop). Inevitably you'll make adjustments.

PENNY-PINCHING IDEAS

You can shave hundreds of dollars off your landscaping price tag with a few cost-cutting tricks:

- **Buy from the source.** Eliminate the middleman and you're likely to get a bargain. Look for brickyards, paving makers, stone and slate quarries, gravel yards, and other nearby sources of raw materials. Ask around or find them online. Do some comparison shopping. Make sure you know how much you need — before you ask for a price.

- **Find a friend with a pickup truck.** Don't strain the springs of your own or a friend's truck with stone or other ultra-heavy materials, but do haul your own lumber and anything else that you can safely carry to save on delivery charges. You can also do a short-term truck rental from some stores.

- **Combine brick with concrete.** Instead of installing costly all-brick walks, combine brick with concrete. Use the brick as decorative strips in the walk.

- **Eliminate mortar between pavers or bricks.** Set the materials into a frame made of rot-resistant lumber or strips of concrete. Set bricks or pavers into a sand base between the edges of the frame and brush sand into the cracks. The frame prevents the paving from shifting.

- **Salvage cool stuff.** Visit architectural salvage dealers for real deals on fencing, arbors, ironwork, and attractive decorative touches. It's a matter of chance what you can find, but we defy you to come away empty-handed. Estate sales and Facebook Marketplace are also good places to trawl.

- **Make a faux stone wall out of free concrete.** Pieces of broken concrete sidewalk can look a lot like fieldstone when you stack them for a dry wall. Next time you see a sidewalk being ripped up, stop and ask if you can have the broken pieces. Most contractors will gladly dump the stuff in your yard so that they don't have to haul it to the landfill, where they pay a fee for dumping.

- **Seek out free or cheap wood chips and mulch materials.** Places to ask include tree services and utility companies or road crews clearing roadside right-of-ways. You can often get a truckload for zero cash. Use the chips for path surfaces and for long-lasting mulch. Also, many municipalities have free mulch pickup areas, but be take a careful look first: these may contain bits of unwanted plants, such as invasive weeds.

The most important thing, though, is to prioritize. Pick a project and plan to get started.

Getting Ready

Preparing for this work requires . . . preparation. All advance groundwork smooths the way ahead. Then, you can proceed with as much confidence and efficiency as possible.

Here we break this down into a logical process. First, we help you examine ways to make even the most ambitious plans manageable. Then we go over things you need to consider and take care of before breaking ground (basically, well-placed phone calls or conversations). Last but not least, we enumerate tasks you can and should attend to before launching into landscaping.

Cutting your project into bite-sized pieces

Renovating your entire yard in one fell swoop can overwhelm even the most dedicated gardener, unless you have an unlimited budget or a staff the size of Martha Stewart's. Consider the following tips for ways to focus on one task at a time:

>> **Establish your priorities.** Plan to work on the areas that you'll use the most. Only you know whether you get more pleasure out of a patio or an herb garden.

>> **Have a long-term plan.** Redo your yard with a plan. A two-to-five-year plan is appropriate if you're doing major installations, such as adding a new deck, a rock garden, and/or a water feature, or if you have a big property. Use your budget estimates to decide which parts of your plan you can have this year and which have to be deferred.

>> **Do a little at a time.** Landscaping can be a bite too big to chew in a weekend of hard labor. If you're doing the work yourself, focus on one small area at a time. Complete it before you move on to the next. Otherwise your entire yard will be torn up for longer than you're probably comfortable with.

>> **Start in the back and move forward to avoid damaging completed work.** Do work at your yard's boundaries or fencelines before tackling more-central areas.

Taking action before you break ground

Before you begin your landscaping project, call your local governing body — town council, zoning board, homeowners association, or any other likely agency — and ask what regulations apply and whether permits are necessary for the work you're planning. Tell them what kind of job you're undertaking; chances are, you'll have some red tape, including permits and permission, to get through.

You may also want to let your neighbors know what you're planning — before a backhoe arrives. Also, before beginning your landscape project, consider which tasks may be too time-consuming — or require too much expertise — for you to tackle alone. Keep reading for more about who to contact and what to remember.

Dealing with City Hall

Local restrictions vary greatly from one place to the next, as the neighbors of the Sultan of Brunei found out when he painted his Beverly Hills palace hot pink and added statues of naked dancing girls along the street. Your plans, of course, won't come close to those of His Highness, but you'll still have to clear them with the authorities before you proceed. In many communities, for instance, the height of a fence is a matter of law. Better to find out ahead of time that 5 feet (1.5 m) tall is the limit before you invest in 6-foot (1.8 m) privacy fencing. Ponds and pools, even small ones, may require a fence to keep neighborhood toddlers or delivery people from wandering in. You may need to have an inspector check your work. At the very least, you'll likely need permits for erecting any kind of permanent structure.

TECHNICAL STUFF

The term *setback* is a popular one with zoning departments. The setback is the distance from an adjoining property line that a structure can be erected. Before you dig, make sure you're putting the new element in the right place. Building a deck or installing a fence is hard work. Taking it down and moving it 2 feet (.6 m) inward is plain aggravation. Keep things easy on yourself by finding out the rules before you begin.

Calling before you dig

You've probably seen it on a million little signs plastered to telephone poles or set along the byways: "Call 811 before you dig." Utility companies have a lot going on under the ground, including gas and water mains, electric lines, fiber optic cables, and so forth. If you think the cost of bricks is high, wait until you get the bill for slicing through a cable! Play it safe, even if all you're doing is planting a tree.

Follow the advice of those cautionary signs to get the okay from those companies or utilities. They usually send someone out to have a look and flag the danger zone.

Keeping the neighbors happy

Keep peace in the neighborhood with a very simple action — talk to your neighbors, before heavy equipment arrives. Let them know what kind of work you're planning. They'll naturally want reassurances from you about noise, debris, whether it might affect their property, and how long you think the project might take.

Some neighbors are as territorial as some dogs about their own places. Be sensitive to how your changes may affect them. Before you plant a row of 12-foot (3.6 m) evergreens or put up a privacy fence, consider whether you'll be blocking their view or creating a shade problem for them. Put yourself in their shoes and determine whether your improvements will be a positive thing for them, or your neighbors will be left staring at the ugly backside of your new fence or swatting mosquitoes attracted by your garden pool.

Preparing your property

Here are a few practical things you should do before the landscape makeover begins in earnest, to minimize disruption and mess:

1. Complete all exterior home repairs.

2. Complete all exterior painting and power-washing of the house and outbuildings as well as fences you plan to keep.

3. Call an arborist to attend to existing big-tree issues: removal (including stump grinding, if applicable) and removal of lower limbs and pruning of damaged or diseased branches.

4. Call in the professionals for an in-ground irrigation systems before any other landscaping work is started (see Chapter 5 for full details).

5. Attend to necessary grading as well as water-flow or flood-mitigation issues (see Chapter 4).

Doing It Yourself or Calling in the Big Guns

As handy and enthusiastic as you are, you probably can't do it all. Before you tackle a new project, such as laying a patio, assess your physical strength and your skills, and how trainable you are. Surf websites, tune into HGTV, watch YouTube videos, and read more in how-to books. Then take a merciless look at your biceps and your already jam-packed free time, and decide whether you and the task are compatible.

Even if you're a beginner, with a little dedication and energy, you can have success with the following projects:

>> Making a path of wood chips or gravel (check out Chapter 7)

>> Laying a brick, flagstone, or concrete paver walkway (see Chapter 7)

>> Planting small trees, shrubs, perennials, and other plants (refer to Part 3)

>> Installing sod or spreading grass seed (see Chapter 16)

>> Planting a groundcover (flip to Chapter 16)

>> Building a raised bed (see Chapter 10)

>> Installing outdoor lighting (see Chapter 10)

>> Building a lightweight shade structure, arbor, or trellis (see Chapter 10)

>> Making a bench or planter (see Chapter 10)

>> Installing a garden pond or other water feature (see Chapter 10)

Here are some bigger jobs that require more time and heavier labor. Feel free to tackle them yourself if you're inclined, but you may want to get professional help. For one thing, a professional can get it done a lot faster, without mistakes or undue waste.

>> Installing a fence and gate (refer to Chapter 6)

>> Building steps (see Chapter 8)

>> Installing an irrigation system (check out Chapter 5)

>> Building stone or stacked-concrete walls (see Chapter 6)

>> Planting large trees (refer to Chapter 11)

>> Pruning or removing large trees (refer to Chapter 11)

>> Doing electrical, plumbing, or gas-line work

>> Building large outdoor structures, such as a shed

>> Pouring concrete (see Chapter 9)

>> Installing a patio (flip to Chapter 9)

>> Building a deck (see Chapter 8)

>> Installing a pool

WHO YOU GONNA CALL?

Should you decide to holler for help, holler in the right direction. When you're ready to call in a pro, talk to trusted friends and neighbors first. Track down a local Master Gardener or Master Gardeners group, or ask at your favorite local garden center or nursery, and see whom they suggest. Ask for recommendations for companies that have done satisfying work; don't hire Jimmy-down-the-street's cousin just because he's the only name on your list. Ask for references, and check them. A drive-by around a former client's property may be all you need to see if the work is up to snuff. You can also check online reviews, but bear in mind that only the happiest and the most-disgruntled people tend to write online reviews.

Work quality isn't the only consideration, though. Ask whether the work was done on schedule, at a fair price, and whether clean-up afterward was satisfactory. Would the client hire the contractor again? When you've narrowed down your list, check with the Better Business Bureau, your state Attorney General's office, and/or professional associations.

If you feel at all shaky about your skills as a designer, call in a landscape designer to give you advice or even draw up a plan for you. You can also show the pro your own plan and ask for suggestions or confirmation of your good common sense — all for a fee, of course. The help of a genuine landscape architect is warranted if you have a large property, are starting from scratch, and/or can afford their more-expensive expertise.

For more on various sorts of landscape professionals, including information on professional associations that can lead you to them, turn to Appendix A.

2

Building Hardscape into Your Yard

Get a handle on your site if you're ready to add a hardscape element, including preparing the land, knowing what tools you'll need, and so on.

Understand the ins and outs of water, including drainage and different watering systems.

Add some privacy to your landscape design by including a fence, wall, and gate.

Incorporate a path or walkway into your garden to highlight your plants and welcome guests.

Create an outdoor living space and place to entertain friends and family by building a deck or patio.

Consider a wide array of fun and creative ways you can bring your garden to life with lighting, fire pits, raised planters, and so much more.

Chapter **4**

Taming Your Site

When you're ready to install or redo a yard, you may feel overwhelmed, wondering where to start. We advise you, whenever possible, to plan and execute major landscape improvements, fixes, and hardscape projects first, before anything else. This chapter shows you how, beginning with some general guidelines for most any type of outdoor construction project. We empower you to do it yourself. If you hire some help or bring in someone to do the whole thing, though, at least you'll have a sense of what's involved.

The first step of landscape construction is to prepare your site for plants and structures. Whether your home is surrounded by bare land or by a mature, established yard, before installing your new landscaping, you have to *lay out* (locate and mark) the site improvements, grade the ground for any structures, stabilize slopes, solve drainage problems, and make sure any underground utilities, such as electrical wiring or water lines for irrigation, are safely installed.

Focusing on Construction Basics

Outdoor structures are fun to build, and many are within the capabilities of a novice builder. Other projects are more complex, requiring an experienced hand. This section provides some basic information for both types of projects — after you review our information, you should be able to determine what you can handle or what you may need help to do.

Looking at site challenges

A building project shouldn't involve a carefree, anything-goes approach. Whatever you build or install outdoors endures constant exposure to the weather and withstands continuous contact with the ground, which teems with organisms that accelerate rotting. The ground is also subject to the following:

>> *Frost heaves* (in areas with severe winters, freeze-thaw cycles cause the ground to buckle)

>> *Natural settling* (natural compaction of soil over time)

>> *Creepage* (the sliding of soil down a slope over time)

>> *Poor drainage* (sodden ground)

>> *Unstable soils* (certain types of soil don't compact well, whereas others can't be depended upon to remain in place without extra support)

Ramping up — a checklist

Many structures, such as decks and large shade structures (like pergolas), must meet building-code requirements. Irrigation systems are subject to plumbing codes, and lighting and wiring projects are subject to electrical codes. Observe the following list of construction basics for outdoor projects, and bring in the professionals for some or all parts of the project that aren't in your wheelhouse:

>> **Investigate regulations.** Contact your local building department to find out which regulations apply to your project and whether you need to obtain a permit. Although states or provinces have standardized building codes, municipalities often refine them even further.

Your home may also be subject to the guidelines or rules enforced by a neighborhood or homeowners' association, which may include a design-review process that usually requires submitting a measured drawing (scaled plan), not just a rough sketch.

>> **Draw plans.** Work out construction details on paper, not on the job, by making scale drawings (quarter-inch, or small-square metric, graph paper makes this task so much easier). Sometimes elevation drawings are helpful; these drawings show plans from the ground up to illustrate height relationships. Part 1 discusses what to draw.

>> **Require adequate foundations.** Structures must be supported on concrete footings, gravel beds, or similar foundations. Designs vary with local climate, soil, and slope conditions, but the basic requirement is to place the weight of a structure on solid ground (below the *frost line* — the depth to which the ground freezes during winter, which can be 4 feet, 1.2 m, or even deeper) or on a stable, well-drained bed. Also all rot-prone wood must be elevated at least 8 inches (20.3 cm) above *grade* (aboveground level).

>> **Choose building materials carefully.** Wood remains popular, but you have other options. See the section, "About Wood Alternatives," later in this chapter.

>> **Utilize corrosion-resistant fasteners and hardware.** Use nails, screws, and hardware that are galvanized or otherwise treated for outdoor use. For galvanized nails, we recommend HDG (which means *hot-dip galvanized*). Use fasteners that grip, such as spiral-shank nails or galvanized deck screws, for better holding power.

REMEMBER

One secret to building long-lasting outdoor structures from wood is to nail, screw, strap, glue, and connect the heck out of 'em!

>> **If you use wood, choose finishes that last.** Preservatives (which protect wood from destructive organisms), sealers (which repel moisture), semitransparent stains (light-bodied stains that reveal grain pattern), solid stains (which mask the wood), and paints help wood structures last for years. Some products contain two or more finishes, such as stains that contain a sealer, preservative, and/or ultraviolet-ray blocker. The most effective finishes are those that penetrate the wood, such as water repellents, water-repellent preservatives, and semitransparent stains, and those that are designated specifically for outdoor wood structures, not just for general use.

>> **Manage materials carefully.** Estimating, ordering, obtaining, delivering, and storing materials is a major part of construction. Many materials are readily available from home centers, but you may have to locate a masonry yard, concrete supplier, fencing specialist, or similar outlet for others. Discuss delivery fees with suppliers.

Plan your job so that you move materials only once by storing them near (6 to 10 feet, 1.8 to 3 m from) the construction site. Stack lumber on a flat, dry, shaded surface, such as a patio or garage floor, to keep it from warping. (Keep lumber off dirt or grass.) Create shelf space to store nails, bolts, screws, and similar hardware. Store bags of cement or mortar mix out of the weather.

Use a wheelbarrow or arrange for a helper to move sand, gravel, and masonry materials from the street to your yard.

Avoid storing materials and equipment under a tree (within a tree canopy area) because the resulting soil and root compaction can lead to tree death, if not right away, in a couple of years.

>> **Have a plan for debris.** Figure out ahead of time where to haul your debris in the likely event that regular trash services won't pick it up. To make disposal easier, separate trash, clean fill, toxins, and reusable scraps. Arrange for a disposal service to haul everything away, if you can't do so yourself.

Understanding wood and its alternatives

Lumber remains the most widely used construction material, certainly for decks and fences; however, lumber isn't your only option. The following sections examine wood and lumber alternatives and help you make your choice of which to use based on your project's size and needs, your taste, and your budget.

About wood

All wood is *not* created equal. Only certain grades (called *heart grades*) of certain species (cedar, redwood, cypress, and some tropical woods) are naturally resistant to decay. Many nondurable woods, such as pine and Douglas fir, aren't decay resistant, but they are available as pressure-treated with preservatives and stains. They're treated for either aboveground use or for ground contact.

Here are some general tips to bear in mind when looking at wood for your projects:

>> **Consider strength.** These requirements vary depending on whether you're considering a deck (that needs to support furniture, perhaps a grill, and a number of people at times) or a structure such as a pergola, arch, or fence that will only support the growth of a vine. Southern pine, Douglas fir, and cypress are stronger than redwood, cedar, and other pines. Black locust is becoming more popular and larch, where available, may be suitable.

In recent years, there has been a disheartening decline in lumber quality as tree plantations grow the wood too fast and/or harvest it too young, resulting in reduced strength and durability.

>> **Inspect your potential purchases for flaws.** Sight along a board looking for warping and twisting. Knots are okay if tight and in-grown, whereas loose ones are a bad sign.

>> **Pay attention to size.** The thickness and width of boards are expressed in nominal dimensions, such as 2x4 or 1x6, but the actual dimensions are less: ½- to ¾-inch (.5 to 1.9 cm) less (a 2x4, for example, is 1½ by 3½ inches, or 3.8 by 8.9 cm). For length, boards come in 2-foot (.6 m) increments from 6 to 20 feet (1.8 to 6.1 m).

>> **Be selective with the type.** Choose boards with a high percentage of *heartwood* (the darker, richer-colored wood) and dense growth rings (at least eight per inch/2.5 cm). In addition, remember the following:

- Some woods, such as the heartwood of cedar and redwood, resist decay naturally. These woods also tend not to warp as much as other species. Although cedar and redwood lack strength for major load-bearing members, such as deck joists, they work well for fences.

- Nondurable woods (southern pine and Douglas fir, for example) that have been pressure-treated with preservatives make good fence materials. Bear in mind that treated lumber fencing really shouldn't be used adjacent to edible plants (or used to make raised beds for food gardening — see Chapter 10), because the chemicals do leach into the soil over time.

REMEMBER

You can improve the appearance of most wood by staining or painting it, so consider durability and strength first.

About wood alternatives

You can construct many hardscape projects from lumber alternatives, principally plastics and composites, which we discuss here:

>> **Plastic materials** such as PVC (polyvinyl chloride) vinyl and fiberglass reinforced plastics (FRP) are generally used for fencing, arbors, deck skirting, and lawn edging. Many styles and sizes are available; they're strong and versatile and require no maintenance. Some plastic fence materials are sold as kits, making installation easy.

>> **Composite decking boards** (CDB) are made from recycled or reclaimed materials with polyethylene (HDPE or LDPE) plastic or PVC mixed with wood fiber, rice hulls, or other fillers as well as a blend of chemical additives to create a rigid product that won't rot, splinter, warp, or crack. These are commonly referred to as Trex. Trex, like Kleenex in the world of facial tissues, is actually a brand name. Similar products include New Tech Wood, Fiberon, and Timbertech.

In recent years, the marketplace and many contractors have embraced non-wood products because they have a lot going for them, such as:

- They have a convincing wood-like look that is truly aesthetically pleasing.

- They're tough, resistant to mildew, mold, and rot.

- They're easy to maintain — just spray off with water from time to time.

- They're available in many colors (though the brightness will fade over time).

Generally they're more expensive, but composites hold up much better and for much longer than wood and, in the end, if you factor in less maintenance, using them could end up being about the same investment or perhaps even a savings for you.

Composites are a good choice for decking, railing systems, and landscape timbers. They may be used pretty much as you would use regular lumber, though we recommend always creating pilot holes for nails and screws. The boards can be cut with a circular saw, require little to no maintenance, and don't need to be painted or stained.

Identifying tools and supplies

Be sure you have the necessary tools on the job before you start. You don't need to purchase all of these tools. You may be able to borrow some from family members, friends, and neighbors (just make sure to return them clean and in a timely manner). Or rent from big box home–improvement stores.

Here are some tools to add to your toolbelt and toolchest:

- **Basic carpentry tools:** A tape measure, hammer, square, screwdriver, handsaw, power/circular saw, power drill, and *chalkline* (a simple gadget that looks a bit like a tape measure; it helps you easily mark straight lines in chalk; see Chapter 2) — more than likely also a wheelbarrow, stepladder, and sawhorses.

- **Carpentry tools:** A jigsaw or even better, a reciprocating saw.

- **Digging tools:** Both square and round shovels, a good trowel, and perhaps a garden rake.

- **Specialty tools:** For instance, a power auger (to dig post holes), scoop loader (for hauling bulk materials), masonry-cutting saw (for brick, tile, or stone), plate compactor (for compacting gravel and sand), or ditch excavator (for irrigation, drain, and electrical pipes),

These specialty tools are perfect examples of ones you can rent or borrow rather than buy.

>> **Hose:** Not necessarily a tool per se, but having a nearby hose is never a bad idea. Rinse off dirty or muddy tools at the end of each work day. Blast soil or dirt out of your way. If you use mortar, you'll need water.

Meanwhile, you'll need stakes and levels for your hardscape projects:

>> **Stakes:** The stakes that we refer to are called *hubs* or *construction stakes*. They're made of wood, and the standard size is 2 x 2 inches (5.1 x 5.1 cm), with lengths varying between 8 and 24 inches (20.3 and 60.1 cm). They're sold in bundles at any lumber yard or home-supply store.

>> **Levels:** Levels are very handy. The three main kinds are as follows:

   • **Line level:** A smaller-size gadget (3 or 4 inches, 7.6 or 10.1 cm long) that can be hung on a taut string (via little hooks); has a bubble level embedded in it.

   • **Carpenter's, spirit, or I-beam level:** The classic metal, wood, or plastic item, typically 2 feet (.6 m) long (but you can get them up to 8 feet/2.4 m long — the longer the level, the greater the accuracy), with one or more bubble levels embedded; fine to use for smaller projects.

   • **Laser level:** This newer gadget is a game-changer, making formerly time-consuming jobs so much easier. Some look like a carpenter's level, and some look like a tin can; they mount on a tripod and rotate (manually or automatically) while emitting a red laser beam. You can rent the setup.

Keeping safety front and center

Always think safety. Proper attire as well as wise work habits and work-site precautions go a long way toward making any project safe for you and any helpers. Use common sense and keep the following in mind at all times:

>> Wear gloves, safety glasses or goggles, a dust mask, or hard hat as needed. If you have long hair, tie it back.

>> Dress in fitted, not loose, heavy pants and long-sleeve shirt.

>> Wear steel-toe boots.

>> Banish kids, pets, and individuals not helping you out of the work area.

>> Lift with your legs, not your back, and avoid lifting and twisting at the same time.

>> Keep the work site clear of scraps, idle tools, and other tripping hazards.

>> Make sure that extension cords and power tools are plugged into outlets with ground-fault circuit interrupter (GFCI) protection.

>> Operate power tools with caution, observing the manufacturer's safety recommendations.

>> Unplug tools if you need to change blades or bits.

Grading Your Property

Grading a site means leveling the soil to the desired contour — usually a flat surface, slightly sloped to allow for drainage. (*Note:* The land under a proposed deck site doesn't need to be level.) Grading for lawns and planting beds may also include adding soil amendments.

In any case, we're talking about pick-and-shovel work. For small areas, hand tools suffice. For a large patio or a complete landscaping overhaul project, rent a small tractor with a scoop loader and grading attachments.

TIP

The basic rule for grading for patios, walks, and foundation sites is the Goldilocks rule: not too much, not too little, just right. Built structures must rest on undisturbed soil, so don't overdig. Where additional soil is required, compact it carefully to minimize settling.

When you're grading your property, start with measuring. Don't rely on eyeballing; always check your work with a level. For larger sites, use the following steps to establish the finished grade:

REMEMBER

For most sites, slope the grade at a minimum rate of ¼ inch per foot, (.6 cm per 30.5 cm), for drainage. Around the house, foundation experts recommend that the ground slope away from the house at a rate of ½ to 1 inch per foot (1.3 to 2.4 cm per .3 m) for the first 10 feet (3 m) (except for patios and other paved areas, which slope at ⅛ to ¼ inch per foot, .3 to .6 cm per .3 m).

1. **Pound 18-inch (45.7 cm) stakes 6 to 12 inches (15.2 to 30.5 cm) into the ground every 10 feet (3 m) or so, with a sledgehammer as shown in Figure 4-1.**

WARNING

If this process begins for you with the soil on your property resisting staking (due to rocks or heavy or highly compacted soil, for example), call in the pros with heavy equipment.

FIGURE 4-1:
Pound stakes into
the ground every
10 feet (3 m) or
so along a grade.

© John Wiley & Sons, Inc.

2. **Identify the stake that you want to be at the highest point, and make a reference mark on that stake at the finished grade level.**

   You may have to dig down a bit to make the mark, or make the mark several inches (cm) above the existing grade.

3. **Mark the other stakes at the same level as the reference mark.**

   Use a laser level.

4. **At each stake, write how far below or above the reference mark the finished grade must be — 2½ inches (6.3 cm), for example.**

5. **Dig and fill the soil, using the measurements written on the stakes as a guide.**

TIP

When excavating, scrape off the topsoil first and place it where you can reuse it in your garden. For more on taking out a lawn, see Chapter 16.

Laying Out Straight Lines and Shapes

A *layout* is a system of stakes and stringlines that establishes the precise location of footings and borders for a building project. This could be the perimeter of your dream deck or patio, or just a fenceline.

You normally do layout *after* grading the site (see the previous section), but you may need to set a few stakes, using basic layout techniques, to guide the grading. Yes, doing so sounds old-school, but the methods are tried-and-true, and you can do it.

If an obstacle, such as a tree trunk, makes it impossible to string a line between two stakes, move both stakes an equal distance, in the same direction, from their original position. Then, stretch a stringline between them. To establish points, such as post locations, where the original stringline would have run, measure an equal distance from the string to the distance that you moved the stakes. This technique is called *offsetting*.

Make sure that you establish precisely what the stringline represents, for example, the inside edge of posts, the outside edge of the finished structure, the center of footings — whatever. It doesn't matter what you choose; just be consistent. Usually, however, stringlines represent the outside edges.

Any sturdy string will do for these tasks, but we recommend mason's twine because it is more durable and stretches less.

These sections help you execute these tasks in your yard. We prefer to use basic and practical techniques that many construction surveyors use on a regular basis.

Stringing lines — The hub and tack method

The simplest example of a layout is a string stretched between two stakes to establish a straight line. Instead of tying the line to the stakes, we recommend the more accurate method of securing the string to nails in the top of each stake. In construction surveying's lingo, this is called the *hub and tack method*; that is, the stake is a *hub* and the nail is a *tack*.

Here's how to do get started for a fence or a square or rectangular patio or deck or even a pathway (refer to Figure 4-2):

1. With a sledgehammer, pound 18-inch (45.7 cm) stakes 6 to 12 inches (15.2 to 30.5 cm) into the ground at each end of the proposed line.

2. Pound in a small nail at the top, in the center, of each stake — only partway.

3. Tie a string from one nail to the other.

Stringing out the rest of a shape

After you establish the first line, finish stringing the perimeter of the rest, whether it's your new patio, deck, or another item. Just follow these steps:

FIGURE 4-2:
Lay out a line.

© John Wiley & Sons, Inc.

1. **To establish a right angle and thus continue laying out the shape, go down your existing line 3 feet (.9 m) and set a stake.**

   Using a carpenter's square, go 4 feet (1.2 m) down in the perpendicular direction and set another stake. Put nails on top of each, as you did when you laid out the initial line.

2. **Measure the diagonal between the two new stakes.**

   If it's 5 feet (1.5 m), you're good, you made a right angle (you have a good carpenter's square). If it isn't, adjust the stake on the line that lacks a string yet (the one 4 feet, 1.2 m away) until it all checks out, that is, the numbers form a triangle with a right angle.

   TIP

   For checking larger distances, use multiples of 3, 4, and 5 feet, such as 9, 12, and 15, or 12, 16, and 20 feet (in metric, that would be .9, 1.2, and 1.5 m, such as 2.7, 3.6, and 4.8 m, or 3.6, 4.9, and 6.1 m).

3. **Continue down your new line the designed/desired distance, and put in another stake at the end, again topping it with a partially pounded-in nail.**

   Run mason's twine the full length.

4. **Double-check your diagonals.**

   This step requires math. Get out a calculator. We deploy the Pythagorean Theorem. (Yes, this is your tenth grade trigonometry class, back to haunt you!):

   $a^2 + b^2$ should $= c^2$

   a is the length of one side, b is the length of the other side, and c is the diagonal distance between the corners.

Adjust the stakes until it all checks out.

TIP

In some situations, such as attaching a deck or patio to the house, your layout may look cockeyed because the house walls, driveway, or other existing features aren't square. If so, fudge the layout slightly to bring the side of the layout in line with the existing feature.

5. **When you're satisfied, mark the layout on the ground.**

   If the stringlines are for guiding excavation — for fence posts or a patio base, for example — you need to mark the ground for digging. Where such marks must be perfectly accurate, hold a plumb bob close to the ground, with its string brushing against the stringline, and mark the ground directly under the bob with spray paint, flour, chalk, or colored cloth held down with a nail. Make several marks, as needed.

Working with Slopes

Installing one or more retaining walls on a slope does two good things for a landscape:

>> It prevents erosion.

>> It creates flat plantable areas where there wasn't before.

You can build a low (3 feet, .9 m, or less) retaining wall yourself out of timbers, stacked stone, or stacked block using the techniques in these sections.

WARNING

A wall higher than 3 or 4 feet (.9 or 1.2 m) is more of an engineering feat than a low one (it has to be able to withstand the considerable pressure from the earth behind it). It generally requires permits. Have a professional — a landscape architect or a stonemason, depending the material — design and build it.

Understanding challenges unique to installing retaining walls

Be prepared to contend with these major issues when you're installing retaining walls (they're certainly not deal-breakers when your wall is 3 feet (.9 m) or less):

>> **It's hard work.** Even for a wall of low height, you have to dig a lot. Depending on the materials you choose, you'll also be doing heavy lifting and maneuvering — all the more so if you plan several successive ones, that is, if you're terracing a slope (see the nearby sidebar about terracing).

TERRACING DEMYSTIFIED

Terracing is a great solution for turning an otherwise unusable or difficult-to-landscape slope or hillside into garden space. Just fill the completed terraces with soil and plant away. Or, customize the soil in each one — we've seen some great rock gardens on this plan. (For rock-garden information, turn to Chapter 20.) Because you'd still be scrambling up and down a hillside to care for whatever plants you install, we recommend low-maintenance choices. Check the color insert for a photograph of how one homeowner worked terracing into their landscape.

Remember: One 3-foot (.9 m) retaining wall is a retaining wall; installing a succession of two or more is basically *terracing*. It's the same project as the ones we describe in the section, "Working with Slopes," in this chapter, just bigger. You'll do more measuring, more excavating, devote more time, and spend more money on materials.

Before you start the project, you need to establish a plan that accommodates two things:

- **Rise** (the height you want your project to climb/occupy)
- **Run** (the length, measured from the highest point to the lowest — the horizontal distance)

This basic information will determine how many terraced beds you're going to need.

After doing that, it's just math. Decide how long each of your beds will be, say, for example, 10 feet (3 m). Divide by the total run (say, 50 feet, 15.2 m), so you need five beds: 50 divided by 10 = 5 (or 15.2 divided by 3 = 5).

When the rise is greater than your height, measure the hillside in increments.

Start work from the bottom, trenching and building as you work your way up the hill. The back of the last bed should be as high as the front wall of the first bed.

If you plan to stabilize your wall with *deadmen* (horizontal braces; refer to the nearby sidebar about jargon), you'll need additionally to create trenches every 4 feet (1.2 m), perpendicular to the wall, to accommodate them.

REMEMBER

One item that makes the work easier and faster is a tamping machine that you can rent. A tamping machine smooths out and compacts the soil surface so it's as solid and level as possible, without ruts or air pockets; a minimum of two or three passes over a project area is recommended. Follow all instructions about operation and safety.

>> **Get cleared for takeoff.** Make sure the project area doesn't have any underground pipes or buried cables. If there's any chance there's natural-gas lines, call your utility company so they can come out and check, and mark spots to avoid — a free service. To make sure, call 811, a nationwide service that checks for utility lines.

>> **Water can ruin your wall.** You must install provisions for drainage in order to prevent water from saturating the soil behind your retaining wall and exerting pressure on it, which can destabilize it or move it or parts of it out of position — a snafu you want to avoid.

To do so, either create *weep holes* (holes or gaps that allow drainage) or install a perforated drainpipe (perforated, to facilitate absorption and drainage). Working and backfilling with stones will also help stabilize the project. (You know the neighbor's wall that's falling down? We wager that if you look for weep holes, you won't find them.)

Positioning a retaining wall

Properly positioning a retaining wall is important because you want it to be stable. Here are the two main ways to do this:

>> **Set the retaining wall well away (say, several feet, or a meter, or more) from the original hillside, and then fill in behind the wall.** When you install the wall, you still create a base and backfill with some gravel, but the rest of the gap between the original hillside and your wall will require extra soil to be brought in.

>> **Set the retaining wall close to the top of the original hillside.** In this case, you need far less extra soil. In fact, you may be able to simply reuse the soil removed from the base of the hill, shoveling it in near the top of the wall.

Installing a retaining wall

To orient you to this project, the following steps generally apply to installing retaining walls of any kind:

1. **Clean up the designated area by removing plants, grass, and any loose debris.**

2. **To create a base, start at the bottom of the hill or slope and dig a trench with a shovel.**

   Dig an inch (2.5 cm) for every 8 inches (20.3 cm) of wall height. For example, if your wall will be 3 feet, or 36 inches, tall, do the math: 36 inches divided by 8 inches = dig 4½ inches deep (or, in metric: dig 11.4 cm deep).

   The length and width depends on the materials you're using.

3. **Tamp down the soil in your 4½-inch (11.4 cm) deep trench.**

4. **Install something to relieve the pressure of water building up behind your new wall.**

   Provide either weep holes along the base of the wall or a perforated drainpipe behind the wall.

5. **Add several inches (cm) of stones (#1 stones are best).**

   If you're using a perforated drain pipe, surround/bury it. Tamp down the stones. Check that the stone base is level, adding or shifting stones as necessary until it is.

6. **Line the bottom and perhaps also the sides with landscape or geotextile fabric.**

   Use plenty of extra extending beyond the boundaries; you can always trim after your timbers or stones are in place, but you can't extend too-short pieces. Try to use one continuous piece, but if that isn't possible, use overlapping pieces. (Doing so not only helps hold the soil down, but it will also prevent weeds from encroaching.) Don't trim it yet; wait until you're done.

TIP

You don't want soil to come through and cause clogs. Use washed stone because unwashed stone is loaded with silt.

7. **Begin to install the wall material.**

When putting in more than one tier, two things are important:

- *Batter* them so each succeeding layer leans back into the hill (in other words, it won't be perpendicular; this slight slant helps your wall counteract gravity).

- Backfill each tier with gravel as you go to strengthen it and aid drainage.

There's more than one way to make an effective retaining wall. Other construction materials to consider include timber, concrete blocks, and stacked stones. Here's some details about each, including how to erect them properly.

Timber retaining wall

To build a retaining wall out of *landscape timbers* (pressure-treated 6 x 6 boards specified for ground contact) or composite timbers, follow these instructions (see Figure 4-3):

1. **Start by creating the outer wall.**

Lay timbers horizontally on the tamped-stone base (the first one and part or all of the second may be below ground level, embedded in your base). Stagger the end joints; this forms stronger corners. Stagger joints at least 3 feet (.9 m).

WARNING

Don't use old railroad ties! They've been soaked in the toxic and messy preservative creosote. When it leaches into the soil, it contaminates groundwater and can also kill or harm plants. Railroad ties should never be used in the vicinity of edible plants.

2. **Add successive rows, but batter them atop one another ever-so-slightly back into the hill about a half inch (1.3 cm).**

Do so until you reach the desired height (typically 3 feet, .9 m, tall; generally speaking, taller ones require additional stability; construction of taller ones is best left to the pros).

3. **Anchor the ends of each timber to the underlying timbers.**

Every 2 feet (.6 m) or so, drill pilot holes and insert long spikes of rebar. Drive them deep enough so that the tops align just below the top of the finished wall.

4. **Midway up the wall, perpendicular to it, dig level trenches back into the hillside every 4 feet (1.2 m), back far enough to accommodate a 4-foot (1.2 m) *deadmen* (horizontal lengths of timber).**

Attach the deadmen flush with the outside of your wall, using 12-inch (30.5 cm) spikes or Torx drive screws. (If you lined the back of the excavation with landscape or geotextile fabric, you'll have to cut holes to accommodate the deadmen.) After they're placed, anchor them with 12-inch (30.5 cm) spikes or Torx drive screws.

REMEMBER

You'll need additionally to create trenches every 4 feet (1.2 m) for deadmen perpendicular to the wall, to accommodate them.

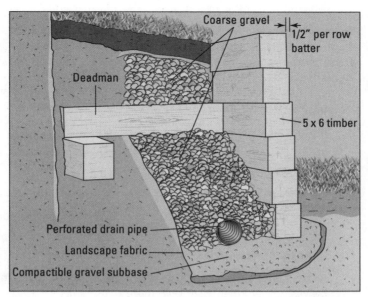

FIGURE 4-3:
Give a low retaining wall deadmen for stability.

5. **Install the remaining rows of timbers, again securing with rebar.**

Finish backfilling behind the wall, including the space between the deadmen.

6. **Drill weepholes, about 4 feet (1.2 m) apart.**

A good location is in the second row of timbers above ground level. Angle the weepholes upward.

Concrete block retaining wall

Manufacturers have created decorative concrete blocks that are specifically designed for dry-stacked retaining walls — that is, you don't need mortar. Modular in dimension, they're easier to work with than stone. Sometimes they are called *Allan blocks*, referring to a specific manufacturer.

Most blocks are designed to be battered, and many have predrilled holes for inserting stabilizing pins or rebar to lock them together. When you follow the manufacturer's directions to the letter, this project is straightforward!

Stacked-stone retaining wall

A stacked-stone retaining wall should have a backward slant (batter) of 2 to 3 inches (5 to 7.6 cm) for dry-set stones and 1 to 2 inches (2.5 to 5 cm) for mortared stones. This slant helps your wall counteract gravity. If you prefer to use mortar, see Chapter 5 for full details.

Building a 2- or 3-foot (.6 to .9 m) high wall of dry-stacked (no mortar) stones requires considerable lifting and adjusting of stones, but it's enjoyable work if you aren't in a hurry. It pays off with a handsome wall. Follow these steps, and consult Figure 4-4:

1. **Dig into the hill, about 15 to 18 inches (38.1 to 45.7 cm).**

2. **Dig an ample base.**

We recommend a trench 2 feet (.6 m) deep and wide enough for the broadest stones plus a 4-inch (10.1 cm) drainpipe.

3. **Place gravel in the trench and compact it, 4 inches (10.1 cm) deep.**

Lay the drainpipe along the back corner, sloping it toward the outlet end. Then add another 12 inches (30.5 cm) of stones to the trench.

4. **Using the largest stones, set the first course in place.**

Tilt the stones back slightly, toward the bank. Check frequently that the top of the wall is level. When it isn't level, make adjustments.

5. **Drape landscape or geotextile fabric against the inside back wall, and backfill with gravel or drain rock as you lay each course.**

6. **Build up the wall with stones.**

As you lay each course, lean the wall into the hill at a rate of 2 to 3 inches per foot (5 to 7.6 cm per .3 m) of wall height. A 3-foot (.9 m) wall, for example, must lean 6 to 9 inches (15.2 to 22.8 cm) into the hill.

7. **Within 12 inches (30.5 cm) of the top of the wall, fold the filter fabric over the stones and backfill the rest of the wall with topsoil.**

If you want, install a capstone.

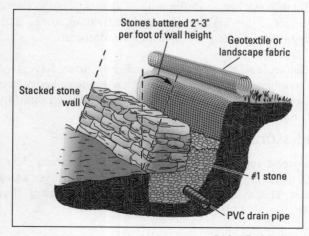

FIGURE 4-4: Building a stacked concrete or stone wall, without mortar, requires careful placement of the stones.

© John Wiley & Sons, Inc.

Chapter **5**

Dealing with Water

There's a lot of talk about water these days. If you live in a drought-prone area, your design and needs are likely to differ dramatically from areas that are flush with water. The best practices, in any case, involve keeping water on your property. That's true whether you're working with water that arrives naturally or working with water that you wish to supply efficiently.

So important is water in home landscapes that we focus this entire chapter on it. Don't worry, we don't give a treatise on *hydrology* (the study of the movement, distribution, and management of water on this planet). Rather we stick to the need-to-know information for home landscapers like you and keep it basic and useful.

We can't emphasize this point enough: Deal with water in your yard early and properly. That way, you can avoid some seriously vexing problems. You can also save yourself unnecessary and perhaps onerous work later, after all your other landscape elements such as decks, patios, or flowerbeds have been put in place. Grandma was right, an ounce of prevention is worth a pound of cure.

Routing Water and Improving Drainage

Water in a landscape involves *infiltration*, the distribution of water through layers of soil; effectively infiltration removes contaminants and replenishes groundwater supplies. You may have seen signs near or on storm drains that prohibit or warn people from dumping oil and other waste products (for example, "drains to the sea," or "drains to the Ohio River," sometimes with a picture of a fish). Do what you can to prevent excess water from going down these drains. The more water that sinks *into the ground* to get cleaned and distributed through natural channels, the better!

REMEMBER

If your property is in a low spot and you have very wet soil, other tricks can help convey water in a natural way. Trees, for example, are like columns of water, and their roots help prevent erosion during periods of heavy rain.

Unless your entire site has no low spots where rainwater and melted snow accumulate, you probably have some drainage problems to solve — especially if water accumulates under a deck, around a patio and walkways, under the shed, or around the house. Don't forget the basement either; a wet basement is often a warning sign of water table or drainage problems on your property.

Water exists or appears in your yard in two main places: on the surface and below the surface. Although you may or may not specifically observe the water itself, you'll surely notice its effects. The following sections discuss drainage and how to route water prudently and correctly through your landscape.

Focusing on surface drainage

You can divert water away from low spots by creating *swales* (shallow gullies with gently sloping sides), dry streambeds, or ditches along the surface of the ground, or by installing a subsurface drainage system. Here we consider each.

WARNING

Make sure you don't do the following:

>> **Send water into your neighbor's yard.** Not only will you not win Neighbor of the Year, but you may face a lawsuit and even fines from many municipalities.

>> **Divert water into the street.** In many places it's not legal (the exception being extraordinary circumstances like pumping out a basement after a major flood).

To address surface drainage, follow the following steps:

1. Identify an outfall on your own property, to which water can be diverted.

The *outfall* (discharge point) must be lower than the problem areas and mustn't spill large amounts of water onto your neighbor's property or into the street. If necessary, plan a catch basin to collect surface water and divert it underground to a suitable outfall (refer to the next section for instructions).

2. **Plot a route for a ditch or swale between the problem area and the outfall.**

   Choose a meandering course to slow down the flow of water and create an interesting landscaping feature. This step takes more than skill; it takes observation. Water follows the path of least resistance.

3. **Dig the ditch or grade the swale.**

   Check the bottom with a level and 8-foot (2.4 m) straightedge to make sure it slopes 1 inch (2.5 cm) per 8 feet (2.4 m) of horizontal run for bare soil and 2 inches (5 cm) per 8 feet (2.4 m) for a lawn or planted beds. Remember the following:

   • For steeper pitches or where heavy rainstorms occur, line the bottom of the waterway with strips of PVC (polyvinyl chloride) membrane that is designed for lining ponds. Or, better yet, get the steep area terraced.

   • For a decorative effect, place stones along the water course to resemble a dry streambed during dry months.

Installing subsurface drainage

To put in subsurface drainage, follow these steps:

1. **Find a low point in your yard where you can run an underground drain pipe.**

   The pipe should be 3 or 4 inches (7.6 or 10.1 cm) in diameter and slope away from the problem site at a rate of ⅛ inch per foot (.3 cm per .3 m). The outlet of this pipe must disperse the water into your yard, not into your neighbors' yard or the street.

   If that isn't possible, terminate the drain pipe in an underground *dry well,* an excavation approximately 8 feet (2.4 m) deep and 3 to 4 feet (.9 to 1.2 m) wide that you fill with stones and rubble and cover with topsoil. The dry well enables water to percolate into the soil more quickly than from the surface.

   Dry wells don't work in deep clay soils with a low percolation rate. There the only solution is a concrete-lined pit with a sump pump.

REMEMBER

2. **After you identify where the drain pipe is to terminate, excavate a trench from that point to the problem site and another trench along the site perimeter, about 14 to 16 inches (35.5 to 40.6 cm) deep.**

   Slope the ditches toward the termination point at a rate of ⅛ inch per foot (.3 cm per .3 m).

3. **Place 2 inches (5 cm) of #1 stone in the bottom of the perimeter trench and lay 4-inch (10.1 cm) diameter plastic (PVC or ABS) perforated drain pipe atop the stone as Figure 5-1 shows.**

   Continue this pipe to the termination point or connect it to 4-inch (10.1 cm) diameter (unperforated) plastic pipe, which goes to the outfall. (*#1 stone* is masonry jargon for the largest of the crushed-stone, or gravel, grades; it's widely used in drainage projects.)

4. **Backfill the trenches with 8 inches (20.3 cm) more of #1 stone, surround with geotextile fabric, and fill the trenches with top soil.**

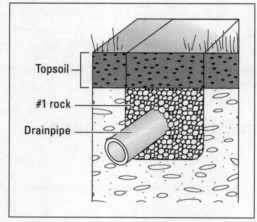

FIGURE 5-1:
Use underground drainpipe and #1 stone to provide subsurface drainage.

© John Wiley & Sons, Inc.

Returning water to the land — rain gardens

Rain gardens are a relatively new and increasingly popular type of garden is a win-win landscape feature. Basically a *rain garden* is a trench or garden bed, approximately 6 inches (15.2 cm) deep that receives rainfall runoff from your home's roof, driveway, and/or yard. The runoff soaks into the area, which is typically landscaped with shrubs and perennial plants. Water thus remains in your own yard, sustaining a garden area and also naturally replenishing the groundwater table. For example, water from your home's gutters is routed with a pipe to the rain garden area (see Figure 5-2).

REMEMBER

A rain garden mitigates stormwater runoff, reduces erosion, and diminishes flood damage. The plants in a rain garden thrive with little extra attention as soon as they're established.

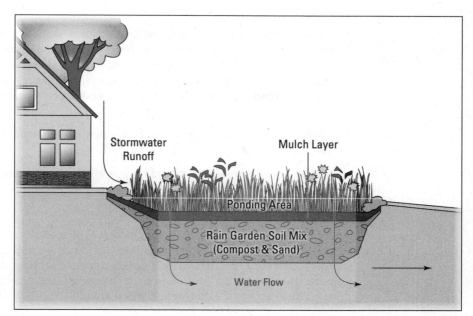

FIGURE 5-2:
A rain garden routes gutter water to a small garden area.

If you want to create one in your landscape, you can stick to the following steps: (Alternatively, some contractors specialize in them; get an estimate and hire someone experienced to do the work.)

1. Walk around your property to identify an appropriate spot.

The best one is in a flat or only slightly sloping area.

WARNING

Don't pick a low, perpetually wet spot in your yard because chances are it drains poorly, and you'd only get long-term sogginess. Stay at least 10 feet (3 m) from your house, especially if it has a basement, to avoid creating a water problem. Also, if you have a well or septic field, stay away from it.

2. Dig a test hole about a foot (.3 m) deep, fill it with water, and observe how long it takes to drain.

It should drain off in a day or less. If it doesn't, try another spot until you find one that drains off in a day or less.

3. Calculate the size/footprint of your rain garden, based on the size/footprint of your home.

REMEMBER

Here's a good general rule: A rain garden should be about one-sixth the size of your home. Research has shown that this size works for receiving routed gutter runoff without any major problems.

TIP

Make your rain garden square, round, oval, whatever shape you like, just within the size range calculated. For example, if your home's footprint is 1,600 square feet (488 square meters), make your rain garden about 260 square feet (7.2 m). This translates (approximately) to a rectangular rain garden that measures 26 × 10 feet (7.9 × 3 m), or perhaps you'd prefer 15 × 17 feet (4.6 × 5.2 m).

You can fool with your options using this handy online calculator: www.propertycalcs.com/area/.

Mark its boundaries with stakes and string, a length of rope or cord, or a flexible hose.

4. **Dig out the area.**

   A mere 6 inches (15.2 cm) may be fine, though if you plan to mulch the plantings, you need to dig a bit deeper. Work to keep the bottom of the hole fairly level; it doesn't have to be perfect, but you don't want to route water to a corner. If the area is on a slope, use some of the excavated soil to create a berm on the downside to prevent runoff.

5. **Run a pipe from the nearest house downspout into the area.**

   You may choose to bury it from view in a shallow trench. A standard PVC drainpipe works.

6. **Fill the rain garden with good soil (see Chapter 17) and plant thickly.**

   Choose plants that like moist ground (see Part 3) or get advice at the nursery or garden center where you're buying the plants. Perennials, shrubs, and even ornamental grasses all work.

Recognizing the Different Options of Watering Systems

Planning ahead and getting watering systems installed *before* plants are put in is obviously preferable. Otherwise, you may be looking at creating some temporary but significant havoc, that is, digging up planted areas and having to re-landscape them afterward.

Conserving water, a precious resource in many areas, is the prize. You want to supply your plants with just enough, with little or no waste. The following sections identify your options, starting with the low-tech choices and working up the trouble-and-expense ladder.

You can conserve a lot of water not only by watering efficiently and growing drought-tolerant plants, but also by grouping thirstier plants together. Group plants by water needs, and water them together. Or — better still — group them in a lower part of the yard where the water naturally goes, especially after a rainstorm.

Watering cans

Before you dismiss hand-watering with a watering can, think again. This time-honored method not only allows you to deliver directly to certain plants and, if you bend down a bit, to send it straight to the roots (rather than inefficiently watering the foliage), it also enables you to slow down and observe your plants one by one. Using a watering can lets you to notice your plants' water needs better, not to mention perhaps the early signs of any pest or disease problem. You're also going to enjoy their beauty.

Our favorite cans are durable galvanized steel with a *rose* (the device at the end of the spout, like a cap but with tiny holes) to shower the plants lightly and evenly. The water soaks in well with them. Just don't go too big, or you'll be staggering to manage your watering can when it's full.

Rain barrels

In recent years, as rainfall has become sparser or homeowners become thriftier, rain barrels have become quite popular. In the past people would use anything handy, including old 55-gallon drums (which may be contaminated with whatever used to be in them) and heavy-duty plastic trash cans. Nowadays you can buy a special rain barrel at a garden center, home-supply store, or even online.

If water is really dear where you live, especially in the hot summer months, but even if it isn't — ask yourself why you dump tap water on your garden. The expense begins in your area's watershed where water is removed to your municipality's water-treatment plant. There it's treated with various chemicals and filters until it's *potable* (safe for drinking). You'll pay for all this later when your water bill arrives. By the way, even gardeners with well water have filtering and disinfecting treatments in place.

Your landscape plants *don't require potable water.* Collecting rainwater in a rain barrel is a great way to stockpile water for the garden at barely any cost or trouble. You can get a big one and position it strategically (like under a roof gutter).

Although you can use any durable barrel, you can find ones sold solely for this purpose. They come with nice features, such as a fitted top screen to keep out debris and critters (including breeding mosquitoes), and a spigot for easy access or to attach a hose.

REMEMBER

Make sure you pick the right site. A full rain barrel is incredibly heavy, but even a partially full one is impossible to maneuver. Choose a site that's firm, level, and well-drained (so the weight doesn't cause it to sink or tilt). In freezing climates, empty it before winter sets in.

Hoses of all kinds

Living in a house without a garden hose is nearly impossible, even when you have other watering systems in place. You'll always have a need for a hose, even if it's just spot-watering or rinsing something off. Here are the main types of hoses:

>> **Traditional garden hose:** You get what you pay for. Poor-quality hoses kink, break down in sunlight, and end up having to be discarded. Treat yourself to a quality hose. As for length, we find that longer is better, just because of extended reach.

>> **Soaker or leaky hoses:** These types of hoses are great. Wend them through a flowerbed or vegetable garden, turn on the water, and let them *sweat* (dribble out) water slowly, evenly, and steadily — directly into the plants' root zones. Black ones are barely visible, if you want to leave them in place.

>> **Extras:** You can find lots of accessories, such as watering wands and spiffy bubbler attachments (which are screwed on to the delivery end of the hose), not to mention timers (which are installed at the water source). Look around in a well-stocked garden supplier or in an online catalog, and treat yourself to something that makes your watering life easier and more efficient, not to mention perhaps even nicer for your thirsty plants.

Irrigation systems

If you're interested in having an irrigation system in your yard, you have options. The kind you ultimately install depends on your climate, the size and needs of your landscape, and your budget. Approach this important element prudently. Start by finding out what your neighbors are doing, visit their yards, and ask questions. If you want to proceed, call a contractor who installs systems for an estimate and the different options, which include the following.

TECHNICAL STUFF

Traditional in-ground sprinkler systems, certainly, are a thing of the past, thanks to the rise of superior in-ground irrigation systems and the fact that the old ones wasted so much water to runoff and evaporation. You occasionally may still see them at work on golf courses and some corporate and college campuses, but they're being phased out in favor of new, greatly improved technology.

TIP

Conserve water by operating watering systems during early morning hours. (Don't water during evening hours because doing so can lead to disease issues in your plants; see Part 3.)

In-ground systems

Irrigation technology for home landscapes has experienced a boom in recent years, as research has advanced and demand has soared. The efficiency and durability of in-ground systems are impressive.

However, installing one is a major and sophisticated project, especially if you want full-yard coverage. In fact, your whole yard may have to be dug up or disrupted. If you're contemplating such an installation, it's really not a DIY project. Find a good contractor by weighing their experience, completed projects, references, insurance, and so on.

Aboveground micro-irrigation

Aboveground micro-irrigation systems deliver water to emitters, microsprinklers, or drip hoses that you place at the bases of individual plants or clusters of plants. The only parts of the system that you need to install during site preparation are the main water-supply lines, but most of the system is aboveground and can be installed after you put in plants.

The basic components of a micro-irrigation system include the following items:

>> A filter (to keep the tubing free of minute debris that can clog the drip holes)

>> A pressure regulator (to keep the water pressure in the system constant for optimum performance)

>> A backflow preventer (a simple device, usually a vacuum breaker, that prevents water in the system from backing up into the public water supply)

>> Valves — manual or electronic (to control water flow to different circuits)

>> An automatic controller (includes valve controllers and a timer)

>> Tubing

>> Emitters, microsprinklers, or drip hoses

TIP

Most manufacturers provide excellent step-by-step instructions for installing their systems. Before you begin planning yours, visit a home center or irrigation supplier and pick up product specifications and instructions, or dig around online (being careful to research ones that are actually marketed to home, and not commercial, landscapes). Also watch some instructional YouTube videos.

TIP

You can buy components in kits or individually. Kits are less expensive than the same parts bought individually, but they may include components that you don't need. The major components, such as the pressure regulator and filter, may also be too small if you intend to expand your system beyond the kit size.

Your main planning task is to decide what type of drip emitter or microsprinkler to use at each plant. These devices are calibrated for different flow rates, such as half a gallon per hour, so that each plant receives an individualized amount of water. Manufacturers provide recommendations for the size and number of emitters to use for certain plants. Most container plants require one emitter rated at a half-, one-, or two-gallons per hour (GPH), depending on size. Some plants, such as ferns or bromeliads, may also require *misters* (devices that create mist) to keep their leaves moist.

Old-fashioned sprinklers

You may have grown up chasing your siblings or friends through the path of a sprinkler on a hot day, which did double-duty watering the lawn and entertaining and cooling off the kids. In areas where water isn't scarce, people still use them. Elsewhere, their day in the sun has faded in favor of the more efficient watering gear earlier in this section. The fact that fewer people have sprawling lawns may also have something to do with their popularity decline.

And yet, they're not altogether gone. If you don't mind hooking a sprinkler up to a hose, and/or don't mind moving one around for coverage, you may be pleased to discover that sprinklers today have some nifty improvements. Some sprinklers allow you to adjust the width and range of the spray, and others are weighted so they don't scoot around. Others oscillate, others offer multiple different patterns, and some are programmable.

INSTALLING WATER-SUPPLY LINES

You're considering undertaking the momentous project of installing your own water-supply lines. Perhaps you're installing an outdoor kitchen or an outdoor stall shower, running water to a utility sink or potting shed, or adding places to hook up garden-watering hoses and equipment.

Remember: If you live in a cold climate, enjoying the use of your outdoor plumbing is seasonal. Drain your water-supply lines when cold weather comes, even if the plastic you used was touted as flexible. You won't be needing the water supply again till warmer days return. To simplify this annual chore, attach a valve adjacent the shutoff to your house and blow the lines out with an air compressor.

Plastic pipe and fittings make outdoor plumbing fairly simple and inexpensive. Pex (plastic tubing made from high-density polyethylene) is great stuff. To install water lines, follow these steps:

1. **Connect a new pipe to a convenient *fitting* (such as a connector, elbow, or tees) in the existing main line, just before it goes into the house.**

   Look for a short branch pipe, such as a pipe that supplies a faucet, so you don't have to cut into the main water supply line. In areas with severe winters, this point of connection must be protected from frost, either by locating it within the basement or burying it deeply (below the frost line).

   For public health reasons, plumbing codes require a backflow device to be installed between this point of connection and the first outlet for the garden system.

(continued)

(continued)

2. **Dig a trench for the new pipe from this connection point to the new faucet or irrigation valve location.**

   For short runs, dig by hand, using a narrow shovel called a trenching shovel. For long runs, rent a ditch excavator.

3. **Lay out the new pipe next to the trench.**

   Pipe comes in 20-foot (6.1 m) sections of various diameters. For a single faucet, use ¾-inch (1.9 cm) diameter pipe. For multiple faucets or valves, use 1- or 1¼-inch (2.5 or 3.2 cm) diameter pipe, depending on the available water pressure.

4. **Plan the fittings that you need.**

   Join pipes end-to-end, using the bell end; 90- and 45-degree elbows for changing direction; tees for branching additional lines off the main line; adapters for converting from plastic pipe (slip joints) to threaded fittings (MIP or FIP joints — male or female iron pipe); and nipples (rigid pipe threaded at both ends) for short extensions. Although you eventually terminate the water lines at faucets and/or sprinkler valves, you don't need to install those yet — simply attach threaded or slip caps to the ends of the pipe. Where winter freezes are common, install a drain-down valve at the lowest point of the system to empty the pipes for winter.

5. **Install a gate valve (manual shutoff valve) where the new piping connects to the old.**

   Shut off the main water valve, remove the existing faucet and riser, and install a tee. Reattach the faucet riser to one outlet of the tee and install the gate valve on the other outlet. Turn on the water and test the valve. (If the valve is underground, place a *valve box* — a prefabricated enclosure for underground valves — over it for access.)

6. **Install the pipe and fittings, starting at the gate valve and working toward the remote locations.**

7. **Turn on the gate valve to test the connections.**

   Warning: If a test and inspection are required, don't connect the piping to the gate valve. Instead, isolate the system from the valve, attach a pressure gauge at one of the fittings, and pump air into the pipes to the required test pressure — typically around 100 to 125 pounds per square inch (2.5 cm square). The pressure should hold for at least four hours.

8. **After testing the system, fill the trenches with soil.**

   If the soil is rocky, cover the pipes with sand to prevent punctures; then fill the trench with soil.

Chapter **6**

All Things Fences, Walls, and Gates

Your property needs boundaries around it and access into it. Ever since humans set down roots in residences, it seems, they've had the impulse not only to wrap themselves in the shelter of a home but to define their adjacent outdoor space — whether it's keeping the howling wilderness at bay, creating privacy, or setting the domain apart from neighboring properties.

In your landscape, fences and walls do the job while also providing a vertical background or backdrop for what's within. And don't forget about the occasional gate, which lets you into your yard! Check the color insert to see a couple of photos of fence-gate combos.

Install the elements in this chapter as early in the landscape construction process as possible. Make sure you know where that property line is (if in doubt, refer to Chapter 4). Here we tour some options and walk you through basic construction. If you're not a DIYer, hire a professional for this work.

REMEMBER

Safety is key whenever you're building or installing anything. Review the general safety advice in Chapter 4 about worksites.

Fabricating Fences

Fences tend to be variations on a basic design: posts buried in the ground; horizontal rails installed between them; and some kind of fencing attached to the rails — pickets, boards attached vertically, boards attached horizontally, lattice, wire mesh, solid panels, siding materials, bamboo, wood, or some other durable material worked into decorative designs.

Add to those variables, the height of the fence and the endless possibilities of color, and you can see why no two fences are exactly alike.

Here we delve into the look of your new fence, including dimensions and the many possible materials. You have a lot of great options so you want to choose wisely and well. We also walk you through the building process.

Knowing what to consider before beginning

To narrow your choices, use the following guidelines:

>> **Height:** Six feet (1.8 m) is standard for side and backyards but may not be high enough if you have a raised deck or if neighboring houses are close to your property line. In those cases, you may want to build an 8-foot (2.4 m) fence or install solid screen of tall bushes (see Chapter 12 for hedge and windbreak advice and information). In addition, remember these points:

- For front-yard fences, 3 to 4 feet (.9 to 1.2 m) is sufficient for defining your property line.

- If you have a corner lot with fences along both streets, make sure that neither fence blocks views of traffic.

- Be sure to discuss your new fence with your neighbors. Advise them of the things they'll want to know, especially how high and when construction will begin and end. You may have to ask for permission to work on or carry material across their property.

WARNING

Depending on where you live, zoning ordinances (as well as home-association boards) govern fencing matters, specifically allowable heights and sometimes also materials. You don't want to proceed without a required permit and get fined or put in something too tall and be asked to tear it down and start over.

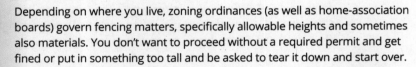

>> **Imposing fences:** A long, tall fence may create the feeling of prison walls. To break up the stockade effect, intersperse decorative elements, such as lattice panels or alternative fencing materials along the fence at regular

intervals, or use shrubs (see Chapter 12) or perennial flowers (refer to Chapter 14). Break up the top of a long, monotonous fence with *finials* (round doodads) at the tops of the posts or top the fence sections with scallop shapes to create a wavy fence line.

>> **Color:** Color is often overlooked when planning a new fence, but it can make the difference between something merely functional and something that contributes to the beauty of your landscape. A white or light-colored fence calls attention to itself and brings a fence forward visually. A dark-colored fence recedes into the background. Painting a fence the same color as your house unifies the two elements. Choosing neutral colors or earth tones for the fence ties your fence to your garden.

>> **Neighborhood:** In some areas, certain fence styles or materials dominate. In other areas, fence styles reflect eclectic tastes. Respect neighborhood and regional traditions in choosing your style.

Choosing fence materials

You may be amazed at the range of materials that can be used in fencing. We encourage you to weigh all your options before deciding. Looking around your street or neighborhood at other fences may also spur thoughts of what you want (and what you don't want), so take the time to do that, too.

Considering wood or composite fencing

To help you decide whether to use wood (and to discover about what kinds) as well as to review the pros and cons of the newer composite fencing materials, refer to Chapter 4. In the end, of course, the material you choose is a matter of your taste and budget.

Wood specifically intended for fence-building should be *pressure-treated* to prevent rot; avoid untreated lumber. Pressure-treated lumber is placed in a depressurized holding tank, then the air is removed and replaced with a chemical preservative. This infusion protects treated wood from insect damage and rot, although it doesn't prevent weathering and corrosion.

TECHNICAL
STUFF

Pay attention to the *retention level* (how much preservative the lumber holds). For posts, choose a retention level of .40, which is suitable for contact with the ground. For other fence members, choose lumber that's treated to a retention level of .25. Unless you buy pressure-treated wood that includes a water-repellent stain, you must seal and finish the wood after your fence is in place.

Keep these tips in mind as you buy lumber:

>> Use lumber cut to standard dimensions (4x4s, 1x8s, and so on), or buy wood that's milled into specialty shapes such as pickets, split rails, decorative posts, or scrolled board patterns.

>> If you're on a smaller budget and don't mind replacing your fence after a season or two (depending, of course, on your climate), you can use plywood. Just make sure you choose exterior grades.

>> Prioritize posts! No matter what type of wooden fencing you buy, always choose a high grade of the most durable wood for the posts.

>> You can also buy prefabricated sections or panels of fencing, but examine them carefully for the quality of wood (avoid sapwood and wide growth rings), the size of lumber, and the number and type of fasteners (staples rather than nails or screws).

>> Alternatively, consider using composite lumber (commonly called Trex, which is actually a brand name). It makes for a more durable fence that stands up to weather and the passing years and is low-maintenance. You can build an entire fence out of composite materials. The steps are the same as for a wooden fence, with only one minor difference: when nailing or screwing, take the time to create *pilot holes* first (pre-drilled holes before moving on to inserting nails or screws).

We walk you through how to build a fence later in the section, "Building a basic fence," later in this chapter.

Going with vinyl fencing

These fences, which come in a variety of styles and heights, are hollow vinyl shapes. They're popular in areas where winters don't batter them until they sag or become brittle. Often they come in white, which may or may not be to your taste. (A downside is that you need to periodically rinse off your white vinyl fence with the hose to keep it clean and nice.) In recent years manufacturers have improved the product so it's tougher and lasts longer. *Remember:* Thicker is better.

Installation of vinyl fencing is too advanced for this book. If you want vinyl fencing, we suggest you consult with a pro. The good news is usually buying this material is a package deal: The supplier is the installer, and you'll likely get a lifetime guarantee on the fence, too.

Recognizing metal options

Depending on your needs, taste, and budget, metal (including tubular aluminum and steel) or wire (including chain-link) may be your choice. These materials are even available as fence kits, complete with assembly/installation directions.

GOING THE NATURAL ROUTE WITH YOUR FENCE

Some other natural fencing materials to consider include the following:

- **Reclaimed wood:** Perhaps you have access to some discarded wood from an old barn or other wooden structure that's been taken down. Here are some considerations, besides the obvious question of whether there is enough for your fence:

  Pros to using reclaimed wood include the fact that it's an environmentally friendly material and gives a rustic look. Because it often comes from old-growth trees, it's harder and more dense. However, if you're buying it from a dealer, it may be expensive. Also the wood could contain toxins from paint and chemicals, like different preservatives or lead. Check for signs of bug infestation. Wear gloves when handling.

- **Hemp lumber:** Some builders and carpenters are looking to this newer material as the wave of the future. Hemp is hard and dense, and it can be sanded, painted, or stained. However, hemp lumber remains expensive, so it's not widely used yet; therefore, it hasn't had time to be thoroughly tested.

- **Bamboo wood:** This is another alternative that is increasingly appearing on the market and may tempt you. Bamboo is eco-friendly, costs less, and is easy to install. However, it's often attacked by fungi and insects if not treated, and it can't resist fire. Also, in most cases, you can't nail bamboo; if you elect to use bamboo, your fence will have to be held together with wire or hemp cords.

For specific installation information, you can always go to the websites of the manufacturers or tune into the many instructional videos on YouTube. Just like any other fence, work on a straight line, consider height, and so on.

After your plain metal fence is up, you can make it more private and more attractive by encouraging a leafy or flowering plant to grow up through and over it. See Chapter 12 for vine advice.

Building a basic fence

If you have a few weekends, some vacation time, some helpers in your network of family or friends, you may enjoy building your own fence. The experience offers an excellent opportunity to practice basic carpentry skills. For a basic one, wood or Trex, stick to the steps in the following sections. Posts go in first, then rails, then the actual fencing boards.

THE MAGIC OF WILLOW FENCING

Willow fencing and screening has long been popular in British gardens, where its light weight and appealing natural look adds a lot of charm. Improvements over the years have included interweaving willow with wire so it's easier to bend to your will and the results are more stable. Some suppliers instituted a process that peels the thin bark off twigs and treats them with high-pressure steam carbonizing, which results in a smooth, mahogany tone.

But you don't have to go that far. Back-to-basics construction is an even older art and results in a more natural, rustic look that you can use for fencing, screening, and even low (say, 6 inches, or 15.2 cm high) decorative borders around flower or vegetable beds.

You can do it yourself, assuming you live somewhere near abundant willow trees (so you can harvest judiciously, without depleting the population or harming individual trees' appearance or health). Willows, both native and introduced, grow widely throughout North America and favor habitats and settings of damp ground. The following basic instructions are adapted from the techniques of the late Heru Hall, an experienced landscaper from San Mateo, California; his work graces many residential and commercial gardens in the Bay Area. You can also find a variety of inspiring willow-fencing instructional videos on YouTube.

Here are some simple steps:

1. **Harvest willow branches in spring when they're young and full of moisture.**

   Cut long lengths, several feet (a meter or so) long if possible. You can shorten them later if you want, but the only way to lengthen them is to weave or wire them together. It's easier to have long whips. Strip off the leaves.

2. **Within a day or two of harvesting, weave, braid, and/or wrap the whips into the design you desire, while they're still fresh and pliable.**

   Allow the design to set for several days to a week. It will naturally cure, dry, and harden, shrinking ever so slightly.

   When erecting a fence or long low border, secure it by driving wooden posts or thick wooden branch pieces (of some other hardwood tree) in at intervals.

Laying out post-hole locations

Start by laying out the locations for your post hole:

1. **Stretch a string between stakes along the fence line.**

   Short 6-inch (15.2 cm) stakes work well. Align the string with the centers — not the edges — of the post positions. If you prefer, you can use a laser level.

2. **Establish the post spacing.**

Posts are typically spaced 5 to 8 feet (1.5 to 2.4 m) apart, depending on the size of framing members, weight of the fencing material, and length of prefabricated fence panels. If possible, choose a spacing that divides evenly into the total fence length.

Don't forget to put in posts for the gate (see the section "Going for Gates," later in this chapter for more information). Try to make fence *bays* (sections between posts) equal on either side of a gate. If you end up with an odd-sized bay, get rid of it by readjusting the post spacing or changing the overall fence length. If neither solution works, split the odd-sized bay dimension in half and place the shorter bays at each end of the fence.

3. **Mark the ground.**

Starting at the uphill end of the fence and holding a tape measure as close to level as possible (rather than laying it on sloping ground), mark the center of each post location with spray paint, a swatch of cloth with a nail through the center, or even a pinch of flour. To align the mark with the stringline, hold a *plumb bob* (a string with a weight on the end) against the string or hold a level vertically against it without deflecting the string.

Installing posts

Now you're ready to put the fence posts in place — an important step to get right so the fence will succeed. There are a couple of additional considerations (posts that come with *mortises*, or holes) and the option of securing the posts into the ground with concrete footings, so consult the nearby sidebars if they apply. Otherwise, here's how to proceed:

1. **Temporarily move the stringline out of the way.**

2. **Determine the post hole size.**

In general, keep the holes as narrow as possible, usually about twice the width of the post. Some additional guidelines include

- Plan an 8-inch (20.3 cm) diameter for posts to be set in crushed stone and/ or earth (plan 12-inch, or 30.5 cm, diameter holes for 4x4 posts that will be set in concrete footings — see the nearby sidebar "Considering Concrete Footings"). If you use larger posts, expand the hole accordingly.

- Each hole should be 6 inches (15.2 cm) deeper than the post footing depth (according to local building codes) or, in cold climates, 12 inches (30.5 cm) past the frost line.

WORKING WITH POSTS THAT HAVE MORTISES

Posts with *mortises* (holes) cut into them to receive rails, or with decorative tops, must all be set to the same level — you *cannot trim the tops to level them.*

Install the higher end post first. Attach temporary *cleats* (short pieces of wood that straddle the hole) to opposite sides of the post to keep it from sinking into the hole. Install the other end post at the same level, using a level to keep them aligned. Brace both posts securely. Then, measure down an equal distance from the top of each post, tack nails at those points, and stretch a line between the nails. Install the remaining posts so that all of the tops are an equal distance above the stringline.

3. **Dig holes.**

No way around it, this is hard work. For just a few holes, use a *clamshell digger* (a hand tool that resembles a large pair of tongs). For long fences, rent a *power auger* (a gas-powered, hand-held machine with a screw-type blade), or hire an excavator. If you rent an auger, specify an 8-, 12-, or 14-inch (20.3, 30.5, or 35.5 cm) diameter. Whichever tool you use, have a 6-foot (1.8 m) long digging bar or crowbar handy to dislodge rocks and loosen hard soil.

Keep the sides of each hole plumb — don't flare the top of the hole; if anything, work to flare the bottom to increase stability.

A power auger generates tremendous *torque* (twisting force), especially a large one, and requires two strong people to operate the beast.

WARNING

4. **Place 6 inches (15.2 cm) of crushed stone in the bottom of each hole.**

5. **Restring lines.**

Move the stringline position from the post centers to the post edges (either side). For 4x4 posts, for example, move the stringline over 2 inches, or 5 cm (1¾ inches, or 4.45 cm, if you use *surfaced* (that is, planed or smooth) posts, which are 3½ inches, or 8.9 cm, thick).

6. **Set the corner or end posts in place first.**

Set each post in its hole, burying the bottom 2 inches (5 cm) into the gravel. Align the post with the stringline(s), using a level to make sure that the post is plumb. Brace the post by driving stakes diagonally into the ground along two adjacent sides. Nail the stakes to the post with *duplex nails* (double-headed nails), again checking with a level to make sure the post is plumb.

7. **String a line between the end posts near the top.**

8. **Set the remaining posts in their holes.**

Align them to the stringlines and brace them, using a level to make sure they're plumb. Then, for now, leave the lines in place.

9. **Backfill the holes.**

Use tamped crushed stone, which offers better drainage than just soil. It also offers improved stability if well-tamped and installed in dense soil. Alternatively, use a mixture of crushed stone and ordinary soil, shoveling in about 3 to 5 inches (7.6 to 12.7 cm) at a time and tamping well after each batch.

Before each tamping, hold a level against the post and adjust until level.

Continue until done. If you plan to plant grass, make sure the last few inches (several cms) are just soil. Mound the top layer to shed water away from the post.

10. **Trim the post tops.**

Re-check that your posts are plumb. The string you used for aligning them and then left in place will help guide you, and/or you can use a laser level (see Figure 6-1). Consider the following as you trim:

- **If the ground is fairly level,** simply start with the post at the highest point of the fence. Mark that post where the top rail rests on top of the post. Using a laser level, transfer this mark to the other end post. You can use a chalk stringline between the two marks and snap the line to transfer chalk marks to the other posts at the same level.

- **If the ground slopes gently,** use a laser level and refer to your plans to determine the best level for cutting.

- **If the ground slopes steeply,** step the fence down the slope by using a laser level, marking only a few posts level with each other and then lowering the marking level a few inches (several cms) for the next few posts, and so on.

In any event, using a square and pencil, extend the mark around the four sides of each post. Cut along the marks.

WARNING

Making horizontal cuts with a circular power saw is dangerous. If you don't have experience making such cuts, use a handsaw. If you do have experience, stand on a sturdy stepladder or bench, and wear safety glasses.

CONSIDERING CONCRETE FOOTINGS FOR FENCE POSTS

Concrete footings for fence posts are the exception, not the rule. They *aren't* needed if a fence post is placed at or below the frost line (3 to 4 feet, or .9 to 1.2 m, below the ground surface). Set posts in concrete footings if stability is critical, which is the case for fences installed in sandy or soft, mucky soil.

If you decide to secure your fence posts in this fashion, the fence project is going to take a bit longer. That's because concrete needs to *cure* (harden) for a minimum of two days.

Be aware: Concrete traps water around a post, which reduces the post's lifespan. You can mitigate this problem by waiting until the concrete sets, then applying high-quality exterior acrylic latex caulk or silicone designed specifically to adhere to concrete to the base of the post. This seals the gap between the concrete and post that's caused by freeze-thaw cycles and thus prolongs a post's life.

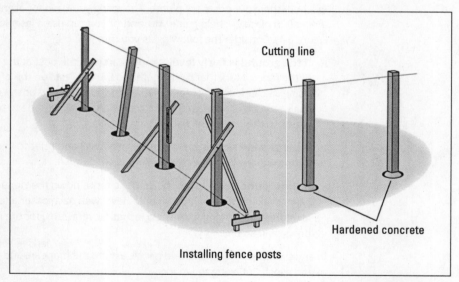

FIGURE 6-1: Using stringlines to align fence posts and mark them for trimming works fine.

Cutting line

Hardened concrete

Installing fence posts

© John Wiley & Sons, Inc.

Building the framework

To build a framework for your fence, follow these steps:

1. Install the top rail.

Use 2x4s or 2x6s long enough to connect at least three posts. Take measure-ments, along a level line, at the *bottoms* of the posts (the tops may be out of line). Plan joints over the centers of the posts. After cutting each board, secure the top rail to each post with galvanized nails or exterior wood screws — drill pilot holes near the ends of boards. You may need to pull post tops into alignment first.

TIP

As boards shrink, joints open up. When joining boards end-to-end, cut the ends at a 30-degree *bevel* (angle, as viewed from the edge — refer to Figure 6-2) so that each board slightly overlaps the previous board. As the joint opens up, the beveled ends appear to touch each other from most viewing angles.

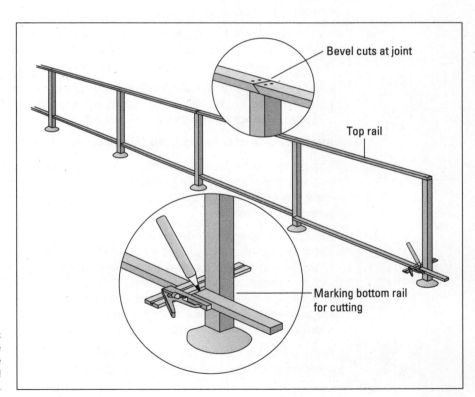

FIGURE 6-2:
Attaching the fence rails to the posts; note bevel cuts at joints.

2. Install the bottom rails between the posts.

Mark the rail locations on each post by measuring *down* from the top rail (which should be level), not up from the ground. Cut 2x4s to fit between the posts at these marks. Install them by drilling pilot holes and toenailing each end to the post with galvanized nails or exterior wood screws. (*Toenailing* means driving a nail in at an angle in order to anchor the board.)

TIP

Kickboards used to be added to fill gaps between the bottom rails and to make the fence stronger. We recommend instead installing a 2x4 perpendicular to the bottom rail in the same position that the kickboard was placed — a far better, more stable design.

Installing the fencing

To put on the actual fencing, follow these steps:

1. Install nailers as needed.

If you install boards or panels between the rails, you may need to attach *nailers* (strips of wood) along the bottom of the top rail and top of the bottom rail to nail the fencing to — and perhaps along the posts, as well.

WARNING

Avoid a fence design that depends on too many nailers. They create more joints for moisture to get trapped in — which, with wood, encourages rot — and provide weaker support than the frame itself.

2. Attach the boards or panels to the framework or nailers.

Attach 1-by (1x3, 1x4, or 1x6) boards and any lattice screening with specialty nails and screws, meant for long life in outdoor/exterior uses. These include metal connector screws, stainless-steel screws, galvanized screws, composite screws, and so forth.

For pickets or other vertical boards with uniform spacing, make a spacer to speed up installation — see Figure 6-3. *Rip* (saw along the board's length) a board to the same width as the required spacing, long enough to extend from top rail to bottom rail. Attach a small cleat to the back side of the spacer, flush with the top edge, to act as a hanger. After installing each board, hang the spacer beside it, butt the next board against the spacer, and nail or screw the board in place. Use a straightedge or stringline to keep the tops level.

TIP

Rent a pneumatic nailer to speed up installation of the fencing. The rental agency provides operating and safety instructions.

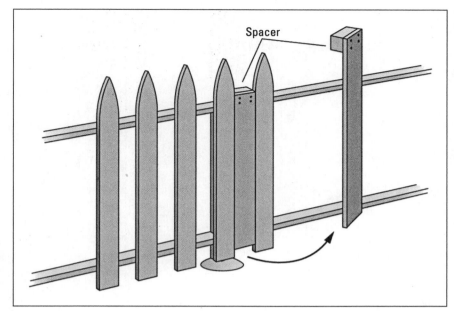

Spacer

© John Wiley & Sons, Inc.

FIGURE 6-3:
Installing pickets
is less tedious
if you use a
spacer to align
each picket.

3. **Trim the top edge.**

   If you attach boards to the edge of the rails (rather than below the top rail), the
   tops may not be even (unless you used a straightedge or stringline to keep
   them level, as with a picket fence). Snap a chalkline along the length of the
   fence (shown in Figure 6-4), at the finished height, and cut along the line. If you
   use a power saw, nail a cleat along the fence to guide the saw.

4. **Add decorative trim.**

5. **Apply the finish.**

   If you've used composite, skip this step. You're done. If you've used wood, allow
   your new fence to season for a week or two and apply a sealer (for natural
   color) or water-repellent stain. If you want to paint the fence, wait several
   weeks for the wood to season.

TIP

Apply white-pigmented shellac to exposed knots to keep resin from bleeding
through the paint.

Then prime the fence (use oil-based primer for redwood and cedar; latex for
other woods) and finish it with one or two coats of latex paint.

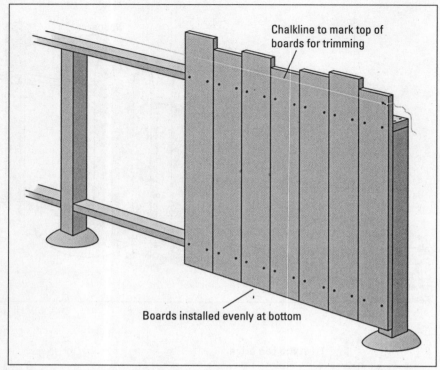

Chalkline to mark top of boards for trimming

Boards installed evenly at bottom

© John Wiley & Sons, Inc.

FIGURE 6-4: For a simple board fence (not pickets), trim the top of the fence after installing all of the boards.

CHECKING OUT PRIVACY PANELS

Here's an alternative that may not have been on your radar. Privacy panels actually aren't fences. They're more like outdoor screens. Some can be temporary or moved around. They're especially great for small yards, urban settings, or even larger gardens that you wish to divide into separate outdoor rooms. Fashionable *and* functional, what's not to love?

Advantages to using privacy panels are as follows:

- They add artistic flair with interesting designs, color, and patterns.

- They're portable, or at least you can take them down if you need to (for example, when winter is coming).

- They're versatile. You can erect or mount where needed.

- They're cheaper than a fence or wall.

- They may let breezes through rather than blocking.

Disadvantages to using privacy panels are as follows:

- They won't last as long as a fence or wall.

- They may not be strong enough to stand at the site without swaying or tipping in a storm.

- They may damage or show wear too easily for your taste.

When shopping for them, make sure the material can stand up, not just to a stiff breeze, but to rain and UV sun rays. Powder-coated steel is fairly tough, but galvanized steel is better still (because it's more durable and heavier).

If you want to discover more about these, search online for "outdoor privacy screens" or dig around on Instagram and Pinterest.

Alternatively, you can fashion a privacy screen from a trellis or two or more similar trellises, with or without climbing plants, install a roll-up bamboo shade or a more-durable plastic look-alike, or hang fabric (some options include tablecloths, drapes or curtains — even theater curtains! — sheets, and painted fabric).

Working with Walls

Garden walls imply permanence — some seem to have been a part of the landscape forever. You can build low walls (6 to 12 inches, or 15.2 to 30.5 cm, high) to establish borders and boundaries. A wall 3 feet (.9 m) high creates a sense of enclosure, and taller walls offer privacy and sound control. As with retaining walls (see Chapter 4), avoid building walls higher than 3 feet (.9 m) yourself unless you have experience with masonry.

TIP

A wall 15 to 18 inches (38.1 to 45.7 cm) high can also serve as a bench, which may come in handy if your garden is small or you're creating an intimate sitting area or courtyard.

You have several materials to choose from:

>> **Concrete block:** Because of their uniform grid patterns, concrete block works well in formal gardens that have a strong axis and regular forms.

Concrete block is the most versatile material because the blocks themselves come in plain or decorative formats and different colors and because you can cover an ordinary block wall with almost any kind of veneer, from smooth stucco to imitation stone patterns.

They are also easy to work with.

>> **Brick:** Brick offers more variations in pattern and is easy to lift, but requires considerable working of the joints. Its earthy texture is appealing.

>> **Cut stone:** You get a slightly more rustic look, but with a modular format, and it fits together nicely. Stone, although heavy and time-consuming to place, is fun to work with and is forgiving of mistakes.

>> **Fieldstone:** For informal and naturalistic gardens, choose durable, handsome fieldstone or irregularly cut stone.

There's a beautiful old book about the art of building mortarless stone walls called *The Granite Kiss.* A *granite kiss* is a smashed finger or thumb, and it comes with the territory. All you can really do to avoid such an injury is to work carefully without rushing. You do need your hands to feel the materials, so heavy–duty gloves don't make sense. Wear lighter, flexible gloves if you can.

The project of building a wall takes time and energy, but it isn't unduly complicated. Go to the type of material you've chosen in the following sections and work your way through our steps with care.

Building a stacked stone wall

To build a *stacked*, or dry, stone wall, follow the same principles as building a stone retaining wall (see Chapter 4):

1. **Set aside some large flat stones for the top of the wall and several *bondstones* (stones long enough to extend from one side to the other) to place every 4 feet (1.2 m) along the middle course.**

Save the largest stones for the base.

2. ***Batter,* or angle, both sides of the wall in toward the top.**

Use a rate of 1 inch (2.5 cm) for every 2 feet (.6 m) of wall height.

3. **Make the base of the wall approximately 2 feet (.6 m) wide for every 3 feet (.9 m) of wall height.**

Build the ends first and work toward the center.

As you build, use small stones to fill cavities and create flat perches for the larger stones.

4. **Interlock the stones as much as possible, and tilt large stones toward the center of the wall.**

Building a mortared stone wall

Binding stones together with mortar creates a stable wall and makes it possible to make the sides plumb (straight, not battered), but the wall is vulnerable to ground settlement. To solve this problem, build the wall on a *footing* (reinforced–concrete base), and follow these steps (see Figure 6-5):

1. **Lay out and dig a trench at least 12 inches (30.5 cm) deep, or to the frost line, and approximately 4 inches (10.1 cm) wider than the wall base.**

    Place two lengths of #4 (½-inch; 1.2 cm) rebar in the trench, held off the ground at least 3 inches (7.6 cm) by stones or *dobies* (small concrete blocks). When splicing rebar end-to-end, overlap the rebar for 2 feet (.6 m) and twist tie wire tightly around both pieces.

2. **Fill the trench with concrete.**

    Make sure the footing is concealed from view when the wall is complete and soil is placed against it.

3. **After the concrete sets, dry-fit a few stones at one end of the wall and remove them.**

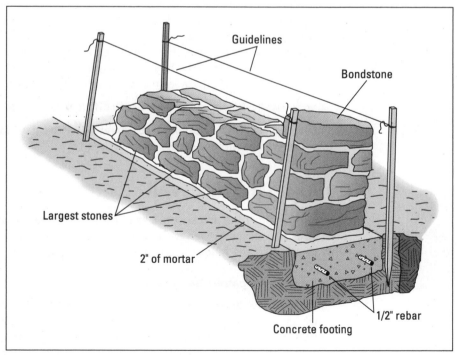

FIGURE 6-5:
A wall of mortared stone, block, or brick requires a reinforced concrete footing.

Guidelines

Bondstone

Largest stones

2" of mortar

1/2" rebar

Concrete footing

4. **Mix a small batch of mortar, place a 2-inch (5 cm) thick layer of it on the footing, and set the bottom stones on the mortar.**

5. **Place small stones and rubble between the large stones and, using a mortar trowel, throw a layer of mortar over them and the bottom stones.**

6. **Set the second *course* (layer) of stones over the first.**

   As you set each stone, strike spilled mortar off of the wall surface with your trowel.

7. **Repeat the process at the other end of the wall.**

8. **Drive a stake into the ground at each end of the wall and string a guideline between the stakes at the level of the second course.**

   Use this line to keep the face of the wall straight and plumb as you lay each course of stones.

9. **As you build each course, start at the ends and work toward the center.**

   Use the largest stones at the ends. To prevent long vertical joints that have to span several courses, strive to place one stone over two and then two stones over one — in other words, stagger the joints.

10. ***Rake* (gouge) the joints as you go.**

    After the mortar has set for 10 or 15 minutes, scratch away enough mortar from each joint to create an indentation up to ½-inch (1.2 cm) deep, using a round stick or piece of pipe. Then, remove excess mortar with a soft brush and smooth the mortar, to make the joints stronger, with a *jointing tool* or *jointer* (narrow trowel that fits between the stones) or curved piece of copper tubing.

11. **Cap the wall with flat stones and brush off all excess mortar.**

12. **Cover the wall with a tent of plastic sheeting for five days to allow the mortar to cure without excess evaporation.**

Building a brick wall

Bricklaying varies from stacking bricks in a simple, repeating pattern to creating intricate artistic designs. Even with no bricklaying experience, you can build a low garden wall using the following techniques:

1. **Plan the brick pattern and layout.**

   Most garden walls are 16 to 24 inches high and 8 inches wide (40.6 to 60.1 cm high and 20.3 cm wide) — or two *wyeths* (width of one brick) — wide. Lay the bricks end-to-end and flat, offsetting the bricks in each course by half a brick length, so that the vertical joints in alternating courses align. This pattern is called a *running bond*.

UNDERSTANDING MORTAR

Mortar is basically the material, the glue, that can fill gaps and hold a stone or concrete wall together. It's a mix of fine sand and Portland cement. Lime and gypsum may be added to improve workability and speed up drying. You just add water.

Follow manufacturer's directions on the bag to the letter. In particular, the amount of water-to-cement ratio is critical for the success of your project.

Warning: Cement is a strong chemical that can cause burns. Be careful and wear gloves and eye protection.

There are different kinds of varying strengths. Some are more cosmetic, whereas others improve load-bearing. Discuss with a salesperson which is best for your needs and how much you need and read labels before you purchase. You'll need not only the dimensions of the wall but also the materials you'll be using.

Keep the following in mind:

- **For stone, brick, and block work:** Use a mortar mix of one part Portland cement, one part hydrated lime, and six parts sand. You can buy the ingredients in bulk or premixed in 60-pound sacks. If you buy mortar mix, specify Type M, which is suitable for ground contact. Mix only enough per batch to use in 30 minutes.

   Add only enough water so that the mortar stays in place without slumping. For bricks, mix a creamier batch that's stiff enough to hold the weight of a brick but moist enough to smooth easily. You may color mortar by adding a powdered tinting agent, available at masonry suppliers.

- **Mixology:** After mixing the mortar in a bucket or wheelbarrow, shovel it onto a piece of plywood close to your work site. Using a pointed brick trowel, slice off a section of mortar, and then scoop it off the plywood and throw it into place — all in one motion.

Always allow mortar to set until crumbly — several days. Temperature will affect how fast or slow this process is. Then you can use a hand broom or stiff brush to brush off excess and tidy up. If there's any remaining residue, scrub it off with a wet, rough-textured rag.

2. **Dig a footing trench, and install an 8- to 12-inch (20.3 to 30.5 cm) wide concrete footing.**

   For walls taller than a foot (.3 m) high, install a vertical rebar, tied to the horizontal rebar, every 2 feet (.6 m) down the center of the wall. See the section, "Building a mortared stone wall," earlier in this chapter.

3. **After the footing hardens, snap a chalkline onto it as a guideline for one edge of the wall.**

4. **Lay out the first course of bricks in a dry run.**

   Space the bricks 3⁄8-inch (.9 cm) apart for mortar joints. Adjust the length of the wall, if necessary, to accommodate full bricks. Then, remove them.

5. **Mix and spread enough mortar at one end of the wall for a row of four or five bricks.**

6. **Set the first brick in place, tapping it to bed it into the mortar.**

7. *Butter* **one end of the next brick with mortar (the same way that you butter bread) and shove it into place against the first brick.**

   Scrape off excess mortar with your trowel.

8. **Repeat the process for the next two or three bricks.**

9. **Lay the same number of bricks in the second wyeth, starting with a half brick.**

   Butter one end and the inside edge of each brick before setting it in place.

10. **Throw a row of mortar on top of the first course of bricks.**

    Using the point of your trowel, create a *furrow* (indented channel) along the center of the mortar.

11. **Lay the second course of bricks, starting with a half brick on the first wyeth and a full brick on the second wyeth.**

    Using a 4-foot (1.2 m) level, or a laser level, check the course to make sure that it's straight and level (refer to Figure 6-6).

12. **Continue building up one end of the wall with courses, until you have room for only one brick on top.**

    The resulting pyramid-like structure is called a *lead*. Each course steps back a half brick from the previous course, creating an incline. Lay a level or straight-edge against this incline to make sure that the bricks are even.

    Every two or three courses, embed *brick ties* (corrugated metal straps) in the mortar at 2-foot (.6 m) intervals to tie the two wyeths together.

13. **Build an identical lead at the other end of the wall.**

14. **After completing both leads, fill in the center area with more bricks.**

    To keep the bricks aligned, stretch mason's line between the two leads as you move up each course.

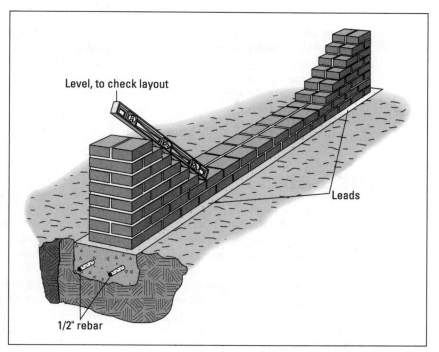

Level, to check layout

Leads

1/2" rebar

FIGURE 6-6: Installing a brick wall requires double-checking levels at intervals.

15. **Remove excess mortar and tool the joints as you go.**

See the section, "Building a mortared stone wall," earlier in this chapter.

16. **Cap the wall with bricks laid across the wall, flat (header) or on edge (rowlock).**

To create an overhanging cap, combine a half brick with each full brick.

Building a concrete block wall

Build a concrete block wall the same way as a brick wall, by pouring a concrete footing, doing a dry run, building a lead at each corner, staggering successive courses, and tooling the joints (see the section, "Building a stacked stone wall," earlier in this section).

One difference is that the hollow units allow you to insert vertical rebar in the footing to reinforce the wall. When setting blocks, place them with the *web* (wider edges) side up.

If you plan to veneer the wall with stone or brick facing, insert wall ties in the mortar of each course, spaced 2 to 3 feet (.6 to .9 m) apart, with 1 to 2 inches (2.5 to 5 cm) of tie protruding out of the wall. When the wall mortar cures, trowel mortar onto the face of the wall, embedding the wall ties in it, and adhere the stone or brick to the wet mortar. Another option for veneering a wall is to cover it with stucco, which doesn't require wall ties — consult a contractor for more information on stucco.

Going for Gates

From grandiose to rustic, gates play a prominent role in landscaping and offer rich fodder for the imagination. Even if you're not building a fence or wall, you may want to place a gate in your garden as a decorative focal point.

If you hang a gate on a fence, plan on using larger posts for the gate than for the fence — 6x6s, for example, if the fence posts are 4x4s — and burying them deeper than the fence posts. If your gate features a trellis over it, hang the gate between two of the trellis posts. Refer to the section, "Installing posts," earlier in this chapter, for more information.

You have two options for attaching a gate to a stone, brick, or block wall:

>> Attach a vertical board to the inside face of the wall opening, using lag bolts or similar masonry anchoring devices, and attach the gate to it.

>> Install two *screw hooks* (L-shaped hinge holders) in the masonry aligned vertically. Either embed them into fresh mortar as you build the wall — one near the bottom and one near the top of the gate position — or drill holes with a masonry bit and install the hooks with *expansive mortar* (mortar specified for embedding hardware into masonry).

Make the gate opening at least 3 feet (.9 m) wide — up to 4 feet (1.2 m) is better for moving garden equipment and materials around. If the opening is wider than 4 feet (1.2 m), install double gates.

Sometimes you may find a pre-made gate that suits you and your fence and, if you're lucky, is a Cinderella fit. In that case, of course, it's a matter of attaching or mounting it. Review the following steps anyway because some of the advice and measurement considerations may apply.

Although nails have been traditionally used, we urge you to put your gate together with screws instead. Screws simply are more secure. You can drill pilot holes (holes a little smaller than the screw, first) for the first pieces — as a good practice.

To build a gate, follow these steps (see Figure 6-7):

1. **Plan the gate width.**

Measure the width of the opening at the top and bottom of the gate location and reduce these measurements by ¾ to 1 inch (1.9 to 2.5 cm) for gate clearance.

2. **Plan the gate height.**

Allow clearance at the bottom for obstacles. Align the top with the fence or, if you prefer, choose a different height to emphasize the gate.

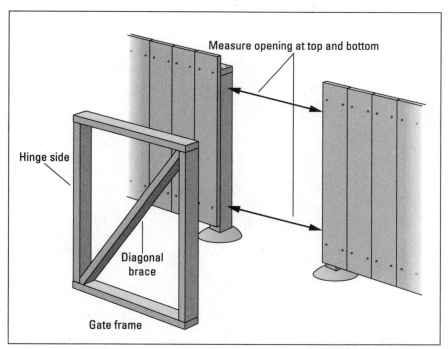

FIGURE 6-7:
Measure the opening at several points when planning the gate frame.

© John Wiley & Sons, Inc.

3. **Build a box frame out of 2x4s.**

Cut the top and bottom cross members to the full gate width (width of opening minus 1 inch, or minus 2.5 cm). Cut each side piece 3 inches, or 7.6 cm, shorter than the total height of the frame. Screw the cross members to the side.

4. **Install a diagonal brace.**

Lay the frame over a 2x4, set on edge. Align the 2x4 so that it extends from the bottom hinge corner to the top latch corner. Square the frame and mark cutting lines on the 2x4 brace by tracing a pencil line against the box frame members. Cut the brace along the lines. Slide the brace into the box frame so that it's flush with the outside face of the frame. Drill pilot holes through the frame and drive screws through them into the brace.

5. **Attach fencing or other material to the frame.**

   Lay the frame down flat with the outside facing up. Lay the fencing material on top of the frame and attach it with screws.

6. **Attach hinges to the gate as shown in Figure 6-8.**

   Use strap hinges, mounted on the front or back of the gate, or butt hinges, mounted on the side of the gate. Mount them so that the gate swings *into* your property.

7. **Position the gate and attach the hinges to the gate post.**

   Support the gate temporarily. Drill pilot holes for the hinge screws and attach the hinges.

8. **Add gate hardware (such as a latch, cane bolt, or closer) and a stop.**

   Use a strip of wood for the stop and attach it to the fence post or gate, depending on the gate swing.

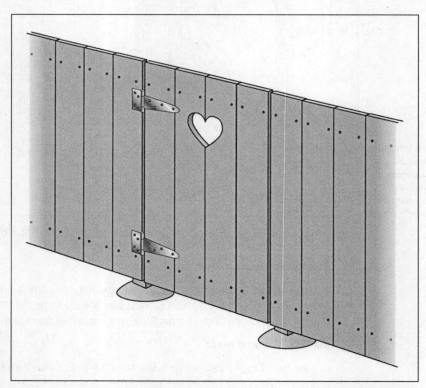

FIGURE 6-8:
Attach hinges
to the gate
first, and then
hang the gate.

© John Wiley & Sons, Inc.

Chapter **7**

Creating Paths and Walkways

Paths or walkways are arguably the most important element because you use them every day. This chapter looks at both the practical side and the pretty side of paths and walkways, so that getting from here to there is not only integrated into your yard but also a pleasure.

Make sure you execute this part of your overall plan before you worry about plants, outdoor furniture, and so forth. In fact, if you don't have good access to your outdoor spaces, then you won't be able to turn your attention to other projects, especially planting. To view some effective and inspiring paths and walkways, check the color insert.

REMEMBER

Safety is key whenever you're building or installing anything. Review the general safety advice in Chapter 4 about worksites.

Getting Started

Creating a path or walkway through your home landscape is a — pardon the pun — step-by-step process. It's a bit like a good recipe; you never want to find out that you should have buttered the pan after the cake is in the oven. Here we begin at the beginning, by first determining how you'll use the path. We then consider which materials are appropriate and will look good.

Considering design and use

In planning a path or walkway, focus on its purpose. If you and your garden visitors want to meander through your yard, passing and admiring plantings or views, then insert curves and jogs along the way. If the goal is to get from Point A (for example, the back door) to Point B (for example, the kitchen garden), lay it out straight.

REMEMBER

No matter what design you ultimately choose, make sure to avoid low areas with poor drainage and steep inclines.

If you choose to put in a narrower path or make a narrow secondary path, that's fine; just be advised that foot traffic on it will be one-person-at-a-time or one-way. Some designers argue for narrower paths, explaining that they encourage exploration.

Deciding on materials and dimensions

The walking surface of your new path or walkway can consist of any number of materials, so choose wisely. You're also going to have to adhere to certain conventions in terms of width and slope, so the result is practical as well as comfortable to use.

Consider the following when choosing materials for your paths or walkways:

>> **For formal, all-weather walks:** Choose concrete, brick, or flagstone.

>> **For informal paths:** Select stepping stones, gravel, crushed stone, or wood chips.

As for width, make paths at least 3 feet (.9 m) wide. Even wider may be better; bear in mind that two people walking side-by-side require a path 4 or even 5 feet (1.2 or even 1.5 m) wide.

For wheelchair use, slope the path no more than 1:12 — 1 inch (2.5 cm) of rise for every 12 inches (30.5 cm) of run, measured horizontally — and provide a 5-foot (1.5 m) long landing every 30 feet (9.1m).

Building Paths

Not all pathways are created the same way; layout and installation vary a bit depending on the material you choose. Take a tour of the four following common options to see what suits your budget and strikes your fancy. After you make up your mind, for best results, stick to our specific directions.

Creating a gravel or crushed stone path

These *loose fill* materials (so-called because you ultimately just pour or shovel them onto the prepared surface) create paths with a classic, old-world feeling. They're lower-priced than the other options and also have the advantage of conforming pretty easily to curves and slopes.

Identifying the differences between pea gravel and crushed stone

However, gravel and crushed stone aren't the same. Here are some of their characteristics:

>> **Pea gravel:** Pea gravel used for landscaping has rounded edges and is uniform in size. It has the sound and feel of loose pebbles. As a path material, it drains quickly and stays clean, but it constantly moves underfoot. Color is usually gray.

>> **Crushed stone:** Also called *crusher run stone,* crushed stone has sharp edges and is a mixture of small rocks and *fines* (sand and fine particles), which enables the material to compact into a solid mass. The ingredients vary in size due to screening. Larger-sized particles and stones, on the other hand, don't compact as tightly, but are cleaner. Crushed stone varies in color from tan and beige to blue and gray tones.

Which one you go with depends not just whether you find it attractive to look at, but also how you want the walking experience to be for you and your garden visitors. If you're not sure, a visit the supplier — to see, handle, perhaps take a test walk in a demonstration area — can help you make up your mind.

Getting to work with your gravel or stone path

To build a gravel or stone garden path, follow these steps:

1. **Lay out the edges of the path using garden hoses or stringlines.**

   For layout techniques, see Chapter 4.

2. **Dig between the edges to a depth of 6 to 8 inches (15.2 to 20.3 cm) (deeper, if your winters are severe).**

3. **Install a border along each side of the path.**

   Set 1x6s or flexible *bender boards* (thin, bendable boards) on edge and nail them to short stakes placed along the outside. You can also buy vinyl edging and install it according to the manufacturer. As another alternative, consider lining the sides of the excavation with something stronger and more durable, such as bricks, stones, or timbers.

4. **Place 4 to 6 inches (10.1 to 15.2 cm) of *road base* (crushed rock used for gravel beds) or class-five gravel in the bottom of the excavation.**

5. **Using a *flat plate vibrator* (a power compactor; you can rent one), compact the base.**

   Add more rock as necessary. If you don't rent a compactor, you can use a hefty hand-tool you can use called (of course) a *tamper*, consisting of a heavy square base (typically 10x10 inches/25.4 cmx25.4 cm) on a sturdy handle like shovel handle. Only contemplate this if the area isn't very big . . . otherwise, you'll be wishing you had rented the machine.

6. **Fill the rest of the excavation with 2 to 4 inches (5 to 10.1 cm) of pea gravel or crushed rock.**

   If you use crushed rock, build in a *crown,* or hump, along the center of the path for drainage. Compact everything firmly.

7. **Finish.**

   Take a mallet and go along both sides of your path, tamping the edging securely into place in case it got dislodged during construction. Then, rake over the surface of the rocks or gravel, or soak it with the hose. The object is settle everything into place and neaten up.

Making a walkway with bricks or pavers

Brick has subtle textures and variable colors that fit into many landscape designs. It's readily available, easy to handle, and has uniform dimensions that make various interlocking patterns possible (head to Chapter 9, where we discuss brick patios for more about the different patterns available). You can install bricks in a bed of compacted sand or on a mortar bed over a concrete slab. Although a mortared installation is more durable, bricks laid carefully on a compacted sand base make a very solid walkway that's fairly easy to build.

Although some types of brick are referred to as *pavers*, the pavers that we refer to in this book are concrete pavers, the modern cousin of brick. Concrete pavers have the same advantages of modular size, compact form, and easy installation, but they cost considerably less, are stronger, and have beveled edges that prevent slightly-raised pavers from becoming tripping hazards.

To install bricks or pavers on a sand bed, follow these steps (see Figure 7-1):

1. **Lay out the walk.**

See the section "Creating a gravel or crushed stone path," earlier in this chapter for specifics.

2. **Dig to a depth of 9 to 15 inches (22.9 to 38.1 cm).**

See the section, "Creating a gravel or crushed stone path," earlier in this chapter.

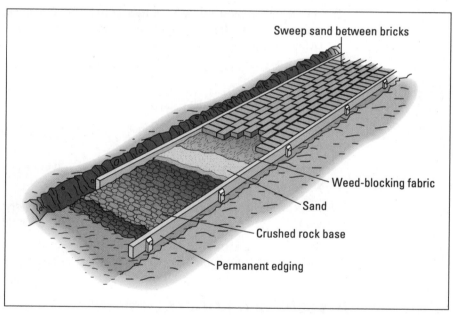

Sweep sand between bricks

Weed-blocking fabric

Sand

Crushed rock base

Permanent edging

FIGURE 7-1:
A well-compacted base and firm edgings are the keys to installing bricks or pavers on sand.

© John Wiley & Sons, Inc.

3. **Moisten the bottom of the area that you just dug out and compact it.**

Compact the entire base with whichever tool you prefer (a power compactor or a hand tool, as we describe in Step 5 of "Creating a gravel or crushed stone path," earlier in this chapter).

4. **Place 4 to 8 inches (10.1 to 20.3 cm) of road base or class-five gravel in the excavation and compact it.**

   Class-five gravel is a good, practical material, commonly used by road crews. It's usually crushed limestone, a mix of sand and small rocks, that compacts well into place.

5. **Install edging along the two sides of the walk.**

6. **Install weed-blocking fabric.**

   This material prevents weeds from coming up but allows rainwater to soak into the ground.

7. **Place 2 to 4 inches (5 to 10.1 cm) of sand over the fabric.**

   Moisten and compact the sand so that the distance from the top to the finished level of the walk is equal to the thickness of one brick.

8. **Dampen the sand bed.**

9. **Tie a length of mason's twine to two loose bricks, and using them for anchors, stretch the line parallel with (and one brick's width away from) either edge of the walk.**

   Use this line to guide placement of the first row of bricks, even if they butt up to the edging.

10. **Set the bricks or pavers in place.**

    Gently tap each one with a rubber mallet to snug it into the sand; avoid displacing any sand.

11. **After laying several bricks or pavers, check your work by laying a straightedge or long level over it.**

12. **After all of the units are in place, spread a layer of fine, dry sand over the walk.**

    Sweep it back and forth, working it into the joints. With the excess sand still on the surface, compact the walk. Keep adding sand, as necessary.

Installing a concrete walk

Concrete walks are composed of layers that assure stability and good looks (see Figure 7-2). You can finish the concrete in one of several ways for the final surface, or you can use the concrete as a base for installing other paving materials.

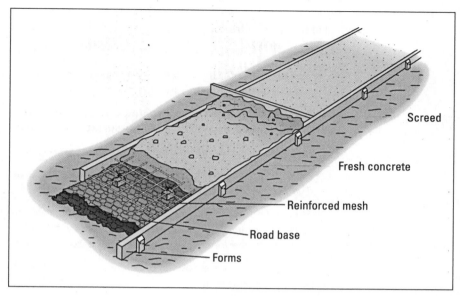

Screed

Fresh concrete

Reinforced mesh

Road base

Forms

© John Wiley & Sons, Inc.

FIGURE 7-2:
The most critical steps in building a concrete walk are setting the forms and finishing the concrete surface.

To build a basic walk, follow these steps:

1. **Prepare the sub-base.**

   In other words, excavate the length of the course. The general rule is to dig twice as deep as the planned thickness. So, for a 4-inch (10.1 cm) thick concrete walk, excavate 8 inches (20.3 cm); for a 6-inch (15.2 cm) thick one, excavate 12 inches (30.5 cm).

   See the section, "Creating a gravel or crushed stone path," earlier in this chapter for relevant information.

2. **Using 2x4s set on edge, build forms along each side of the walk.**

   Set the tops at the finished level of the walk, securing them with stakes. Rather than level the forms from side to side, set one side ⅛-inch (.3 cm) lower than the other for drainage. Use two or three thicknesses of flexible bender board as forms for curved walks.

3. **Place gravel in the excavation and compact it.**

   This is for drainage. We recommend using #4 crushed stone.

4. **Install reinforcing welded wire mesh.**

   Use *6-6-10-10 wire reinforcing mesh* (#10 wire on a 6-inch, 15.2 cm, grid, available in 5-, 6-, or 7-foot wide rolls; 1.5-, 1.8-, or 2.1 m wide rolls). Cut to within an inch, 2.5 cm, of the form walls. Place some sturdy outdoor chairs on the steel to keep it centered in the concrete.

5. **Fill the forms with concrete.**

   For information about ordering or mixing concrete, see Chapter 6.

6. ***Screed*, or *strike off*, the concrete by dragging a 2x4 over the tops of the forms in a back-and-forth sawing motion.**

7. **Finish the concrete (smooth it so that the rocks [aggregates] are fully embedded and the paste floats to the surface) with a joint trowel.**

8. **Create joints at intervals in the concrete using groovers.**

   Doing so controls cracking; concrete expands and contracts with the weather, and you want to create and define where the cracks occur.

   The general rule for intervals is about one-and-a-half times the width of the path. (So, for example, if your path is the standard width of 3 feet (.9 m), create joints every 4½ feet/every 1.4 m.) Use a straight 2x4 as a guide.

   As for the depth of the groove, approximately one-fourth the thickness of the concrete is recommended. (So, your 6-inch/15.2 cm thick concrete path should have joints about 1½ inches/3.8 cm, deep.)

   Tools intended for this work come in brass or steel. Be neat and careful.

9. **Allow the concrete to set slightly and finish the surface.**

   Run an *edger* along the forms to give the edges of the walk a rounded profile. For finishing techniques, see Chapter 6.

10. **Cover the walk with wet burlap material for at least 24 hours to *cure* (allow it to harden without all of the moisture evaporating) the concrete.**

TIP

There is more than one way to cure concrete. After it has set, you can place burlap material on top and keep it wet. Or you can spray a curing compound on the concrete, which helps keep the moisture from evaporating. Either way, you need to wait several days for the process to complete.

Building a flagstone path

Flagstone can be made from any kind of horizontally layered rock, which is then split into flat *flags* or slabs, generally an inch or two (2.5 to 5.1 cm) thick. Natural options include Pennsylvania bluestone and Arizona sandstone. You can also find prefabricated but realistic-looking ones (usually made of concrete and then dyed). If you want a formal-looking path, get rectangular or square flags. The irregularly shaped ones are lovely for a more informal look.

To make a durable and secure flagstone path, follow these steps:

1. **Mark the layout.**

   You can lay out a straight path by using string tied between small stakes. Mark the course of meandering path with flour. Check that the width of the path is consistent as it proceeds by measuring across at intervals.

2. **Dig out the base.**

   Four inches (10.1 cm) down is the minimum. Make it deeper, 6 to 8 inches (15.2 to 20.3 cm), if you live in a colder climate where freeze-thaw cycles over the winter and early spring can dislodge stones, or if water and its drainage may be an issue.

   Cart away this excess soil to another garden area, or perhaps add it in layers to your compost pile. (For details on composting, turn to Chapter 17.)

3. **Fill the excavated area with coarse sand or stone dust.**

   Be generous — go a half or a full inch (1.2 or 2.5 cm) above ground level; doing so will aid drainage. Depending on how wide your path is, mound the sand higher to the middle to direct rain water off.

4. **Tamp and smooth the sand as you work.**

   A short board or a brick works fine.

5. **Set the stones in place (see Figure 7-3).**

   Don't try to seat them immediately; stand back and check your design first. This step is particularly important with irregular flags; you want to avoid continuous joints or an overly busy-looking design. This is called, aptly, a *dry run.*

   Here are two important considerations with this step:

   1. **Seat the stones.**

      Settle each flag into place by wiggling and twisting it. Tap it with a mallet. Take care that the spaces between stones are consistent, an inch or less (2.5 cm or less) on all sides.

   2. **Fill in the gaps between the flags.**

      Toss on more sand or stone dust and then use a broom to sweep the flags clean and to direct the filler into the gaps. Sprinkle with a spray of the hose or a watering can, and keep working until the sand is level with flags. Allow a couple of days for settling, and then return and fine-tune everything.

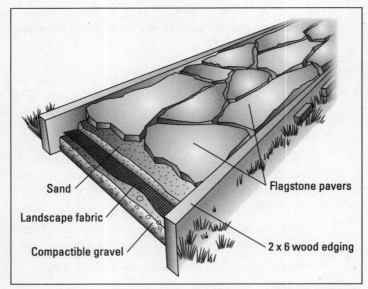

FIGURE 7-3: Set the flagstones atop the base and experiment with the path's design before finishing.

Sand

Landscape fabric

Compactible gravel

Flagstone pavers

2 x 6 wood edging

TIP

You can put plants into the gaps between the flags — a settled look that also helps hold them in place. For plant suggestions for this project, little groundcovers that tolerate foot traffic, check Chapter 15.

Stepping in Style

Gardens with steep slopes or multiple levels require steps. You can build informal garden steps out of timbers or stacked stones, or you can build a more formal set of stairs out of concrete, brick, or mortared stone (for information about building wooden stairs, see Chapter 8).

Whatever materials you choose, your steps must conform to code requirements intended to make stairs safe. If possible, avoid single steps — they're difficult to see and may come as a surprise to the casual stroller. Also, include lighting in your plans (see Chapter 10).

To get down to the work of making steps, you must first do a little simple math, which we're about to explain, nice and clearly. After that, you can start construction, from the bottom step, heading up.

Calculating step dimensions

The following requirements are typical of most building codes (verify with your building department):

» Stairs must be at least 3 feet (.9 m) wide.

» The *total rise* (distance from landing to landing, measured vertically) must not exceed 12 feet (3.6 m). For longer climbs, include at least one landing every 12 feet (3.6 m).

» For each step, the *riser* (vertical measurement) plus one *tread* (horizontal) equals 18 inches (45.7 cm). The vertical measurement, that is, the riser, should be between 4 and 7.5 inches (between 10.1 and 19 cm). See Figure 7-4.

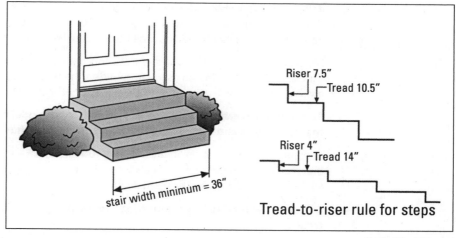

FIGURE 7-4: Stairs and garden steps must maintain uniform, safe dimensions.

» All riser heights and tread widths within a set of stairs must not vary more than ⅜ inch (.9 cm).

» Stairs with three or more risers require a handrail. Handrails must be a uniform height above all stair treads: 34 to 38 inches (86.3 to 96.5 cm) as measured vertically from the stair *nosings* (front edges).

» Landings must be as wide as the stairway and at least 3 feet (.9 m) deep.

Planning your steps

Make garden steps as luxurious as possible, with low risers (5½ to 6½ inches; 14 to 16.5 cm), deep treads, and a generous width. To plan your steps, proceed in the following order:

1. **Measure the vertical rise between landings.**

Measure from the finished surface of the lower path to the finished surface of the upper path. To do this, set one end of a straightedge on the upper path (or on a support that represents the approximate level of the path). Holding the straightedge level, bridge the step location with it and measure down from the bottom of the straightedge to the surface of the lower path.

2. **Divide this dimension by a trial riser height, such as 6 inches (15.2 cm), to determine the number of risers.**

If the answer is a whole number (not likely), proceed to the next step. If not, round the answer up to the next whole number and divide that number back into the original dimension. The result is your actual riser height.

For example, a total rise of 27 inches (68.6 cm), divided by a trial riser height of 6 inches (15.2 cm), yields 4.5 risers. By rounding this number up to 5 and dividing it into 27, you get a riser height of 5.4, or 5⅜, inches (13.7 cm).

3. **Calculate the tread *depth* (width, as viewed from the side) by doubling the riser height and subtracting the answer from 26 inches (66 cm).**

Continuing with example in Step 2: 5⅜ × 2 = 10¾ inches. 26 − 10¾ = 15¼ inches for the tread depth (in metric, the calculation looks like this: 13.65 cm × 2 = 27.3 cm; 66 − 27.3 cm = 38.7 cm for the tread depth).

4. **Calculate the total run by multiplying the tread depth by the number of treads.**

The number of treads is one less than the number of risers, so the total run of a set of steps with five risers and a tread depth of 15¼ inches (38.7 cm) would be 61 inches (154.9 cm).

5. **Test the total run.**

Holding a tape measure level with the upper path and using a plumb bob or level to transfer the measurement down to the lower path, measure a distance equal to the total run to see if you have enough space for the steps. If necessary, reduce the total run by shortening the tread depth dimension by 1 inch, 2.5 cm (remember that the riser-to-tread formula allows a total of 25 to 27 inches, 63.5 to 68.6 cm) or by reworking the ratio using a higher riser height.

Building steps

Use large building materials, such as landscaping timbers, concrete blocks, or large stones, to make informal garden steps. If a timber or stone is taller than the required riser height, simply bury it in the ground a bit. The techniques for building with block or stone are similar to the following techniques for building with timbers (see Figure 7-5).

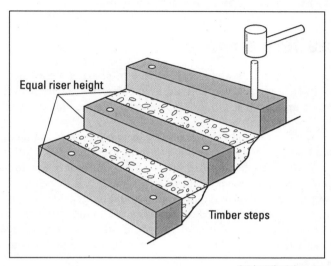

FIGURE 7-5: You can use landscape timbers to build garden steps.

Equal riser height

Timber steps

© John Wiley & Sons, Inc.

Avoid using old railroad ties, which leach toxins into your soil and groundwater. See Chapter 10 when we talk about raised beds for more details.

1. **Cut 6x6 landscaping timbers into 3-foot (.9 m) sections.**

   Bore two ½-inch (1.3 cm) diameter holes through each piece, near the ends.

2. **Set the bottom step in place.**

   Excavate and level the ground as necessary. Backfill and level the space behind the step, using gravel, crushed rock, concrete, or compacted soil for the backfill.

3. **Place the next step.**

   Measure back from the front edge of the lower step, at both ends, a distance that's equal to the tread depth. Place the next step so that the front edge is aligned with this dimension. Backfill and level for the next step.

4. Proceed up the slope.

As you build each step, stabilize the timber by driving a 2-foot (.6-m) length of ½-inch (1.3 cm) rebar through each predrilled hole, flush with the top.

Set each step so that the front edge is ⅛- to ¼-inch (.3 to .6 cm) lower than the back for drainage.

5. For three or more risers, add a handrail along one or both sides of the steps — see Chapter 8 for more information.

Installing a ramp

You may prefer to install a ramp instead of steps. For instance, a ramp can lead into a shed, allowing you to take a wheelbarrow, lawnmower, or heavy riding mower up and down it. Or perhaps you just like the look of one.

If, however, you need to install one to accommodate someone in a wheelchair, be advised that handicap ramps have to meet American Disabilities Act (ADA) standards. Width must be at least 3 feet (9 m), and there are practical rules about steepness (not very steep, a rise of one inch, 2.5 cm, for every 12 inches, 30.5 cm, in length). There are also requirements for landings and safety handrails, depending on the ramp's length and elevation gain. You may want to invest in a pre-built one that meets all the standards. If you'd rather build your own, however, first check with your local building inspector to find out whether a construction permit is required.

Figuring out the dimensions

An ideal shed ramp has a shallow slope and plenty of length for ease of use. Of course, you need sufficient real estate in front of your shed. To determine whether you have space, find out the dimensions by following these steps:

1. Determine the floor-level difference.

Calculate how far it is from the threshold of your shed to the ground. The higher it is, the longer the ramp will have to be (and the more materials you'll need). Most sheds are on a foundation pad or footing, so it will probably be between 9 and 14 inches (22.9 and 35.5 cm).

2. Determine the width.

Measure the door opening, and then add 6 inches (15.2 cm) on either side. No sense in cutting it close; this extra amount gives a good buffer.

3. **Determine the length.**

   You aren't worrying about the ADA standards, but you don't want a steep ramp because it can be at best difficult and at worst slippery and unsafe to be pushing something heavy up such a ramp. We recommend 1:8 at most; that is, 1 inch (2.5 cm) rise for every 8 inches (20.3 cm). Shallower is even better.

4. **Take your measurements to the lumber yard for help buying the materials you'll need, whether lumber or composite.**

   Note that joists need to be *tapered* (higher closer to the shed door, shorter at the ramp's end in your yard; get them pre-cut if you aren't confident of your measuring or sawing skills).

Constructing a basic shed ramp

For best results in constructing a basic shed ramp, drill pilot holes before securing boards with galvanized screws. Stick to these steps:

1. **Attach an exterior support to the shed; attach a board securely under the doorway.**

   Make sure it's level.

2. **Attach joists.**

   You'll probably need at least four, evenly spaced a foot or so (.3 m or so) apart. Attach them to the support using galvanized hangers.

3. **Fit blockings horizontally between the joists for extra stability.**

   Determine how many you need. That amount depends on the size of your ramp, but more is always better, at intervals up and down the length of it.

4. **Attach the decking boards across the joists, starting at the shed door/ exterior support and working downhill.**

5. **Clean up, stain, or paint.**

TIP

If you want, install a nonslip surface on the deck boards. You can get good ones with adhesive backing. Alternatively, use floor paints that have sand in them — a coat or two of this provides a nonslip coat.

Chapter **8**

Constructing Decks

Home life has shifted to the outdoors. Many families spend as much time cooking, dining, entertaining, playing, and working in their yards as they do in their houses. Having an attractive landscape isn't enough — people want an outdoor space that's functional but also has all the comforts of home.

The heart of any outdoor living space is a deck or patio, which you'll most likely build before turning your attention to the rest of the yard. Then, you can let nature provide the ambiance (and nuisances), or you can enhance your deck or patio with such features as an overhead shade structure (pergola), built-in seating, a cooking center, exterior lighting (see Chapter 10), as well as some containers of flowering plants (turn to Chapter 15). Check the color insert for some inspiration.

This chapter focuses on building a deck. Although a deck is a fairly simple structure, building one requires careful planning and workmanship. As a floor system, a deck must support heavy loads. As an outdoor structure, it must endure constant exposure to rain, perhaps snow, and sunlight. These factors alone require that your deck have heavy structural members, strong connections, solid footings, and effective protection from rot.

In addition, your deck must fit in with the site, harmonize with your home and yard, and be large enough for whatever activities you plan. This chapter, along with the basic construction guidelines in Chapter 4, can help you plan and build a basic deck that meets these challenges.

REMEMBER

Safety is key whenever you're building or installing anything. Review the general safety advice in Chapter 4 about worksites.

Understanding a Deck's Components

In simplest terms, a deck is a well-organized stack of lumber resting on rot-resistant supports as shown in Figure 8-1. In technical terms, concrete *footings* buried in the ground support *piers*, which support *posts*, which support one or more *beams*, which support *joists* (a *ledger board* connected to the house may also support the joists). The joists support the *decking boards* that you walk on and any *stairs* or *railings* that attach to the deck.

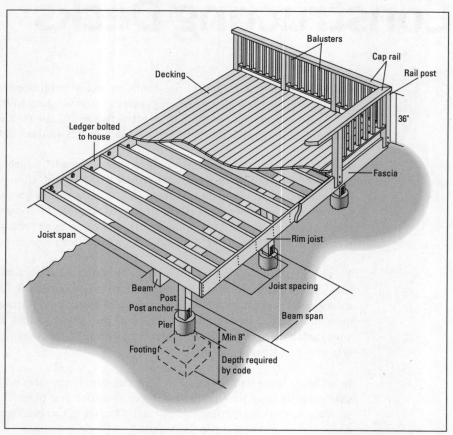

FIGURE 8-1: The basic structural system of a deck.

© John Wiley & Sons, Inc.

The beams and joists bear a critical relationship to each other. The farther apart the beams, the stronger and/or closer together the joists must be. The posts, footings, and beams bear a similar relationship — the farther apart the posts, the larger the footings and the stronger the beams.

Corrosion-resistant fasteners hold everything together and a *deck finish,* such as a water-repellent preservative, retards deterioration. As with any well-built structure, the deck must be *level,* the posts and railings *plumb* (perfectly vertical), and the corners *square* (exactly 90 degrees — unless the deck design includes different-sized angles).

Starting with Building a Deck

Planning and preparation account for at least 40 percent of a building project's time, starting long before construction begins. For a deck, you must draw up a plan, get any necessary permits, order materials, arrange for delivery and storage, and obtain tools. To march through this process logically and efficiently, you must have a good plan first — that means a suitable site as well as a solid, detailed design.

Developing a good deck plan

Most decks measure 12 to 16 feet (3.6 to 4.9 m) wide and 16 to 24 feet (4.9 to 7.3 m) long — approximately 200 to 400 square feet (60.1 to 122 m), or the size of a large family room. You need to decide where you want the deck first, and then you can design it, which we explain here.

Selecting a site for your deck

In choosing a site for your deck, consider the following:

>> **Sun and shade patterns:** Look at how the sun and shade patterns change throughout the day and the seasons.

>> **Access to the house and yard:** Plan for convenient access to the house, especially the kitchen and other public rooms, and to the yard.

>> **Traffic flow:** Take into account furniture arrangements and traffic flow. You may need to reconfigure the deck's shape or size for more efficient use.

>> **Views and privacy:** Use a stepladder to make observations from the proposed height of the deck platform.

>> **Other features that may interfere with the deck:** Inspect your deck site for downspouts, buried utility lines, meters, a septic tank, a crawlspace opening, and similar features.

Designing the deck plan

To design the deck itself, outline the platform first. Draw to scale an outline of the deck's shape from an aerial perspective. Include the house walls — with window and door locations — and other existing features that affect the deck.

Next, plot the direction of the decking boards, joists, beams, and ledger board (refer to Figure 8-1 again) for the shortest joist spans and most convenient footing locations.

Typically, decking runs parallel with the house wall or along the longer deck dimension. To calculate the size and spacing of the joists and beams, use the following recommendations:

>> **Decking:** Use 2x6 boards, which safely span 24 inches (60.1 cm) no matter what type or grade.

>> **Joists:** Plan 2x8 joists, spaced 24 inches (60.1 cm) *on center* (measured center-to-center or from one side of a joist to the same side of the adjacent joist). 2x8 joists of construction grade lumber, such as No. 2 pine, standard and better Douglas fir, or construction heart redwood, can span from 8½ to 10 feet (2.6 to 3 m) safely. For longer spans, use larger joists or space the 2x8s closer together.

>> **Ledger:** Choose a ledger board one size larger than the joists (a 2x10 or 3x8 for 2x8 joists).

>> **Beams:** Place the first beam 9 feet (2.7 m) from the ledger and subsequent beams 8 feet (2.4 m) apart. The joists can extend 2 to 3 feet (.6 to .9 m) beyond the outside beam. This span is called a *cantilever*. The size of beam depends on the spacing between posts. A 4x8 beam, for example, spaced 9 feet (2.7 m) from adjacent beams, can span up to 6 feet (1.8 m). If the posts are farther apart, use a larger beam.

>> **Posts:** Use 4x4s for posts shorter than 6 feet (1.8 m), larger sizes for taller posts.

>> **Piers and footings:** Plan footing locations so that each one supports approximately 50 square feet (15.2 square m) of deck area.

TIP

To get help with figuring out how much lumber to purchase for the project, we highly recommend this useful online calculator (www.omnicalculator.com/construction/decking). Remember to factor in an extra 10 percent in case of flaws or mistakes.

Choosing decking material

Lumber varies widely in durability, strength, appearance, availability, and cost. For decks specifically, for all the obvious reasons, we emphasize that you choose the strongest possible materials. Choose pressure-treated lumber for the structural members to ensure strength and durability. If larger beam sizes aren't available, choose untreated lumber and apply a preservative/sealer on-site.

For the decking boards, you have wider choices. Consider redwood, cedar, pressure-treated pine or Douglas fir, or even tropical hardwoods. You can find excellent nonwood alternatives, including Trex. Turn to Chapter 4 where we discuss wood lumber and its alternatives in more detail and the color insert for a photo of a deck made from composite lumber.

Besides lumber, you need to purchase concrete for the footings and piers, *rebar* (steel reinforcing bars for concrete; use ½-inch, 1.3 cm, diameter), connecting hardware, and deck finish.

Getting the Site Ready

Prepare the deck site by removing weeds and grading the soil to slope away from the house. If necessary, install drainage lines to prevent water from puddling under the deck (refer to Chapter 4). If you're attaching the deck to your house, make any alterations or repairs, such as removing a porch or repainting an area covered by the deck, at this time.

TIP

If you've been thinking of installing a new window adjacent, wait until after you build the deck to do so. The new deck will provide a convenient platform for completing the exterior part of that installation.

If your deck is going to cover an existing patio that slopes away from the house by at least a quarter inch per foot (.6 cm per .3 m), leave the patio in place and break holes through it where the footings for the deck go. The patio enhances drainage, inhibits weeds, provides a convenient storage platform, and keeps the area under the deck clear. If the patio doesn't slope correctly, break it up and remove the concrete; if you don't, puddles may accumulate against the house foundation because of the shade from the deck.

Lay out the deck's perimeter using the techniques described in Chapter 4. If you attach your deck to the house, simplify the layout by installing the ledger board first. A *ledger board* is a horizontal lumber beam attached to an existing wall and used to tie in construction elements such as porch roofs and decks. It makes a convenient batter board, especially for multiple rows of footings, which require intermediate stringlines between the perimeter lines. (*Batter board* refers to temporary wooden frameworks used to suspend the layout strings for a foundation.)

Preparing to attach the ledger board

Before you do anything, check the affected section of the house carefully. You don't want to cut or nail into a water pipe, electrical line, heating duct, and so on. Also make sure that the lag screws holding the ledger board will penetrate into the house framing, not just the siding.

Prepare the wall following these steps:

1. **Draw a level line along the wall for the top of the ledger (2½ inches (6.3 cm) below floor level if the decking boards are 2-by lumber; 1½ inches (3.8 cm) for ⁵/₄-inch/3.2 cm decking boards).**

   This is to save room (thickness) for decking boards and, if needed, undersill trim (which goes between the house siding and the deck boards).

   You can mark a long, level line in any of the following three ways:

   - Having a person help you, hold a long straightedge with a level on it against the house and scribe the line.

   - Link a series of marks that you make by using a long or laser level.

   - Using a level, make two end marks that are level with each other and then snap a chalkline between them.

   If the siding is stucco, plywood, or board siding that makes full contact with the *sheathing* (plywood or similar panels between the studs and siding) behind it, proceed to the steps for installing the ledger board in the next section.

   If the siding is vinyl, aluminum, shingles, or wood lap siding that doesn't make full contact with the sheathing behind it, proceed to the next step.

2. **Remove a section of siding where you intend to install the ledger.**

3. **Cover the exposed sheathing with a piece of metal *flashing* (aluminum or galvanized sheet metal).**

Tuck the flashing under the siding board above it, smooth the flashing flat against the sheathing, and bend the bottom to lap over the siding below it. Bend the loose ends the same way and lap them over the adjacent siding an inch (2.5 cm) or so. Seal the exposed flaps with caulking and nail them tight.

Installing the ledger board

To install the ledger board, follow these steps:

1. **Cut the board to length.**

2. **Mark locations on the board for drilling ⅝-inch (1.6 cm) diameter holes, for ½-inch (1.3 cm) diameter lag screws.**

You may alternatively use ledger lock fasteners, GRK fasteners, or Simpson strong-tie fasteners.

Screw them in using a screw gun or impact driver.

Place two holes within 6 inches (15.2 cm) of each end and a pair of holes every 16 to 32 inches (40.6 to 81.3 cm). Make sure there are no obstructions in the wall to interfere with hole locations and that the holes don't interfere with the joist layout.

3. **Position the ledger against the wall, keeping the top aligned with your guideline.**

Tack it in place using 16d duplex nails, 3½-inch (8.9-cm) exterior wood screws, or prop it up with braces.

4. **Using a pencil, mark the hole locations on the wall.**

5. **Take down the ledger and drill pilot holes into the wall for the lag screws.**

TIP

If you need to drill through metal flashing and the flashing is aluminum, use a hole saw. If the flashing is galvanized steel, use a metal-cutting bit and lubricate it with a few drops of oil as you drill.

6. **Prepare the ledger for attachment.**

Prop the ledger into an upright position and thread all the lag screws through their washers and the ledger holes. Use *malleable* (thick iron) washers.

TIP

You don't want moisture to get trapped between the ledger and the house wall. To prevent this, on the back side of the ledger, place a spacer over each screw. Use aluminum or plastic spacers specifically designed for this function or a group of five or six cut washers.

7. Attach the ledger.

With a helper, carefully lift the ledger into place and start the lag screws in their holes. Slowly tighten them in a random sequence until the ledger is snug and level.

After installing the ledger, complete the layout by building batter boards and stringing lines for the perimeter of the deck and any rows of intermediate footings. Refer to Figure 8-2 (and check out Chapter 4 for more information about layout).

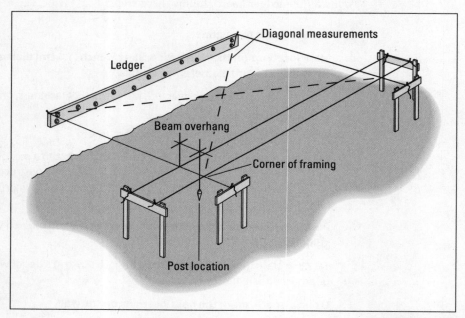

Diagonal measurements

Ledger

Beam overhang

Corner of framing

Post location

© John Wiley & Sons, Inc.

FIGURE 8-2: For a deck layout, attach stringlines directly to the ledger board.

TIP

You may find it convenient to deal with the ground that will be under the completed deck — especially if the finished deck surface will be low. Otherwise, if you want, it can wait till project's end. You'll want to lay down weed-excluding landscape fabric and then gravel. Refer to the section, "Sides and undersides," later in this chapter.

Prepping footings and piers

Dig holes for the footings to the depth required by your local building code, which is typically below the frost line in areas with severe winters, or at least 12 inches (30.5 cm) below grade (18 inches, 45.7 cm, on slopes). Dig the holes using a posthole digger, hand auger, or power auger. Keep the sides straight and the bottom level. Flare or enlarge the bottom of each hole enough to provide at least 2 square feet (.6 square m) of bearing surface for the footing (an 18x18-inch square, or 20-inch-diameter circle; 45.7x45.7 cm square, or 50.8 cm diameter circle).

To build forms for the concrete, follow these steps:

1. **For each hole, cut a length of 8- or 12-inch (20.3- or 30.5-cm) diameter forming tube that's 4 inches (10.1 cm) shorter than the hole depth.**

2. **Center the tube under the stringlines and suspend it so that the top extends 8 inches (20.3 cm) above grade.**

3. **Lay a 2x4 across the hole on each side of the forming tube and, using deck screws and a power screwdriver, secure the tube to both 2x4s.**

   Center the tube again and secure the 2x4s in position by driving a stake next to each end and attaching it to the 2x4 with screws.

4. **For additional bracing, run 1x4s diagonally from the stakes to the upper part of the tube; secure them by using deck screws.**

5. **Cut a length of rebar for each pier the same length as the tube and set it aside for the concrete pour.**

After the building inspector okays your forms and footing holes — if you already obtained a building permit, sometimes they check and sometimes they don't — it's time to order or mix the concrete.

Completing footings and piers

You may finish the supports by pouring concrete and securing reinforcing rebar into them. Take your time and follow these steps:

1. **Place just enough concrete in the bottom of each hole to fill the bottom 1 inch (2.5 cm) of forming tube.**

   Using a stick or rod, jab the concrete to consolidate it.

2. **After the concrete sets for a few minutes, fill the rest of the tube, settling the concrete by jabbing it and tapping the sides of the form with a hammer.**

3. **Using a scrap of wood, strike off the concrete to level the top.**

4. **Push the rebar down into the center of the pier until it's buried 1 to 3 inches (2.5 to 7.6 cm) below the top.**

5. **Using the string lines and a plumb bob to guide you, set the post anchors into the wet concrete.**

   Make sure they're plumb and level. Allow the concrete to cure for five days before removing the forms.

Installing posts and beams

After the concrete hardens, install the posts by following these steps:

1. **Rough-cut the two outer posts slightly long and set them in the post anchors or brackets, plumb them with a level, and temporarily brace them with stakes.**

TIP

   Before reattaching the posts to the post anchors, for maximum rot prevention, soak all the cut ends in wood preservative for eight hours.

2. **Using a laser level, or a long straightedge and carpenter's level, mark each post at the same level as the top of the ledger board.**

3. **Measure down from this mark the depth of the joist material (7¼ inches/18.4 cm, for 2x8s) plus the depth of the beam, and mark the post.**

4. **Using a square, scribe a line around each post at this mark (on all four sides).**

5. **Remove each post, trim off the top at the cutting line, and reattach it to the post anchor.**

6. **String a tight line between the tops of these outer posts and use it to mark the intermediate posts for cutting.**

7. **Cut and install the other posts.**

8. **Attach connecting brackets.**

9. **After installing all the posts, brace each one temporarily with diagonal braces.**

10. **Before installing each beam, cut it to the same length as the ledger.**

    For long spans, cut beams to length so that splices occur over posts.

11. **Set the beam(s) in place.**

    Measure along the beam and mark the precise locations for the post tops.

12. **Using a sledgehammer, knock the posts (not the beam) into alignment.**

    Check to make sure they're plumb and fasten the connectors to the beam. Use 16d galvanized joist hanger nails, common nails, or strong drive connector screws.

Installing the joists

To install the joists, follow these steps:

1. **Starting at either end of the ledger board, draw a vertical line 1½ inches (3.8 cm) from the end, using a square to keep the line accurate.**

   If you don't plan to cover the end joist with a fascia board, trim the ledger along this line so that you can cover the end of the ledger with the first joist (do the same at the other end).

2. **Continue to the other end of the ledger, making similar lines every 24 inches/60.1 cm (or at whatever joist spacing you're using).**

   Mark an X on the side of each line where the joist goes.

3. **Mark the same joist layout on the beam, making sure that you start from the same end.**

4. **Attach joist hangers to the ledger.**

   Using a scrap of joist lumber as a gauge, set the joist hangers so that the tops are flush with the top of the ledger. Nail only one side of each hanger to the ledger, aligning it with the layout line. Use 16d galvanized joist hanger nails.

5. **Attach the first joist to the ledger.**

   Rest it on the beam and slide the other end into the joist hanger. Leave ⅛ to ¼ inch (.3 to .6 cm) of clearance at the end of the joist, squeeze the joist hanger closed, and nail the loose side to the ledger. Then nail the hanger to the joist, holding a sledgehammer against the opposite side of the joist that you nail to keep the board from splitting.

6. **Attach the joist to the beam by toenailing three 8d galvanized common nails or by securing the joist with a metal rafter tie or hurricane tie.**

   Toenailing means driving a nail in at an angle in order to anchor the board.

7. **Install the rest of the joists, securing both ends of each joist before installing the next one.**

8. **Trim the free ends of the joists.**

   Holding a chalkline between the outer joists, snap a cutting line across the tops of all the joists. Mark a cutting line along one side of each joist where the chalkline crosses it. Cut along the marks.

9. **Attach a rim joist (also called a *header*) to the ends of the trimmed joists.**

Mark the joist layout on the back of the rim joist and, working from one end to the other, attach the header to each joist with 16d galvanized spiral-shank nails or 3-inch (7.6 cm) deck screws (drill pilot holes for the end joists).

Make sure that you attach the rim joist on the same day that you install the joists, or they may warp. Also, apply preservative to the cut ends of all boards before you install them.

10. **Install blocking between the joists along the beam.**

Snap a chalkline across the joists. Measure each joist bay and cut a 2x8 block for it. Tap it into place between the joists and nail it with four 16d nails at each end. Stagger the blocks on each side of the chalkline to facilitate nailing.

Laying decking boards

Before laying the decking boards, apply sealer to the joists, especially the tops. You should also apply a coat of finish (sealer or sealer/preservative, depending on type of lumber) to the decking boards if you have sufficient room to lay them out in a shaded, well–ventilated area. Otherwise, apply finish to the bottom sides, after laying them out, before you attach them.

To install the boards, follow these steps:

1. **Sort through the stack of lumber and select the best boards for prominent locations, such as in front of doorways and stairs, and along the outer edge of the deck.**

Likewise, select the worst boards for hidden locations.

2. **Starting along the house wall, lay out the decking boards loosely over the joists.**

Be careful walking near the ends of boards until they're fastened to the joists.

3. **Fasten the first board by doing the following:**

1. Tip it on edge and snap a chalkline across the joists, measuring out from the wall the width of one board plus ⅜ inch (.9 cm).

2. Align the outer edge of the board along this line.

3. Fasten with two *deck screws* (3-inch/7.6 cm galvanized screws installed with a power screwdriver), two 12d galvanized common nails, or a *deck clip* (hidden fastening device) at each joist.

4. Drill pilot holes for deck screws or nails at the ends of the board.

4. **Fasten the remaining boards.**

Maintain a $\frac{1}{16}$- to $\frac{3}{16}$-inch (.16 to .5 cm) gap between boards. Straighten bowed boards by driving a chisel into the joist and using it to pry the board into alignment.

If the boards are shorter than the deck, join them end-to-end over joists. Stagger the joints at least three joists apart from each other.

TIP

5. **Trim the ends of the boards.**

Snap a chalkline along the edge of the deck, either flush with the outside edge of the joist (if you're adding a fascia board) or ½ inch (1.3 cm) beyond the joist. Cut along the chalkline.

6. **Attach the fascia.**

Use 1-by or 2-by lumber one size wider than the joist size (a 1x10, for example, for 2x8 joists). Apply preservative and sealer to the joists and back of the fascia (not to the *front* of the fascia). Cut the fascia boards at 45 degrees for mitered joints at the corners. Attach them by driving screws through the back of the joists into the fascia, every 6 inches (15.2 cm) along the top and 12 inches (30.5 cm) along the bottom.

Adding deck stairs

Deck stairs consist of two or more stringers and treads attached between them (see Figure 8–3). The width of the treads and height of the risers are critical measurements and *must be consistent.*

Make sure you remember the following when adding deck stairs:

» Build to standard code, which is typically a total of 18 inches (45.7 cm): for example, 12-inch (30.5 cm) steps with 6-inch rise (15.2 cm). For additional information about stair requirements and calculating dimensions, see Chapter 7.

» Buy lumber with *nosing* (the edges of lumber pieces are rounded or sanded, that is, not sharp-edged). Use the nosing edge for the leading edge of each step.

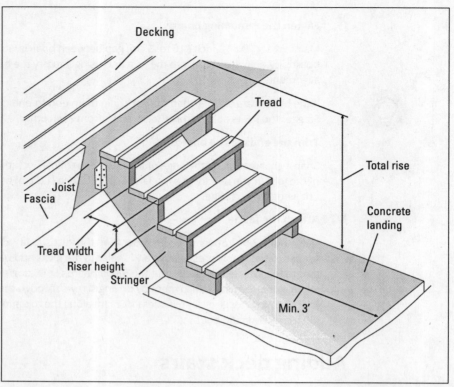

Decking

Tread

Total rise

Joist

Fascia

Concrete landing

Tread width

Riser height

Stringer

Min. 3'

FIGURE 8-3:
Components
of simple
deck stairs.

© John Wiley & Sons, Inc.

Study Figure 8–4, and then use the following techniques for building deck stairs:

1. Choose 2x12s for the *stringers* (the vertical support boards), 4 feet (1.2 m) longer than the total run.

2. Lay out the first stringer, using a framing square.

1. Use tape to mark the riser dimension on the *tongue* (short leg) of the square and the tread dimension on the *blade* (long leg).

2. For each step, align these marks with the top edge of the stringer and trace along the lower edge of the square.

3. Move the square to the next position and trace again, until you have enough risers.

3. Cut out the stringer.

Mark a cutting line for the bottom step by subtracting the thickness of the tread material (1½ inches, or 3.8 cm, for example, for 2-by boards) from the bottom riser. If you're using a circular power saw to cut out the steps, stop the saw before you reach the corners and finish each cut with a handsaw.

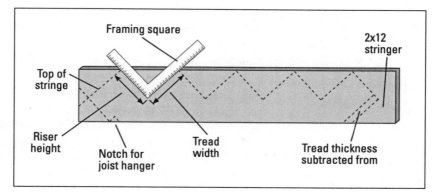

FIGURE 8-4:
Building stairs
requires precise
measurements
and careful
carpentry.

Framing square

2x12
stringer

Top of
stringe

Riser
height

Notch for
joist hanger

Tread
width

Tread thickness
subtracted from

© John Wiley & Sons, Inc.

4. Test the stringer by setting it in place.

The bottom should rest flat on a concrete landing or a wooden cleat bolted to a concrete footing. Use a level to make sure that the treads are level and the risers plumb. Note any necessary adjustments and cut out a new stringer.

5. Trace the first stringer onto a second 2x12 and cut it out.

6. Install both stringers.

Secure them to the deck joist with joist hangers. Secure them to the landing by bolting 2x4 cleats to the landing along the inside edge of each stringer. Drive deck screws through the stringers into the cleats.

7. Install the treads, starting at the bottom.

Align the front edge of each tread so that it overhangs the stringer cutouts by 1 to 1½ inches (2.5 to 3.8 cm).

Adding deck railings

Stairs with three or more risers require a handrail on each open side of the stairway. For the railings to be safe and useful, certain standards must be met:

>> Handrails must be *grippable* — that is, a continuous portion of the handrail must be 1¼ to 2 inches (3.2 to 5 cm) wide so that you can easily grip it, with at least 1½ inches (3.8 cm) of clearance above and behind the rail and a maximum projection out from any wall of 3½ inches (8.9 cm).

>> The ends of handrails mustn't be exposed (they're sleeve-catchers), so face the ends to a post or wall.

>> Handrails must be uniform height above all stair treads: 34 to 38 inches (86.4 to 96.5 cm) as measured vertically from the stair nosings.

>> Handrails for any drop-offs more than 30 inches (76.2 cm) must include childproof *screening* (that is, a 4-inch/10.1 cm sphere can't pass through it) between the handrail and stairs.

REMEMBER

Be sure to treat cut surfaces with wood preservative before installing.

To install a handrail, attach posts at the top and bottom of the stair stringer and every 4 to 6 feet (1.2 to 1.8 m) in between. Attach a string from the bottom post to the top post that's parallel with the stringer and at a uniformly consistent height of 34 to 38 inches (86.4 to 96.5 cm) above the tread nosings. Mark where the string intersects each post and attach the handrail at these marks.

Decks higher than 30 inches (76.2 cm) require railings, which must adhere to very strict safety standards. Most codes require that the rails be 36 inches/91.4 cm high (42 inches/106.7 cm in some areas), have closely-spaced members (called a *screening*) that prevent a 4-inch/10.1 cm sphere from passing through, and also be strong enough to resist a *lateral force* (sideways pressure) of 200 pounds per square foot (2153 pounds per square meter). Most railing designs consist of posts, horizontal rails, and some type of screening.

Use the following techniques to build railings:

1. **Bolt the railing posts to the outside of the joists.**

   Use 4x4s and space them evenly, 4 to 6 feet (1.2 to 1.8 m) apart. For a more finished appearance, cut a 1½-inch-wide (3.8-cm wide) notch out of the bottom of each post so that it overlaps the decking, and bevel the bottom of the post tail at a 30-degree angle. Bolt each post with two ½-inch/1.3 cm diameter carriage bolts, anchors, or fasteners (as shown in Figure 8-5).

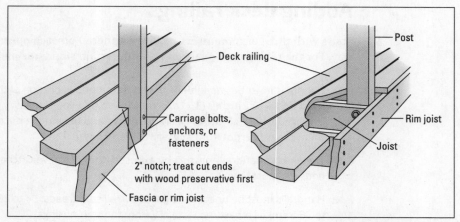

Deck railing

Post

Carriage bolts, anchors, or fasteners

Rim joist

Joist

2" notch; treat cut ends with wood preservative first

Fascia or rim joist

FIGURE 8-5: Bolting a railing post to the deck.

© *John Wiley & Sons, Inc.*

2. **Mark and cut pairs of 2x4 rails (horizontal supports) to fit between the posts.**

   Set the bottom rails 4 inches (10.1 cm) above the decking. For *balusters* (vertical slats), set the rails on edge and flush with the inside face of the posts. For wire screening attached to the outside face of the framing, set the rails flat.

3. **Attach the rails to the posts by drilling pilot holes and driving two 3-inch (7.6 cm) galvanized deck screws at an angle through the face of each post and into the rail.**

4. **Drive additional nails at an angle up through each end of the rail and into the post and then down through each end of the rail and into the post.**

5. **Install a 2x6 cap rail on top of the 2x4 top rails.**

   Use miter joints at the corners and attach the cap rail by driving deck screws up through the top rails at an angle.

6. **Attach the screening to the top and bottom rails.**

Finishing Your Deck

Congratulations, you're almost done! The last two steps, dealing with what's underneath and finishing the surface, complete the project. Then, call your family to admire your good work and invite people over for drinks or a grilled meal.

Sides and undersides

For finishing touches, you have several items to attend to, including the following:

>> **Add weed control fabric.** If you haven't already done so, put down weed control fabric before spreading gravel under the deck (easy enough with a higher deck). To do this, stick to these steps:,

   1. Lay down two or three layers of landscape fabric, overlapping by at least 8 inches/20.3 cm (layering them perpendicular to one another for best coverage).

      Make sure to leave a 2-inch/5-cm overhang around the edges, so you know you won't come up short.

   2. Cover the area with a layer of gravel (not mulch, which holds in moisture).

>> **Attach lattice panels and/or screening.** Attach it to the deck posts so that the area under the deck is concealed, and animals and children can't crawl under and hide or get trapped (we know a dramatic story about a trapped possum family; you can imagine!).

>> **Dress up the railing and post edges.** You can use a router with a round-over bit (which produces a rounded edge) or other decorative bit.

Protective finishes

For the finish itself, apply a water–repellent preservative or a semitransparent stain that's specifically designed for deck surfaces (not for general outdoor use, including masonry). Other products, such as paint or solid stains, make attractive finishes but are more difficult to apply and maintain.

Before applying the finish, test it on a hidden part of the deck or some scrap wood. Choose a sunny day on which the air temperature is between 40 and 90°F (4 and 32° C), but try to avoid working in direct sunlight. Apply the product according to manufacturer's recommendations. Using a brush or pad increases penetration, but avoid overapplying the finish because an excess can lead to filming. For stains, coat the full length of each board to avoid overlap marks and puddle stains.

> » **Creating a base for a patio**
>
> » **Arranging bricks or pavers on a sand bed**
>
> » **Constructing a concrete patio**

Chapter **9**

Building Patios

Patios offer more design options than decks, but even with those options, patios are, in some ways, simpler to design and build than decks. The four basic building steps are as follows:

- » Planning the size and shape of your patio

- » Choosing the surface (paving) material

- » Constructing the base

- » Installing the surface

The techniques vary primarily with the type of surface you install.

Constructing the base, though, is similar for most materials. What you then put on top of that base foundation is up to you. Choose surface materials with an eye to how your new patio will blend in with your home's architecture and other features of your yard.

Here we address the most common surfacing materials: concrete, brick, pavers, and broad stones. We explain what you need to know about the different surfaces.

REMEMBER

Safety is key whenever you're building or installing anything. Review the general safety advice in Chapter 4 about worksites.

As with decks (refer to Chapter 8), the size and shape of a patio reflect the uses you intend for it and the available space to fit it in. More than decks, patios lend themselves to curves, freeform shapes, and flowing transitions into paths and walks. (See the color insert for ideas on patio shapes and uses.) Patios can be slightly larger than decks because, being at ground level, they aren't as prominent a structure.

However, any large expanse of paving is monotonous, so break up your patio with tree wells, planters, benches, fountains, low walls, borders, and similar features. Minimize the impact even more by softening the edges with plants (see Part 3 for more on plantings).

Selecting Materials

Determining what your new patio will look like deserves some careful thought. Here we guide you through the factors to consider, including what materials you'll need, which materials to use, and how much you'll need. You may decide to mix it up, that is, using one material for the main surface but another to form an attractive border.

Recognizing factors to evaluate

Your primary decision is what the patio's surface will look like. Consider the following factors:

>> **Texture:** Smooth surfaces tend to be monotonous and may become slippery. Excessively bumpy surfaces create the risk of people tripping and may make outdoor furniture wobble.

>> **Color:** Just like flooring or an indoor rug, the surface's color can add character and beauty to its surroundings. Terra cotta and brick colors complement greenery but have strong red or orange tones that seem artificial or overwhelming in some settings. Very light and very dark colors call attention to themselves and accentuate the patio. Mid-tones blend with their surroundings. Bold colors create interesting accents and contrasts. Color also affects the capability of the patio to absorb or reflect sunlight, which can be a factor in exposed locations.

>> **Scale and proportion:** For small patios, choose finely textured paving, such as brick, tile, or small stones. For large patios, choose flagstone, large pavers, or concrete.

- >> **Durability:** Brick and stones that absorb moisture, such as sandstone, are vulnerable to frost damage and moss. Materials set on a sand base endure unstable ground quite well.

- >> **Drainage:** Solid paving sheds water, whereas paving that's set on sand absorbs it.

- >> **Availability:** Most stone and brick is distributed within a small geographic region, although choices are abundant within most areas. Consider ease of transportation and storage.

- >> **Handling:** All masonry materials are heavy and have different handling characteristics. Pallets of flagstone are difficult to maneuver. Bricks and concrete pavers stack easily and are fairly easy to move.

- >> **Ease of installation:** The easiest installations are brick or pavers on a sand base. Concrete is easy to place but requires skillful handling and finishing. Bricks are easy to lift and handle but require great patience to set in patterns.

- >> **Cost:** In pricing materials, verify the unit of measurement (cubic yard or meter for concrete, square foot (.3 m) for tile or cut stone, weight for stone, and unit for brick or pavers). Generally speaking, concrete is the least expensive material and flagstone is the most expensive.

REMEMBER

As you price various materials, factor in the delivery cost. Also order about 10 percent more than what you need because breakage or flaws are inevitable.

Considering your choices

Materials for a patio surface include concrete, brick, pavers, and various stones, natural and manufactured. To help you decide, here's some more details about them:

- >> **Concrete:** Concrete is a relatively inexpensive choice that offers durability, a uniformly smooth surface, and a wide range of finishes — from smooth grays to colorful textures. Over the last few years, embossing techniques (referred to as *stamped concrete*) have revolutionized concrete finishing. If you associate concrete with drab slabs, consider surfaces that resemble huge slabs of natural stone or realistic patterns of cut stone, colored with permanent stains in warm earth tones. Other finishes include exposed aggregate and *broomed finishes* (a finish created by dragging a concrete-finishing broom across the fresh concrete), which add subtle patterns of straight or wavy lines.

>> **Brick:** Bricks vary in color and texture, depending on the manufacturing method and source of clay. Brick that is suitable for patios includes the following two types:

- **Common brick:** Common brick, also referred to as *standard* or *building* brick, is the most common (surprise!). Choose type *SW* (severe weathering) for areas with subzero temperatures, and SW or *MW* (moderate weathering) for areas where temperatures frequently dip below freezing but seldom below zero Fahrenheit (–18°C).

- **Paving brick:** Designed for mortarless installations, paving brick is half the thickness of common brick and has straight, even sides.

Bricks also vary in size but always have modular dimensions that enable them to fit into different patterns. The basic module is 4 x 8 x 2½ inches (10.1 x 20.3 x 6.3 cm). Actual dimensions vary to take the mortar joints into account, ranging from 3½ to 3¾ inches (8.9 to 9.5 cm), for example, for the 4-inch (10.1 cm) dimension. Paving brick is usually a full 4 x 8 inches (10.1 x 20.3 cm) wide.

WARNING

Don't buy or salvage unfired clay bricks, sometimes also called *NW* (no weathering) bricks. They're unsuitable for patios because they absorb water and are subject to damage from freeze-thaw cycles.

>> **Pavers:** A younger cousin of brick, modular pavers have swept the patio scene as the ideal paving material for do-it-yourself installations. They're cheaper and more durable than brick but lack the rich variations of color and texture, although manufacturers are continually striving to improve their appearance. Shapes vary from mock bricks to hexagon and herringbone patterns. Some patterns require two different shapes of paver. Thickness varies — choose between 1½ and 2½ inches (3.8 and 6.3 cm).

REMEMBER

Always install pavers over a sand bed. Most paver designs have rounded edges to prevent sharp transitions between pavers because they settle and move at different rates.

>> **Flagstone and other stones:** Basalt, bluestone, granite, limestone, sandstone, and slate are common types of stone for paving. You can buy quarried stone cut into regular or modular shapes, much like tile, or in random sizes and shapes, which require fitting together like a jigsaw puzzle. If you live in an area with cold winters, avoid sandstone and limestone, which absorb water and crack when they freeze. Some stones, such as granite, become very slippery when wet.

REMEMBER

The best stone is rough enough for good traction but smooth enough for tables and chairs to rest stably upon. Install stone on a concrete slab or over a sand base (which requires thicker stones).

ADDING BORDERS: YES OR NO?

Patio materials that you install on a sand bed do require a permanent edge to hold them in place. Even a patio that you install on a mortar bed or concrete slab may look better with some kind of border.

Materials for permanent borders include bricks laid flat or on end, stones, a concrete curb, wood timbers, composite "wood" timbers, 2-by lumber set on edge, and concealed heavy-duty plastic or metal edging held in place with spikes.

Calculating how much material you'll need

To estimate the quantity of materials you need, start with the overall dimensions of your patio and calculate the total area. If the patio is a simple geometric shape, such as a rectangle, multiply the length times the width. If the patio is free-form, draw it to scale on graph paper and tally the squares that it covers. Then, convert the surface area into the amount of each material that you need, starting with the surface material/paving.

Here's how to do these area calculations:

>> For concrete, multiply the surface area by the thickness of the slab, which is usually 4 to 6 inches, or 10.1 to 15.2 cm.

>> For base materials, figure 4 to 8 inches, or 10.1 to 20.3 cm (refer to the next section for more details). Then, convert the answer to cubic yards by dividing by 27 (or by dividing by 35.3 to get cubic meters).

>> If the paving is brick, figure five bricks per square foot (.3 m). If it's dimensioned stone, use the square footage (m).

>> For flagstone, divide the surface area (square feet or m) by 100 to arrive at a figure for tons needed.

TIP

If math isn't your thing, turn to these handy online calculators (www.omni calculator.com/construction#s-104 or www.homeadvisor.com/r/brick-paver-calculator/), which work well for geometric shapes but aren't as useful for a free-form or unusual-shape patio.

Building the Base

Patio construction isn't mysterious. You excavate an area of the size and shape you want, and then you fill it in. The base comes first, the surface comes second. No matter what paving material you choose, the most important component of your patio is actually the part you don't notice when it's all completed — the *base*.

Begin by excavating, then install a firmly compacted subbase. Follow these steps:

1. **Establish the layout of the base.**

   Create a grid of stakes with mason's twine strung between them. Use the same techniques as for a deck (refer to Chapter 8), with two differences:

   - Rather than leveling all the lines to each other, lower the outer line so that the patio slopes ⅛ inch (.3 cm) per foot (.3 m) away from the house, for drainage.

   - In addition to the perimeter lines, string additional lines 3 to 5 feet (.9 to 1.5 m) apart to create a grid of lines crisscrossing the patio site. These intermediate lines allow you to take depth measurements throughout the patio as you dig (although they're a nuisance to navigate around).

2. **Excavate the soil within the patio perimeter.**

   Go down 4 inches (10.1 cm) deeper than the thickness of the material you've chosen for the surface. (For example, if you're planning to install a surface of bricks, which are about 3.5 or 4 inches [8.9 to 10.1 cm] thick, dig down about 8 inches, or 20.3 cm.) To gauge the depth as you dig, measure down from the grid of string lines.

   TIP

   You can monitor the depth of your excavation with a handy stick. Here's how: Mark a stick at a distance equal to the distance from the string line at the site's highest elevation (if it slopes) + the thickness of your planned surface (for example, 4-inch, or 10.1 cm, bricks) + 4 inches, 10.1 cm, to account for the gravel subbase layer. If your string line is 6 inches, or 15.2 cm, above ground level, for instance, your depth stick should be 14 inches (6 + 4 + 4), or, in metric: 10.1 + 10.1 + 15.2, which is 35.4 cm. As you dig, use the mark on the stick to gauge the depth of your excavation.

3. **Add crushed rock or gravel (about 5 inches'/12.7 cm worth), and then firmly compact it.**

   Using a rented vibrating flat-plate compactor, compact it to the desired 4-inch (10.1 cm) thickness.

4. **Remove the grid of strings and install the edging material.**

   We advise adding edging, a border around your patio for stability and also because it looks neat. Refer to Figure 9-1 for some ideas (bricks/pavers, timber, and concrete curbing).

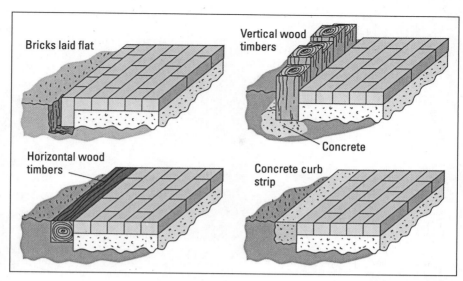

FIGURE 9-1:
You have
several options
for creating a
border around
your patio.

Installing the Surface

The patio surfaces that most homeowners undertake on their own are brick or pavers laid on a thin bed of sand or stone dust (the easiest installation), and a concrete slab.

Even if you're not comfortable building your own concrete patio, the information in this section helps you work with professionals — for example, building the forms and having a professional concrete finisher handle the pouring and finishing.

Installing brick, pavers, or flagstones

After the subbase is in place and firmly compacted, you can move on to the part you've been waiting for — installing your surface. You'll be setting the surface materials into sand, plus adding a bit more sand around them. The sand helps keep them in place but still allows them to shift slightly as the ground expands and contracts seasonally. See Figure 9-2.

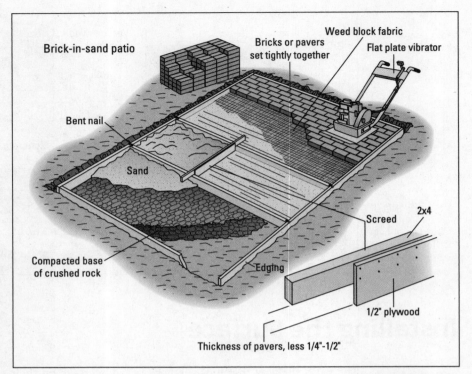

FIGURE 9-2:
A brick or paver patio installed over a sand bed requires a firmly compacted base, a stable border, and tightly packed paving units.

Labels in figure:
- Brick-in-sand patio
- Bricks or pavers set tightly together
- Weed block fabric
- Flat plate vibrator
- Bent nail
- Sand
- Compacted base of crushed rock
- Screed
- 2x4
- Edging
- 1/2" plywood
- Thickness of pavers, less 1/4"-1/2"

To install bricks, pavers, or flagstones, follow these steps:

1. Choose a pattern.

Bricks offer a variety of time-honored patterns, shown in Figure 9-3. The easiest to lay, called *jack-on-jack,* is bricks lined up next to each other in even rows. Staggering each row so that the joints fall at the midpoint of bricks in the adjacent rows creates a pattern called *running bond.* Other patterns, such as *basketweaves* and *herringbones,* involve placing bricks at right angles to each other. *English* and *Flemish* styles alternate brick lengths and widths.

TIP

Avoid patterns that require cutting lots of bricks in half or into other shapes. Jack-on-jack, running bond, and basketweave patterns require minimal cutting. (Cutting bricks, or pavers, is a fairly dangerous and frustrating project, and is beyond the scope of this book. If you need to cut your patio's surface materials, consult a professional.)

Pavers may or may not have as wide a choice of pattern options, depending on which shape you choose. If your pavers require two different shapes to complete the pattern, be sure you have enough of both shapes.

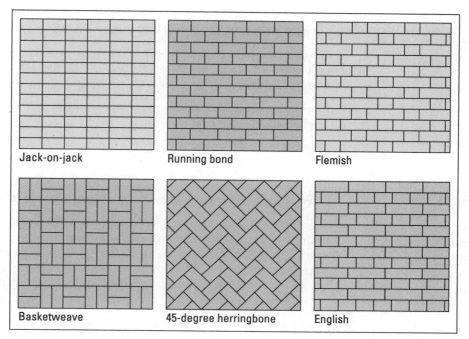

Jack-on-jack   Running bond   Flemish

Basketweave   45-degree herringbone   English

© John Wiley & Sons, Inc.

FIGURE 9-3:
These brick
patterns are
designs that any
do-it-yourselfer
can duplicate.

2. **Lay down weed-blocking landscape or geotextile fabric atop the prepared, compacted subbase.**

   Overlap cut edges by about 6 inches (15.2 cm). Extend beyond the outline so you're not short; you can always trim excess later.

3. **Add the layer of sand or stone dust, an inch (2.5 cm) deep.**

   The trick is to lay it down evenly. We suggest you use 1-inch depth spacers, either plywood strips or lengths of 1-inch (2.5 cm) pipe. Set these about 3 feet (.9 m) apart. Then dump in the sand or stone dust and rake it until the surface is approximately smooth (your spacers will be just barely showing). Water thoroughly with a gentle spray from the hose to settle the sand or stone dust.

   After that, *screed* (smooth over) the surface to a nice even layer by drawing a 3-foot (.9 m) or more length of board (a 2x4 will do fine) across the surface with the ends resting on the embedded spacers. Water, tamp, repeat. Then carefully extract the spacers and fill in and smooth over the void where they were.

4. **Use a guide line.**

TIP

   Tie a length of mason's twine to two loose bricks, pavers, or stones. Using these for anchors, stretch the line parallel with (and one brick's width away from) the starting edge. Move the line over and use it as a guide as you lay each row.

5. **Set each piece in place without sliding it.**

   Tap each piece lightly with a rubber mallet to snug it into the sand or stone dust — avoid displacing any. Pavers should protrude above the edging a little bit, for compaction later on, about ¼ to ½ inch (.6 to 1.2 cm).

6. **After laying several bricks, pavers, or stones, check your work by laying a level or straightedge over it.**

   Reset the pieces as necessary to align them. As you work your way across the patio, place 2-foot (.6 m) square pieces of plywood (with a kneeling pad or kneepads for you!) on the surface to kneel on, to distribute your weight.

7. **After all the bricks, pavers, or stones are in place, compact the patio.**

   Spread more sand or stone dust over the patio and then sweep it back and forth into the cracks. With some excess still on the surface, go over the patio with the rented vibrating flat plate compactor. Sweep again, as necessary, to force and pack the sand or stone dust into the joints and tightly compress the paving. For a final cleanup, sweep away the excess and hose off the patio.

Installing a concrete slab patio

No matter the size, building a proper form is within your abilities. If you focus on preparing the base, building the forms, and setting the reinforcing steel, you're halfway there.

The actual placing of concrete — technically, it's *placed*, not poured, although using the word *pour* is customary — isn't as important an event, despite the high drama, as what happens before and after.

WARNING

If you're planning a concrete slab patio larger than 4 x 6 feet (1.2 x 1.8 m), we recommend you hire a professional concrete finisher. That's because larger slabs require numerous control and expansion joints — precision work best left to the pros. (Take note of the sidewalks in your town to understand what we mean.)

So, unless you're making a smaller patio and plan to finish the surface with a simple broom finish (as we mention in the following list in Step 14), engage a professional do the final finish work.

To visualize the full process, look at Figure 9-4.

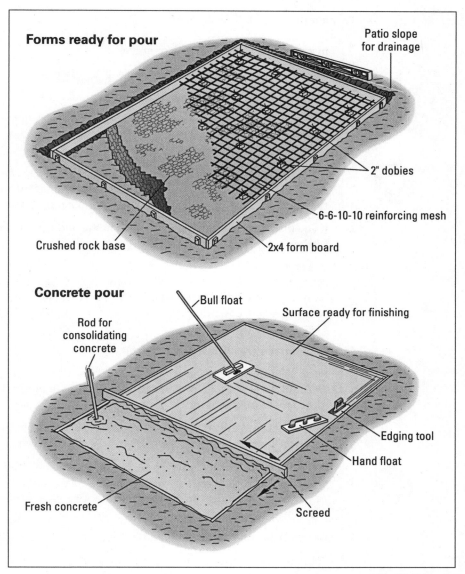

Forms ready for pour

Patio slope
for drainage

2" dobies

6-6-10-10 reinforcing mesh

2x4 form board

Crushed rock base

Concrete pour

Bull float

Surface ready for finishing

Rod for
consolidating
concrete

Edging tool

Hand float

Fresh concrete

Screed

FIGURE 9-4:
Save money by
preparing the
base and forms,
but unless your
concrete slab
patio is small, it's
wise to call in the
professionals to
pour and finish it
for you.

© John Wiley & Sons, Inc.

To build the form, follow these steps:

1. **Install a base of crushed rock or gravel.**

See the section, "Building the Base," earlier in this chapter.

2. **Build 2x4 forms around the patio perimeter.**

Set them on edge and hold them in place with steel or wooden stakes every 3 to 4 feet (.9 to 1.2 m), adjusting the boards so that the tops are exactly at the finished height of the patio.

TIP

If the patio is adjacent to the house foundation, install a strip of expansion joint material (available at concrete and masonry suppliers) against the foundation to absorb pressure from the patio as it expands during hot weather.

3. **If you install permanent divider boards in the patio, place them no farther apart than 10 feet (3 m).**

Use pressure-treated or a durable species of lumber, sealed with a water-repellent preservative. Drive standard framing (or 16d) galvanized nails partway into the sides of each board, every 16 inches (40.6 cm), for the concrete to grip. Cover the tops of the boards with masking tape to protect them from concrete stains.

4. **Dampen the gravel base to compact it.**

5. **Place *welded-wire reinforcing mesh* (mesh consisting of 6 x 6-inch, or 15.2 x 15.2 cm) squares formed by 10-gauge wire running in both directions) over the base.**

Overlap edges by at least 6 inches (15.2 cm), and place 2-inch (5-cm) *dobies* (small concrete blocks) under the mesh to raise it off the base.

WARNING

Wear gloves when handling reinforcing mesh. Be extremely careful when unrolling it because it can recoil with terrific force if you don't straighten it out as you go. Cut the mesh with bolt cutters, a hacksaw, or a circular power saw with a metal cutoff blade.

6. **Get an inspection, if required, and order the concrete delivery.**

Calculate the exact volume of concrete you need.

You may do this by multiplying the width times length times thickness of the slab (measured in feet/meters or fractions of a foot/meter). Divide the result by 27 to give you the number of cubic yards (or by 9 for meters), which is how concrete is ordered. Add 5 or 10 percent for waste.

You can find out how much you need by plugging the numbers into this online construction calculator (www.omnicalculator.com/construction).

Stop, unless it's a patio 4 x 6 feet (1.2 x 1.8 m) or smaller. Call in professionals (in fact, you can call them in even sooner if you need help ordering the concrete, including discussing the options). You'll save money and impress the crew when they show up to find a prepared form waiting for them. They'll also have the necessary tools and experience to pour and finish the slab correctly.

7. **Place concrete in the forms, starting in one corner.**

   Have a helper place the fresh concrete up and down with a rod or shovel to consolidate it and fill any voids in the mix. Pile the concrete just slightly higher than the forms.

8. **Smooth *(strike off)* the concrete by dragging a screed (a 2x4 or 2x6 long enough to span the patio) across it in a back-and-forth sawing motion.**

9. **After placing and screeding all the concrete and before water collects on the surface, smooth the concrete further by using a wood or magnesium *float,* which resembles a flat trowel (a *bull float* has a very long handle).**

10. **Smooth the hidden edge of the slab by running the blade of a brick trowel between the slab and forms.**

11. **Using an *edger* (small hand trowel with a curved lip along one edge), glide back and forth along the edges of the slab to round them and smooth 2 or 3 inches (5 or 7.6 cm) of concrete surface.**

12. **Using a 1-inch (2.5 cm) *groover* (a tool with a ridge on the bottom), cut control joints into the concrete every 10 feet (3 m).**

    Control joints (or grooves) help to confine cracking of the concrete, which is inevitable. To keep the joints straight, snap a chalkline on the concrete or lay a straightedge on it. Use knee boards to keep your knees and feet off the concrete as you run the groover back and forth.

13. **After the concrete becomes a bit firm, steel-trowel the surface very smooth, being careful not to leave any trowel marks or ridges.**

    Then re-edge the slab and recut the joints.

14. **Have lunch and wait for the concrete to begin to cure so that, when you touch it, you barely leave an impression.**

    To apply a basic nonskid *broom finish,* drag a soft, *wet,* concrete-finishing broom with fine nylon bristles gently over the concrete, in straight lines or a wavy pattern.

Chapter **10**

Enhancing Your Landscape

After you're satisfied with the placement and look of the more substantial elements in your home landscape — hardscape elements such as a deck or patio, perhaps a new fence — you'll feel ready to furnish the rest of your yard.

This chapter is a sampling of manageable projects you can undertake to make your garden more productive, practical, and beautiful. Dig in, pick a few. Investing in some of these enhancements serves to make your outdoor living space more of a haven from the hectic pace of daily life.

Adding a Raised Bed to Your Landscape

Raised beds relieve the tedium of bending over to plant, weed, and care for your vegetables and flowers. They also offer a way to terrace a sloping yard or solve soil problems, such as excess clay or rocks. You can even gopher-proof your raised beds to control those pesky varmints. Figure 10-1 shows some examples (check out the color insert for a photo). The following sections break down what you need to know about adding one to your landscape.

FIGURE 10-1: Three types of raised beds.

© John Wiley & Sons, Inc.

Recognizing the details

Although a raised bed is really nothing more than a large, bottomless box set on the ground, the most appealing designs include a wide edge around the top for sitting or setting things down.

Keep the following details in mind when you're thinking of building a raised bed or two:

>> **Dimensions:** Raised beds vary in height from 8 to 18 inches (20.3 to 45.7 cm), depending on the material you use. Make the beds no wider than 5 feet (1.5 m), so that you can reach the interior areas. Raised beds can be any length you want, from 5 to 20 feet (1.5 to 6.1 m).

>> **Spacing:** If you plan several raised beds or devote an area to them, we recommend 3 feet (.9 m) of space between beds for wheelbarrows and easy access. Use gravel, bark chips, or bricks for the pathways, after first installing weed-blocking fabric under the walkway material.

>> **Materials:** You can make raised beds from brick, stone, timbers, or dimensioned lumber.

Landscape timbers, stacked log-cabin-style, make a sturdy bed that's easy to build. Stack 6x6 timbers two or three high. Check the first *course* (layer) with a level before adding the second two courses. Drill ½-inch (1.2 cm) diameter holes through each timber, aligning the holes over each other. Drive ½-inch (1.2 cm) *rebar* (steel rods used for concrete reinforcement) into the holes after you stack the timbers to lock them in place.

For a lumber bed, use 2-by boards, such as a single 2x12 or a pair of stacked 2x8s. For a bed measuring 5 feet wide by 12 feet long (1.5 m wide by 3.6 m long), for example, use two 12-foot (3.6-m) lengths and two 5-foot (1.5 m) or one 10-foot/3m) lengths of lumber for each layer. Use heartwood lumber of a durable species. Refer to Chapter 4 for more basics about lumber.

WARNING

Don't use railroad ties for raised beds. They've been drenched in toxic creosote; the poisons leach into and harm soil and groundwater.

Building the raised bed

To build a lumber bed, do the following:

1. **Get 4x4 posts into the ground at the four corner locations and every 4 feet (1.2 m) along the long sides.**

   Pre-dig holes to accommodate those corner posts. Use stringlines to keep them aligned and a level to keep them plumb (check out Chapter 4 for more information).

2. **Cut the side pieces to length and place them around the outside of the 4x4s to make a box.**

3. **After you level each piece, clamp it to the 4x4s, drill ⅝-inch (1.6 cm) diameter holes through the lumber and stakes, and bolt them together with ½-inch (1.3 cm) carriage bolts.**

   If you stack boards, overlap the corners, log-cabin style.

4. **After you attach all the side pieces, trim the 4x4s flush with the tops of the sides.**

   For a seat, install 2x8s around the top of the box. If necessary, reinforce the 2x8s by attaching a 2x4 cap piece around the top of the box.

5. **Cut the ends at 45 degrees for miter joints.**

   Miter joints are boards joined with angled, rather than square, ends.

6. **Position the 2x8s on the 4x4s and the top edge of the side pieces, and attach them with 3-inch (7.6 cm) galvanized deck screws.**

TIP

To keep burrowing and nibbling animals, such as gophers and voles, out of your box, use wire mesh netting to line the bottom of the box. Cut an oversize piece so you can bend it to go partway up the sides; secure with poultry-netting staples. After that, you may fill the box with soil.

Making a Built-in Bench

A built-in bench is like a magnet, making a deck or patio instantly inviting. The easiest way to provide a bench is to buy an attractive ready-made bench that you can set anywhere in your landscape. If you want to build your own, you can design a simple bench with no back, or blend a bench into a railing or planter and use those as the back of the bench.

The following can help you:

>> For basic dimensions, the seat should be 15 to 18 inches (38.1 to 45.7 cm) high and at least 15 inches (38.1 cm) deep.

>> If you add a back, it should be at least 12 inches (30.5 cm) high and ideally (for comfort) lean back at an angle of 20 to 30 degrees from vertical.

>> If the bench is part of a deck railing, extend the back 3 feet (.9 m) above the *seat* (not just the deck) and observe the screening requirement (see Chapter 8), including the area below the bench seat.

We discuss some ins and outs to making benches in these sections.

An elegant, low bench

A classic design for a deck bench of any length is to make the seat out of 2x2s, 2x4s, or 2x6s (or a combination) running lengthwise and trim with a *fascia* (an edge board meant to give a project a finished look) of 1x4s or 2x4s (see Figure 10-2 for an example). Stick to the following steps to make your own:

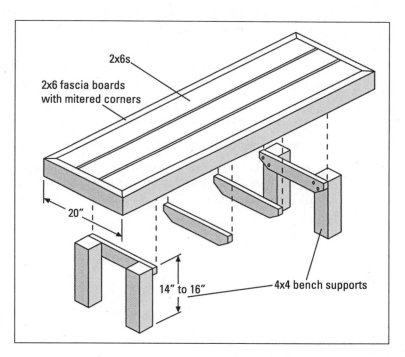

2x6s

2x6 fascia boards with mitered corners

20"

14" to 16"

4x4 bench supports

FIGURE 10-2:
The basic garden bench is easy to build.

1. **To prevent nail heads or screw heads from showing on the top surface, construct the bench seat face-down by laying out the long boards and attaching 2x4 cleats to them every 3 to 4 feet (.9 to 1.2 m) with deck screws.**

   A *cleat* is piece of wood, a short board, installed at 90 degrees to secure and add stability to multiple cross pieces (it isn't visible).

   Leave a ¼-inch (.6 cm) gap between the seat boards.

2. **Hide the ends of the cleats from view behind the fascia.**

   The way to do this is to bevel the ends to 2 inches (5 cm) deep.

3. **Attach the cleats by using 3-inch (7.6 cm) deck screws driven down through them into the seat boards (after first drilling countersink holes, of the same diameter as the screw heads, 1¾ inches (4.4 cm) into the cleats so that the screws will reach the seat boards).**

4. **After assembling the seat, attach legs to the cleats.**

Cut the legs out of 2x8 or 2x10 lumber, 14 to 16 inches (35.5 to 40.6 cm) long, or cut pairs of 4x4s to the same length.

5. **Attach the legs to the cleats by using 3½-inch (8.9 cm) carriage bolts and use a framing square to align the legs.**

6. **Turn the bench back upright, set it in place, and attach it to the decking by driving deck screws through the legs into the deck boards or by using angle brackets that you screw to the deck and then into the legs.**

To conceal angle brackets, screw all of them down to the deck first and then set the bench in place with the legs on top of the lower flanges.

TIP

If you're building a new deck, attach the bench legs to the deck joists and/or beams prior to installing the deck boards, to increase stability.

7. **To complete the bench, install 1x4 or 2x4 fascia boards around the seat.**

Cut the corners at 45 degrees to make miter joints and attach them by driving screws into them from the back, not from the face. Smooth all the edges by using a plane and sandpaper.

TIP

To give the bench a more substantial look, replace the legs with simple boxes measuring 12 inches (30.5 cm) square. The boxes can also be planters, as shown in Figure 10-3.

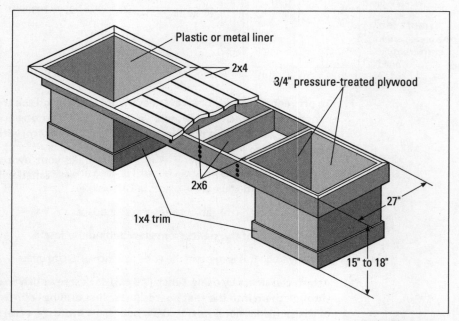

FIGURE 10-3: Enhance a bench with planter boxes.

© John Wiley & Sons, Inc.

Masonry benches

Although you can build a freestanding bench out of brick, stone, or concrete block, it may tend to look like a lost pile of masonry unless you integrate it with a garden wall, steps, fountain, or similar feature. Portions of a low garden wall can easily be modified into benches if you plan the dimensions carefully. Make the seats 15 to 18 inches high, 15 inches deep (38.1 to 47.7 cm high, 38.1 cm deep), and at least 4 feet (1.21 m) wide, so two people can sit comfortably.

Building (or Buying) a Planter

Although you can buy attractive planters made out of wood, fiberglass, acrylics, ceramics, metal, and other materials at garden centers and other outlets, building wooden planters of your own has some advantages. You can design planters to match the dimensions and details of your deck or landscape, you can build larger planters than are available for sale, and you can incorporate planters into a deck as built-ins.

REMEMBER

If you build planters for a deck, keep in mind that large planters are heavy. A planter 2 feet high, 2 feet wide, and 6 feet long (.6 m high, .6 m wide, and 1.8 m long) holds almost a ton of moist soil — too heavy for a deck without reinforcement. If possible, place such planters within openings in the deck and support them on a concrete or gravel bed on the ground. Another option for large planters is to build a wooden enclosure with a shallow shelf and place container plants on the shelf, leaving most of the wooden planter empty.

The following sections provide information and instructions for two of the most popular types of DIY planters: wooden ones and masonry ones.

Going with a wooden planter

Here's what you need to know if you want to make your own wooden planter, whether it's a bigger one to go on a deck or even a basic small windowbox:

>> Construct planters out of redwood, cedar, or preservative-treated wood (including plywood) and use corrosion-resistant screws or bolts. If you plan to put edible plants in the planter, use naturally durable species of wood, rather than treated wood.

>> Because a box full of moist soil exerts considerable pressure against the sides, take time to reinforce the corners. Bolt the side boards to vertical 4x4s (2x2s for small planters) that you place inside the corners.

>> If necessary, reinforce the corners even more by lapping the alternating boards, log-cabin fashion, or by attaching a band of 2x4s or other trim boards around the top of the box and bolting them together at the corners.

Drainage holes in the bottom of a planter are important so the plants don't sit in soggy soil, which leads to rot. Drill ¾-inch (1.9 cm) drain holes in the bottom of the box. Cover them with a bit of window screen so soil mix doesn't wash out when you water.

Going with a masonry planter

Masonry planters, placed around the edge of a patio, within a patio, or elsewhere in the garden, add an elegant touch to your landscape. They can also double as dividers, benches, and — on slopes — retaining walls. Brick, stone, and concrete blocks covered with a veneer are all attractive materials for these planters. You can incorporate them into benches or low walls for even greater effect.

To build a masonry planter, form and pour a concrete base with openings in its longitudinal center for drainage directly into the ground below. (See Chapter 7 for more information about working with concrete.) An easy way to provide such drainage is to set short lengths of plastic pipe, such as 2-inch (5 cm)-diameter PVC (plastic) pipe, vertically within the planter area before pouring concrete for the footing. Simply insert them into the gravel base and then trim the tops flush with the finished concrete surface.

You can also build a box form that's the same size as the interior dimensions of the planter and pour concrete around it — something like a doughnut — and then lay the brick, stone, or concrete blocks on the reinforced concrete ring.

Considering Hot Ideas

If you enjoy spending time in your new, improved yard, it's only a matter of time before you begin entertaining outdoors — season and weather permitting. For most people, outdoor living means outdoor cooking. Preparing food over an open flame appeals to ancient instincts and the latest grilling craze alike. (Get a copy of the latest edition of *Grilling For Dummies* by Marie Rama and John Mariani [John Wiley & Sons, Inc.] to find out more about grilling equipment and get some great recipes for grilled food.)

Grilling is the old standby, but you have quite a few other options. Perhaps a chimenea or a fire pit will make your backyard cozier. If you're an avid cook, you may want to consider an outdoor bread or pizza oven or a mini-kitchen. We discuss all of these ideas in the following sections.

WARNING

Before we delve into any of these enhancements, we remind you to always keep safety and practicality in mind with such projects. Open or even partially enclosed fires can be a danger to people and to pets (keep everyone at a safe distance), as well as flammable elements in your landscape from your deck to garden plants and trees.

Here are our safety tips:

>> When locating, plan the item away from traffic areas. Never put one against your house or any other building. The recommended safe distance from structures is 10 to 30 feet (3 to 9.1 m). That said, it's good if you can see it clearly from an indoor window or door, for extra monitoring.

>> When locating, site it downwind from windows and doors.

>> Don't place anything that gets hot or involves flames inside an unvented enclosure or under low-hanging tree branches.

>> Avoid placing any of these items on a deck unless you can provide a hearth, that is, *at least* 2 feet (.6 m) of fireproof material underneath it on all sides (such as bricks or pavers).

>> Keep a means of putting a fire out handy: water, an extinguisher, sand, a blanket, or all of the above. Never leave a fire unattended.

Installing a chimenea or fire pit

Both chimeneas and fire pits (check out the color insert for an example) are essentially freestanding fireplaces. On summer nights, they're lovely to gather around — standing is fine, but arraying adjacent seating is better. Maybe you and your guests, including supervised kids, can roast hot dogs or marshmallows. A bit of smoke discourages mosquito traffic. The flames are mesmerizing. On the cooler evenings of spring and fall, people can gather 'round for warmth. (Even in winter! Just bundle up, and serve hot cocoa or warming adult beverages.) In our opinion, any time is the right time for making s'mores.

WARNING

Always check the weather before lighting one of these. If it's windy, not only will lighting the fire and keeping it going be difficult, but it will toss smoke into everyone's eyes. Also wayward sparks can be carried to flammable spots, whether a shed or dry leaves. It's not worth the risks.

TIP

Burn regular, seasoned firewood in your chimenea or fire pit. Construction scrap lumber or pallets may have been treated with chemicals or contain remnants of adhesives, which lead to stinky and potentially toxic smoke.

Chimeneas

Chimeneas tend to be narrow, vertical items, typically around 5 or 6 feet (1.5 or 1.8 m) tall, perched on squat legs (the legs are important — you don't want hot fire right on the ground). A burn basket holds the burning wood or coals, and a slender chimney funnels away the smoke. Traditionally, they've been made of clay, but more durable options include cast iron and steel.

Set it up where you won't be moving it (except, perhaps, in areas of harsh winters where you'll want to drag it into a garage or shed for storage).

Additional factors to look for include the following:

>> **Heft:** You want something heavy so there's no chance a storm or even a person can tip it over (even when there's no fire going). In other words, give the cute 20-pound models a pass. Fifty to a hundred pounds is best!

>> **An ample burning basket:** Too small, and you'll not only have to chop up wood to fit, but you'll find the fires go out too soon or require constant fussing.

>> **A grate for the logs:** This elevates them slightly so air can help feed the flames.

>> **A mesh screen:** Hinged ones are easier to use than sliding ones. The idea is to give you easy access for adding logs as needed, but after that, to close it so sparks don't trouble spectators.

Fire pits

A *fire pit* is a bigger deal. It can accommodate a bigger fire, with all the safety concerns that implies. Check first with your local municipality or homeowners association because some have size limitations or even require a permit for installation. (In fire-prone areas of the West and Southwest, these structures are often flat-out prohibited.)

Fire pits can be either homemade or come as a kit, assembly required. The standard size for small, cozy family gatherings is about 3 to 4 feet (.9 to 1.2 m) across. Some are in-ground, some are aboveground (about a foot/.3 m high is nice — people seated around it can see the flames well). Calculate plenty of room in an open area so those gathered or seated around the fire can be both comfortable and keep a safe distance.

Common to all safe fire pits is an outer wall, inner wall, and often a decorative cap. The outer wall and the cap can be fire-resistant material such as flagstone, bricks, stones, or blocks. The inner wall, which will be in contact with the flames, must be fireproof: fire brick and/or a steel fire ring.

REMEMBER

Fire pits aren't low-maintenance landscape additions. After the ashes are cold (a day or two after a good fire), you'll want to clean them out so they don't build up. This is a constant and important chore.

Installing an outdoor brick or stone oven

What's old is new: Outdoor ovens have long been used, especially in rural areas, to bake bread over a wood fire or to roast vegetables in glowing coals. Outdoor-cooked pizza is just a slightly more modern use.

Yes, installing an outdoor oven is a big, ambitious project, but mainly because of the need for heavy-duty and safe construction (heed our general cautions about siting at the start of this section). You can buy one as a kit and assemble it, buy one as a kit and hire someone to install it, or watch dozens of YouTube videos and undertake one from scratch. Putting it up will take several days, and then you'll want to refrain from using it until any concrete used has cured, around a couple of weeks.

Make sure you elevate the bake oven so you're not stooping while cooking and so the fire is conveniently positioned below the baking food. Elevating a substantial brick or stone oven, meant to reach high temperatures, requires a very heavy stone or cinderblock base. Additionally, you may well want the base to be bigger than the oven, so you have counter space.

As for the oven itself, shapes include rectangular, square, or domed; just make sure it's wide and deep enough to accept a pizza paddle or several sourdough loaves. A chimney or at least a rudimentary flue will be necessary. Insulation (hidden from view when the project is finished) is worthwhile.

Planning a cooking center

An outdoor cooking center also allows you to entertain guests on your deck or patio. How elaborate you make it and what materials you choose will be contingent on what your climate allows.

A cooking center can be as simple as a table and portable grill, or as elaborate as a gourmet outdoor kitchen (in a mild year-round climate). Even if your kitchen is only steps away from your deck or patio, consider at least having an outdoor grill.

For more-distant locations, such as a poolside patio, consider a mini-kitchen, complete with sink, grill, counters, cabinets, and a refrigerator. Protect it from rain and snow with an overhead structure (see the "Installing a pergola or overhead" section later in this chapter) and plan at least one wall behind it — or at least provide weatherproof enclosures for the cabinets and appliances. Use tile or similar durable materials for countertops. Plan the location of plumbing, electrical wiring, and gas lines carefully *before* you install a patio or deck.

TIP

Although they can stand alone, outdoor cooking structures and gadgets are more attractive and easier to use if you set them into a permanent enclosure, with table or countertops handy.

To create a complete cooking center, you can adapt kitchen cabinets for outdoor use. They'll likely need an extra coat or two of oil-based exterior enamel paint, renewed every year or so as needed. (This scheme is best-suited to yards in mild-climate areas, of course.)

Installing Lighting

If you think that lighting your deck or patio means putting up a few floodlights, you're in the dark about outdoor design. Today's decks and patios bring high fashion into their lighting schemes. This trend doesn't mean high expense, thanks to affordable solar, LED, and low-voltage outdoor lighting.

REMEMBER

Consider the following when choosing and installing lighting in your yard:

>> **Light up your lifestyle.** Identify your lighting needs. Some lighting is for traffic and movement; some is for activities, such as cooking or eating; some is to create moods, or ambiance; and some is for decoration.

>> **Avoid overlighting.** You don't need to illuminate the entire outdoor landscape or to light every feature or point of use with its own light. Plan light schemes so that pools of light spill over into other areas. Instead of lining a path with lights that shine directly onto it, for example, light the garden areas along one side of the path enough to illuminate the path, too. Motion-sensing lights are well worth considering.

>> **Avoid underlighting.** A common mistake is to illuminate a deck or patio beautifully, but not light the rest of the yard. Rather than surround your deck with darkness, create variety and security by *uplighting* (aiming light fixtures upward) a few trees and bathing distant flower beds in soft light.

You can introduce lighting to your landscape to light it so people can see at night (practical) and to decorate (fun). Often you may wish to accomplish both objectives — not a problem! Read on.

Illuminating your landscape

At the bare minimum, plan lighting for doorways, stairs, and main traffic areas, and whatever else your local building codes may require.

Placing fixtures close to the ground illuminates stairs, paths, and plants in soft pools of light. Use stronger 120-volt (standard house voltage) lights for doorways and cooking areas. Also consider using solar-powered lights in locations where they'll receive abundant sun and a limited amount of light is all you need. Motion-sensitive lighting may startle away intruders of the human or raccoon-and-possum kind.

Follow these principles for the best and most pleasing results:

>> **Light your yard, not the neighborhood.** Avoid lights that shine onto your neighbors' property. In fact, try to place all lights so that nobody can see the light bulb — only the results. You can't enjoy even the most exquisite patio or deck with a light glaring into your eyes.

>> **Hide ugly fixtures.** Many outdoor lighting fixtures are works of art and should be on display, but you don't need to rely completely on these money-eaters. You can use lots of plain, ordinary fixtures and hide them.

>> **Step into the light.** Light all stairs and traffic paths. To light stairs, set a fixture close enough to illuminate all the steps or install an in-wall fixture into the riser of each step. To light traffic paths, place lights high and direct them straight down or place several lights close to the ground to illuminate areas along the path, spilling light onto the pathway.

>> **Light for work.** Use higher-intensity lighting for task areas, such as a cooking center or game area. Just as for paths, place several lights in trees or overhead structures and aim them straight down. Don't illuminate eating areas with harsh lighting. Use low-intensity lights or lanterns.

>> **Know your limits.** Don't undertake a wiring project yourself (except low-voltage lights) unless you have experience with electrical wiring *and* have obtained the necessary permit.

WARNING

Low-voltage lighting systems consist of light fixtures, cable (or wire), and a transformer, which you plug into a standard 120-volt receptacle. Because the wire between the transformer and light fixtures carries low-voltage current, you don't need to bury it or enclose it in conduit (although you may want to conceal it).

Simply run it along the ground, up tree trunks, under deck railings, or wherever needed, securing it by using staples or clips. Avoid suspending wires overhead. Low-voltage fixtures produce a fairly low level of light (three to five *foot-candles*, in the lingo), which is desirable for most outdoor lighting needs.

Adequate lighting, however, requires many fixtures, for example:

>> Eight to ten for an average deck

>> Two to three for a short run of stairs

>> Three per tree for effective downlighting

>> One for every 6 to 8 feet (1.8 to 2.4 m) of pathway

Because transformers have a limit to the number of fixtures they can power and the distance the wire can run, divide the lighting load into several circuits of six to ten lights each (depending on the size of bulbs and transformer — consult the manufacturer's specifications). No run should be longer than 100 feet (30.5 m).

Incorporating decorative lighting

This is an opportunity to have fun while making your yard appealing to view or to lounge in during the evening hours and after dark. Don't overdo it, though; it's nighttime, not a stage. Here are some of our favorite, successful ideas in this realm:

>> **Create special lighting effects.** Place two or three lights, aimed downward, high in a tree to create interesting shadows from branches and leaves. Light other trees or plants along walls from below, using well lights set into the ground or low floodlights. (*Well lights* are inground light fixtures, typically circle-shaped.) Conceal the light source behind plants or rocks.

>> **String ceilings.** Originally a trend for restaurants with outdoor dining areas, this tack has become wildly popular in even the smallest yards, patios, porches, and decks. Simply create lines or even a grid of string lights over a seating area. Where daytime light is good, solar strings are easy; otherwise, Christmas strands or suspended *Edison bulbs* (incandescent or LED bulbs that are shaped for a vintage look, like the original Edison bulbs) fill the bill. Just make sure they're well above the heads of the tallest standing people.

>> **Defining lines.** Strands of lights, either as bare bulbs or something more decorative such as tiny lanterns, can be arrayed along a porch or deck railing, wound up a tree truck and/or along branches, and more. The ideas is to outline a shape so it stands out (in a new way) by night.

Go shopping. Visit the outdoor-lighting section of your favorite home or big-box store, or go online and search the websites of home-décor companies. You *will* be inspired.

Adding Wooden Support Structures

Wooden supports can bring order to the garden. They not only provide a framework for plants to grow on, but they also frame your plants and can provide a dramatic focal point themselves. Although the terms are often used interchangeably, in this book, a *trellis* is a vertical frame for supporting plants and an *arbor* is an overhead structure. A *pergola* or *overhead* is more substantial, sheltering a patio, deck, or seating area; its vertical posts support overhead beams or lattice.

The most common and, in our view, deservedly popular garden structures are trellises, arbors, and pergolas. Following is a discussion of each, to help orient you not only to what exactly they are, but how best to use them.

Growing up: Trellises

You can buy ready-made trellises at nurseries and home centers, or shop online and order ready-to-go or assembly-required ones. At one end of the scale, you can buy or commission one from an artisan; at the other end, you can fashion your own from small-dimensioned lumber, bamboo, or wire mesh (green or black vinyl-coated wire mesh, galvanized wire mesh, or steel-reinforcing mesh left to rust naturally).

Most trellises have a basic square or rectangular shape, much like a picture frame, or a vase shape that mirrors the spreading foliage of many plants. If you make a trellis, space cross members 6 to 12 inches (15.2 to 30.5 cm) apart and attach them securely to each other at all joints using screws, nails, or tie wire.

Mount trellises on fences or walls, or make a free-standing trellis by joining two vertical trellises at right angles to each other. Support your trellis with stakes driven into the ground and secured to the bottom rungs of the trellis.

Check out the color insert for examples of trellises (complete with colorful plants adorning them).

WARNING

Don't mount a trellis or other vine-support directly to a wall or fence. There's little or no space for the plant to grow and operate, so to speak, which is bad for its appearance and health. You can still attach a support to something sturdier for extra stability, but keep it at least several inches/cm away, never flush.

Putting arbors in their place

An arbor is more substantial than a trellis and offers many design variations, from an archway to a crisscrossing framework. Build a small arbor over a gate, bench, or path to add a dramatic focal point to your landscape, and support it with a single post or a pair of legs on each side.

When planning your arbor, keep in mind that the standard lumber sizes that are most readily available aren't well-proportioned: The ubiquitous 2x4, for example, is more awkward than graceful at most lengths; a 2x3 has more appealing proportions; and a 3x4, which must be custom-milled, has the same proportions as the classical golden mean (a 5:7 ratio).

TIP

You want to match the climbing or vining plant to the structure. Roses and wisteria, for example, are heavy plants; morning glories are lightweights; a clematis vine can be either. This is a practical matter of sufficient support, of course, but it's also a design concern. We think the slim tendrils of morning glories look better climbing a trellis than draped on a heavy pergola. For much more advice and information about recommended vines, flip ahead to Chapter 12.

Installing a pergola or overhead

A pergola or overhead shade structure (also simply called an *overhead*) can enhance your outdoor living in many ways. It provides shade, defines space, and delights the eye. It can also support vining or climbing plants, which integrates it into your landscape and provides some welcome shade.

Here are some important considerations:

>> **Freestanding or attached to the house:** For an attached structure, the height of the house's roof overhang determines some of your design options. If the overhang is at least 9 feet (2.7 m) above the patio or deck surface, you can probably tuck a patio roof under the eave. Otherwise, plan to attach the overhead to the house roof itself or build a freestanding structure that clears the roof eave.

- » **Made in the shade:** To provide minimal shade, plan a structure without any *canopy* (slats or solid covering) above the rafters or a canopy consisting of very few slats. For more shade, space slats no farther apart than their depth. If the slats are 2x4s, for example, space them 3½ to 4 inches (8.9 to 10.1 cm) apart. If you orient the slats east to west, they provide shade all day, except during early morning and late afternoon hours. If you orient them north-south, they admit the sun at noon but provide shade in the late afternoon. For maximum shade, build a solid roof. To avoid heat buildup, plan the roof with a vented ridge or similar openings.

  A good compromise between an open structure and a solid roof is to plant vines, such as grapes, clematis, or wisteria, that fill out the canopy during the summer and drop their leaves in the fall. For more about vines, consult Chapter 12.

- » **Scale and proportion:** Plan the overhead structure so that it's large enough for comfortable seating under it (at least 10 feet/3 m square) and high enough to leave approximately 8 feet (2.4 m) of clearance.

- » **Durability:** As does any outdoor structure, an overhead must resist deterioration caused by constant exposure to sun, rain, snow, and other elements. All connections must be corrosion-resistant. Wood members must be at least 8 inches (20.3 cm) above ground unless they're treated with a preservative specified for ground contact. Wood members must also be well-secured to resist warping and cracking and should be treated with a preservative and sealer.

TIP

To calculate the size and spacing of the joists and beams of a structure you intend to build, first make a scale drawing. Take it to the lumber yard or home-supply store to get an associate's help, or come prepared with rough numbers based on the estimate from an online calculator:

- » For a trellis or arbor, we find online calculators intended for fencing work well, such as: www.omnicalculator.com/construction/fence or https://yardgardselect.com/fencecalculator.php.

- » For pergolas and similar shade structures, we recommend https://pergoladepot.com/resources/tips/how-to-measure-pergola/.

Utilizing a Shed

A shed is a wonderful addition to any home landscape, space permitting. You can store tools and supplies, use it as a puttering space, or even make it into a little retreat. Invest enough time and effort to create a shed that's tidy, durable, watertight, and attractive.

A small outbuilding also provides a rationale for an inviting path or two and the suggestion of a secret destination that adds an element of charm or whimsy to your garden.

Pay attention to these important practical matters:

>> **Location:** If you place your shed in the open, soften the impact by siting it under a tree, if possible, or place large shrubs around it to blend it into the natural scenery. If it's privacy you seek or you want the best spots in your yard to be full of plants, tuck your shed in a back corner or side yard.

>> **Elevation:** Setting a shed on flat ground, assuming you have or can create sufficient space, is an option, but you may regret it the first time it rains and the floor, dirt, or otherwise, gets saturated. Some people raise their shed up a few inches/cm on a concrete pad or a base of gravel or support it on cinder blocks to avoid this vexing problem. (Should you need steps or a ramp, we direct you to Chapter 7.)

>> **Integration:** Fresh paint and real shingles may be enough to dress up your shed, or you can attach a trellis to one or two sides, paint a *trompe l'oeil* (fake) window on the outside, or conceal the shed completely behind a fence or lattice screen.

The following sections explain the three main types of sheds you may want in your new, improved home landscape.

Storage sheds

A shed for storing tools not only corrals clutter, but it also frees up storage space in the garage, on the patio, in the basement, or wherever you're keeping gardening supplies.

Shed designs vary from utilitarian boxes to replicas of distinctive architectural styles, such as a log cabin, Swiss chalet, Japanese tea house, or Greek temple.

A typical do-it-yourself shed usually measures 8 feet wide, 6 feet deep, and 7 feet tall at the peak (6 feet, 8 inches inside) (in metric, that's 2.4 m wide, 1.8 m deep, and 2.1 m tall; 2 m inside) — plenty of space for a lawnmower, rotary tiller, wheelbarrow, dozens of implements, and other gardening gear and supplies.

See your local building-supply store for plans and materials, or you can purchase a pre-made one.

She sheds

The she shed is the female answer to the man cave. It's a place to retreat, to dec-orate, to entertain, to read, to write, to paint, to nap, or just to escape for some me time. It may be related to the yard and gardening, certainly, with potted plants, windowboxes, a vine clambering over the roof, and supplies within, but it more often is just a little place to call your own.

You can view a wide array of adorable and inspiring ones on Pinterest and Insta-gram, and upscale suppliers offer pre-made ones. But there's a certain victory in taking over the long-neglected, already present backyard shed and transform-ing it.

Potting sheds

A potting shed is a time-honored British classic that anyone anywhere else can create. It's a practical outbuilding, devoted to gardening projects, outfitted with tools and supplies. No longer do you have to clear a kitchen counter or outdoor table in order to divide houseplants or pot seedlings. Now you will have a spot to hang dry herb bundles or store the gladiolus corms.

Such a shed not only cheers and motivates a gardener, it also benefits your garden as well. Because you're working more efficiently, you tend to think up more proj-ects and execute them more successfully. Neatness and productivity in the potting shed translate to healthy new plants out in the yard and inspired ideas for their placement. When you have a potting shed, your garden gains a new sense of purpose — and pleasure.

The basic elements are as follows: a table or flat surface, storage shelves, bins, hooks, good light, and access to a water source.

Pondering Water Features

Adding water to your home landscape may be easier and more rewarding than you now imagine, especially if you start small. You don't have to call in a backhoe or hire a contractor to convert the old in-ground swimming pool into an extensive water feature — although you certainly can if you have the resources and space.

Water always transforms a scene because it's captivating. Everyone who visits your yard is immediately drawn to the display. The presence of water restores you to nature's rhythms and allows you to contemplate the arc of the sky, the passing clouds, the path of the sun. Jarring noises and distractions drop away. In a busy, crowded world, something as simple as a backyard pond is a balm to the spirit.

You do have a range of options:

>> **Fountain:** This can be anything from a small gurgling feature with a (hidden) recirculating pump tucked into a flowerbed, corner of the patio, or shady spot, to a formal pool with a big spray shooting high into the air.

>> **Container water garden:** Water-garden suppliers sell water-tight pots as well as liners you can fit into half-whisky barrel planters and offer plants that will thrive in a smaller space. You can even get miniature waterlilies.

>> **Small inground pool:** You can invest in a preformed shape (or line your own shape with heavy plastic meant for this use). Dig an ample hole for it and settle it into place atop a bed of sand, then fill it with waterlilies, lotus, water irises, floating plants, fish — basically a contained little ecosystem.

>> **Large inground pool with waterfall or cascade:** This is a job for experienced professionals, but you can make this dream a reality when you work closely with them on the siting and design as well as get their assistance and advice regarding plants and fish. We suggest you have a maintenance contract so the investment remains good-looking and its many living residents are kept in good health.

You may be interested to find out — as was discovered and promoted many years ago by amateur members of Denver's Colorado Water Garden Society — that an area converted to water garden consumes less water than the same area covered by lawn. Yes, even in an arid climate! Properly built, the feature simply recirculates its water and loses a minimal amount to evaporation, especially when water-lily pads spread over the surface.

Some general considerations include whether you have a good, sunny spot out in the open. Avoid big rocks and tree roots — water plants don't bloom well in shade and you don't want leaf litter from overhead trees falling in — as well as utility lines. You also must determine whether your yard's soil and terrain will accept a substantial hole in the ground. Choosing a site is also, of course, a matter of aesthetics. Assess whether you can make a comfortable sitting and viewing area adjacent, or place it next to a deck, patio, gazebo, or pergola so it's easy to observe.

After it's installed, a water feature is surprisingly low-maintenance because the most basic need of the plants within — water — is constantly present. You'll groom off spent leaves and flowers, place a decoy if water birds drop by for a fishy snack, and top it off with the hose from time to time. Most of all, you'll really enjoy it.

The soft silver-green foliage of catmint, *Nepeta*, not only flatters its own light purple flowers but also looks beautiful with the bolder blue of *Delphinium*.

A duet in purple ('Purple d'Oro' daylily) and silver ('Silver King' artemisia) creates a gorgeous garden scene. Explore more about designing with color in Chapter 2.

Lighten up dim areas with shade perennials that have variegated (green-and-white, green-and-yellow) leaves. Refer to Chapter 14.

You don't need flowers to create a beautiful landscape. If shade is your lot, plant a riot of green (see Chapter 2).

When you have big trees in your yard, try stepping down, landscaping with shorter trees and medium-height ornaments like this stone birdbath.

One well-placed, large, handsome ornament — such as this ceramic urn — gives a garden scene focus (refer to Chapter 2).

Make a small garden rich with interest by simple layering, installing plants of different sizes.

Mix textures, bold with fine, evergreen with deciduous (see Chapter 2). Green is a color with many shades.

After your fence and entryway or gate are in place, complete the picture and soften the lines by planting compatible-colored flowers adjacent, such as a rosebush.

A metal fence and gate, an ugly liability? Certainly not! Try securing containers of lovely flowers to them.

Have a long fenceline to pretty up? Repetition is really successful; notice how this landscaper kept the color theme simple as well as compatible. (Chapter 2 has more design principles.)

A sloping landscape can be transformed by low stone walls, essentially stone terraces (refer to Chapter 6).

When you need an all-weather, more formal path, concrete serves well (check out Chapter 7).

PHOTO BY KATHY FORTON

Brick paths aren't difficult to install and give your garden an appealing established look. Chapter 7 has more about paths.

PHOTO BY PAUL SMITH

This impressive planting at the base of an aspen tree is composed entirely of annuals — quick, long-lasting color! More about landscaping with annuals in Chapter 13.

A path made of paving stones is both practical and handsome.

When you want a natural, informal-looking path, choose flagstones. To find out more how to choose stones and install a path, consult Chapter 7.

If your deck is small, create a sense of privacy by enveloping it in flowering plants to soften the lines and inject color.

For longer life and less maintenance, consider a composite lumber deck. (See Chapter 8 about building a deck and Chapter 4 for more on composite lumber.)

While stone pavers are often used in paths, they make excellent, durable patios as well. More in Chapter 9.

Judicious placement of potted plants, both large and small, bring a greater feeling of

You can match materials. The gray urn and weathered bench flank a stone patio (see Chapter 9).

When you install a brick patio, you have attractive options for patterns, like this herringbone

Be sure to mu
the spaces
between your
raised beds to
thwart weeds
and keep the
area looking t
(explore more
about raised b
in Chapter 10)

Trellises can be useful,
dividing areas and
creating garden rooms
as well as enhancing
privacy (consult Chapter
10). Adorn them with
flowering vines (see
Chapter 12).

To enjoy your garden after hours, install lighting. Here carefully placed uplighting enhances a beautiful scene (check out Chapter 10).

Chapter 10 explains the main principles of installing a firepit: a fireproof area and

A pergola (basically a trellis that extends with a roof to cover more area) creates a sense of retreat, making a sprawling or unexciting yard feel more enclosed and intimate (see Chapter 10).

Landscape trees need not be large. Many worthy smaller-statured ones also provide spring flowers (like these dogwoods) or fall color. Chapter 11 discusses trees.

A food garden has be as pretty as it is practical. Just add annuals, ornaments, and stylish structures (see Chapter 13).

Many bright flowers, including these California poppies and the purple scabiosa (in the left foreground), do just fine in dry, sunny growing conditions (see Chapter 13).

Keep it simple, and make it bright. White pansies and red coleus
liven up a dim area.

Tuberous begonias are fabulous for bringing
big color, wherever they are planted, in the
ground, in a pot, even in shade. (Chapter 13
discusses different annuals. Chapter 20
explains shade gardening.)

This low-maintenance border is made spectacular with dramatic ornamental grasses and carefully chosen evergreens (see Chapter 14).

Pretty and durable, daylilies are a wonderful perennial plant for reliable color for weeks on end in summer (this is 'Doll House'). Find out more about perennial gardening in Chapter 14.

Welcome pollinators like this bee to your garden by planting pollen-rich perennials, like this cranesbill geranium. More information in Chapters 14 and 21.

Brighten a shady area in your yard with hostas. You have many choices, but ones with variegated leaves and white flowers stand out best. (See Chapter 14 for more on shade perennials.)

Perky snowdrops *(Galanthus)* are often the very first flower to appear in early spring in colder climates.

You can dress up tree-shaded areas by planting perennials that produce colorful blooms. (View our top selections of shade perennials in Chapter 14.)

Spring splash is yours with bright tulips and blue brunnera. Many bulbs are easy to grow and show off in containers.

Jazz up a plain green hedge backdrop with pots of vivid blooming tulips (see Chapter 14 for

Have fun, mix it up! Containers of different types of plants can really liven up a patio.

Want color under a tree? Some annuals, such as these begonias, bloom in shade. Others, like caladium (left) and coleus (right) have colorful leaves (see Chapter 15).

Chapter 15 explains how you can transform your yard with pots of pretty plants, from herbs to annuals.

The thriller-filler-spiller formula works even better when you choose contrasting colors.

Gorgeous compatible and contrasting color, and plenty of plants, equals a pot to be proud of!

One dramatic potted display can be a real scene-stealer!

Repurpose decorative objects as planters, such as this birdcage. For more ideas for using offbeat containers, see Chapter 15.

When your garden needs extra color, cluster pots of flowering annuals (taller blue salvia, back center), perennials (taller red bee balm, *Monarda*), and shorter herbs (basil, tan pot in front), and more.

Placing a variety of succulents (refer to Chapter 15) close together is an easy and unique way to cover a lot of ground.

This gardener knows the secret to colorful dry-climate gardening: a variety of painted pots featuring diverse succulents (see Chapter 15).

Sometimes the best use of a lawn is as a border, a rest for the eye, between landscaped areas (see Chapter 16 for more discussion about lawns).

One hallmark of a bountiful garden is the ever-shrinking lawn. Make it easier to care for by choosing perennials and annuals that bloom generously.

You don't have to banish lawn grass altogether, but you can encroach on it, adding mixed beds of trees, shrubs, and perennials, as Chapter 16 explains.

Behold some of the secrets of a low-water-use landscape: less lawn, strategically placed stones, drought-resistant plants, and plenty of mulch to hold the soil in place (see Chapter 20).

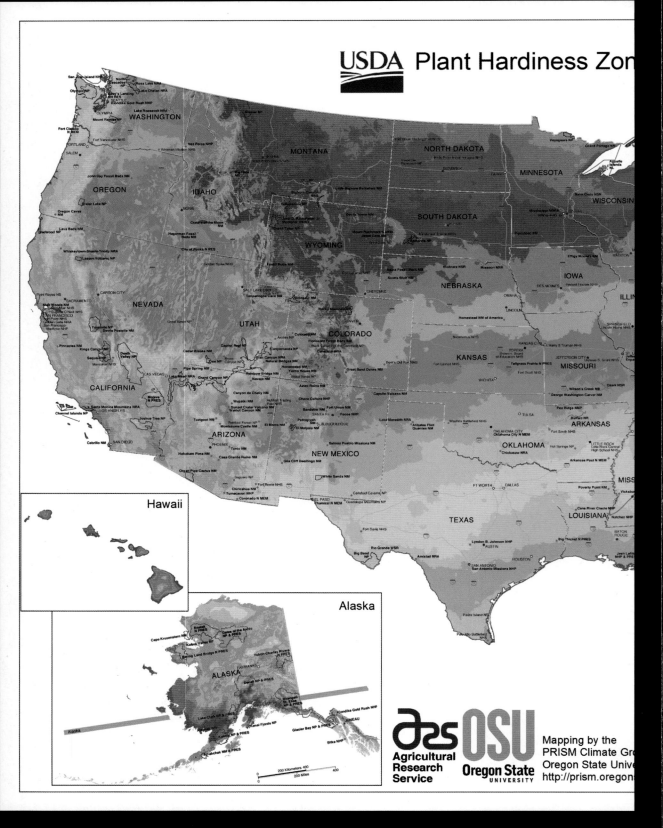

USDA Plant Hardiness Zon

Hawaii

Alaska

Agricultural
Research
Service

Oregon State
UNIVERSITY

Mapping by the
PRISM Climate Gr
Oregon State Univer
http://prism.oregon

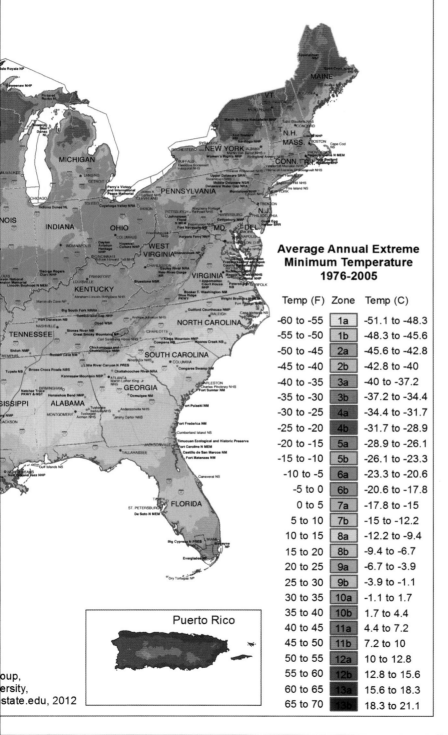

Average Annual Extreme Minimum Temperature 1976-2005

Temp (F)	Zone	Temp (C)
-60 to -55	1a	-51.1 to -48.3
-55 to -50	1b	-48.3 to -45.6
-50 to -45	2a	-45.6 to -42.8
-45 to -40	2b	-42.8 to -40
-40 to -35	3a	-40 to -37.2
-35 to -30	3b	-37.2 to -34.4
-30 to -25	4a	-34.4 to -31.7
-25 to -20	4b	-31.7 to -28.9
-20 to -15	5a	-28.9 to -26.1
-15 to -10	5b	-26.1 to -23.3
-10 to -5	6a	-23.3 to -20.6
-5 to 0	6b	-20.6 to -17.8
0 to 5	7a	-17.8 to -15
5 to 10	7b	-15 to -12.2
10 to 15	8a	-12.2 to -9.4
15 to 20	8b	-9.4 to -6.7
20 to 25	9a	-6.7 to -3.9
25 to 30	9b	-3.9 to -1.1
30 to 35	10a	-1.1 to 1.7
35 to 40	10b	1.7 to 4.4
40 to 45	11a	4.4 to 7.2
45 to 50	11b	7.2 to 10
50 to 55	12a	10 to 12.8
55 to 60	12b	12.8 to 15.6
60 to 65	13a	15.6 to 18.3
65 to 70	13b	18.3 to 21.1

This USDA Hardiness Zone Map (see Chapter 19) is a useful tool in determining which plants should be hardy (will overwinter) in your growth area.

Natural Resources
Canada

Ressources naturelles
Canada

Canada's
Plant Hardiness Zones

Zones de rusticité des
plantes au Canada

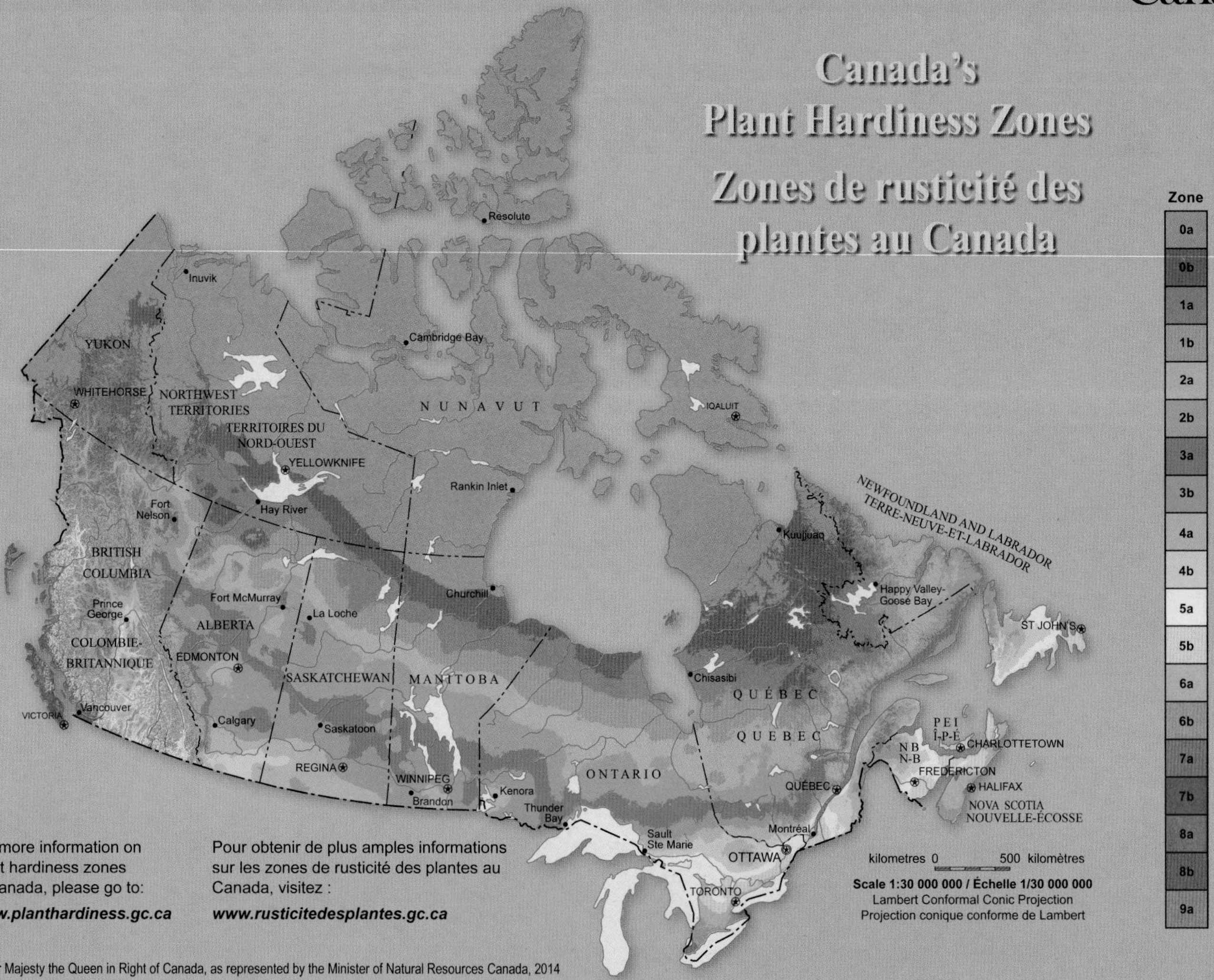

For more information on
plant hardiness zones
in Canada, please go to:
www.planthardiness.gc.ca

Pour obtenir de plus amples informations
sur les zones de rusticité des plantes au
Canada, visitez :
www.rusticitedesplantes.gc.ca

Zone

| 0a |
| 0b |
| 1a |
| 1b |
| 2a |
| 2b |
| 3a |
| 3b |
| 4a |
| 4b |
| 5a |
| 5b |
| 6a |
| 6b |
| 7a |
| 7b |
| 8a |
| 8b |
| 9a |

kilometres 0   500 kilomètres
Scale 1/30 000 000 / Échelle 1/30 000 000
Lambert Conformal Conic Projection
Projection conique conforme de Lambert

© Her Majesty the Queen in Right of Canada, as represented by the Minister of Natural Resources Canada, 2014
© Sa Majesté la Reine du chef du Canada, représentée par le ministre de Ressources naturelles Canada 2014

Want to create a butterfly sanctuary in your landscape? You'll need to nurture the caterpillars, too. Milkweed (*Asclepias*) is a must (refer to Chapter 20).

When you mainly enjoy your garden later in the day or in the evening hours, be sure to plant white: plants with white-variegated leaves and those with white flowers (see Chapter 21).

Get cottage-garden charm with a rustic fence.

This cottage garden successfully mixes lovely pastel bloomers *(Geranium maculatum)* with an old-fashioned wheel as an ornament. Chapter 21 can provide more inspiration.

3

The Planting o' the Green

Choose plants based not just on beauty, but also on function and suitability. You want plants that adapt well to your area, are easy to care for, and will live for a long time.

Examine what you need to know about adding trees to your landscape.

Include shrubs and vines that best fit your garden and avoid common pitfalls when adding them.

Incorporate some color and variety in your yard with annuals.

Find suitable perennials and bulbs that can come back year after year.

Add succulents and container plants to include even more color and variation in your landscape.

Fill open areas wisely and well with groundcovers, a smaller lawn, mulch, and more.

Chapter **11**

Barking Up the Right Tree

No home or neighborhood should be without trees. They bring a home into scale with the surrounding wide-open landscape and give a neighborhood a sense of identity. (What makes the difference between a new neighborhood and one that's 30 years old? The trees!) Trees provide protection from the elements by buffering strong winds and blocking hot summer sun. In crowded neighborhoods, trees can provide privacy, screening you from your neighbors or from unpleasant views.

Trees also offer beauty to your landscape — beauty in flowers among the branches, in the leafy green canopy, in colorful fruits and seedpods dangling among the limbs, and in dazzling hues created by their autumn leaves. Trees can even be attractive in winter, when the texture of their bark and the silhouette of their branches adds structure and form to their surroundings.

This chapter tours the world of trees, specifically the ones suited to today's home landscapes. You'll be amazed at and enticed by the many wonderful choices. After you make a selection, we tell you how to plant it.

Choosing the Perfect Tree

People who work with trees like to say that the perfect tree doesn't exist — and they're probably right. As with people, every tree's personality has its good and bad aspects. Before you plant one, try to find out everything you can about the tree, both the good and the bad. Most get big and live a long time (possibly longer than you!), so if you make a mistake and plant the wrong one or in the wrong place, the result may be a costly removal or replacement project. (Removing a tree may even be dangerous to people and property.) Check out the color insert for a breathtaking example of fully grown trees in a landscape.

REMEMBER

Trees come in many, many sizes and shapes, but can also be divided into two main categories:

>> **Deciduous:** They drop their leaves in autumn and grow new ones the following spring.

>> **Evergreen:** These trees include *conifers,* such as pine and fir, and also *broadleaf evergreens,* such as the southern magnolia. Evergreen trees retain their leaves (or needles) throughout the winter.

Before committing to any new tree for your landscape, think about the following and questions:

>> **Size:** How fast does it grow? Fast growth isn't always a virtue — fast-growing trees tend to have weaker wood.

>> **Shape:** How tall and wide will it eventually get? Determine whether you can give it the elbow room it will need.

>> **Adaptation:** *Adaptation* basically means whether or not it will grow well in your area. Is the tree you like adapted to your climate and the sun, soil, and water conditions . . . at the proposed planting site? Your best choice may be a native species; refer to the section, "Making the case for native trees," later in this chapter.

>> **Possible drawbacks:** Does the tree tend to have problems? Some examples include strong or invasive roots (that can lift concrete or harm your lawn), weak limbs (that can fall on your house), or being prone to insects or diseases (that can mar its appearance before killing the tree).

>> **Maintenance:** Does the tree need any special care, such as yearly pruning? Consider a compact-growing or dwarf version if you'd rather not have that chore. How messy is it? Find out if it drops excessive amounts of flowers, fruits, or leaves; you'll have to clean up, or live with the mess.

TIP

A local nursery is a good place to find out how a tree performs in your area; so are city or county parks departments. Your nearest Cooperative Extension office can also help you with information about trees. Parks, university campuses, and established cemeteries often have fine plantings to study. Botanical gardens and arboretums, of course, are also especially good places to observe a wide variety of (labeled!) trees.

Considering important details before making the purchase

After deciding on the type of tree (deciduous or evergreen), you have a wealth of ornamental characteristics from which to choose. Before you can make an informed decision, make sure you know what climate zone you live in. Check Chapter 19 for an explanation of these zones, and consult the color-coded map in the color insert.

Here are some other important points to consider before spending any money:

>> **Seasonal color:** Many trees, including flowering fruit trees, bloom in early spring. Others bloom later in spring, and some, such as crape myrtles, in midsummer. You can choose almost any flower color.

By planting trees such as sourwood and parrotia (check out their descriptions in the section, "Discovering Some Favorite Trees," later in this chapter), you can have stunning autumn color even in warmer-winter climates.

Conifers, on the other hand, are attractive year-round. If you're attentive, you'll appreciate seasonal changes, including new, light-green growth in spring and cone production later in the year.

>> **Colorful fruit:** Trees such as crabapples, hawthorn, and serviceberry follow their blooms with colorful fruit, which can (if the birds don't eat it all) hang on the tree into winter, after the leaves have fallen.

TIP

Don't overlook trees that produce edible fruit when you're making your choices. Many fruit (and nut) trees are also good-looking landscape plants and have the added bonus of bringing food to the table. Refer to the section, "Planting some fruit trees," later in this chapter.

>> **Attractive bark:** The white bark of birch trees is familiar to most people, but many other trees have handsome peeling or colorful bark. Stewartia (see the section, "Listing our favorite flowering trees" later in this chapter) is a stunner in this regard — check it out.

You can appreciate the bark of conifers if you *limb up* (remove lower limbs, which may start to die back on their own when shaded by ones overhead). Red pine bark is especially pretty.

Finding a healthy tree at the nursery

Before you buy, check out these tips for buying a healthy tree:

>> **Avoid trees that are clearly unhealthy and growing poorly.** They'll probably be disappointing after they're in the ground.

>> **Take a closer look at the whole trunk.** Some unscrupulous nurseries wrap paper around the trunk of trees to hide bark damage. If the tree you're considering is wrapped, ask to have the paper removed so you can see the condition of the trunk.

>> **Examine the rootball.** Also make sure the visible roots are in good shape and not mashed, nicked, or rotten. Avoid trees that have large, circling roots (roots that go round and round at the outside edge of the pot) near the surface — that's a sure sign that the tree has been in the container too long.

>> **Steer clear of trees that are the smallest or largest of a group.** Select ones that are well-proportioned with foliage and branches evenly spaced along the trunk. Choose a tree without closely spaced, crisscrossing branches, multiple leaders (dominant upright stems), or tight crotches (the crotch is the angle formed where a branch joins the trunk).

>> **Pick a tree with a trunk that is evenly tapered from top to bottom.** This indicates the tree is growing naturally and properly and will continue to develop a durable structure, as it should.

>> **Look for healthy, even-colored leaves.** Certain tree diseases and pests cause discolored or yellowed foliage, so plentiful green leaves is a good sign.

>> **Choose a tree that's free of insects and signs of disease.** Avoid ones with chewed or misshapen leaves, goop oozing from the trunk, or dead branches.

GETTING COOL WITH TREES

In this fast-paced world of concrete, asphalt, and hazy sky, trees are the great equalizers. They shade your street and cool your neighborhood, they absorb dust and air pollution, and their roots hold the soil in place and prevent erosion.

Providing cooling shade is one of a tree's greatest assets, especially in regions where summers are hot and dry. If you plant *deciduous* trees (trees that drop their leaves in autumn) on the warmest side of your house (usually the south or west side, but the east side can also be warm), the shade that they provide keeps your house cooler in summer and reduces your air-conditioning expenses. The best shade trees spread wide and tall enough to shade a one- or two-storied home, but you can effectively shade a patio or deck with smaller trees, especially if you plant several. You can also use smaller trees to shade windows as a way to prevent the sun from shining through and quickly warming the house.

Of course, you don't have to worry about overcooling in winter: Trees lose their leaves — right when you need them to — so the warm sun can get through, thus reducing heating costs.

You can save energy by planting trees as windbreaks. Planted close together and at right angles to the prevailing wind, dense-growing trees can reduce the chilling effects of winter winds and help lower heating bills.

Making the case for native trees

Trees may have once been growing where you now live, and they were removed to make way for development. Putting a native tree (or trees) back into the landscape has practical advantages:

>> **Native trees are regionally and/or locally adapted.** That is, they'll prosper in your climate and soil and grow well.

>> **Native trees are tough and healthy.** They're likely to be naturally resistant to pest and disease problems that trouble trees introduced from other areas.

>> **Native trees help sustain the food web in your area.** You'll definitely see more birds, probably also squirrels as well. Native trees also support a lot of life you may not see at a glance, such as the insects and caterpillars that the birds feed on, pollinators, and so on.

But aren't native trees far too big for your yard? Some are. No worries — a good tree nursery will have options for you. They may point you to a smaller-growing species. Also, horticulturists have selected and promoted many excellent variations or *cultivars* (cultivated varieties), for example, smaller-size native oak trees. To be clear: Nonnative trees aren't automatically bad or unsuitable, but native ones may be a better choice.

We list North American–native trees in the next section.

Discovering Some Favorite Trees

With so many good trees to choose from, you may need some advice on the best ones. We divide the following suggestions according to common landscape uses — shade trees, flowering trees, trees for small spaces, fruit trees, and some evergreen trees that are valuable for their winter appeal and screening capabilities — with each list arranged alphabetically according common name, with the botanical name following in case you need it when shopping. Consider combining them all into your landscape; refer to the color insert for a photo showing deciduous trees providing shade and privacy.

Naming our shade tree faves

We find that the ideal shade tree is between 25 and 50 feet (7.6 to 15.2 m) high. For most homes that size is appropriate to partially shade the roof, but not get too big so the tree becomes a liability. However, different-size lots and homes may call for different-size trees, so not all the trees listed here have the perfect size and shape.

The best shade tree is also deciduous, so that sun can warm the house in winter. (Besides the trees in this section, you can also effectively use any of the deciduous trees we list in the section, "Tagging top trees for small spaces.") In southern climates, where winters can be quite warm, you may be able to use some evergreen trees as shade trees.

Look for shade trees with a *spreading canopy* (the leafy top portion of the tree).

>> **Chinese pistache:** *Pistacia chinensis.* A wonderful, spreading shade tree with dependably healthy dark-green foliage in spring and summer and stunning yellow, orange, or red autumn color — even in the middle to deep South. Grows 30 to 35 feet (9 to 10.6 m) high, has divided leaves, and is hardy to Zone 6. Tolerant to drought and pollution and adapts to many soils.

>> **European white birch:** *Betula pendula.* Loved for its papery white bark, multiple trunks, and golden autumn color. Hardy to Zone 3, but not well-adapted to areas with hot, dry summers or to areas where birch borers are prevalent. Call your extension office or local nursery to check about birch borers. (An alternative is the river birch, *Betula nigra,* which is widely adaptable and borer-resistant. It's also a North American native tree.)

>> **Katsura:** *Cercidiphyllum japonicum.* A really elegant tree, pyramidal in habit when young and maturing to a more oval shape. Foliage emerges bronze-purple in spring, turns light green over summer, and becomes rich yellow to orange in autumn. Insects and diseases rarely trouble this tree. Can attain 40 to 60 feet (12 to 18 m) high and wide. Hardy in Zones 4 to 8. A graceful weeping form is called 'Amazing Grace.' If you want it quite a bit smaller, look

for 'Heronswood Globe,' which tops out at 15 feet; 4.5 m) and, as the name implies, has a more rounded profile.

>> **Linden:** *Tilia cordata.* With dense branching and dense foliage, this makes an impressive landscape tree. Widely adaptable, it can grow in heavy clay, drier soils, and acidic ground and still look great. Pretty heart-shaped leaves. Late spring brings fragrant yellow flowers that bees love; sticky sap can be a problem if your car is parked under or you have an outdoor table under this tree. Fall color is yellow. Can reach 60 feet (18 m) high and half as wide. Zones 3 to 7. 'Summer Sprite' is a little one, reaching only about 20 feet (6 m) high and wide. ***Note:*** The native American version, basswood, *Tilia americana*, shares many of the same qualities but is a bigger tree.

>> **Maple:** *Acer* species. The maples are a large group that includes many trees known primarily for their wonderful autumn color. Most are hardy to at least Zone 5. Sugar maples (*A. saccharum*), North American natives, are hardy to Zone 3. But they're big trees; smaller cultivars include 'Apollo,' compact and columnar in habit (30 feet high, 10 feet wide; 9 m high, 3 m wide) and 'Southern' (20 to 25 feet high, 15 to 20 feet wide). 'Legacy' (ultimately 40 feet, or 12 m, high and wide) is a beauty, deservedly popular. Red maple (*A. rubrum),* which can reach up to 50 feet (15.2 m) high, is a fine native species that doesn't get as tall as sugar maple and has brilliant fall color.

TIP

Most maples perform poorly in areas with mild winters or hot, dry summers.

>> **Oak:** *Quercus.* A large family of varied evergreen and deciduous trees, many of them grow very large and are only suitable for open areas. Some deciduous types have good autumn color. Red oak, *Q. rubra,* native to the eastern United States, the English oak, *Q. robur*, throughout western Europe, the cork oak, *Q. suber,* of northern Africa and southern Europe — are often good choices. However, many species are widely adapted. Oaks support a lot of wildlife. Regional nurseries usually have appropriate cultivars for you to choose from if you're interested.

>> **Red horse chestnut:** *Aesculus × carnea.* Large roundish leaves and huge spikes of pink to reddish flowers top this bold-textured tree. Grows up to 50 feet high and about 30 feet wide (15.2 m high and about 9 m wide), casting dense shade. Roots can be invasive. Leaf edges turn brown in hot summer climates. Hardy in Zones 4 to 7.

>> **Sourwood:** *Oxydendrum arboretum.* North American native. Makes a truly handsome *specimen tree* (planted solo), with a pyramidal profile, maturing to around 25 to 30 feet high and 20 feet wide (7.6 to 9 m high and 6 m wide). Nice, long, dark-green leaves are joined in summer by panicles of tiny white scented flowers. Bees adore them, and beekeepers rave about the resulting honey. Fall brings spectacular color: vivid maroon, garnet, and gold. Zones 5 to 9.

>> **Thornless honey locust:** *Gleditsia triacanthos* f. *inermis.* North American native. Finely cut foliage casts a wonderful shade from this adaptable tree.

Leaves turn yellow before dropping in autumn; they leave little mess. Grows 40 to 60 feet (12 to 18 m) high with a spreading habit. Has some pest problems in parts of the western and southern United States (check with your nursery). Hardy into Zone 4. 'Majestic,' 'Moraine,' 'Shademaster,' and 'Skyline' are all good selections.

>> **Tupelo:** *Nyssa sylvatica.* North American native. Does best in deep, moist, acidic soil. Form is pyramidal. Lustrous dark-green leaves turn a beautiful glistening red in autumn. Can reach 30 to 50 feet high and 20 to 30 feet wide (9 to 15.2 m high and 6 to 9 m wide). Hardy in Zones 4 to 9. 'Green Gable' is an especially healthy, strong grower. 'Red Rage' is magnificent in fall.

Listing our favorite flowering trees

Trees that flower often do so for a stretch in spring or summer. We savor their period of glory and accept that they're less showy the rest of the gardening year. That said, their foliage is handsome. Here are our top choices, with something for every climate.

TIP

Take tree–flower color into account when planning your displays. Pink magnolias look lovely in the company of tulips, but clash with bright–yellow blooming forsythia. Crape myrtles flower so abundantly that they're scene–stealers — but fortunately, they come in many hues, so you can pick one that works for your landscape.

>> **Crape myrtle:** *Lagerstroemia indica.* Summer-blooming. Beautiful, small trees (usually 10 to 20 feet (3 to 6 m) high but can also be grown as a multi-trunked shrub), hardy to Zone 7. Flowers are huge, crinkly, and crepelike, in shades of white, pink, red, and purple. Crape myrtles also have shiny, peeling brown bark and orange-red autumn color. Grow best in areas with hot, dry summers. Elsewhere, plant mildew-resistant varieties, such as 'Cherokee' and 'Catawba.' Dwarf varieties are available as well.

>> **Dogwood:** *Cornus florida.* North American native. Key attributes are deep-red autumn color and large white or pink midspring flowers followed by bright-red fruit that birds enjoy eating. An excellent small (20 to 30 feet; 6 to 9 m) tree that's hardy to Zone 5. Not well adapted to hot, dry climates but can be grown successfully in partial shade. Anthracnose and borers can be serious problems. Hybrids 'Aurora,' 'Galaxy,' 'Constellation,' and 'Stellar Pink' are less prone to anthracnose disease; 'Pluribracteata' is especially resistant.

TIP

If dogwoods in your area are affected by the debilitating dogwood disease anthracnose and/or late frosts damage the spring flower display, try instead the Kousa dogwood (*C. kousa*). This species is highly disease-resistant and flowers later in the season so is rarely damaged by frost. It has attractive red fruit in autumn.

>> **Flowering crabapple:** *Malus* species. Crabapples differ from apples in that they have fruit less than 2 inches (5 cm) in diameter. You have many species and varieties to choose from, ranging in tree size and shape. Spring flowers come in white, pink, or red and are followed by colorful red, orange, or yellow edible fruit that often hangs on the bare branches into winter. Most are hardy to at least Zone 5 and grow best where winters are cold. Flowering crab apples are subject to severe diseases, including fire blight, powdery mildew, and scab. Seek out disease-resistant varieties.

>> **Flowering fruit:** *Prunus* species. A large family of trees that bloom in early spring that includes flowering cherries and plums. Flowers are usually fragrant and come in shades of white, pink, or red. Most are hardy to at least Zone 5 and range in height from 15 to 20 feet (4.5 to 6 m). Favorite fruitless types include Kwanzan flowering cherry, *P. serrulata* 'Kwanzan' with drooping clusters of double pink flowers. Another favorite is a purple-leaf plum, *P. cerasifera* 'Krauter Vesuvius,' which has pink flowers and bronzy-purple leaves.

>> **Goldenrain tree:** *Koelreuteria paniculata.* A well-behaved, round-headed tree with divided leaves and large, bright-yellow flower clusters in summer. Unusual, papery, Japanese lantern-like fruit follow the flowers. Grows 25 to 35 feet (7.6 to 10.6 m) high and grows well in many different climates. Hardy to Zone 5.

>> **Magnolia:** *Magnolia* species. Some native, some not. The deciduous magnolias bloom stunningly on bare branches in early spring. Flowers are huge, often more than 10 inches (25.4 cm) across, and come in shades of white, pink, and purple. Some flowers are bi-colored. Leaves are large and leathery. Trees usually grow 15 to 25 feet (4.5 to 7.6 m) high, are often multi-trunked, and are hardy to at least Zone 6. One of the best is the saucer magnolia, *M. × soulangeana,* a multi-trunked tree that bears large, cup-shaped flowers, usually white on the inside, purplish on the outsides.

The southern magnolia, a North American native, *Magnolia grandiflora,* bears fragrant, white summer flower that are huge — up to 12 inches (30.5 cm) across — and held among bold, deep green leaves. One of the all-time favorite evergreen trees for mild-winter climates. The species gets large, upwards of 80 feet (24.4 m) high. Where space is limited, seek out the aptly named 'Little Gem'; hardy to Zone 7.

Magnolia lovers with smaller gardens or in a colder climate, take note! Shorter and oh-so-pretty, the Little Girl series are a cross between the lily magnolia (*M. liliiflora*) and star magnolia (*M. stellata*). They bloom a bit later in spring, thus avoiding damaging late frosts — great news for gardeners in colder regions (they're hardy in Zones 4 to 8). Low-branching, almost shrubby, they reach between 8 and 15 feet (2.4 to 4.6 m) high. Look for 'Ann,' 'Betty,' 'Judy,' and more.

>> **Palo verde:** *Parkinsonia aculeata.* Actually a Caribbean native that does quite well in the South, Southwest, and southern California. It has a light, airy profile and is generous-flowering. Individual flowers are on the small side, an inch

(2.5 cm) or less, bright yellow with orange markings, and sweetly scented. Blooming starts in spring and continues on and off through the summer months. The tree gets about 15 feet (4.6 m) high and wide. Tolerant of drought, alkaline soil, seaside conditions; hardy in Zones 8 to 11.

>> **Redbud:** *Cercis* species. North American native. Most popular is the eastern redbud, *C. canadensis,* which reaches 20 to 30 feet (6 to 9 m) high and spreads almost as wide. It has the prettiest maroon-to-pink flowers every spring. Hardy to Zone 4. 'Alba' and 'Royal White' have white flowers; 'Royal White' is a more cold-tolerant choice, if you live in Zone 4. 'Forest Pansy' has maroon foliage, and the flowers are more intensely colored than the species. 'Ruby Falls' is a weeping selection.

The western redbud, *C. occidentalis,* is a multitrunked, small (12 to 15 feet; 3. 6 to 4.6 m), drought-tolerant tree particularly well adapted to dry-summer areas. Hardy to Zone 8.

REMEMBER

>> **Stewartia:** *Stewartia.* The North American native species is *S. ovata*; the showier Japanese species is *S. pseudocamellia.* Each gorgeous creamy-white flower is around 3 inches (7.6 cm) across, with a dramatic boss of golden stamens in the center (like a camellia). Dark green leaves, fall foliage may or may not be colorful. In winter, admire the exfoliating bark with its beautiful shades of gray, red-brown, and orange. *S. ovata* only gets 10 to 15 feet (3 to 4.6 m) high and wide and is hardy in Zones 5 to 8; *P. pseudocamellia* gets 20 to 40 feet (6 to 12 m) high and wide and is hardy in Zones 4 to 7.

Tagging top trees for small spaces

The following are well-behaved, smaller-size trees (usually 15 to 30 feet, 4.6 to 9 m, high), especially suitable around patios or in small gardens where larger trees won't fit.

>> **Crape myrtle:** *Lagerstroemia indica.* See the previous section for a full description.

>> **Dogwood:** *Cornus florida.* North American native. Refer to the previous section for a full description.

>> **Fringe tree:** *Chionanthus virginicus.* North American native. This charming tree has medium-green leaves, scads of fleecy fragrant white flowers in spring, and blue-purple fruits that attract birds in autumn. It gets 12 to 20 feet (3.6 to 6 m) high and wide and is pretty cold-hardy; it does well in Zones 4 to 9.

>> **Hawthorn:** *Crataegus* species. Most are North American natives. These small trees (most are 20 to 25 feet, 6 to 7.6 m, high) offer a long season of color: white, pink, or red flowers in midspring, bright-orange-to-red berries in

autumn and winter, and usually orange-to-red autumn leaf color. Most are hardy to at least Zone 5. Branches have thorns. Fire blight and rust can be problems. An important food source for wildlife, especially birds.

>> **Hornbeam:** *Carpinus caroliniana.* North American native. A handsome and adaptable tree that grows slowly to 20 to 30 feet (6 to 9 m) high and about half as wide. Like its cousins the birches, it has serrated leaves; fall color can be lovely. You mostly can depend on this tree for healthy, hearty greenery. Also like birches, it has pendulous yellow-green catkins (flowers) in spring. Bark is hard and blue-gray, something to appreciate during the winter months. Hardy in Zones 3 to 9.

>> **Japanese maple:** *Acer palmatum.* The Japanese maple is one of the most popular small trees (ranging from 5 to 25 feet (1.5 to 7.6 m) high, depending on the variety). It comes in dramatic weeping forms with finely cut leaves and bright autumn color, mostly in shades of red, orange, and yellow. Some varieties like 'Bloodgood' have purplish leaves during the entire growing season. In hot, dry-summer areas, Japanese maples are best planted in partial shade. Most are hardy into Zone 5. Another great small-growing maple is paperbark maple, *A. griseum.* It has gorgeous cinnamon-colored exfoliating bark.

>> **Magnolia:** *Magnolia* species. Refer to the previous section for a full description.

>> **Parrotia:** *Parrotia persica.* There's a lot to love about this tree, which generally matures at 20 to 30 feet (6 to 9 m) high and half as wide. It has tough, trouble-free lime-green leaves in spring and summer and puts on a spectacular color show in fall (a vivid blend of yellow, red, and orange). When the leaves are off in winter, it has an interesting, textural profile and develops multihued bark (green, white, tan). The reddish springtime flowers have appeal, but honestly, the rest of the plant overshadows them. Hardy in Zones 4 to 8.

>> **Redbud:** *Cercis* species. North American native. Refer to the previous section for a full description.

>> **Serviceberry:** *Amelanchier canadensis.* North American native. Because it has a multi-stemmed habit, this handsome plant is sometimes considered a shrub, but it can easily grow to between 6 and 20 (1.8 to 6 m) feet. It has lots of small white flowers in spring, nice green leaves in summer, red fall foliage, and fall berries for wildlife to enjoy. It prospers in damp ground or beside water, and is hardy in Zones 3 to 7.

TIP

If you're seeking a more modest–size, slower–growing evergreen tree, we recommend dwarf conifers, which vary in size from 1 to 2 feet high (.3 to .6 m) to as tall as a person (that is, 5 to 6 feet; 1.5 to 1.8 m). They're popular for hedges and rock gardens, but there's no reason why you can't feature one or more in your smaller garden. Flip to Chapter 12 for more details.

Planting some fruit trees

If you suspect that there is a lot to know about growing fruit trees well — well enough to harvest fruit from your own yard — you suspect correctly. But you can do it. The following can help.

You don't have to put in rows of trees, or become an expert on what to spray and when. The art and science of homegrown fruit isn't as complex or as much work for homeowners as it is for an orchardist. You don't have to know and follow all their rules. Put in one or two trees and, after you taste success, expand.

REMEMBER

You do need to follow the rules concerning two factors:

>> **Siting:** To do well, fruit trees need to be out in the open, where they can enjoy plentiful sunshine and good air circulation.

>> **Soil:** Like any other food crop (refer to Chapter 17), fruit trees need good, fertile soil, and regular watering and attention.

Why not raise peaches, pears, or cherries in the middle of the lawn? Or put in one or more trees near the back of your property or adjacent to the kitchen garden? You'll get attractive trees in your yard with the added bonus of spring flowers and fresh fruit to eat later.

Do remember that when harvest time comes, you may not be able to pick every ripe fruit. Some will fall, so you don't want any branches to be extending over a patio or deck, or garden path, where small mushy messes happen or critters and insects gather to feast.

TIP

Always opt for disease-resistant varieties of fruit trees. It will make managing the health of your selections so much easier, right out of the gate!

REMEMBER

Solo fruit trees tend to be sad fruit trees. Many fruit trees require a nearby companion: a tree or two of the same kind but perhaps of a different variety. (Sorry, no, pear trees can't pollinate apple trees, although they're botanically cousins.) Otherwise, although you might get pretty spring flowers, they won't be followed by an abundant fruit crop — you'll get little or no fruit set. That's because many fruit trees aren't self-fertile. The bees and other pollinators, or even just a nice breeze, need to move the pollen between separate trees.

Among the fruits that need a nearby partner (within 50 feet, or 15 m, or so, is a good general rule) are apples, pears, Asian pears, plums, and sweet cherries. You can discover more in the second edition of *Gardening Basics For Dummies* by Steven A. Frowine and the National Gardening Association (John Wiley & Sons, Inc.) as well as from nurseries that specialize in fruit trees.

CONSIDER AN ESPALIER OPTION

If your garden space is really limited or you have a patio or courtyard area, here's some fun news: You may be able to grow *espaliered* (trained to grow more-or-less flat against a wall or fence) fruit trees. Some dwarf selections fit well in compact spaces, plus their limbs are trained to grow on a horizontal plane, that is, flat against a south-facing wall, for example. This option is popular in stylish European gardens and courtyards where they join other edibles or flowering plants or herbs and add more beauty and abundance.

If you're intrigued, search online for information, read specialty fruit-growing books, and check with nurseries that sell such plants. Just remember your espaliered fruit trees will need and deserve plentiful sunshine, good air circulation, good fertile soil, and lots of love from you.

Among the fruits that can manage/produce fruit on their own (are *self-pollinating*) are certain apricots, peaches, nectarines, and sour cherries.

Looking at evergreen trees

We divide evergreens into two groups: *conifers* and *broadleaf* evergreens. Always check with a local nursery for selections that are adapted to your climate. Here's a bit more about some good ones for home landscapes, and yes, we name names:

>> **Broadleaf evergreen trees:** The following are good selections in the milder climates where they can be grown.

- **Camphor:** *Cinnamomum camphora.* Dense-foliaged tree with light green, aromatic leaves. Grows 40 to 50 feet high (12 to 15.2 m) with a round head. Hardy to Zone 8. Withstands drought. Has aggressive surface roots.

- **Oak:** *Quercus.* Evergreen oaks come in many species, most of which get quite large and spreading.

  Widely adapted species include the southern live oak, *Q. virginiana,* which grows 40 to 60 feet (12 to 18.3 m) high, is wide-spreading, and is hardy to Zone 7.

  Another good one is the holly oak, *Q. ilex,* which reaches 20 to 35 feet (6 to 10.7 m) high and is hardy to Zone 8.

  The coast live oak, *Q. agrifolia,* is a California native that is widely planted in that state and hardy in Zones 9 to 11.

>> **Conifers:** *Conifers* are cone-bearing evergreens, most with needlelike leaves, consisting of the diverse group of pines, junipers, spruces, firs, hemlocks, arborvitaes, and cedars. Many are North American natives. Although similar in their overall pyramidal appearance, foliage density, color, and texture varies. They're widely grown throughout the world and are especially valuable for year-round greenery and are often used as windbreaks and screens.

Even though most are large trees (some get taller than 100 feet, or 30.5 m) and need lots of room to grow, many garden-suitable dwarf forms are also available (see Chapter 12).

TIP

We recommend tall and skinny columnar selections to those who want year-round greenery in their garden but have limited space. These are also less vulnerable than their bulkier, wider counterparts to being smashed down and damaged by winter snow and ice.

Even though these are sometimes used to form tall hedges (also known as *living fences*), a pair can look magnificent flanking an entry to your home or back garden. Or place one or more out in the open — they can make your yard look a bit like a garden in Italy or Greece.

Among our favorites are the arborvitae cultivar, *Thuja occidentalis* 'Degroot's Spire' (15 to 20 feet, or 4.6 to 6 m, tall and only 4 or so feet, 1.2 m, wide) and the Norway spruce cultivar *Picea abies* 'Cupressina' (up to 20 feet tall and around 4 feet, or 6 m tall and around 1.2 m wide).

Steering clear of these trees

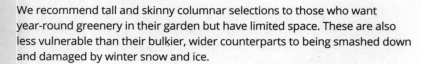

WARNING

Although we appreciate trees, some simply don't make good yard or garden citizens. We give a big Warning icon to this, our Nope List:

>> **Ash:** *Fraxinus.* Sadly, these days, the emerald ash borer is a destructive pest that debilitates and kills ashes. It's increasingly widespread, so avoid planting these trees.

>> **Black walnut:** *Juglans nigra.* Not only do black walnuts get really large, but they're allelopathic, that is, they exude a toxin into their growing area that harms or kills many other plants. If you have one already, don't cut it down unless you have a compelling reason. Harvest and enjoy the nuts. Hang a tire swing. But don't go out and buy and plant one.

>> **Bradford pear:** *Pyrus calleryana* 'Bradford'. Ugh, what a dreadful tree. Once widely planted, it has worn out its welcome. It's short-lived, falls apart/has weak and brittle branches, has smelly flowers, is invasive, and generates thorny seedlings.

- **Cottonwood:** *Populus* species. Although some people may consider these trees to be cherished shade trees, iconic even, the truth is that cottonwoods can become sprawling beasts, getting huge and unfortunately with soft wood. And the fluff that follows flowering blows around and sticks to everything.

- **Leyland cypress:** *Cupressus × leylandii.* This tall evergreen is very adaptable and grows quickly — that's the positive spin. The other side of the coin? It's weedy and weak-wooded and also turns out to be quite disease-prone. Established trees end up looking awful and aren't easy to remove.

- **Lombardy poplar:** *Populus nigra* 'Italica'. Its super-fast growth (up to 6 feet, or 1.8 m, in a year) means weak wood, prone to breakage. Its root system aggressively invades and disrupts pavement, sidewalks, as well as water and sewer pipes. It's disease-prone. Just no.

- **Mimosa:** *Albizia julibrissin.* Lush growth, ferny leaves, pink puffball flowers in summer (when not many other trees are blooming). It's also short-lived, vulnerable to many pests, and weedy. It sheds loads of beanlike seedpods, which lead to loads of seedlings. You'll rue the day you plant this.

- **Mulberry:** *Morus alba.* Fast-growing with aggressive roots. Sure, the little berries are sweet, but often there's so many you can't begin to keep up with harvesting, which means a red-purple, staining mess, especially on deck, patio, or sidewalk surfaces. Furthermore, a seedling can take up to a decade to produce fruit. Not worth the aggravation in our opinion.

- **Norway maple:** *Acer platanoides.* This nonnative maple is an invasive bully of a tree, spreading seedlings around and sucking the life out of its real estate. Plant native maples instead.

- **Russian olive:** *Eleagnus angustifolia.* Once in favor as an ornamental tree, now definitely not because it's invasive and aggressive, crowding out competition. Hogs nitrogen and nutrition in its soil environment. Thorny and hard to eradicate. Don't even give it a toehold.

- **Silver maple**: *Acer saccharinum.* Though at first you may think it's pretty, it will wear out its welcome. It's notorious for splitting in storms; in fact, some municipalities have outlawed it for this reason.

- **Tree of heaven**: *Ailanthus altissima.* More of a rangy, multistemmed shrub than a true tree, it can reach treelike height and girth if given a chance. It's fast-growing, weedy, and sheds it messy seeds everywhere. Unwanted seedlings follow.

IN DEFENSE OF GINKGO

The ginkgo biloba didn't make our Nope List, although it's often on other "avoid at all costs" lists! The reason is the female trees (yes, some trees although not many are either male or female, and ginkgo is one) litter the ground in the late summer and fall with stinky fruit (the fruits are edible, but there's a lot and they stain and make a big mess). The plain fact is, a nursery won't sell you a female ginkgo tree unless you specifically request it. And the male ginkgos are gorgeous, especially when their unique fan-shaped leaves turn golden in autumn. These trees grow up to 50 feet (15.2 m) high and wide and are hardy in Zones 4 to 9.

Ginkgos are also quite tolerant of air pollution, so many cities have planted them as street trees. Another important quality: Ginkgo root systems are well-mannered. They stay deep and don't ruin pavement and patios.

Demystifying Tree Planting

Proper planting ensures that your trees get off to a good start and thrive for years to come. Newly planted trees need special attention (especially with watering) until they can stretch their roots out into the surrounding soil and fend for themselves.

Planting a tree is also planting for the planet and the future. All too often, when we humans build, we remove trees to make way for our homes, yards, businesses, sidewalks, and streets, so let's restore! Remember that, through the amazing process of photosynthesis, trees literally remove and store the carbon and release life-sustaining oxygen back into the air we breathe — such an important and valuable service. Planting a tree (or several) benefits us now and is a gift to future generations.

TIP

Adding a tree to your curb strip: First, find out if it's allowed. Call your city or county planning or parks department. If it is, they may have a list of suitable street trees. Sometimes, you may discover that they have nursery plants to give out or sell inexpensively in order to encourage such planting!

The following sections discuss the way trees are sold, which affects the way to plant them. We also explain in five easy steps how you can plant a tree.

Shopping for trees — pro tips

Trees are sold three different ways:

>> **Bare-root trees:** Deciduous trees are available for planting during the dormant season (late fall to early spring, before new growth starts) without

soil on their roots. Bare-root trees look kind of like an old witch's broom, but with a trunk and roots instead of a handle and straw. They're lightweight and easy to handle. Fret not, they aren't dead, only dormant. Bare-root is also the most economical way to purchase a tree.

>> **Balled-and-burlapped trees:** These trees are dug and sold year-round in mild climates and most of the year elsewhere, with the *rootball* (the mass of soil and roots) intact and wrapped in burlap. Check for major cracks or breaks in the rootball and make sure the trunk doesn't rock or move in the soil ball. As long as the rootball is mulched and not allowed to dry out (watered regularly), these trees can be planted at almost any time the ground is workable.

>> **Container-grown trees:** These trees, sold in large plastic or clay pots, are easy to handle and available year-round. Check for circling or densely matted roots, signs that the tree has been in the pot too long and may not grow well after it's in the ground.

Planting a tree in five easy steps

After you purchase your tree, follow these steps for planting it:

1. Dig a large hole.

The hole should be deep enough to accommodate the roots (use a stick to determine depth) and two to three times as wide as the rootball. Slant the walls of the hole outward and loosen them with a shovel or garden fork to allow easy root penetration.

Reserve the excavated soil to one side, for backfilling at the end.

2. Insert the tree into the hole based on the type of tree you purchased (see the preceding section for more information):

- **Bare-root trees:** If any of the roots are damaged, soft, broken, or mushy — prune them off.

  If your new tree has a single, thick taproot that extends directly down from the trunk, place the tree in the hole so its nursery soil line (you'll see a color change from light to dark along the trunk) is even with the surface of the soil.

  For fibrous-rooted trees, set the base of the roots on a cone of soil in the middle of the hole, adjusting the cone height so that the plant's nursery soil line is even with the surrounding soil. Spread the roots in different directions. (You can see how this is done in Chapter 12 in the shrub-planting instructions.)

- **Balled-and-burlapped trees:** Remove the burlap, nails, and any twine or wire used for wrapping after setting the ball in place in the hole (very gently so the rootball doesn't break). Otherwise, those things may interfere with future growth or strangle the trunk (especially if the twine is plastic or nylon, which doesn't degrade). Burlap is supposed to break down quickly in the soil, but we prefer to remove it to make sure that it doesn't get in the way of root growth. If you can't get it all off, use a sharp knife to cut off everything except what is directly beneath the ball.

- **Container-grown trees:** Loosen any roots that have become tangled inside the pot by spraying off the soil from the outer inch or two (few cm) of the rootball. Cut off roots that are broken or permanently damaged; after all, they're not going to recover.

TIP

If the rootball seems dense, that is, you discover it's fairly rootbound, you can score the roots vertically (lengthwise) with a sharp knife, every few inches (cm). This will have the effect of preventing them from continuing to grow in a circle and will also inspire the growth of new fibrous roots.

3. **Backfill.**

Don't bother to amend (improve) the reserved soil from when you dug the hole — the roots may have a tough time growing beyond the amended area if you do. Of course, if your soil is especially poor (mucky clay or gravel), do work in some compost or other organic matter such as composted fir bark. In any event, water and tamp as you work, to prevent air pockets.

4. **Create a basin and water the tree well.**

To help direct irrigation and rainwater to new roots, create a basin at least 4 to 6 inches (10 to 15.2 cm) high just outside the rootball.

Deliver water to the basin by letting a hose trickle in until the soil is soaked deeply. Continue to water the tree any time that the soil begins to dry out during the next six months to a year — even longer if your summers are hot and dry.

5. **Mulch.**

To hold in soil moisture and keep weeds at bay, lay down several inches of mulch in the planting basin, but not in direct contact with the trunk (which could cut off air and invite pests or disease).

TIP

The only time staking is recommended is when you're planting in a windy location. (Otherwise, tightly tied stakes can be like crutches, preventing a tree from developing a strong trunk.) To stake, drive two tree stakes in the soil beyond the roots. Attach ties to the tree at the lowest point at which it stays upright. Use soft ties and tie *loosely* so the trunk can move in the wind. Remove after a year or two.

» **Landscaping with vines and avoiding expensive mistakes**

» **Getting to know our favorite shrubs and vines**

Chapter **12**

Bulking Up with Shrubs and Vines

B ecause they're both versatile and hardworking, shrubs can work wonders in your landscape. They tie the landscape together, bringing unity to all the different elements — from tall trees to low-growing groundcovers. Simply put, shrubs bring together the voices of many different plants and landscape features and turn them into the song of a well-planned landscape — look at the color insert for an example. Vines are equally as versatile, are able to fit into the narrowest places, and provide shade by sprawling over the largest arbor or trellis. We start this chapter with shrubs and then wind our way down to the vines.

Finding Out about Shrubs

The term "shrub" covers a wide variety of plants. Shrubs can be deciduous or evergreen, and they provide a variety of valuable ornamental qualities, from seasonal flowers to colorful fruit to dazzling autumn foliage color. But of equal importance is the diversity of foliage texture and color that shrubs offer — from bold and dramatic to soft and diminutive. Shrubs are substantial players in your yard, always visible, whether or not they're in bloom. So be sure to consider the foliage, color, texture, and form of the plant when selecting shrubs and deciding where to place them.

TECHNICAL STUFF

An oft-repeated horticulture-instructor joke is that "shrub is a fancy word for bush!" But, to be serious here, a *shrub* is defined as a woody plant that branches from its base. But that's actually too simple a definition. Shrubs can range from very low-growing, spreading plants that work well as groundcovers (see Chapter 16 for a list) to taller, billowy plants that you can prune into small, multi-trunked trees. In general, though, shrubs cover themselves with foliage from top to bottom. They come in a wide range of sizes, most falling into the 1- to 15-foot range.

In the following sections ahead, we take a closer look at all things shrubs, including considering shrubs as design elements, using native shrubs, and ways to rehabilitate existing shrubs.

Looking at design considerations

Shrubs serve so many functions in landscapes. Here are some useful categories to better understand how they function in your yard's design:

>> **Foundation plantings:** One of the most common uses of smaller shrubs is to plant them around the base of a house to conceal the foundation. These shrubs are usually evergreen, so they continue the job year-round and give the area appeal even in winter. But maybe you can break this rule. Any shrub can serve, as long as it meets your criteria.

TIP

Using too many of one type of plant leads to monotony and an unnatural look. Try mixing groups of plants with different sizes (bearing in mind eventual sizes) and textures. For example, instead of dotting your landscape with yews, put in a variety of evergreen shrubs (hollies, junipers, boxwoods, low-growing pine). Take a look at the photo in the color insert; it may inspire you!

Also, don't plant shrubs too close to your house. Bring the plantings out some distance — 3 to 4 feet — to give them room to grow. This way, they'll be able to optimize rainwater (saving you the work of watering), and their branches won't end up rubbing against the house.

Picking out varieties of shrubs that are naturally slow-growing or specifically labeled as "dwarf" will increase the longevity of your foundation plantings.

TIP

>> **Unifiers:** Using the same plant in different spots can unify a yard or an area — shrubs are perfect for this role. Avoid using plants in pairs, though, which leads to an awkward-looking formality. Odd numbers in groupings is a landscaping cliché, yet an effective principle.

Similarly, shrubs work well when planted among shorter-lived perennials in border plantings. Because shrubs are usually larger and bulkier, they provide a design foundation for the more extravagant perennials and a structure for your landscape in the off-season. In other words, shrubs provide consistent beauty and unity even when everything isn't looking its best. For more about perennial plants, see Chapter 14.

» **Backgrounds and barriers:** Shrubs can be the perfect backdrop for flower-beds. A consistent, deep green background is one of the best ways to highlight blooming plants. If you want to keep pets (or people) out of a certain area, plant a row of sharp-leaved hollies or rose bushes. They'll get the "point."

» **Accent plantings:** Some shrubs, such as azaleas and rhododendrons, are spectacular bloomers and bloom at different times. Others have stunning berries or autumn color. Just a small selection in a special place can light up a whole yard. And don't forget foliage — a substantial viburnum, for example, makes a dramatic presence among plants with smaller leaves, like azaleas.

» **Hedges, screens, and groundcovers:** Many shrubs, usually ones with smaller leaves, can be planted close together and maintained as hedges and screens. Some, including boxwoods and arborvitaes, can be clipped regularly into the rigid shape of a formal hedge to give a landscape a tidy look. (Refer to the section, "Planting shrubs," later in this chapter for how to prune a hedge.) Many others can be left to grow more naturally, creating screens for privacy. Many *prostrate* (low-growing) shrubs make excellent groundcovers. For more information, see Chapter 16.

REMEMBER

Evergreen shrubs are usually the best choice for year-round screening.

Making the case for native shrubs

In recent years gardeners have been alerted to the potential pitfalls of nonnative shrubs in their yards. Researchers (notably Doug Tallamy, author of the popular book *Nature's Best Hope; A New Approach to Conservation that Starts in Your Yard*, [Workman Publishing]) have confirmed that many nonnative plants don't sustain native wildlife — from insects to birds, including butterflies, important pollinators, songbirds, and more. When gardeners fail to provide these creatures with food and shelter, their populations decline and the food web falters.

Planting, or keeping, native shrubs in your yard is a wise and responsible way to reverse this unintended consequence. And, good news, you have plenty of handsome choices. Furthermore, if a plant is locally or regionally adapted, it transplants and grows well.

TIP

But how will you know what's native and what's not? Check out the following sources for this information:

>> **Look on the nursery tag.** The tag not only provides the plant's full common and botanical (Latin) name, but it also states which USDA Hardiness Zones it performs best in (zones are explained for you in Chapter 19), expected mature size (believe this!), and whether the plant is suitable for sun or shade.

>> **Ask.** If the information isn't on the nursery tag or in the catalog description, flag down one of the store's associates or call the supplier and ask. Or, because you're now empowered with its name, you can search online for a prospective plant choice or go online to the ever-helpful NGA website (https://garden.org).

>> **Scan the various special lists in this chapter.** We note which plants are natives. (Local nurseries tend only to offer suitable native shrubs because, they want the plants to thrive; they want you to be a happy customer.)

Grow native, it's a win–win!

SHRUB REHAB

More than likely you already have shrubs on your property, and their presence is okay with you. But they look like they've seen better days. What to do? Bring them back with these suggestions:

- **Tidy up.** March out there with loppers, clippers, and a pruning saw. Take out all dead and diseased wood — it's never going to come back to life. You can also cut off suckers right at the ground level. Do this work at any time of the year, even winter when a shrub is dormant.

- **Rein in.** Too much growth? The time to chop back is spring when growth is beginning. Shrubs are most resilient at this time. Remove no more than a third of the profile at any one time.

- **Let in light and air.** Opening gaps in dense, overgrown foliage helps penetrate the shell of darkness and allows many plants to generate healthy growth closer to their main trucks or branches. The result? Before long, the shrub looks and feels better.

- **Fix legginess.** Neglect or bad pruning makes some shrubs develop bare ankles. If you don't like that look, you can change it, but it will take time and patience — a few years. Remove up to a third of the old major stems or branches each year, allowing the plant to recover each time.

As for *cultivars* (cultivated varieties) or special selections of native plants — sometimes called *nativars* — using them to support native wildlife is probably fine. To clarify, a cultivar would never be found in nature. Horticulturists have selected or created worthwhile variations, whether it's a more compact-growing version, a flower of a different color, or even better cold-hardiness. Some interesting research is being done on these to see how wild creatures, particularly insects, respond to such plants; often the original plain one appears to be preferable, but, not always.

Discovering Some Favorite Shrubs

This section lists shrubs that we consider to be good ones, arranged by common name first and botanical (Latin) name second for full clarity. All are widely available and many are *broadly adapted* (they can grow in many different climates). We also note the North American natives. Regarding specific soil needs, refer to Chapter 17 to see how to adjust soil as needed for certain plants and Chapter 19 for more information about hardiness zones. The shrubs are as follows:

» **Azalea and rhododendron:** *Rhododendron* species. Evergreen and deciduous. Huge family of much-loved flowering shrubs. You can find many types to choose from, but all grow best in acid soil.

A frequently asked question is: What is the difference between azaleas and rhododendrons? All azaleas are rhododendrons (in the genus *Rhododendron*) but not all rhododendrons are azaleas. Most azaleas are deciduous, but true rhododendrons are usually evergreen.

- Azaleas are generally lower-growing, deciduous plants that cover themselves with brightly colored, funnel-shaped spring flowers in shades of pink, red, orange, yellow, purple, and white. Some are bi-colored.

- Rhododendrons are usually taller with larger flower clusters (rhodie flowers tend to be bell-shaped) and larger leaves. Most are spring bloomers, but a few bloom in the fall. They come in basically the same color range as azaleas, but they aren't as well adapted to hot-summer climates.

Most azaleas and rhododendrons prefer moist, shady conditions and soil rich in organic matter. Some can take full sun. Hardiness varies.

Rhododendrons include some of the most cold-hardy evergreen shrubs, a few of which tolerate winters in Zone 4. Deciduous azaleas share the rhododendron's cold tolerance (the Northern Lights series is hardy to Zone 4). Evergreen azaleas are much less tolerant of cold (Belgian Indicas are hardy to Zone 9 and Kurumes to Zone 8).

- » **Bayberry:** *Myrica pensylvanica.* Native. Deciduous. Yes, this bayberry is the one of holiday candles; once, the waxy blue-green fall berries were boiled and the fragrant wax collected from the female plants (nowadays, the wonderful scent is artificially recreated because this process is too labor-intensive).The sage-green leaves are thick and also aromatic. This choice is good for lean, acidic soil in full sun; it can stabilize a slope, define a property line, or even serve as a low-care foundation plant. The root systems are able to fix atmospheric nitrogen, which means bayberries improve the soil they grow in. Many wild birds appreciate the berries and the thick shelter these plants offer. Grows 5 to 10 feet (1.5 to 3 m) high and wider. Zones 3 to 6.

- » **Beach plum:** *Prunus maritima.* Native. Very hardy. It tolerates salt, drought, lean soil, and wind. Late spring brings a flurry of white flowers and fall can bring little edible fruits. Transplanting from the wild inevitably fails; get your plants from a reputable nursery. You'll need more than one for cross-pollination if you want the little plums. They can grow up to 15 feet (4.6 m) high; some people like to prune off the lower branches to give the plants a more domesticated look. Zones 3 to 6.

- » **Boxwood:** *Buxus* species. Evergreen. The boxwood is one of the finest plants for a tightly clipped, formal hedge. Small, dark green leaves densely cover the branches.

  - The Japanese boxwood, *B. microphylla (*synonymous with *B. japonica),* is one of the most popular types. Unpruned, it grows about 4 to 6 feet (1.2 to 1.8 m) high. 'Winter Gem' and 'Green Beauty' are two varieties that stay bright green all winter. Others pick up a brownish tinge. Grow in full sun to partial shade. Hardy to Zone 5.

  - The English boxwood, *B. sempervirens,* is the classic boxwood of the mid-South. Many named varieties are available. It's hardy to Zone 6.

    English boxwood seems to be most susceptible to the devastating boxwood blight disease. Resistant larger ones include 'Dee Runk,' 'Green Beauty,' and 'John Baldwin' — resistant dwarf/smaller cultivars include 'Green Gem' and 'Harland.'

WARNING

- » **Camellia:** *Camellia* species. Evergreen. With its glossy, deep green leaves and perfectly formed flowers, it's one of the finest shrubs for shady conditions in milder climates. Flowers come in shades of red, pink, and white, with some bicolors. Most types bloom in winter and early spring.

  - The Japanese camellia, *C. japonica,* is the most commonly grown camellia, usually reaching 6 to 12 feet (1.8 to 3.6 m) high. Many varieties are available, varying by color and flower form. Most are hardy into Zone 8.

  - Sasanqua camellia, *C. sasanqua,* has smaller leaves and earlier flowers (often in autumn). These shrubs range from small shrubs to more spreading, vine-like plants. Hardy to Zone 8.

- New varieties are more cold hardy to Zone 6a. These shrubs are hybrids of the Japanese camellia and *C. oleifera.* Named varieties include 'Winter's Beauty,' 'Winter's Interlude,' 'Winter's Star,' and 'Winter's Waterlily.'

» **Chokecherry:** *Aronia* species. Native. Deciduous. A multi-stemmed shrub suitable for groups or massing. Its time of glory is in the fall when the lustrous green leaves turn crimson and purple and it produces scads of brilliant red berries (that persist into winter). Very adaptable, 6 to 10 feet tall and half as wide; hardy in Zones 4 to 9. 'Brilliantissima' is a sensational, bright cultivar.

» **Elderberry:** *Sambucus canadensis.* Native. Deciduous. These small, blue-black berries have enjoyed a surge in popularity in recent years because of their immune system–boosting reputation. Whether that's verifiable or not, they're delicious in jam, jelly, pie, and syrup. Just beat the neighborhood critters to the harvest (Chapter 18 discusses ways to fend off critters.) Summer flower clusters are white to pink. The plants have a casual, relaxed form and reach between 5 and 12 feet high, so they're best for the back of a garden or anywhere they have sufficient room. Zones 4 to 9.

Interestingly, you can find the European species *Sambucus nigra* in ornamental cultivars, such as purple-leaved 'Black Beauty' and lacy-leaved 'Laciniata'. Zones 5 to 7 for these shrubs.

» **Flowering fruit:** *Prunus* species. Evergreen or deciduous. You can find many valuable shrubs in this large family.

- Carolina cherry laurel, (*P. caroliniana)* and Portugal laurel (*P. lusitanica*) are evergreen with white spring flowers, handsome foliage, and tall stature (20 feet, 6.1 m, high or more).

- English laurel (*P. laurocerasus),* has fallen out of favor due to being invasive. The evergreen types are useful as tall screens but their smaller varieties are more appropriate for most landscapes. Laurels are generally hardy to Zone 8 and grow best in full sun.

- The purple-leafed sand cherry, *P. × cistena,* is a hardy deciduous flowering fruit with white spring flowers, purple foliage, and small edible plums. Reaches 10 feet (3 m) high, is hardy to Zone 3. Plant in full sun.

» **Flowering quince:** *Chaenomeles.* Deciduous. Among the first shrubs to bloom in early spring, flowering quince are tough, reliable plants that never let you down. The flowers are borne on bare stems in shades of mostly red and pink, but may also be white. Plants range in size and shape depending on variety, but generally grow 5 to 10 feet (1.5 to 3 m) high, are upright, and have thorns that can create an impenetrable barrier. They can be clipped as a hedge, espaliered, and usually look best with regular pruning. Plant in full sun. Hardy to Zone 4.

» **Fothergilla:** *Fothergilla species.* Native. Deciduous. What a great three-season shrub. Spring features white, sweetly scented bottlebrush flowers before or while the plant is just starting to leaf out. Foliage tends to be a medium green, until autumn comes, when, wow! Vivid hues of orange, red, and yellow, sometimes all on the same leaf; the full effect is gorgeous. *Fothergilla major* is a big shrub, reaching up to 10 feet (3 m) high and wide. For smaller spots or a flowerbed, go with *F. gardenii*, which grows 2 to 4 feet (.6 to 1.2 m) high and wide. Full sun to partial shade. Moist, organically rich, acidic soils bring out their best. Zones 4 or 5 to 9.

>> **Gardenia:** *Gardenia jasminoides*. Evergreen. Intensely fragrant, pure-white summer flowers and beautiful deep green leaves make gardenias a favorite shrub wherever they can be grown. Plants usually grow 3 to 6 feet (.9 to 1.8 m) high and must have acid soil and consistent moisture. Plant in full sun in cool climates, partial shade in warmer areas. You can find big-flowered ones and miniature varieties. Hardy to Zone 8.

>> **Highbush blueberry:** *Vaccinium corymbosum.* In addition to the delicious fruit, you get good-looking shrubs in the bargain. And, fall foliage color is often vivid red. In winter, admire the red twigs. They do need acidic soil and regular watering, and yes, full sun. Zones 3 to 7.

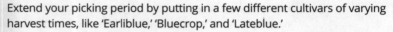
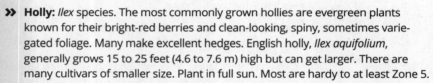

TIP

Extend your picking period by putting in a few different cultivars of varying harvest times, like 'Earliblue,' 'Bluecrop,' and 'Lateblue.'

>> **Holly:** *Ilex* species. The most commonly grown hollies are evergreen plants known for their bright-red berries and clean-looking, spiny, sometimes variegated foliage. Many make excellent hedges. English holly, *Ilex aquifolium*, generally grows 15 to 25 feet (4.6 to 7.6 m) high but can get larger. There are many cultivars of smaller size. Plant in full sun. Most are hardy to at least Zone 5.

Several native hollies are outstanding shrubs, including the following:

● Inkberry, *Ilex glabra,* has smooth, shiny, evergreen leaves. It can reach 10 feet (3 m) high and wide, but responds well to pruning and shaping. Zones 5 to 7 or 8.

● Winterberry, *I. verticillata*, is prized for its abundant red berries (but you'll need a nearby male plant to get them). It grows slowly to 10 feet (3 m) high and wide; it's hardy in Zones 3 to 9.

● The American holly, *I. opaca*, also requires both male and female plants for fruit set. It's very popular on the East Coast and in the South, prospering in Zones 5 to 9.

>> **Hydrangea:** *Hydrangea* species. Deciduous. The big, bold leaves and huge summer flowers of these unique plants put on a great show in shady and semi-shady landscapes. The bigleaf hydrangea, *H. macrophylla,* is most commonly grown. Flower clusters are up to a foot across and are light to deep blue in acid soil, pink to red in alkaline soil. Plants usually grow 4 to 8 (1.2 to 2.4 m) feet high and must be pruned heavily to encourage compactness and heavy bloom. Many cultivars give you a wide range of choices of flower colors and plant sizes. Hardiness varies by species.

The popular "peegee" *H. paniculata* 'Grandiflora,' is a big shrub or small tree with beautiful white flower panicles in summer; these age to pastel hues in autumn. The blooms form on new growth, so it's safe to prune the plants in late winter or early spring. As such, the flowering show is rarely affected by late frosts. The plants also tend to be more drought-tolerant than *H. macrophylla.*

A handsome native species, oakleaf hydrangea, *H. quercifolia*, sports great clusters of pyramidal flowers and oak-like leaves. It matures between 4 and 6 feet (1.2 to 1.8 m) high and wide, and is hardy in Zones 5 to 9.

>> **Juniper:** *Juniperus* species. Evergreen. The low- and wide-spreading growth pattern of most junipers makes them most useful as groundcovers (see Chapter 16). However, you can find many upright, shrubby types, including forms of the Chinese juniper, *J. chinensis.* Look also for very columnar varieties, like 'Wintergreen' and 'Spartan.' Plant in full sun. Hardiness varies; most can be grown into at least Zone 5.

A versatile native is the Eastern red cedar, *J. virginiana,* (not a cedar at all). It's tough, resilient, and widely adaptable, growing in Zones 2 to 9. It can be everything from a specimen plant to a full hedge, with annual trimming. For more refined-looking landscape specimens, check out the many attractive cultivars.

>> **Lilac:** *Syringa vulgaris.* Deciduous. Wonderfully fragrant clusters of spring flowers make lilacs a favorite wherever they grow. Blooms are in shades of lavender, purple, white, and rosy pink. Plants usually grow 8 to 15 feet (2.4 to 4.6 m) high and have dark green leaves. Plant in full sun. Lilacs grow best where winters are cold; they're hardy to Zone 3. The Descanso Hybrids will flower where winters are milder. 'Bloomerang' is a miniature *S. meyeri* (Korean lilac) — it's spectacular.

>> **Mountain laurel:** *Kalmia latifolia.* Native. Evergreen. The state flower of Connecticut and Pennsylvania, it certainly deserves a place in more gardens and can be used with or instead of other evergreen shrubs like rhododendrons. Shiny, dark green leaves are almost never bothered by pests or diseases, and the early-summer saucer-shaped flowers are very pretty — there are cultivars with red, pink, white, and bicolor blooms. The plant grows best in acidic soil and partial shade. Reaches 10 to 15 feet (3 to 4.6 m) tall if you never prune, but it takes very well to periodic trimming and can be easily kept around 4 to 6 feet (1.2 to 1.8 m) tall and wide. Zones 4 to 9.

>> **Ninebark:** *Physocarpus opulifolius.* Native. Deciduous. Few shrubs are as tough and dependable. They grow easily to about 6 to 10 feet high and not as wide, with arching branches. Good for hedges and screening due to thick growth. Untroubled by pests or diseases. Masses of white to slightly pink flowers (they look a bit like spirea flowers) appear in spring. The red- to purple-leaved cultivars are popular.

'Diabolo' gets mildew, but the newer ones don't, such as 'Coppertina' and 'Summer Wine.' 'Lemon Candy' has chartreuse foliage. Full sun, part shade. Zones 2 to 7.

>> **Oleander:** *Nerium oleander.* Evergreen. Oleander is a tough plant that puts on an incredibly long show of color throughout summer and into autumn. The flowers are born in large clusters in shades of white, pink, and red. The plants are low maintenance and thrive in hot summers. Oleanders are densely foliaged and generally grow 10 to 20 feet (3 to 6.1 m) high but can be kept lower with annual pruning. You can also choose dwarf varieties. Plant in full sun. Hardy to Zone 8.

All parts — leaves, stems, flowers, and seeds — of all types of oleander are toxic to humans, dogs, and cats.

>> **Photinia:** *Photinia* species. Mostly evergreen. Several species of useful shrubs that show bronzy-red new growth in spring followed shortly by clusters of small, white flowers, and later black or red berries.

- *P. fraseri,* which reaches 10 to 15 feet (3 to 4.6 m) high, is popular because of its resistance to powdery mildew, but it doesn't have berries.

- 'Red Robin' and 'Pink Marble' are two especially showy cultivars.

- Japanese photinia, *P. glabra,* is slightly lower-growing and has red berries that gradually turn black.

Photinias tolerate the full spectrum of light conditions. They're hardy to Zone 6.

>> **Rockrose:** *Cistus* species. Evergreen. Particularly well-adapted to dry summer climates such as in the western United States, rockroses are tough, colorful plants that can get by on little water. You can find several species and hybrids, most growing between 3 and 6 feet .9 to 1.8 m) high and blooming in late spring to early summer. The round, silky blooms are 1 to 2 inches (2.5 to 5 cm) wide and come in shades of white, red, and pink, often spotted or marked. Foliage is gray-green. Plant in full sun. Hardy to Zone 8.

>> **Rose:** *Rosa* species. Deciduous. All want full sun and well-drained ground; they thrive when they're fertilized and well-cared-for, which is a nice way of saying they're generally not low-maintenance plants. But they're gorgeous, though, right? Most are hardy into Zone 5 or 6.

Just choose wisely, so you can enjoy their beauty and not have to pamper or fret over them. Certain diseases and pests are a problem in certain areas; get good, local advice when shopping. All that said, here are some of our favorite landscape roses, organized by class. For more information, check out the latest edition of *Roses For Dummies* by Lance Walheim and the Editors of the National Gardening Association (John Wiley & Sons, Inc.).

- *Floribundas* are stiff, bushy, and not tall, with large clusters of flowers. They usually grow 3 to 5 feet (.9 to 1.8 m) high and can be used as informal hedges, mixed in perennial borders or planted in masses. Favorite varieties include 'Iceberg,' with white flowers, 'Hot Cocoa' with unique red-rust blossoms, and 'Sexy Rexy' with rose-pink flowers.

- *Shrubs* are a catch-all group of roses that includes many diverse plants, including ones that can be used as groundcovers (we revisit them in Chapter 16). They're heavy bloomers compared to the floribundas or hybrid teas. Height can range from 18 inches (45.7 cm) to more than 10 feet (3 m) high, but most are in the 4- to 6-foot (1.2-to-1.8-m) range. They tend to be tough, durable plants. Want heavy-flowering, low-care ones? Try the Knock Outs or the Easy Elegance series. Want super-cold hardy ones? The Morden (varieties that have Morden in the name) and Explorer roses (named after explorers) are hardy to –25°, or –32°F. If you don't mind a coarser form and thorns, beach roses, *Rosa rugosa* varieties, are super-tough and have spicily fragrant blooms on and off for most of the summer, followed by abundant, edible fruit (*rose hips*).

- *Miniature* roses grow 6 to 30 inches (15.2 to 76.2 cm) high. They have small leaves and small flowers (less than 2 inches wide) but are very useful as edgings, small informal hedges, or mixed in with flowering perennials. Favorite varieties include 'Magic Carousel' with red flowers edged in white, 'Black Jade' with red blooms, and 'Gourmet Popcorn,' which has white flowers with yellow centers.

- *Climbers* are vigorous-growing, long-caned roses that can be trained to a wall, fence, or trellis. For more information, see the "Using Vines in Your Landscape" section, later in this chapter.

- *Hybrid* teas are the most popular type of rose, loved for their beautifully formed flowers. Breeders have worked hard in recent years to create ones that are more pest- and disease-resistant, so newer varieties tend to be better plants than the old classics.

- *Old garden roses* are the grandparents of modern roses. A very diverse group of plants, many only bloom once a season and may get huge. However, their charms are undeniable, and if you do your homework, you may find one suited to your yard.

- *Austin or English* roses combine the glorious full-petaled forms and fragrances of the old-fashioned shrub roses and the repeat-blooming capabilities of modern ones. Some are big plants, some are compact, but all are gorgeous.

TIP

When you're worried that your climate may be hard on roses, own root plants are a wise choice and increasingly widely available. Unlike grafted roses, *own roots* are the same plant from head to toe. Winter (or anything else) may kill or damage the top-growth, but these plant are able to come back, bearing the flowers you expect.

>> **Shrub cinquefoil:** *Potentilla fruticosa.* Native. Deciduous. Particularly valuable in cold-winter climates, this small shrub has bright green, ferny foliage, and colorful wild-roselike blossoms. Plants bloom from late spring into autumn, usually yellow, but you can find cultivars with red, orange, or white flowers. Ranges in height from just under 2 feet up to 5 feet (.6 to 1.5 m). Plant in full sun. Hardy to Zone 3.

>> **Shrubby dogwood:** *Cornus species.* Native. Deciduous. These fine shrubs are related to dogwood trees. Some have colorful stems, some have variegated foliage — you have a lot of fine choices! Full sun to part shade for all.

- Red osier dogwood, *C. sericea*, is prized for its showy red stems, particularly valued in the winter months. It can reach 8 to 10 feet (2.4 to 3 m) high. Cut the old stems back to the ground every year to encourage new red ones to form. It produces white to light blue fruits. The cultivar 'Kelseyi' grows only to 3 feet (.9 m); it works really well in mixed beds and foundation plantings.

- Silky dogwood, *C. amomum*, is similar if a bit less showy but has blue fruit; it's very cold-hardy and adapts to almost any soil. It grows 6 to 10 feet (1.8 to 3 m) high and wide.

- Gray dogwood, *C. racemosa*, has gray stems but, in fall, bears white fruits on red stalks. It can reach up to 15 feet (4.6 m) high and wide; for a smaller site, seek out 'Muskingum', which only gets 2 by 4 feet (.6 by 1.2 m) and has scarlet fall foliage. Zones 3 to 7.

>> **Spicebush:** *Lindera benzoin.* Native. Deciduous. Its name comes from the spicy aroma of the foliage, stronger if you stand next to it or crush some leaves in your fingers. It's very early-blooming in spring with tiny yellow flowers along the branches. In fall, there's shiny red berries (popular with many birds) and bright yellow foliage. Gets about 6 to 12 feet (1.8 to 3.6 m) high and wide. Grow in full sun or part shade, but moist soil is a must. Zones 4 to 9.

>> **Sweet pepperbush:** *Clethra alnifolia.* Native. Deciduous. Candlelike spires of small white flowers, between 3 and 8 inches (7.6 to 20.3 cm) long, waft a delicious, sweet fragrance for up to a month in mid- to late summer, when other shrubs are no longer blooming. They're followed by small brown seed capsules that stay on all winter. Foliage is lustrous and green and never troubled by pests or diseases. The multi-stemmed plants get 3 to 8 feet (.9 to 2.4 m) high; they respond well to pruning. Although it's a wetland shrub and does best moist ground and full sun, it's quite adaptable. 'Ruby Spice' has dark pink blooms that are slow to fade. 'Hummingbird' is a smaller-growing variety. Zones 4 to 9.

>> **Sweetfern:** *Comptonia peregrina.* Native. Deciduous. Not a fern, although the dark green foliage is reminiscent of ferns and is spicily fragrant when brushed against. Forms a nice, woody plant 2 to 4 feet (.6 to 1.2 m) high, then it *peregrinates,* that is, travels to the sides. Tolerates poor soil and does fine in sun or partial shade. Makes a great low hedge or driveway-side planting. Zones 2 to 6.

>> **Sweetshrub:** *Calycanthus floridus* (also referred to as Carolina allspice). Native. Deciduous. The plant earns its common names in the spring, when its small maroon flowers appear and fill the air with a spicy-fruity scent that has been compared to ripe pineapples or strawberries. For that reason alone, you may wish to place one or more near your front entrance. Lustrous dark-green leaves soon join the fabulous flowers. Plant form is rounded and casual. Fall color is soft yellow. 'Athens' has yellow flowers. Typically the plants attain 6 to 10 feet (1.8 to 3 m) high and wide. 'Michael Lindsey' is a more compact version. Zones 5 to 9.

>> **Tobira:** *Pittosporum tobira.* Evergreen. A handsome, well-behaved shrub with glossy deep green leaves and clusters of white, fragrant spring flowers. The species is rounded and can reach more than 10 feet (3 m) high but can easily be kept lower with pruning. 'Wheeler's Dwarf' grows into a neat, mound-shaped plant that reaches only 2 to 4 feet (.6 to 1.2 m) high. A number of variegated-leaved cultivars are available. Plant in full sun to light shade. Hardy to Zone 8.

>> **Viburnum:** *Viburnum species.* The viburnums represent a large family of evergreen and *deciduous shrubs* (ones that drop their leaves in autumn) that are wonderful additions to the landscape. They offer great variety of form and function, and their ornamental characteristics include pretty, sometimes scented flowers, brightly colored berries, and often, autumn color. There are old introduced favorites such as Korean spice viburnum, *V. carlesii*, the tiered-branched *V. plicatum,* and the handsome Burkwood viburnum, *V. × burkwoodii.*

However, we encourage you to consider the native species. Birds and other wildlife will spread about berries, and it's better for ecosystems if they're doing so with native plants. You can choose from quite a few native viburnums, all attractive garden candidates and easy to prune and shape. Plant them in full to part-day sun in fertile soil. They're all hardy to at least Zone 5. They include

- Clump-forming arrowwood, *V. dentatum*, grows 6 to 15 feet (1.8 to 4.6 m) tall and wide; white flowers; bunches of red to purple berries

- Thicket nannyberry, *V, lentago,* grows 15 to 20 feet (4.6 to 6.1 m); white flowers; wine-red fruits hanging from long stalks

- Tall cranberry viburnum, *V. trilobum,* grows to 20 feet (6.1 m); distinctive three-lobed leaves; white flowers; showy bright-red fruit

All are trouble-free candidates for your home landscape, provided you have sufficient space.

Considering Characteristics

Shrubs come in all different colors, shapes, and sizes. Some have showy flowers for part of the growing season (so color, and fragrance, become considerations), some have colorful fall foliage or fruit (more things to think about!), and some are steady-as-you-go (reliable evergreens). The following sections help you figure out which shrubs are right for your preferences. After you find a shrub or two that interests you, check out the preceding section where we provide more details about them.

Colorful shrubs

If you're after color, you can plant shrubs that provide it in abundance through a combination of flowers, fruit, and fall color. In other words, the following are shrubs that provide more than one season of color:

>> **Azalea:** Flowers, fall color

>> **Chokecherry:** Colorful fall foliage, berries

>> **Fothergilla:** Flowers, colorful fall foliage

>> **Flowering fruit:** Flowers, colorful foliage

>> **Holly:** Berries, colorful foliage

>> **Hydrangea:** Flowers, colorful foliage

>> **Ninebark:** Flowers, colorful foliage

>> **Photinia:** Flowers, colorful foliage

>> **Roses:** Flowers, fruit

>> **Tobira:** Flowers, colorful foliage

>> **Viburnum:** Flowers, fall color, fruit, colorful foliage

Drought-tolerant shrubs

Many of popular shrubs, such as junipers, oleander, and rockrose, withstand periods of drought. Rosemary and lavender, tender in colder climates, grow into substantial, long-lived shrubby plants in the West and can also serve a dry landscape heroically.

However, once again we urge you to look to native plants that are naturally adapted to such conditions. Here are our top favorites, but certainly consult your local water district, the *Sunset Western Garden Book of Landscaping*, or visit a native-plant nursery, for a wealth of options:

» **California lilac:** *Ceanothus* species. Evergreen shrubs and groundcovers with dark green foliage and blue or white spring flowers. Native to Western states. Range in height from low-growing shrubs just a few feet high to taller shrubs 15 to 20 feet (4.6 to 6.1 m) high. You can kill this one with overwatering; it's that well-adapted to dry conditions!

» **Manzanita:** *Arctostaphylos* species. Varied group of plants native to Western states. Includes trees, shrubs, and groundcovers. Handsome shiny bark, small pink to white flowers. Range in height from low growing groundcovers (only a foot or two high) to tall shrubs that are more than 15 feet (4.6 m) high.

» **Toyon:** *Heteromeles arbutifolia.* Evergreen with shiny dark green leaves, white flowers, and bright red berries. Grows 15 to 25 feet (4.6 to 7.6 m) high.

Evergreen shrubs

Many kinds of dwarf conifers (needled evergreens) are available and useful as landscape shrubs. Think beyond the overused red cedars and yews. Here's a list of our favorites:

» **Arborvitae:** *Thuja occidentalis.* A dense grower with short ascending branches; height varies by cultivar, and you can choose from many excellent options. Hardy to Zone 2.

» **Cedar:** *Cedrus* species. *C. deodara* 'Compacta' forms a 30-inch (76.2-cm) mound of weeping, green-gold foliage. Hardy to Zone 7.

» **Cypress:** *Chamaecyparis* species. *C. lawsoniana* 'Ellwoodii' is pillar-shaped and grows to 30 inches (76.2 cm) high, with blue-green leaves. *C. lawsoniana* 'Minima Aurea' is bushy and golden yellow; grows to 24 inches (60.1 cm) high. Both are hardy to Zone 6.

» **Fir:** *Abies* species. *A. koreana* isn't truly miniature, but it's so slow-growing that it's regarded as such. *A. koreana* 'Aurea' grows to around 6 feet (1.8 m) tall, has green needles with silvery undersides, and sports appealing bluish cones. *A. nordmanniana* 'Golden Spreader' is compact and irregularly shaped. Grows to 20 inches (51 cm). 'Cis' and 'Nana' are great compact plants. Hardy to Zone 5.

» **Juniper:** *Juniperus* species. *J. communis* 'Compressa' is columnar, grows to 18 inches (45.7 cm) high; has blue-green foliage. Hardy to Zone 3.

» **Pine:** *Pinus* species. *P. strobus* 'Nana' grows 3 to 4 feet (.9 to 1.2 m) high with dense, blue-green needles. *P. mugo* is similar-size, with a neat, compact habit. Both are hardy to Zone 3.

» **Spruce:** *Picea* species. *P. glauca* 'Conica' is a neat, conical shrub with bright-green needles; grows to 4 feet (1.2 m). Hardy to Zone 3.

Fruiting shrubs

When you choose to add a fruiting shrub or a group of them to your yard, be attentive. If you wish to harvest the fruit yourself (for fresh eating or jams and jellies and more), you may have to compete with birds and other wildlife for the harvest. Prevent them from stripping off the ripe fruit by covering the plants early with bird netting, available wherever garden supplies are sold.

If you're choosing these plants to nurture wildlife (birds, mainly), bravo, and your best bet will be to watch the activity from a distance, even with binoculars, so you don't scare them away. Even when they aren't eating or the food is depleted, birds and small mammals seek shelter from predators and severe weather in our shrubs.

Here are our top choices:

>> **Beautyberry,** *Callicarpa*

>> **Blueberry,** *Vaccinium*. Depending on the plant's role in your landscape, you can get taller highbush types or lower-growing lowbush ones. Gardeners in mild-climate areas, seek out "Rabbiteye" types.

>> **Chokeberry,** *Aronia*

>> **Dogwood,** *Cornus*

>> **Elderberry,** *Sambucus*

>> **Juniper,** *Juniperus*

>> **Serviceberry,** *Amelanchier*

>> **Viburnum,** *Viburnum*

Shopping: Finding High-Quality Shrubs

Like trees, shrubs are large and long-lived plants, so select ones that can thrive in your region and at your specific site. Consider the advice offered in Chapter 19 regarding climate, hardiness, and quantity of light or shade.

No matter what the condition of the soil in your landscape, so many shrubs are available that you're sure to find several that will suit. However, if you make even modest improvements in your soil, such as improving the drainage of heavy soils or the moisture retention of sandy soils, adjusting pH, or increasing the fertility of poor soils, the number of shrubs you can consider increases dramatically. (You can read more about improving your soil in Chapter 17.)

Buy your shrubs from local nurseries because they're most aware of your zone and climate. As with trees (see Chapter 11), you can buy them in containers, as bareroot plants, or balled-and-burlapped, but the vast majority of shrubs are sold in containers. Check for quality as follows:

>> Examine the container-grown shrub carefully to be sure it isn't damaged. Avoid plants with broken branches, or chewed foliage (a sure sign of bugs). Look on the undersides of leaves for congregating insect pests.

>> Slide the rootball out — this is easy if the shrub is in a plastic pot — and look for young, white roots; they're essential for efficient uptake of water and nutrients. If a plant is stubbornly *rootbound* (really wedged and stuck into its pot), give it a pass. Older, darker roots function primarily to stabilize the plant.

You can easily easy to be swayed at the nursery by a bloom-covered shrub. Although knowing what the flowers look (and perhaps smell) like is nice, you're better off choosing a specimen that has no flowers, or maybe only some buds. So often flowers fall off a new plant, either in the hot car on the ride home or soon after being planted. A newly arrived shrub will invest energy in its root system. After it's well-established, we promise, buds will develop and bloom.

A dirty little secret of the nursery trade: Some growers infuse young plants with a cocktail of growth stimulants. After these stimulants run out, a plant falters. Be patient and take good care of new purchases.

Planting Shrubs and Hedges

The key to success with your new shrubs begins with correct planting. Sure, buying a healthy plant and handling it gently certainly helps, but a good new home is so important. It gets the newcomer off to a strong start, so it can thrive and you can enjoy it! The following sections explain how to do it right.

Getting new shrubs into the ground

Shrubs grown in containers are planted the same way container-grown trees are planted, as Chapter 11 discusses. When you're ready to plant bareroot shrubs, follow these steps:

1. **Set the base of the roots on a cone of soil in the middle of the hole (see Figure 12-1).**

   Adjust the cone height so that the plant sits slightly higher (1 to 2 inches, 2.5 to 5.1 cm) than it was originally planted in the nursery (you can see a change in color from light to dark along the trunk, which tells you where the original soil line was. To check planting depth, simply lay a stick across the top of the hole.) Spread out the roots in different directions and then refill the hole.

FIGURE 12-1:
For bareroot shrubs, set the plant on a cone of soil in the middle of the hole.

© John Wiley & Sons, Inc.

2. **Build a soil basin and water deeply, as shown in Figure 12-2.**

The basin allows the water to soak in right where needed, instead of running off.

FIGURE 12-2:
Soil basin directs water to roots.

© John Wiley & Sons, Inc.

3. **Apply an organic mulch 2 to 3 inches (5.1 to 7.6 cm) deep.**

Doing so helps hold in soil moisture and keep weeds at bay. Don't push the mulch up against the main trunk.

Betting on hedges

Hedges are basically shrubs planted in a row, for the purpose of creating privacy/blocking a view, enclosing a garden room, defining a property line (what we land-scapers like to call a *living fence*), or blunting the force of the wind. Sometimes they just form a backdrop for other plants and flowers.

You can create different types of hedges depending on the type of shrub you use:

>> **Evergreen hedges:** Hedges created from evergreen shrubs afford privacy all year because the shrubs keep their leaves.

- **Pros:** Foliage works for your landscape year-round.

- **Cons:** They can be rather dull to look at.

- **To bring out the best:** Don't neglect the plants. Regular water and fertilizer during the growing season makes a big difference.

   Consider a *tapestry hedge,* which is a mixture of different evergreens so you get a variety of textures and hues of green.

TIP

- **Pruning:** Get out the hedge trimmers or clippers in spring or summer when the plants are actively growing, and they'll tolerate the haircut. In addition to shaping, the object is to let in light for healthy growth (see Figure 12-3). Never prune or shape in autumn when cold weather is coming; new growth inspired by the cuts can get damaged or killed.

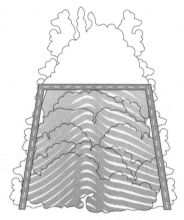

FIGURE 12-3: Keep formal hedges full-foliaged by lightly tapering the sides so that the whole hedge receives light.

© John Wiley & Sons, Inc.

>> **Deciduous hedges:** A hedge composed of deciduous shrubs offers a different look in each season.

- **Pros:** You have so many beautiful choices.

- **Cons:** They aren't as interesting in the off-season.

- **To bring out the best:** Don't neglect the plants. Regular water and fertilizer during the growing season makes a big difference. Groom them from time to time too, removing spent flowers and raking debris from their feet.

- **Pruning:** Know when to prune and shape (if you pick the wrong time, you'd clip off next year's flower show). Generally speaking, you can swoop in right after the last flowers fade.

When you're ready to plant a hedge, keep these points in mind:

» **Start with young, healthy plants.** You may plant in spring (after danger of frost is past) or in fall (6 to 8 weeks before first frost); the idea is to get them into the ground when the soil and weather conditions are hospitable (avoid cold weather and/or muddy ground, too stressful).

» **Space them closely, with the goal of them growing into one another.** How far apart? It depends on your plant choice. Ask at the nursery, emphasizing that you're installing a hedge.

» **Allow for setback.** Hedge plants fill out and bulk up. In time, they'll jut across a property line, push into the driveway or walkway they're adjacent to, or crowd plants in front of them. They need sufficient space to mature on all sides — examine the plant tag, catalog, or other reference to figure out the expected mature width. Have faith this number is correct and allow enough space.

Using Vines in Your Landscape

Vines are constantly on the move. Usually vigorous growers, these plants sprawl over, twine around, climb up, or attach to whatever is in their path.

REMEMBER

Vines are versatile. They can create privacy, provide shade, and conceal unattractive landscape features — sometimes all at once.

As long as you keep them within bounds and under control, vines can be used as groundcovers (covered extensively in Chapter 16), as a covering for a fence or blank wall (fences are discussed in Chapter 6), or as shading on an arbor or trellis (see Chapter 10) to cool a deck (check out Chapter 8).

Selecting a vine with a spot in mind

The most popular use is vertical coverage. Vines are great for adorning attractive and sturdy supports, such as a trellis, pergola, or arch. They can also decorate or conceal a wall, fence, or even an old dead tree that's too large or difficult to remove.

CLIMBING THE WALLS — BE CAREFUL

Some vines can attach so firmly to walls (and fences) that getting them off without damaging the structure becomes almost impossible. And sometimes the attaching parts of the plant work their way into cracks and crevices. As the plants enlarge and grow, they can lift shingles and damage even the sturdiest materials, such as concrete and brick. Examples include English ivy, Virginia creeper, and wisteria, all of which once enjoyed popularity but are now widely considered to be aggressive and invasive.

As for all other vines you may be considering, letting one attach directly to a wall of your house usually isn't a good idea, unless the house is made of brick, stone, or aluminum siding. And even then you can have problems.

Erecting a trellis a few feet away from the side of the house and letting it support the vine is better. That way, you can also paint the wall (behind the trellis) if you need to.

Heavy fences or the walls of outbuildings are another place to plant climbers, and these supports require little work from you. A chain-link fence can be transformed from an eyesore to a wall of color with a handsome climbing rose, hops, or morning glory. In winter, the leaves will drop from deciduous plants, but the eyesore will still look better than without the vine.

TIP

Vines can be ideal in tight spots where few other plants would fit. If your space is limited, look for kinds that offer more than one pleasure, usually those with handsome foliage as well as beautiful flowers or delectable fruit.

Choosing a vine with a purpose in mind

Like other plant groups (trees, shrubs, and so on), vines offer a variety of valuable characteristics and benefits. These plants add a lot of dimension and interest to a home landscape. Determine what your highest priority will be, and start your search:

» **Colorful flowers:** Some vines and climbers bloom in spring, some on and off all summer.

» **Colorful foliage:** Your choices include plain green, variegated (leaves marked, rimmed, or splashed with cream, white, pink, or yellow).

» **Fall color:** Some deciduous vines turn spectacular hues of yellow, orange, or red when cooler weather arrives. Some have bright berries in autumn. Some have both.

» **Winter interest:** Some vines provide handsome bark on artistically twisting branches, easy to view and appreciate in the winter.

» **Fruit:** If you want to harvest homegrown fruit, or invite birds to stop by, then look at vines that produce fruit.

Selecting some fine vines

Here are some of our favorites, arranged alphabetically according to common name and followed by their botanical name:

» **Bougainvillea:** *Bougainvillea* species. Evergreen or partially deciduous. These can be spectacular flowering vines. Stunning flowers in electric shades of purple, red, pink, orange, yellow, and white cover the plant all summer and beyond. Leaves are an attractive bright green. Plants are shrubby and must be tied to a sturdy trellis or arbor and given room to grow. Plant in full sun or, in the hottest climates, partial shade. Plant carefully, being sure not to disturb the roots. Needs only a little water after it's established. Can be grown in mild-winter areas with light frosts (Zones 10 and 11) or protected areas in Zone 9.

» **Chinese jasmine:** *Jasminum polyanthum*. Evergreen. The wonderfully fragrant flowers of Chinese jasmine perfume the air for months in spring. The small blooms are borne in clusters, white on the face, pink on the back. The twining stems hold bright green, divided leaves and are fast-growing to 20 feet (6.1 m) high. A good choice to cover a fence, trellis, or arbor. Prefers partial shade. Hardy to Zone 8.

» **Clematis:** *Clematis* species and cultivars. Mostly deciduous. A diverse family of eye-catching flowering vines with hundreds of selections available. Large-flowered hybrids, with summer blooms up to 10 inches across in shades of white, pink, red, blue, and purple, are most popular. They can twine more than 10 to 15 feet (3 to 4.6 m) high. Plant where the roots are cool and shaded but where the top can grow into full sun. For example, set the plant at the base of a large shrub or tall trellis and let it ramble through to the sunny top. Or plant one where it suits you and cover the roots with a thick mulch. Hardy to Zone 5.

WARNING

Sweet autumn clematis, *C. terniflora* (synonym, *C. paniculata*), grows thickly and produces scads of small fragrant white flowers later in the summer and on into autumn. It is considered invasive in many places, however. Plant it only where such qualities are not a problem, such as on a very sturdy support in need of heavy coverage.

» **Climbing hydrangea:** *Hydrangea anomola*. Deciduous. Enjoy beautiful lacecap flowers on a vigorous-growing vine, which can clamber 20 feet (6.1 m) high or more, clinging with ivylike *holdfasts* (tiny adhesive disks that help them attach to supports) along its stems. A pergola is ideal. You'll be shaded by the textured green leaves and admire the pretty flowers all summer. Winter reveals the muscular stems and branches. Zones 4 to 8.

» **Climbing roses:** *Rosa* species. Many types of vigorous-growing roses can be used as vines; however, they need to be securely tied to a sturdy support like a fence, trellis, arbor, or post to remain upright. Favorite varieties include 'Altissimo' with single (just five petals) deep red flowers, 'Improved Blaze' with large clusters of red flowers, 'America' with fragrant coral pink blooms, and 'White Dawn' with white flowers. Height varies by variety. Prune annually to promote flowering and keep in bounds. Winter protection usually necessary in Zone 5 and colder areas. Plant in full sun.

>> **Creeping fig:** *Ficus pumila*. Evergreen. A vigorous, compact-foliage vine that tightly adheres to any surface it touches. Good-looking, small, heart-shaped leaves. Best grown on stone or masonry. Plant in sun or shade. Hardy to Zone 8.

>> **Star jasmine:** *Trachelospermum jasminoides*. Evergreen. One of the most attractive and well-behaved vines for mild climates. Showy clusters of fragrant white flowers almost obscure the shiny, dark green foliage in late spring to summer. Twining stems reach up to 20 feet (6.1 m) high — they need support. Great for climbing through lattice or on fences in warmer climates. Plant in full sun or light shade. Hardy to Zone 8.

>> **Trumpet creeper:** *Campsis radicans*. Deciduous. Although an undeniably aggressive grower, this vine gives a lot of coverage and tons of gorgeous orange, red, or yellow blooms in summer, which hummingbirds in particular adore. The clinging rootlets aren't sufficient to hold the weight of the plant, so tie and guide the branches on the support. Pinch back growing tips to encourage bushier, fuller form. Hardy in Zones 4 to 8.

Considering some annual vines

Generally a vine becomes a long-lasting fixture in your garden, not so very different from a shrub or a perennial flower. Maybe you've installed a pergola or arch and the climber you want (a clematis or a climbing rose, for instance) will take a couple of seasons to really cover it. In the meantime, you can plant an annual vine close by to do the job, knowing it will die when cold weather returns. Annuals grow quickly and often flower, so "they pay their rent" for the short time you need them.

REMEMBER

If you really prefer annual vines, you have to replant each spring. Start seed indoors in late winter or buy seedlings locally. Put them in the ground outdoors near their support after danger of frost is past. Here are a few good ones:

>> **Black-eyed Susan vine:** *Thunbergia alata*. With loads of yellow, orange, or white blossoms with dark centers, they do indeed look like a smaller-flowered black-eyed Susan. They're popular for hanging baskets and pots, but you can easily get them to ascend and cover a support. Raise them in pots and set the pots at the base of your trellis or arch; pot-bound plants seem to grow more lushly.

>> **Morning glory:** *Ipomoea*. Get seeds or seedlings into the ground as soon as you can and let 'em take off. The grasping tendrils are easy to train (you can guide them with string stretched in the direction you want them to go). And who doesn't love the flowers? Big-bloomed 'Heavenly Blue' remains an all-time favorite, but you might also enjoy something with smaller flowers, a different color, or a bicolor. Check the seed catalogs.

TIP

For coverage all day and into the evening hours, plant both morning glories and closely related, night-blooming white moonflower (*I. alba*).

>> **Sweet peas:** *Lathyrus odoratus.* Colorful and sweetly fragrant, these are a sentimental favorite. They come in every color of the rainbow except yellow and their scent is lovely in the garden or in long-lasting bouquets. Some varieties grow really tall, 10 feet (3 m) or more! One caution: They don't love hot weather. Gardeners in cooler climates have the best luck with these beauties.

Shopping for Vines

Vine-shopping is best done in the spring or, in mild-climate areas, in the fall. The idea is to get the plants into the ground, into their spot, when they're still young so their roots can develop in place. Buying larger plants or digging up a big vine plant and transplanting it to a new location is often a dicey proposition because these plants develop substantial root systems. We say don't bother with such a project. Start them young.

TIP

As when shopping for any new plant, look for healthy topgrowth (no signs of pests or diseases); a few yellowing or bedraggled leaves are no big deal. Favor ones with flower buds rather than wide-open blooms, which may decide to fall off on the ride home or once the vine is planted. Always, when possible, pop the roots out of their pot for a peek — you're looking for a good rootball of crisp, healthy roots.

Planting Vines

Like any new perennial, vines need a good deep and wide planting hole, filled with good soil (follow the planting instructions for perennials in Chapter 14). The secret to a happy, hearty vine? Proper planting, and we don't just mean a spot with good soil and drainage and sufficient sunlight. The support is your vine's partner; consider them a pair. Keep reading for more details.

Providing sturdy support

As vines grow, the branches enlarge and the plant gets heavier. If the supports aren't strong enough, they can buckle or lean under the weight. Install or build supports that are sturdy and long-lasting. Two-inch galvanized pipe and pressure-treated 4x4 lumber are both good choices.

Always install the vine's support before planting the plant. Otherwise, you risk poking into its root system and perhaps damaging it.

Don't crowd! Set the baby vine in the ground several inches away from its support; it will find its way (or can be guided with string) and start growing up.

Vines need to grow on something, either another plant or a trellis, arch, or similar structure that you provide. Most climb by clinging or twining, so be prepared to intervene either by gently tying branches or tendrils to their support or at least tucking new growth in and around the support to encourage heading in the desired direction.

Plan the supporting device in advance. Make sure it's strong enough to bear the weight, and design it to fit the growth habit of the vine.

The classic structure for most any vine is an arbor. The simplest of these may be a pair of posts with a timber or arch spanning the top. You train the vine to grow up the posts and then over the arch. You can use a series of these arches to make a shady outdoor tunnel or to cover an entire patio. Attach wire to the posts to help the young vine find its way to the top. (See Chapter 10 for more about arbors and trellises.)

Pruning and training your vines

Pruning prevents vines from getting out of control, becoming too heavy, or growing into places that you don't want them. Prune heavily to keep a vine healthy and attractive. Keep the following in mind as you prune:

>> Winter is a traditional time for pruning in mild climates; early spring in colder ones. You can clip out rampant growth or dead pieces at any time.

>> Prune flowering vines immediately after the plants drop their blooms. They won't yet have started to form buds for next year's display.

>> The best time to do your major pruning of vigorous-growing fruiting plants, such as grapes and kiwi, is during their dormant season (late in winter or early in spring).

Training is the finer work — we call it "encouragement" or "persuasion" to get the plant to go or stay where you want it. You can effectively secure a vine stem or stems to its support in various ways:

>> Wire is rarely called for, because it damages tender growth.

>> Zip ties, twist ties, and soft strips of cloth are best. Whenever possible, secure the tie to the support first, and then loop it around the stem you're trying to guide — the result looks like a figure 8. Doing so allows the stems a little leeway, especially on windy days.

GETTING RID OF INVASIVE VINES

Sometimes a vine just grows too rampantly, wrapping itself around other plants, a tall tree, or a fence. Here's the easiest way to put a stop to its aggressive ways:

1. **Pinpoint where it emerges from the ground, and cut it off low or at soil level, with clippers, loppers, or even a saw if its base is woody or substantial.**

2. **Dig up the root system as best you can, then cover the spot.**

   Use a tarp, an old carpet remnant, a big rock, or at least mulch. The idea is to discourage resprouting.

3. **Give the topgrowth a couple of days or weeks to die.**

   The foliage will wilt, then brown, then dry out. You may be surprised to see the extent of its reach, now that it's been made more obvious by the color change from green to brown. At that point, it's much, much easier to tug down or extract the limp, dry remains.

4. **Dispose of the remnants.**

   If you're not certain the vine is 100 percent dead, send the remains away with the household trash. Or add the dead pieces to your compost pile (if its stems are very wooly, though, they will take a long time to decompose), or burn them where safe and allowed.

Here is a short list of vines and climbers to be avoided or eradicated:

- Bindweed (*Convolvulus arvensis,* annual)

- Bittersweet (*Celastrus orbiculatus,* perennial)

- English ivy (*Hedera helix,* perennial)

- Porcelain berry (*Ampelopsis brevipedunculata,* perennial)

- Sweet autumn clematis (*Clematis terniflora,* perennial)

- Virginia creeper (*Parthenocissus quinquefolia,* perennial)

- Wintercreeper *(Euonymus fortunei, perennial)*

» Listing our favorite annuals

» Knowing what to look for when buying annuals

» Planting annuals in your landscape

Chapter **13**

Adding Color and Texture This Season with Annuals

When landscape professionals talk about flowers, they're usually talking about annuals, perennials, and bulbs. These words refer to different types of plants, but the distinctions between them are not as clear-cut as you may like.

» **Annuals** usually grow for one season and then die.

» **Perennials,** which we discuss in Chapter 14, live on year-to-year if they're grown in the proper zone (see Chapter 18 for more about zones).

» **Bulbs** (which we also discuss in Chapter 14) arise from some type of swollen below-ground, rootlike structure that allows them to live on year to year in many areas, so technically they can be considered perennials.

We also offer even more planting possibilities with succulents and containers in Chapter 15, and groundcovers and lawns in Chapter 16.

Annuals are the workhorses of the flowering landscape — they provide the quickest and showiest color. If you want flower color, if you want your landscape to be bright, and if you want your landscape to look good *right away*, annuals are your answer. This chapter examines annuals in greater detail and suggests ones that are best for your climate. You also find out what you need to know when shopping for and planting annuals.

Knowing What An Annual Is

An *annual* is a plant that lives for one season and dies. Annual-flowering plants grow quickly, put on a spectacular flower show for up to several months, and then expire. When the plants die, they're usually removed and replaced. Annual plants come in all shapes and sizes, from low-growing alyssum (which rarely gets more than 6 inches, 15.2 cm high) to the tallest sunflower (which can be more than 10 feet, 3 m, high).

Our definition of *annual*, however, is a bit misleading for a couple of reasons:

>> First, some plants that are actually perennials (that is, the plants live on from year to year) are often used as annuals in climates where they can't survive year-round, because of extreme heat or cold. Some flowering plants, such as geraniums and mums, are long-lived in some climates, but because their bloom is so spectacular in a particular season, they're planted for that seasonal bloom and are then removed from the landscape after their show is over.

>> Secondly, our definition of annual plants is also a bit misleading because two kinds of annuals exist: cool-season and warm-season annuals. The distinction between these two types is important because it determines when you plant annuals and when they bloom.

The following sections list some of the most reliably colorful annuals, divided into cool-season and warm-season types, and arranged alphabetically according to common name (but supplying the botanical name in case you need it while researching or shopping).

Annuals can be planted by sowing seed directly in the garden, by starting seeds indoors and moving small transplants (seedlings) outside later, or by purchasing small transplants at the nursery.

TECHNICAL STUFF

Bedding plants are plants for planting in beds in quantity, en masse, filling up an area, whether a wide area in a garden or entire planter boxes. Annuals are the top choice because, when planted in groups or closely, they readily fill in. So the two terms — *bedding plants* and *annuals* — are effectively interchangeable. And, you seem to never buy only one plant when shopping for them!

Cool dudes

Cool-season annuals (such as pansies, violas, and sweet peas) thrive in spring and autumn. Planted in late summer or early spring, these plants grow quickly and bloom while the weather is still on the cool side. When the days get longer and hotter, most cool-season annuals slow down and cease blooming. At that time, we advise taking them out of the garden, although they may live a while longer if you choose to leave them. In mild-winter climates, many cool-season annuals that are planted in late summer and bloom throughout winter. Generally speaking, cool-season annuals are able to withstand mild frosts.

Here are our suggestions for cool-season annuals:

>> **Annual chrysanthemum:** *Chrysanthemum paludosum.* A glorious miniature bloomer from seeds or transplants. Small white-and-yellow daisylike flowers cover the plant. Annual chrysanthemums grow best in full sun and reach 12 to 18 inches, 30.5 to 45.7 cm high. (To clarify, the bigger, colorful florist-type mums sold widely in the fall at home stores, grocery stores, and garden centers aren't hardy in most places and thus are treated like annuals.)

>> **California poppy:** *Eschscholzia californica.* The much-loved California wild-flower is easily grown from seed and reseeds readily. California poppies bloom mostly in shades of yellow and orange (sometimes white); hybridizers have been fooling with this species in recent years and now you can find bicolors and fluffier ones (more petals per flower). The plants reach 10 to 24 inches, 25.4 to 60.1 cm, high. Best in full sun.

>> **Chinese forget-me-not:** *Cynoglossum amabile.* Wispy clouds of tiny, deep blue, pink, or white flowers; a classic for shady landscapes. Chinese forget-me-nots grow 12 to 18 inches, 30.5 to 45.7 cm, high. The plants are easy to grow from seed and *reseed* (grow the next year from seeds spread by their flowers) readily. *Myosotis sylvatica*, the common forget-me-not, is similar and is equally good in shady landscapes.

>> **Geranium:** *Pelargonium* species. Old-time favorites that are often used as perennials in mild-winter climates. Geraniums have huge clusters of white, pink, red, purple, orange, or bi-colored flowers in spring and summer. The plants grow from 8 to 36 inches, 20.3 to 91.4 cm, high, and some have variegated leaves, which adds interest. Start with small plants and grow in full sun to light shade. In colder climates, you can overwinter them indoors where the plants won't freeze.

>> **Larkspur:** *Consolida ambigua.* Pretty, delicate spikes of spurred flowers in pastel shades of white, blue, pink, and purple. Larkspurs grow 1 to 4 feet, .3 to 1.2 m, high, depending on variety. The plants are easy to grow from seed and do best in light or partial shade.

» **Nasturtium:** *Tropaeolum majus.* Sprawling annual with neat round leaves and orange, yellow, pink, cream, or red flowers. Nasturtiums grow about 15 inches, 38.1 cm, high. There are varieties specifically meant for climbing that can grow up to 10 feet, 3 m, when given support from a trellis or fence. Cheerful, bright nasturtiums are easy to grow from seed; plant in full sun or light shade.

» **Pansy and viola:** *Viola* species. The adorable flowers often resemble colorful little faces. These annuals bloom in almost every single color and multicolor except green. Pansies have slightly larger (but fewer) blooms than violas. Both feature neat, compact plants that seldom grow more than 8 inches, 20.3 cm, tall. Pansies and violas can be grown from seed, but they're usually started from transplants. Plant in full sun or light shade.

» **Pot marigold:** *Calendula officinalis.* Easy-to-grow annuals with yellow or orange (or sometimes white) daisylike flowers. Pot marigold is a nice cut flower. The compact plants reach 12 to 30 inches, 30.5 to 76.2 cm, high. Plant in full sun from seed or use transplants.

» **Primrose:** *Primula* x *polyanthus.* Technically perennials in mild climates, but usually grown as annuals. These hybrid ones have brightly colored flower clusters atop straight stems that seldom reach more than 12 to 18 inches, 30.5 to 45.7 cm, high. Many colors are available to choose from, including mixes. Plant in full to partial shade and start with transplants.

» **Snapdragon:** *Antirrhinum majus.* Plants with wonderfully colorful spikes of white, yellow, orange, red, purple, and multihued flowers. The common name comes from the hinged blossom, which opens and shuts like tiny jaws when squeezed on the sides; it's fun to do if you have a child visiting your garden (or even if you don't). Varieties range from 1 to 3 feet, .3 to .9 m, high. Plant them in full sun from transplants (already-growing plants).

» **Stock:** *Matthiola incana.* One of the most deliciously fragrant annuals, with intense, spicy scents. Flower spikes reach 12 to 30 inches, 30.5 to 76.2 cm, high (depending on variety) in shades of white, pink, purple, and red. Stocks are best started from transplants. Grow in full sun.

» **Sweet alyssum:** *Lobularia maritima.* Ground-hugging annual (usually under 6 inches, 15.2 cm, high) that covers itself with tiny, bright white, purple, or pink blooms. Alyssum flowers best in cooler weather and is quite hardy, but it often blooms into summer, too. Alyssum is one of the finest edging and container plants. Easy to grow from seed and reseeds readily. Plant in full sun.

» **Sweet peas:** *Lathyrus odoratus.* Much-loved annual vining plant with intensely fragrant blooms. Sweet peas come in single colors and multicolors — almost every hue except true blue and green. Sweet peas make a wonderful cut flower. Most varieties need a fence or trellis for support (see Chapter 6 for more on fences and Chapter 10 for the scoop on trellises), but bushier, low-growing types, such as 'Little Sweetheart,' don't need supports. Plant in full sun from seed.

When it's hot, they're hot

Warm-season annuals (such as zinnias, marigolds, and petunias) prefer the hot months of summer. Planted after the last frost in spring, these plants grow quickly and bloom when the weather has heated up. Warm-season annuals usually continue to flower until the first frost in autumn, but because they bloom poorly in cool weather, we recommend pulling them out of the ground and discarding them before a frost does them in.

TIP

If you're vigilant, you can actually extend the lives of warm-season annuals — and the pleasure they bring — for a few more weeks beyond an early frost, assuming they're still blooming. If they're in the ground, cover them with sheets or light blankets for frosty nights, removing at daylight. If they're growing in pots, bring them into a warmer, sheltered spot for the night, such as a garage or sunporch, and put them back in their outdoor spot the next day.

Some overlap in bloom time between cool- and warm-season annuals exists, so if you orchestrate your plantings just right, you may never be without blooms.

>> **Bedding begonia:** *Begonia semperflorens.* Versatile annuals that are most useful in shady landscapes (although some types can take more sun). The flowers of bedding begonias come in shades of white, pink, and red. Red-flowering plants, which can take more sun, have bronzy-red leaves. Most varieties grow about 12 inches, 30.5 cm, high. Bedding begonias are best started from transplants (because the seeds are so tiny and hard to handle; leave this task to the professionals).

>> **Cleome:** *Cleome hassleriana.* Easy and fabulous! Because the stems are tall (3 to 5 feet, .9 to 1.5 m) and the flower clusters atop them are big (4 to 6 inches, 10.1 to 15.2 cm, across), they're a substantial addition to any flower display. The airy flowers have a spidery look, hence the other common name of spider flower. As the flowers wave in a summer breeze, they draw butterflies and hummingbirds to your yard. They often re-seed but don't tend to become rampant.

>> **Cosmos:** *Cosmos bipinnatus.* Bright green, airy plants with a brilliant bloom of white, pink, lavender, purple, or bi-colored daisylike flowers. Most types grow tall (upwards of 5 feet, 1.5 m, high), but dwarf varieties stay more compact. Easy to grow from seed or transplants, and the plants reseed. Plant in full sun.

>> **Flowering tobacco:** *Nicotiana alata.* Small, tubular, sweetly scented blooms in shades of white, pink, red, and purple. Flowering tobacco plants grow 1 to 4 feet, .3 to 1.2 m, high, depending on variety. Plant flowering tobacco in full sun or light shade. Can be grown from seed or from transplants.

>> **Impatiens:** *Impatiens walleriana.* The stars of the shady landscape and one of the most popular annual flowers. The 1- to 2-inch (2.5 to 5 cm)-wide blooms

come in bright shades of white, red, pink, and lavender. Bi-colored varieties of impatiens are also available. Plants have dark green or bi-colored leaves and grow 12 to 30 inches, 30.5 to 76.2 cm, high. Grow from transplants. (For sun-loving New Guinea impatiens, refer to the later entry in this list.)

» **Lantana:** *Lantana* species and cultivars. The flowerheads are wonderfully bright and colorful, often multihued, which is fun. The blooms keep coming for practically the entire summer, particularly if you groom the plant regularly. The fragrance doesn't appeal to everyone (it's a bit sharp), but butterflies and hummingbirds adore the flowers. Average soil, full sun. 2 to 4 feet, .6 to 1.2 m, wide, will sprawl several feet, a meter or so, in all directions if you don't trim it back.

» **Lobelia:** *Lobelia erinus.* Low-growing (and often spreading) plants covered in deep to light blue blooms. Few blues are as bright as those of lobelia, but white- and pink-flowering forms are also available. All lobelias reach about 4 to 6 inches, 10.1 to 15.2 cm, high. They can be grown from seed but are more easily started from transplants. Plant in full sun to light shade.

» **Madagascar periwinkle:** *Catharanthus roseus.* Also known as annual vinca, these cheery plants are workhorses in the summer landscape. Compact with deep green leaves, Madagascar periwinkles produce an abundance of white, pink, red, or lavender blooms that often have a pink or white spot in the center. They grow 12 to 20 inches, 30.5 to 50.8 cm, high and are best in full sun (but can take some shade). These plants can be grown from seed but are more easily grown from transplants.

» **Marigold:** *Tagetes* species. Marigolds are one of the most popular summer annuals with blooms in sunny shades of yellow, orange, and red. Many varieties are available. Blossoms can be big or small, as can the plants. Plant in full sun. Easy to grow from seed (sow directly in the ground in the spring after danger of frost is past) or transplants (plant after danger of frost is past). Because of the strong scent, marigolds are often added to gardens as a natural and pretty insect-pest repellent.

» **Million bells:** *Callibrachoa.* These heavy-flowering, easy-care plants are justly popular. The blooms look like mini petunias. The plants can tolerate periods of steamy weather and neglect but look best if their soil is kept evenly moist; they grow 6 to 8 inches, 15.2 to 20.3 cm, tall with a trailing habit, 1 to 2 feet, .3 to .6 m.

» **New Guinea impatiens:** *Impatiens hawkeri.* These are quite a different kettle of fish compared to the standard shade-garden impatiens. They actually thrive in full sun and have huge flowers in a plethora of colors; butterflies love them! They're easy and trouble-free, growing 12 to 18 inches, 30.5 to 45.7 cm, tall and about half as wide.

>> **Petunia:** *Petunia hybrida.* Much-loved annuals with single and double, usually trumpet-shaped flowers in a myriad of single and bi-colored shades. Petunias are compact plants that range from 10 to 24 inches, 25.4 to 60.1 cm, high. Start from transplants and plant in full sun.

>> **Sage:** *Salvia* species. Tall spikes of bright white, red, blue, or purple flowers atop compact, sun-loving plants. Some types are perennials in mild-winter climates. The plants range in height from 10 to 36 inches, 25.4 to 91.4 cm. Site in full sun and use transplants.

>> **Sunflower:** *Helianthus annuus.* Few annuals make a bold statement the way that sunflowers do. Most sunflowers reach 8 to 10 feet, 2.4 to 3 m, high and are topped with huge, sunny, yellow blooms. But sunflowers also come in small-flowered forms in shades of red, orange, and white. Some dwarf varieties, such as 'Sunspot,' stay under 2 feet, .6 m, tall. Plant from seed in full sun.

>> **Verbena:** *Verbena hybrida.* Brightly colored clusters of white, pink, red, purple, or blue flowers on low-growing, spreading plants. Verbenas grow 6 to 12 inches, 15.2 to 30.5 cm, high. Plant in full sun. Easiest to start from transplants.

>> **Zinnia:** *Zinnia elegans.* A cut-flower lover's dream. Zinnias come in a huge range of flower colors (except blue), flower shapes and sizes, and plant heights. Small types, such as 'Thumbelina,' stay under 12 inches, 30.5 cm, high. 'State Fair' grows up to 5 feet, 1.5 m, high and has long stems for cutting. Plant in full sun. Easy to grow from seed (sown directly into the soil after danger of frost is past) or transplants. They frequently reseed themselves, so you'll see zinnias again next year.

ANNUALS FOR FOLIAGE-ONLY USE

Use these tough and versatile leafy annuals to dress up your displays, or — why not? — feature them on their own, massed in ribbons or as a bedding groundcover for a slightly different and durable look:

• **Caladium:** *Caladium* varieties. Big, beautiful heart-shaped leaves with mixes of green, pink, red, and white. Warm-season (grows from a tuber; refer to the section, "Discovering some great bulbs," in the next chapter for our favorites). Hard to beat for bold splashes of color or low-maintenance beds. However, the leaves burn a bit in full sun, so they're best grown in partial shade. Keep them good-looking with evenly moist soil.

(continued)

(continued)

- **Coleus:** *Coleus hybridus*. Warm-season. Grown for its intensely colored foliage, which comes in a variety of color combinations and different leaf shapes — you can find some amazing, unusual choices these days. Coleus typically thrives in the shade, but some of the newer varieties perform splendidly in full sun and display blazing colors all summer long. Coleus is best planted from transplants. Pinch off the flowers to keep a plant compact.

- **Dusty miller:** *Centaurea cineraria*. Cool-season. One of the most valuable gray-foliaged plants for highlighting other colors. Dusty miller makes other plants look brighter. It's perennial in mild climates and produces yellow flowers in summer, starting when the plant is in its second season. The plants have finely cut leaves and a mounding habit, and they grow about 18 inches, 45.7 cm, high. Plant in full sun from transplants. *Senecio cineraria* is another gray-foliaged plant that is often sold as dusty miller. *Senecio cineraria* grows slightly taller (to about 2½ feet, .76 m, high).

- **Flowering cabbage or kale:** *Brassica* species. Cool-season. These vegetable relatives look very much alike. They're grown for their brightly colored, ruffled or frilly foliage arranged in a head. The beautiful foliage is usually green with purple, pink, or white markings. Plants grow 12 to 18 inches, 30.5 to 45.7 cm, high. Plant in full sun from seed or use transplants.

- **Sweet potato vine:** *Ipomoea batatus*. Warm-season. Wowza — the lush, chartreuse to lime-green leaves resemble Matisse cutouts. Fabulous massed together or combined with, say, hot pink or scarlet flowers . . . or any other bright, fun, wild color combination that may occur to you. Growth habit is rambling; just snip back if the stems get too long or there's too much of a good thing. For a different look, try the cultivar 'Blackie' with dark purple foliage.

Understanding Your Options When Buying and Planting Annuals

When planting annuals, you have three choices in what you start with:

>> **Seed outdoors:** Some annuals can be planted from seed that is sown directly where the plants are to grow and bloom.

>> **Seed indoors:** Other annuals can be started from seed indoors and transplanted to the landscape later.

>> **Transplants:** You can purchase *transplants* of varying sizes (from small plants in six-packs to larger ones in gallon cans) at nurseries and plant them in your landscape. If you're not interested in or ready to try your hand at raising annuals from seed, you can rely on someone else doing that for you.

Transplanted annuals at the nursery can give you instant color because they're already or almost in bloom. And if your landscape is full of young plants, some instant bloom really helps make things look better. You can wake up in the morning to a dull, immature green landscape and turn it into a riot of color before noon by simply visiting your nursery or garden center. Besides, with all the other things you may have to deal with when improving your landscape, you probably won't have time to spend six to eight weeks doting over germinating seeds.

TIP

At the nursery, do a quick quality check to make sure the plants look healthy. Check to see whether they've been watered lately (nursery neglect makes for weaker plants). Inspect to ensure they're well-rooted in their little pots or flats (if you can tip one over and it falls right out, the answer is no).

The following sections explain in easy steps how to transplant seedlings, how you can add some splash to your flowerbeds, as well as what you need to know if you're considering foodscaping, that is, adding some veggies or other edibles into your beds for color (and food).

Transplanting your annual seedlings

Before planting, make sure that you prepare the soil properly (see Chapter 17), and make sure that you match the requirements of the plant — sun or shade — with the conditions at the planting site.

To transplant annual seedlings, follow these steps:

1. **Use a hoe, spade, or trowel to make a small hole for each transplant and fit the pot to make sure it fits.**

   Just make sure you don't plant the pot or flat the plant comes in.

2. **Unpot the seedling by turning the pot upside down, cupping the seedling with your hand, as shown in Figure 13-1.**

   If you're planting from six packs (small plastic trays that contain six seedlings), use your thumb to press on the bottom of the individual cells to remove the seedling. Be sure to keep the roots and soil intact. If the seedling seems stuck, gently rap the edge of the pot or squeeze the sides of the pot gently on all sides to loosen the root system.

WARNING

   Don't yank a plant out by its stem, which can fatally damage a baby plant.

3. **Gently tease out matted roots (as shown in Figure 13-2) and check their condition.**

   For larger plants, you can gently cut the bottom of the rootball with a knife and *butterfly* (spread) the rootball apart.

FIGURE 13-1:
Gently turn the pot upside down to remove the seedling.

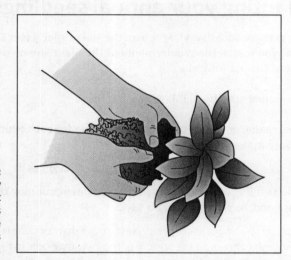

FIGURE 13-2:
Breaking a few roots won't hurt the plant, as long as the mass of roots remains intact.

TIP

If the roots are wound around the outside of the pot, work them loose with your fingers so they can grow out into the soil. Unwind larger roots and break smaller ones until their ends are all pointing outwards.

4. **Fill each planting hole with water.**

   You may also want to add a diluted liquid fertilizer to help your plants get off to a fast start.

5. **Put each prepared seedling in the hole that you made.**

Set the seedling in the hole so the top of the rootball is at the same level it was in the pot (refer to Figure 13-3).

6. **With your hands, firm the soil around the roots, as shown in Figure 13-4.**

Try to make a small basin sloping toward the plant to hold water.

After planting, water thoroughly. Keep the bed moist until the seedlings are established and begin to grow strongly. In extremely hot, dry weather, provide temporary shade for the transplants with paper tents (made like party hats) or wood shingles pushed into the ground on the south or west side of the plant.

FIGURE 13-3:
Set the seedling so that the top of the rootball is level with the surrounding soil.

© John Wiley & Sons, Inc.

FIGURE 13-4:
Firm the soil around the plant just enough so it can remain upright.

© John Wiley & Sons, Inc.

TIP

Many plants that bloom easily from seed can reseed themselves and come back year after year on their own. Most annual wildflowers reproduce themselves this way. Leave annuals such as alyssum, calendula, cosmos, forget-me-nots, marigolds, pansies and violas, sunflowers, spider flower, vinca, and zinnias to go to seed for a landscape full of "freebies" next season.

Creating splashy flowerbeds

Working with a variety of annuals to create colorful displays is a lot of fun. Here are some best practices for bringing some zing to your flowerbeds:

>> **Plant plenty.** The diversity among flowering annuals makes them very useful in the landscape. For the brightest blast of color, we like to plant annuals in large groups. Low-growing types usually work best for this type of planting, and you can go with just one color or mix a number of colors. But the important thing is to plant many annuals and plant them close together (usually 6 to 12 inches, 15.2 to 30.5 cm, apart). Space the transplants evenly in staggered rows (like the groundcovers discussed in Chapter 16) — the plants will grow quickly and fill in the spaces to give you a solid bed of bright color.

>> **Placement counts.** If you prefer a less-regimented look, try mixing many different types of annuals together in one bed. Try to keep the lower-growing plants in front and the taller ones in back, but really, no hard rules about plant placement exist. We also like to keep to a particular color scheme, such as mixing only complementary colors, but you can go with whatever color scheme you like.

Low-growing annuals, such as alyssum and lobelia, are useful as edgings. You can plant these low-growers along walkways or in front of other annuals, in front of perennials, or even in front of flowering shrubs, such as roses.

TIP

The best way to use annuals is to put them wherever you have room. Just one or two plants can turn a blank spot into a colorful focal point. Simply scattering some seed in open areas, where newly planted groundcovers have yet to fill in, for example, can result in a colorful carpet that changes with the seasons.

>> **Grow up.** Some annuals have unique habits that call for special treatment, but these plants also present special opportunities. Most sweet peas and morning glories need some kind of a support, such as a trellis. (See Chapter 10 for information about trellises.) Place the trellis right by a window so you can enjoy them (and in the case of sweet peas, let their sweet fragrance waft in). Tall sunflowers are spectacular focal points for any spot where you have room for them, but they also make a beautiful tall wall around a vegetable garden or along a back fence.

>> **Make them last.** For the longest season of color, pick off faded blossoms to encourage new bloom, referred to as *deadheading* (see the nearby sidebar). When the plants look like they're flagging, you have our permission to pull them out (toss them on the compost pile) and put in something else!

Foodscaping: Vegetables are the new annuals

Many of the crops that home gardeners like you enjoy growing and harvesting are annuals, right? You plant them in spring or summer, and they finish up sometime in fall. If you don't have a vegetable patch, or even if you do, consider breaking the rules and giving a few plants spots in other places in your yard. Invite them into your flowerbeds, create larger plantings, and even use them as edging plants.

DEADHEADING AND SELF-CLEANING TO GIVE YOUR PLANTS NEW LIFE

Deadheading simply means removing spent flowers, which inspires the plant to pump out fresh new ones. The normal cycle of an annual is to flower and go to seed and finish its short but glorious life cycle. But when you deadhead, the flower doesn't expend its energy on making seeds and instead returns to making more flowers. Geraniums are a classic example.

Self-cleaning annuals are those that, basically, self-deadhead. They drop their spent flowers and keep on blooming. You may have to tidy up under or around such plants, or you may not even notice as the blossoms naturally break down and contribute a little organic matter to the soil. Most of the petunias, million bells, and marigolds on the market today are like this.

Additionally, some annuals are bred to be sterile. That just means that they drop their flowers and produce more in a continual effort to produce seed, which they never do. An example is some of the newer alyssum varieties (the Princess and Knight series). You get to enjoy a longer period of bloom.

In case you're wondering, all this also applies to perennial flowers. That is, they too can be persuaded to bloom longer if spent blooms are removed, or may go ahead and bloom longer as fading flowers fall and new ones come along. Read more about perennials in Chapter 14.

TIP

For easy maintenance, when you combine food crops with traditional annuals (or other ornamental plants), pair plants with similar requirements.

Here are a few other ideas if you're interested in adding some vegetables to your landscape plan:

>> **Leafy crops:** Rainbow chard has beautiful red, orange, and/or yellow stems. Interplant it with annuals in those colors. Cabbage and kale come in colorful hues, often nice shades of purple. Lettuces come in different colors and leaf shapes, and mixes; here again, you can tuck some in and among your flowers. Harvesting the leaves for a meal doesn't automatically ruin your display; if you leave the roots, these plants may generate another show and another harvest.

>> **Flowering crops:** On their way to producing an edible crop for you, certain types have attractive flowers that can enhance your garden displays. Artichokes and cardoons are big plants with dramatic flowers. Members of the onion family, such as leeks, garlic, chives, and scallions, sport interesting and good-looking blooms.

>> **Fruiting:** You're probably aware that tomatoes, peppers, and eggplants can generate beautiful fruits, including some different sizes, colors, and shapes. They need space to grow well, but putting them way at the back of a flower-bed may mean you won't see the fruit as easily (both for their developing beauty but also so you remember to harvest). Experiment. You may be pleasantly surprised — and so will garden visitors.

>> **Annual grain crops:** Many grains grow quickly to become comparable in size and appearance to ornamental grasses, which the gardening world embraced some time ago. Some are beautiful: barley, oats, buckwheat, millet, even rice. Planting just a few plants introduces you to these, in case you have a baker or brewer in the family. Additionally, pollinators may appreciate their presence.

REMEMBER

Foodscaping tends to involve fewer plants and therefore a smaller harvest. Still, it can be quite rewarding. Also, pests and diseases that trouble larger grouped plantings in a kitchen garden may be thwarted because the culprits either won't discover or won't build up in a mixed planting.

Chapter **14**

Striving For Long-Lasting Beauty with Perennials and Bulbs

The commonly heard joke amongst gardeners is that a perennial is a plant that, had it lived, would have bloomed again next year. That's not too funny if you've tried and struggled with perennials or feel daunted by them. No worries, though, because this section brings you right up to speed and points you toward success with perennials.

Perennial plants, grown for their flowers, their foliage, or both, are around like the seasons — they return with their beauty, year after year. Compared with annuals (which have to be replanted every year; see Chapter 13), *perennials* are meant to be left in place to grow, get bigger, look better, and bloom more, season after season.

Perennials are a diverse group and include some of the best-loved flowering plants, such as daisies, coneflowers, and daylilies. Spectacular foliage plants, such as hostas, heucheras, and lamb's ears, are also perennials.

TIP

Perennials can be planted in containers (see Chapter 15) or worked in among trees and shrubs for seasonal color. Many perennials also make excellent groundcovers (refer to Chapter 16).

However, some plants that are technically perennials, including some bulbs, are usually grown as annuals. And some annuals, perennials, and bulbs aren't grown for their flowers, but for their foliage texture or color. But don't fret about all this — we clear everything up here.

Creating a Perennial Border

The classic use of perennials is to combine many of them in a large planting bed, known as a *perennial border.* A well-designed perennial border has something in bloom throughout the growing season. It not only has a well-thought-out color scheme, but it also relies on plant texture for visual interest. Designing a beautiful planting can take years of trial and error as well as experience, but even beginning landscapers can create a workable, pleasing border, adding to it over the years as their knowledge increases.

A perennial border is constantly evolving, which is part of the joy of creating it. If certain plants don't work, you replace them with something else. If the border has some downtime when nothing is in bloom, simply tuck in some flowering annuals to fill in the gap, or include some long-flowering shrubs, such as floribunda roses.

Many landscaping books give specific plans for perennial borders and some nurseries even sell plants or seeds that fit predesigned borders. Although the use of these plans and designs may be a good way to start a perennial border, blooming times and growing conditions vary so much from place to place that you may end up making changes. In any case, you'll want to make changes because designing your own, unique landscape is such fun.

TIP

We can't emphasize this enough: prepare the soil first. You won't be remaking this bed every year. Dig deep, add organic material and, most important, eliminate weeds. This effort invested on the front end of the project makes a huge difference and prevents all sorts of heartaches! (For more detailed advice, read the soils section in Chapter 17.)

Even though individual experience is the best teacher, here are some things that we find useful in designing a perennial border:

>> **Start with a plan and keep records.** Sketch out your design on paper, making sure to give plants the room that they need to grow. Work with a simple color scheme, such as three of your favorite colors, and plant only

things that bloom in those hues. (For tips on garden color and beautiful combinations, check Chapter 2.)

>> **Aim for a succession of bloom.** Think seasonally, aiming to have something always in bloom. Keep records of blooming times so that you know where there are gaps to be filled the next planting season. And don't forget winter. Even in cold climates, you can use shrubs that have colorful berries or attractive twigs or bark.

>> **Plant in groups.** One plant, alone, gets lost in the masses. We find that grouping plants in odd numbers — threes, fives, and sevens — looks the most natural.

>> **Vary!** Plants of varying heights next to each other allow each to stand out. Intersperse mounding and sprawling forms. That old saying is right: Variety is the spice!

>> **Don't forget the foliage.** Use plants with dramatic foliage to set off the flowers. Ornamental grasses, irises, even bold-textured shrubs make excellent focal points.

>> **Repeat colors or have a color theme.** There's such a wide palette of perennials, blooming at different times, that mastering an ongoing color show that pleases the eye is a learning curve. Don't be afraid to take plants out and move plants around. If you like yellow, put in different types of yellow bloomers; if you like pastels, experiment with different combinations — and so on, you get the idea. You can always refine and change your mind.

>> **Make use of grays and whites.** Gray foliaged plants (such as lamb's ears or artemisia) and plants with white flowers highlight other colors and tie everything together. (These plants also reflect light and look great on those summer nights when the moon is bright.)

TIP

>> **Consider the background.** A dark green background enriches the color of most flowers. If it's a fence, shed, garage, or wall, consider can you painting it dark green (or even dark brown or dark gray). Alternatively, site your perennial border in front of an existing hedge or install one first (of flowering shrubs or evergreens — if you need ideas and planting instructions, consult Chapter 12).

Listing Perennials by Season

Here are our favorite high-performance perennials, arranged alphabetically according to the common name first, followed by the botanical name for full clarity (nurseries and plant catalogs may use either or both names).

Spring bloomers

When spring returns and the garden comes back to life, it's so heartening. In addition to these perennials, you may be growing spring-blooming bulbs for bright color now (we discuss bulbs in the section, "Packing Beauty into Bulbs," later in this chapter.)

» **Basket-of-gold:** *Aurinia saxatilis.* Brilliant gold blooms cover the gray foliage in spring. Basket-of-gold grows about 12 to 15 inches (30.5 to 38.1 cm) high and spreads. The plant also withstands drought. Plant in full sun. Use in the foreground. Hardy to Zone 3.

» **Candytuft:** *Iberis sempervirens.* Why plant the same old white alyssum as an edging or in a rock garden when you can get bigger, brighter white flowers on a perennial plant? Candytuft forms tidy mounds or mats of thin, glossy leaves that look good before, during, and after blooming. The 1- to 2-inch (2.5 to 5 cm) lacy flower clusters are terrific. Full sun, well-drained soil; hardy in Zones 3 to 9.

» **Creeping phlox:** *Phlox stolonifera.* Spreading and mat-forming, this stalwart is a springtime classic in cooler climates where it thrives and keeps spring bulbs company. It does fine in sun or partial shade alike, but prefers moist ground. Flowers are white, pink, magenta, or purple. Grows 6 to 12 inches (15.2 to 30.5 cm) tall. Hardy in Zones 5 to 9.

» **Hellebores:** *Helleborus* species and hybrids. These beauties are among the first signs of spring. The nodding flowers are slightly cup-shaped and come in gorgeous shades of cream, pink, rose, lavender, or purple, often speckled or blushed with a darker hue. Named cultivars are harder to come by, but you may try some seed-grown ones and see what comes up. Most are about 1 to 3 feet (.3 to .9 m) tall and wide. Pamper them with cool, moist, slightly alkaline soil. Hardy in Zones 4 to 8.

» **Peony:** *Paeonia* cultivars. Truly tough and easy to grow, these plants make you look like a pro. Plush, hauntingly fragrant flowers in many hues with some nifty variations in flower forms. Plant breeders have made significant improvements to stem strength, so that the big flowers no longer need to hang their heads in spring rains. They do need moist, enriched, well-drained soil. Larger plants, they can reach 3 to 4 feet tall and wide (.9 to 1.2 m). Hardy in Zones 3 to 7.

» **Woodland phlox:** *Phlox divaricata.* Showy, fragrant purple or rosy flowers adorn this native, drought-tolerate beauty in mid-spring. Hummingbirds and butterflies may stop by. Grows approximately 12 inches (30.5 cm) high and wide. Does well in shade and organically rich soil. Hardy from Zones 3 to 8.

Summer stars

Summer is generally prime time for perennial gardens, with some plants peaking in early summer, and others at their best in mid– or late summer. Bloom times and duration vary depending on where you live and somewhat on your selections. As you become a more confident and accomplished gardener, you'll be tweaking your displays or adding new items. Here are some of our summer favorites:

» **Bellflower:** *Campanula species.* Much-loved family of mostly summer-blooming perennials with bell-shaped flowers in shades of blue, purple, or white. There are many species, varying from low-growing spreading plants to taller types, some of which can reach 6 feet (1.8 m) high. Flower size and shape also vary.

Our favorite bellflowers include the following:

- **Serbian bellflower:** *C. poscharskyana.* A low, mounding plant, 4 to 8 inches (10.1 to 20.3 cm) high, with blue flowers.

- **Peach-leaf bellflower:** *C. persicifolia.* Can reach up to 3 feet (.9 m) high and has blue or white blooms.

Bellflowers grow best in light shade but can take sun in cool-summer climates. Hardy to Zone 3.

» **Black-eyed Susan:** *Rudbeckia* cultivars, hybrids. Free-blooming, easy to grow. These plants have large yellow, orange, maroon, or mahogany daisylike flowers with dark, domelike centers. These plants bloom from summer to autumn. The plants grow 2 to 4 feet (.6 to 1.2 m) high. Plant in full sun. Hardy to Zone 4.

» **Blanketflower:** *Gaillardia grandiflora.* These sunny-colored, daisylike flowers are a combination of red and yellow or are straight red or yellow. Blooms heavily in summer and grows 2 to 3 feet (.6 to .9 m) high. Plant in full sun. Hardy to Zone 2.

» **Catmint:** *Nepeta* species and cultivars. Perky, light-purple flower spires abound on neat gray-green foliage; bees and other pollinators love them. The plant habit is mounding or bushy and size varies by cultivar. Reaches from 1 to 2 feet (.3 to .6 m) high and wide. Best in full sun. Hardy in Zones 4 to 9.

» **Columbine:** *Aquilegia* species. Widely adapted perennials with fernlike foliage and beautiful, spurred flowers (named varieties and mixes often have bigger flowers). Columbine blooms in late spring and early summer in many single colors and multicolors. The plants range in height from about 18 inches (45.7 cm) to 3 feet (.9 m). Easy to grow from seed and will reseed. Plant in full sun to light shade. Hardy to Zone 3.

» **Coneflower:** *Echinacea purpurea.* Tall, purple, rosy, or white, daisylike flowers top this fine, long-lasting perennial. New cultivars extend the color range and vary the look of the flower (fluffy forms and more). Typically reaches 3 to 5 feet (.9 to 1.5 m) high and blooms in summer. Plant in full sun. Hardy to Zone 3.

>> **Coreopsis:** *Coreopsis* species. Easy-to-grow plants known for their sunny yellow, daisylike flowers borne from spring through summer. *C. grandiflora* is one of the most common. This variety grows about 3 feet (.9 m) high and has single or double flowers. Plant in full sun. Hardy to Zone 5.

>> **Daylily:** *Hemerocallis species.* Daylilies are a dependable group of summer-flowering perennials with stalks of large, trumpet-shaped flowers in single and bi-colored shades of yellow, orange, pink, red, and violet. Some daylilies are fragrant. They have grassy foliage that reaches 1 to 2 feet (.3 to .6 m) high. Plant in full sun. Hardy to Zone 3.

>> **Dianthus:** *Dianthus species.* Lovely family of usually fragrant, spring- and summer-flowering plants that includes carnations, *D. caryophyllus*. Favorites include Sweet William, *D. barbatus*, which grows 6 to 18 inches (15.2 to 45.7 cm) high and has tight clusters of white, pink, red, purple, and bicolored flowers), and cottage pinks, hybrids that have very fragrant, frilly, rose, pink, white, or bicolored flowers on stems reaching about 18 inches (45.7 cm) high above a tight mat of foliage. Plant in full sun or light shade (in hot-summer areas). Hardy to Zone 3.

>> **Gaura:** *Gaura lindheimeri.* Slender wands arise with willowy foliage, topped with delicate-looking, pretty flowers in white or pink. Once established, the plant is a champ in hot, dry summers. It remains in bloom a long time. 'Crimson Butterflies' has reddish leaves and stems and hot pink flowers. Full sun, Zones 6 to 9.

>> **Hosta:** *Hosta* species. Useful foliage plants that make a nice contrast to other shade-loving flowers. Hosta leaves are usually heart-shaped and are often crinkled or variegated. Flower spikes appear in summer. Plants and leaves range from quite small to huge. One favorite is the blue-leaf plantain lily, *H. sieboldiana,* which has large (10 to 15 inches, 25.4 to 38.1 cm), crinkled, blue-green foliage and pale purple flowers; it grows 3 feet (.9 m) high. Hardy to Zone 3. Note that some of the newer varieties can be grown in sunnier spots.

>> **Lamb's ears:** *Stachys byzantina.* A lovely foliage plant with soft, fuzzy, silver-gray leaves. It grows 6 to 12 inches (15.2 to 30.5 cm) high and has purplish-white flowers in summer. Lamb's ears is a fabulous edging plant for flowering perennials. Plant in full sun. Hardy to Zone 4.

>> **Penstemon:** *Penstemon gloxinioides.* Mounding plants that grow 2 to 4 feet (.6 to 1.2 m) high. Garden penstemon features spikes of tubular flowers in many single and bicolored shades of white, pink, red, and purple. Plant in full sun; starts blooming in early summer and goes for weeks and weeks. Hardy to Zone 8. Check nursery catalogs for other species that are hardier.

>> **Phlox:** *Phlox paniculata.* Large clusters of small white, pink, red, salmon, and purple flowers bloom in mid- to late summer. The plants grow 2 to 4 feet (.6 to 1.2 m) high. Plant in full sun. Hardy to Zone 3.

- » **Russian sage:** *Perovskia atriplicifolia,* or its new name *Salvia yangii.* A well-grown plant is a breathtaking sight. It has a shrublike form, with long stems of aromatic leaves spray upward and outward in all directions from the central crown, each stem laden with lovely small flowers. The leaves are gray-green, and the flowers are lilac-purple — the contrast is beautiful. No pests or diseases to speak of. Usually 3 to 4 feet (.9 to 1.2 m) tall and wide. Best in full sun, well-drained ground. Zones 4 to 9.

- » **Salvia:** *Salvia* species. So many excellent perennial salvias are available that we could write a book about them alone. Most are best adapted to dry-summer areas with mild winters. Many are shrublike; others are perennials that are usually grown as annuals. Still others are valuable herbs.

  Favorite flowering types include the following:

  - **Hybrid sage:** *S.* × *superba,* with violet-blue summer flowers reaching 2 to 3 feet (.6 to .9 m) high.

  - **Pitcher sage:** *S. azurea* var. *grandiflora,* with 4- to 5-foot (1.2 to 1.5 m) high, rich royal-blue flowers in late summer.

  Plant in full sun. Hardy to Zone 6.

- » **Spike speedwell:** *Veronica spicata.* This is a super plant for dependable color. Dense, beautiful flower spikes start in early summer and continue for many weeks, longer if you take the time to *deadhead* (remove faded flowers). Usually a fine shade of blue; the plants are about 1 to 2 feet (.3 to .6 m) high and wide. Full sun, Zones 4 to 9.

- » **Yarrow:** *Achillea* species. A useful group of easy-care, summer-blooming perennials with ferny gray foliage and tight, upright clusters of yellow, red, or white blooms. Yarrows range in height from low-growing groundcovers to tall plants (up to 5 feet, 1.5 m, high). One favorite is *A. filipendulina* 'Moonshine' with bright yellow flower clusters atop 2-foot (.6 m) stems. Plant in full sun. Where summer rain is common, some types can become invasive and weedy. Most are hardy to Zone 3.

Autumn stalwarts

A lot of wonderful, colorful perennials are at their best later in the gardening year, and you'll be thrilled if you add them to your landscape to extend the show for more weeks. Here are our top choices:

- » **Asters:** *Aster* species. Colorful, late-blooming perennials with daisylike flowers, mostly in shades of blue, purple, red, pink, and white with yellow centers. Asters usually bloom in late summer to autumn. Some begin flowering in early summer or late spring. *A. frikartii* produces blue flowers almost year-round in mild-winter climates. Asters grow about 2 feet (.6 m) high. Plant in full sun and divide every two years. Hardy to Zone 4.

» **Boltonia:** *Boltonia asteroides.* Covered with countless white daisies late every summer and fall, this is an outstanding choice for a sunny late-season display. The white flowers seem to glow in the evening hours. The plant can get fairly big and floppy, though, so it needs careful placement (to give it enough room) and perhaps staking as well. Moist, organically rich soil is best. Zones 4 to 9.

» **Fall mum:** *Chrysanthemum* and *Dendranthema* hybrids. A very diverse, useful group of perennials, often used for temporary color and discarded (actually treated like annuals). There are so many types! You're probably familiar with the decorative or florist ones, but you may have fun making plantings of others: pom-pom or button; single and semi-double; spoon; quill; anemone; spider; and more. Although mum plants vary in height, flower color, bloom season, and hardiness, one exists for almost every landscape and situation. Most grow best in full sun. Zones 5 to 9.

» **Goldenrod:** *Solidago* cultivars. When horticulturists took a closer look at this native wildflower, they found plenty to admire and work with a clump-forming, non-invasive growth habit, no pest problems, good cold-hardiness, and the ability to tolerate average to dry soil and still look great. Depending on your choice, plants can be 2 to 6 feet (.6 to 1.8 m) tall and 2 to 4 feet (.6 to 1.2 m) wide. Fine for Zones 3 to 9.

» **Japanese anemone:** *Anemone × hybrida.* Most of the summer, the plant is a medium-size mound of good-looking green foliage (3 to 5 feet, .9 to 1.5 m, tall and 2 to 3 feet, .6 to .9 m, wide), but by August slender stalks arise, topped with appealing, daisylike flowers in pink or white. The plant is sometimes called "windflower," which refers to the way these enchanting blooms toss in a breeze. Zones 5 to 7.

» **Sedum:** *Sedum* or *Hylotelephium* 'Autumn Joy' and many others. These are fall classics, tough and beautiful. Flower clusters segue from green to shades of pink, red, and purple. For extra impact, look for cultivars that have contrasting colorful fall foliage. For example, 'Matrona' has pink-rimmed gray leaves and soft pink flowers. Generally these are 1 to 2 feet (.3 to .6 m) tall and wide, and hardy in Zones 4 to 9.

The best long-bloomers

Your mileage may vary, but the following perennial plants generally give weeks and even months of summer color. We discuss these perennials in more detail in the section, "Listing perennials by season," earlier in this chapter:

>> Black-eyed Susan

>> Catmint

>> Coneflower

>> Daylily

>> Gaura

>> Phlox

>> Salvia

Growing native perennials

Native perennials are already well-adapted to your growing conditions and pre-disposed to perform long and well. They'll also shore up the food web in your area, including but not limited to butterflies, bees, a range of pollinators, and birds.

TIP

To find ones suitable in your particular area, visit your nearest botanical garden or shop at a local nursery that sells natives. Never dig up and try to transplant flowers from wild areas; doing so not only depletes an existing habitat, but it also isn't guaranteed to succeed (for reasons of soil biology).

Cultivars or selections of native plants, by the way, are okay. Indeed, they're meant to be more suitable for a garden landscape. Here are some examples:

>> **A sundrop:** *Oenothera fruticosa* 'Fireworks' produces way more flowers, and brighter, longer-lasting flowers, than the original wildflower, and, the plant is not invasive.

>> **A hybrid goldenrod:** *Solidago* 'Golden Baby,' at 2 feet tall and 1 foot wide (.6 m tall to .3 m wide), is significantly smaller and more compact than the wild version, and has more and fuller flower spires.

Discovering ornamental grasses

The term *ornamental grasses* designates a large group of wonderful plants grown for their grassy foliage and feathery, plumelike flowers. Ornamental grasses make stunning focal points among other blooming plants. The dried flowers often look good well into winter.

Here are some favorites:

>> **Purple fountain grass:** *Pennisetum setaceum* 'Rubrum' with purplish-red leaves and plumes that reach over 6 feet (1.8 m) high.

>> **Eulalia grass:** *Miscanthus sinensis* 'Zebrinus' variegated and huge (often more than 8 feet, 2.4 m) with yellow-striped leaves and broomlike plumes.

>> **Blue oat grass:** *Helictotrichon sempervirens,* with gray-blue foliage 2 to 3 feet (.6 to .9 m) high. Growing conditions and hardiness vary.

WARNING

Some ornamental grasses get quite large, outgrowing their allotted space, and can become invasive. To avoid that problem, either plant them in large containers or cut them back to a size you consider acceptable if they get too enthusiastic, once or twice during the growing season.

Shopping For Perennials

You have two main options when shopping for perennials. They are as follows:

>> **Buy them locally.** Sometimes you can meander around the aisles with little pressure and have your choice with what you want.

 Sometimes shopping locally is a little more harried when you join the mobs at the garden center on the first warm Saturday in spring. In that case, you probably won't get every plant you want. Just be prepared to accept substitutes for the exact perennials you had in mind.

>> **Order through a mail-order supplier.** Many mail-order suppliers ship a wide selection of plants bare-root or in rooted in small pots, to keep shipping costs down, with top-growth trimmed off for the journey.

No matter where you buy them, perennial plants are usually sold in six–packs, 4–inch (10.1 cm) pots, or 1–gallon pots.

Here we look at these three methods in greater detail, and then we explain what you need to do to ensure you buy high–quality plants.

Buying locally

Here are some tips to remember when purchasing plants locally, no matter if you're shopping alone on a Monday morning or on a busy Saturday:

>> **Draw up a shopping list or wish list beforehand.** That way you don't get overwhelmed by the choices or the jostling crowds.

>> **Examine each plant carefully.** Check to see if it's well-rooted by turning it over or sideways and thumping the pot lightly. Neither the plant nor the soil mix should fall out, and you may see a few roots peeking out of the bottom drainage holes.

>> **Make sure it's pest-free.** Look on leaf undersides and in the *nodes* (where stalks meet the stem) for small bugs, sticky residue, or webs.

>> **Check that it's disease-free.** You want little or no spotted, curled, or yellowed leaves or deformed buds.

>> **Don't be seduced by a blooming plant!** The petals may drop off on the car ride home or after a few days in their new home. Better to buy a plant that's full of unopened buds, or at least one that's showing signs of fresh new green growth.

Purchasing through a mail-order supplier

Remember these characteristics about buying plants from mail-order suppliers:

>> **They have a great selection.** Shopping by mail allows you to get exactly the plants you want. Mail-order suppliers are specialists and would rather not compete directly with your local garden center, so they instead offer you unique and special plants, the latest-greatest varieties, and/or a really wide selection.

>> **Buying is low risk.** Mail-order suppliers monitor weather conditions and shipping routes and will send you your purchases at the right time for planting in your area. Often they ship early in the week, correctly assuming that you'll get the plants in the ground on the upcoming weekend. Mail-order companies have got shipping plants down to a science. If they didn't, they'd quickly go out of business.

TIP

Do read the fine print in the supplier's catalog or on the website, both to find out exactly what form the plants are in (potted or bareroot), to find out if the supplier substitutes, and to check their guarantee, returns, and refund policies.

TIP

Before placing an order with a mail-order nursery, we suggest you read online reviews by other gardeners on the Dave's Garden website, under the "Garden Watchdog" heading. https://davesgarden.com/products/gwd/.

When your shipment arrives, unpack it immediately and follow the information tucked inside. Typically they advise you to put the roots in lukewarm water to rehydrate. If your planting plans are delayed, you may store bareroot plants in your fridge for a week or so.

Bareroot plants look like dead little twigs — a bit of roots and minimal topgrowth,. They're dormant and thus can be shipped without a pot. Handle them gently, especially the all-important root systems. They're most likely one- or two-year old plants and, once planted, will take off like gangbusters in your garden.

Planting and Pampering Your Perennials

Take the time to get your plants into the ground correctly and to get them off to a good start; these grateful perennials will repay your care. See Chapter 15 for information on planting from pots, Chapter 13 for planting from six-packs, and Chapter 12 for how to plant bare-root. Before planting, be sure to prepare the soil site, as we describe in Chapter 17.

Container-grown perennials can be planted any time that you can work the ground. However, the best time to plant such perennials is in autumn or early spring because the plants have time to get established before stressful (hot or cold) weather arrives.

You can always do a bit more to keep them happy and looking their best. Many perennials benefit from being cut back at various times during their growth cycles. Remember the following as you pinch, cut, trim, and pamper your plants:

>> **To stimulate branching on lower stems and make the plant bushier, trim or pinch off the top of the plant.** Yes, even if it has leaf or flower buds, do it. This literally thwarts upward growth and redirects the plant's energy to the remaining parts.

>> **To get a longer bloom cycle, deadhead.** *Deadheading* is the process of pinching or cutting off faded flowers while the plant is in bloom. Deadheading forces the plant to spend its energy on developing more flowers instead of setting seed.

>> **To get plants to rebloom, cut after the initial bloom cycle.** Some perennials, such as coreopsis and gaillardia, rebloom if cut back by about one-third after the initial bloom cycle.

>> **To prevent falling over, stake plants.** Taller perennials, such as delphiniums, and bushy types, such as peonies, may need to be staked to prevent the flowers from flopping.

>> **To rejuvenate older plants, divide them.** If older plants become overcrowded or bloom poorly, they can be rejuvenated by *dividing*.

Packing Beauty into Bulbs

For many people, especially people who have never had much luck growing plants, bulbs are a dream come true. Think of bulbs as flowering powerhouses: plants that have packed most of what they need for a season's worth of growth into some type of below–ground storage device — the bulb. Plant a bulb at the right time of year and at the proper depth, and you're almost guaranteed a spectacular bloom. It's not really an exaggeration to call them boisterous — you'll see!

When you think of bulbs, you probably think of daffodil or tulip bulbs — brownish things that look something like an onion — which are indeed bulbs. But the term *bulb* as used in landscaping refers to a great number of different plant bulbs. Besides the true bulbs, such as tulip bulbs, there are corms, rhizomes, tubers, and tuberous roots, and each one of these looks somewhat different from the others. But they're all underground stems surrounded by modified fleshy leaves, swollen underground stem bases, thickened and branching storage stems, or swollen roots.

All you really need to know is which bulbs to plant, where and how deeply to plant them, and — most important of all — which end is up!

You can separate bulbs into two groups:

>> **Naturalizers:** This group, which includes daffodils, some tulips (mostly the small growing ones commonly referred to as *species tulips*), crocuses, snowdrops, and grape hyacinths, are left in the ground, year after year. Over time, their numbers tend to increase, and the show gets better and better. Some, notably tulips, need more cold than others. In climates where the ground freezes, the bulbs bloom on. If the ground rarely freezes, which is the case in many mild-winter climates — Zones 9 to 11 (see Chapter 19 for information about zones) — the blooms get smaller each year and eventually stop coming altogether.

>> **Annual bulbs:** This second group of bulb-like plants (which includes begonias and dahlias that technically arise from enlarged roots called *tubers)* has to be replanted every year. They may need to be replanted for many reasons: some may not be cold-tolerant enough to survive over winter in your climate, whereas others may rot in wet soils. Still other ones may not get enough chilling to rebloom year after year.

   Although some of these have to be replanted every year, you don't have to buy new ones every year. After they finish blooming, you can dig them up, store them for the winter months in a cool (non-freezing), dry spot such as your garage or a sunporch, and replant them at the appropriate time to bloom again next season. Dahlias and glads, which grow from bulblike structures called *corms,* for example, work out beautifully with this regimen.

   If, however, you garden in a milder climate (Zones 7 and higher; see Chapter 19 for a full explanation of zones), it may be possible to get these more tender types through the cooler winter months. Simply cut them down to stubs and mulch heavily (4 to 6 inches, 10.1 to 15.2 cm) after the first autumn frost; remove the mulch the following spring after the ground warms up and they should revive.

Discovering Some Great Bulbs

Here are our favorite kinds of bulbs (and similar corms, tubers, and rhizomes), arranged alphabetically according to common name. We also include the botanical names because you may need them for some of the specialty catalogs/websites:

>> **Caladium:** *Caladium hortulanum.* Brightly colored foliage plant, mostly for shady situations (some do well in sun; ask at your source if this interests you). Caladiums feature large leaves, which are tropical-looking and painted with shades of green, white, pink, and red. The plants grow from 1 to 2 feet (.3 to .6 m) high and are great in containers. Hardy only in Zone 10 but can be dug up and stored or grown as an annual in any zone.

>> **Calla lily:** *Zantedeschia* species. Spectacular, tropical-looking plants with large, usually white, cup-shaped summer flowers and bright green, arrow-shaped leaves. Yellow, pink, and red shades are also available. Calla lily plants generally grow from 2 to 3 feet (.6 to .9 m) high, but dwarf forms are also available. Best grown in light shade, but can take sun in cool climates. They do need regular watering and are hardy to Zone 8.

>> **Canna:** *Canna* species. Upright, summer-blooming plant with showy flowers in shades of yellow, orange, salmon, pink, and red. Some have bicolored flowers. For many gardeners, though, the main attraction is their large, beautiful, tropical-looking leaves (in plain green, or colorful). Some cannas grow more than 5 feet (1.5 m) high, but many are lower-growing. Plant in full sun. South of Zone 7, cannas can be naturalized with little care. Elsewhere, dig and store them over winter.

>> **Daffodil:** *Narcissus* species. Carefree bloomers that flower spring after spring, even in mild climates. If you plant only one type of bulb, this should be it. Narcissus plants generally bear clusters of small, often fragrant, flowers. Daffodils have larger blooms. You can choose from many daffodil and narcissus varieties (mostly in white and yellow shades). Plant in full sun to light shade. Hardy to Zone 4.

TECHNICAL STUFF

What is the difference between a daffodil and a narcissus? The answer: none! *Narcissus* is just the Latin/botanical name for daffodil. What is the difference between a daffodil and a jonquil? A jonquil is a particular type of daffodil (referred to in catalogs as Division 7) treasured for its sweet fragrance.

>> **Dahlia:** *Dahlia* species. A huge, diverse family of hybrids with an incredible array of flower forms and sizes. Some dahlia blossoms are tiny balls; other blossoms are huge, star-shaped blooms more than 8 inches (20.3 cm) wide. Summer-to-autumn-blooming in almost every color but blue, dahlia plants range in size from 6 inches (15.2 cm) high to more than 5 feet (1.5 m) high. Plant in full sun and water regularly. Hardy to Zone 9, but they grow in any

zone as long as tubers are dug and stored over the winter. Smaller varieties are often grown as annuals.

» **English bluebell:** *Hyacinthoides non-scripta.* Some shade and rich soil is all they ask. Spikes of scented, bell-shaped, dark violet flowers grow about 1 foot (.3 m) tall appear in late spring and form gorgeous carpets. But, alas, the leaves yellow as the plants fade, and you have to leave the leaves to fuel next year's show. Hardy in Zones 5 to 8.

» **Freesia:** *Freesia* species. Dependable spring-blooming bulb that naturalizes freely in mild climates. Freesia's arching clusters of trumpetlike flowers come in almost every color. Some are splendidly fragrant. The plants grow to about 18 inches (45.7 cm)high. Plant in full sun or light shade. Hardy to Zone 9, but the bulbs must be dug or used as an annual elsewhere.

» **Gladiolus:** *Gladiolus* species. Often just called *glads.* Much-loved cut flower with tall spikes of trumpetlike flowers. Comes in almost all shades except blue, and sensational bicolors and multi-hued ones. Most bloom in summer and grow to 4 to 5 feet (1.2 to 1.5 m) high, but smaller and cold-hardier types are available. Plant in spring in full sun. Hardy to Zone 9, but dig the corms or use the plants as annuals elsewhere.

» **Grape hyacinth:** *Muscari* species. Wonderful little bulbs that form carpets of fragrant, mostly blue, spring flowers and grassy foliage. Grape hyacinths grow from 6 to 12 inches (15.2 to 30.5 cm) high and naturalize freely. They thrive in full sun or light shade. Hardy to Zone 3.

» **Hyacinth:** *Hyacinthus orientalis.* Wonderfully fragrant spikes of white, red, pink, yellow, blue, or purple bell-shaped flowers in early spring. Common hyacinth grows to about 12 inches (30.5 cm) high. Hyacinths look best when planted in masses or containers. Plant in full sun or light shade. Hyacinths do best in cold-winter climates, needing chilling elsewhere. Hardy to Zone 4.

» **Iris:** *Iris* species. A huge group of elegant, spring-to-summer–blooming plants. You can choose from many different types. Favorites include the bearded iris, which has huge blooms and gracefully arching petals. Irises come in many shades and reach from 2 to 4 feet (.6 to 1.2 m) high. The plants spread freely. Plant in full sun or light shade. Most need to have water regularly. Hardiness varies, but most survive into at least Zone 5, some to Zone 3.

» **Lily:** *Lilium* species. Large family of beautiful, mostly summer-blooming bulbs. Most have large, trumpet-shaped flowers, but a great diversity of lilies exists. Colors come in almost every shade but blue, and plant heights range from 2 to 6 feet (.6 to 1.8 m). Some have a strong fragrance, wonderful wafting through your garden as well as in homegrown bouquets. Plant lilies so that the roots are in the shade but the tops can reach for the sun. Water consistently during summer. Most are hardy to Zone 4.

Lilies are different than other bulbs in that they're fleshy and thus much more susceptible to drying out in storage. Be sure to buy them as soon as they appear in the garden store, or order them from lily specialists who know how to keep them fresh. Get them in the ground or into pots quickly.

Beware of lily beetles. These greedy, destructive little red bugs (and their sluglike larvae) eat all parts of all sorts of lovely lilies — it's very upsetting, to the point where in some areas, gardeners have given up on growing lilies. Check around locally before you buy and plant lilies to avoid this heartbreak.

>> **Lily-of-the-Nile:** *Agapanthus orientalis.* Very dependable, summer-blooming bulb with tall stalks of bright blue flowers reaching from 4 to 5 feet (1.2 to 1.5 m) high. Its straplike foliage is evergreen in mild climates. Dig and store the bulbs over winter in cold-winter climates. Lily-of-the-Nile gets by on little water. Varieties with white flowers are also available. Plant in full sun or light shade. Hardy to Zone 9.

>> **Ornamental onion:** *Allium* species and hybrids. They're easy to grow: Just plant them in well-drained soil in full sun, even in a perennial border. There's a great range of choices, from the super-dramatic giant ball-shaped ones like the enduringly popular purple *A. giganteaum* 'Globemaster,' to "drumstick" types (purple, pink, white, or blue), to adorable smaller-flowers bunch-formers. Most are between 1 and 2 feet (.3 and .6 m) high; hardiness varies. Bees love them, deer don't. Hardiness varies.

>> **Persian buttercup:** *Ranunculus asiaticus.* Bright-colored, spring-to-summer flowers in shades of white, yellow, orange, red, and purple. Some are multicolored. The plants grow from 1 to 2 feet (.3 to .6 m) high and have deeply cut leaves. Plant in full sun or light shade. Hardy to Zone 8 but dig and store the bulbs in autumn.

>> **Snowdrops:** *Galanthus* species. Lovely, drooping, bell-shaped white flowers. Bloom in very early spring and naturalize nicely in cold-winter climates. Snowdrops grow from 8 to 12 inches (20.3 to 30.5 cm) high. Plant in full sun or partial shade (snowdrops are great under trees). Hardy to at least Zone 4. The giant snowdrop, *G. elwesii,* naturalizes farther south, into Zone 9.

>> **Tulip:** *Tulipa* species. Much-loved, spring-blooming bulbs with the familiar cup-shaped flowers in almost all shades (including multicolors) except blue. Tulips usually grow from 10 to 24 inches (25.4 to 61 cm) high and are best planted in full sun. They rebloom only in cold-winter climates; they're hardy to Zone 3. Elsewhere, the bulbs must be dug and chilled before replanting. However, many species of tulips, such as *T. clusiana,* naturalize even in mild-winter areas. Most tulips thrive as far south as Zone 8.

Buying and Taking Care of Your Bulbs

Bulbs, like perennials, are sold through the mail as well as at local nurseries. Nurseries should have the best supplies at the appropriate planting time for your area.

Always purchase top-quality bulbs — they give you more bang for your buck. Always remember that, with bulbs, bigger *is* better. Larger bulbs, although more expensive, give you more bloom; bargain bulbs are often poor performers. Avoid bulbs that are soft and mushy or have obvious signs of decay. You wouldn't buy a mushy onion in the grocery store, would you?

After you buy your bulbs and bring them home, you're ready to plant and take care of them. The following sections provide specifics about planting, caring for, and fertilizing your bulbs so they grow into flowers that will add vibrant colors in your landscape.

Planting bulbs

Plant bulbs wherever you want to see them bloom: in the smallest little spot by the front door, in pots, in large swaths under trees, or among other flowering plants. Some bulbs, such as the English bluebell, look particularly good in woodland settings, while others, such as tulips, do well in more formal landscape designs.

One of our favorite designs involves planting large beds of tulips or daffodils. We then plant low-growing annuals or perennials (such as sweet alyssum, pansies, violas, or creeping phlox) right on top of these bulb beds. The bulbs come up through the other flowers and create wonderful combinations. And after the bulbs are through blooming, the other flowers cover up or at least distract from the leftover foliage of the bulbs.

Here we give you some general tips when planting bulbs and explain how you can easily plant bulbs yourself.

Getting ready to plant your bulbs

Remember the following important pieces of information when you're preparing to plant bulbs:

>> **Plant at the right times.** Plant hardy bulbs, such as daffodils and tulips, in autumn whereas plant tender bulbs (corms, tubers), such as begonias, classic glads, and dahlias, a few weeks before the last frost date in spring.

>> **Plan for a long season of color.** Even though some of the most familiar bulbs (such as daffodils and tulips) bloom in spring, others (such as dahlias) bloom in summer and autumn.

>> **Use containers.** Bulbs work especially well in containers (we discuss containers more in Chapter 15). With containers, you can really pack bulbs in tightly for a spectacular bloom (but the tighter you pack the bulbs, the less likely they'll bloom the following year).

TIP

If you live in a warm-winter climate, you can still grow hyacinths, tulips, and other bulbs that require winter chilling (snowbirds, take notice!). You just have to provide that necessary cold period before planting. Check the package for such a recommendation or ask where you purchased them. To chill bulbs, place them in the refrigerator (not the freezer) for six to eight weeks prior to planting.

Planting a bulb, easy as 1-2-3

Most bulbs require well-drained soil because bulbs can rot in soggy, overly wet ground. Before planting your bulbs, mix a slow-release, complete fertilizer into the soil in the bottom of the hole. You can find appropriate fertilizers (labeled *bulb food*) in nurseries and garden centers. After planting the bulbs, water the area thoroughly.

When you're ready to plant your bulbs, just follow these simple steps:

REMEMBER

1. **Set the bulb at the right depth.**

   Figure 14-1 shows the recommended planting depths and proper positioning for common bulb types. As a general rule, most should be planted at a depth equal to three times their diameter.

2. **Make sure to put the bulb in the hole right-side up.**

   Remnants of roots on the bottom should tell you which side of the bulb should go down. Some, like tulips and snowdrops, have a pointy end — that goes up. (If you still aren't sure, just plant the bulb on its side.)

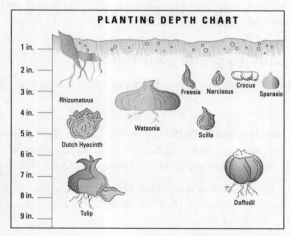

FIGURE 14-1:
Use this bulb-planting depth chart as a guide when you plant your own bulbs.

© John Wiley & Sons, Inc.

3. **Press each bulb firmly into place.**

   The idea is to make sure there are no air pockets; the emerging roots need to be in contact with the soil.

You can plant bulbs individually by using a hand trowel or bulb planter, available at garden supply stores. If you're planting many bulbs, digging a trench and lining up the bulbs along the bottom is usually easier.

Giving your bulbs some TLC

With many bulbs (especially those bulbs that bloom in spring), you won't have much else to do. Plant the bulbs and forget them. The bulbs grow, bloom, die back, and come back again the following year.

Summer-bloomers, like dahlias, classic glads, and begonias, however, need to be watered regularly, especially if rain isn't dependable. It's amazing how well they do if you keep their area consistently, evenly moist. (Extremes cause them to flag — don't get in a cycle of neglecting them till they wilt and then dumping on lots of water. Slow and steady wins the race!)

TIP

Pinch off faded blooms just as you would for most flowers. But after the bloom is finished, don't cut down the bulbs' foliage. Let the foliage die down naturally so that it can continue to feed the bulb and build next year's bloom. That's why planting them with spring perennials and/or annuals is wise.

Digging and storing is necessary for begonias, dahlias, and glads. To do so, just stick to these steps:

1. **Wait until the foliage is almost dried out, and then gently dig up the bulbs or corms.**

   A spading fork works well.

2. **Brush off the dirt and allow them to dry for a week in a cool, dark place, a process called *curing*.**

3. **After drying them for a week, discard any damaged or rotting bulbs or corms.**

   For an extra measure of protection, you may dust the remaining ones with powdered garden sulfur or another fungicide.

4. **Store them in a cool, dark place until replanting time.**

   Brown paper bags, mesh bags, even old pantyhose will do — something that breathes just a little, to prevent rot. Some people even store their bulbs or corms in dry peat moss or perlite.

Fertilizing bulbs

You'll get mixed messages when it comes to fertilizing. Some gardeners feel well-planted bulbs (quality bulbs in decent soil) don't really need to be fertilized. Others insist you must: at planting time and again when flowers are forming, and/or after blooming is over (to bulk up the bulbs for next year). Garden centers and bulb nurseries sell special bulb fertilizers with persuasive names like bulb booster or bulb food.

Here's what we suggest:

>> **Skip bonemeal.** Modern-day bonemeal is so sanitized that most bulbs will have bloomed and done by the time its nutrients become available.

>> **Use compost.** For aboveground fertilizing of bulbs, put down compost from your composting pile (see Chapter 17).

>> **Try organic fertilizers.** Ones that should be beneficial include greensand and rock phosphate, or even just good, organically rich compost.

If you use inorganic granular fertilizers, the 5-10-10 formulations are just fine.

REMEMBER

Whatever you use, bulbs benefit best from fertilizing if the plant food is available to their roots, which are on the bottom of the bulb, so you want to put that food at the bottom of the planting hole. Mix it in a bit, though, so the roots won't come into direct contact with a heavy dose or clump, which can burn them.

THE LOWDOWN ON NATURALIZING

You see this term a lot in bulb catalogs/on bulb websites advertised as "naturalizing mixes" or "great for naturalizing!"

The root word "nature" is your clue. You make it possible for the bulbs to grow and reproduce as they would in nature, in the wild. Start by planting a few and, if the conditions are what they like and there's space for them to spread, you'll have many more in the coming years.

Of course, you want your initial efforts to look natural. To do so, take a handful of bulbs out to the area you've designated and prepared. Simply toss them lightly into the air, and plant them where they land.

Among the best bulbs for naturalizing are crocuses, daffodils and narcissus, grape hyacinth, dwarf iris, and snowdrops — or mixes that include some or all of these. Read more about each kind in the section, "Discovering Some Great Bulbs."

Chapter **15**

Including Succulents and Containers for More Color and Texture

S ucculents open up all kinds of possibilities — and not just for those of you who garden in arid climates. While we're down to earth at their level, we also look closely at other modest-size players: container-grown plants. This is a horizon-broadening chapter. Many interesting and helpful discoveries and inspiring ideas about garden color and texture are ahead.

Including Super Succulents

Succulents are varied, beautiful, versatile, and so easy to grow. Whether in the ground or in pots, they have great potential.

Their thick, fleshy leaves are succulent, hence these plants are called *succulents*. The leaves store life-sustaining water (as do their stems and roots, of course). Succulents are native to deserts and dry landscapes worldwide, including far-off Africa and North America's own Sonoran and Mohave deserts. Cacti are the most familiar examples, but there is a lot of range, from adorable hens and chicks, to aloes and agaves, to the huge sedum tribe.

The following sections examine why succulents are such great plants to add to your garden, identify which succulents are our favorites, explain how to create a succulent vignette, give some shopping and planting tips, and share what you need to know if you want to plant succulents in containers.

Eyeing the many plusses that make succulents so easy to love

Succulents are popular with many gardeners in many areas (not just dry climates). They give a lot of beauty, asking little in return. More reasons why you may want to include them in your garden:

>> **They adapt to most climates.** Because the majority of succulents do fine in hot weather and require minimal water, they're clearly practical for gardeners in mild climates. To you we say, your landscaping options are much wider than you may know. For those in climates with cold or snowy winters, don't feel left out. In the next section we introduce many succulents that will do just fine for you.

>> **They're diverse in shape and color.** In addition to trim rosettes, you'll find paddle-shaped leaves, chubby clusters, dramatic spears, even trailing stems. Some are bulky plants, suitable for flowerbeds or planter boxes. Some are low-growing or little, inviting as groundcovers or in potted displays. As for colors, you can find hues of powder blue, rust red, gold, and every imaginable variation of green from soft sage to bold emerald green. Some even have multicolored leaves. Nor is foliage their only feature. Many produce flowers, big or small, in many colors. Nothing dull or boring here!

>> **They're unfussy and difficult to kill.** The vast majority of succulents are practically self-sufficient, truly low-maintenance plants.

>> **Most are safe for pets.** You don't have to worry about little Piper getting sick or suffering any ill effects from eating or brushing against a succulent.

>> **Most are disease- and pest-free and untroubled by bigger garden pests like rabbits, gophers, and deer.** On rare occasions when a succulent shows a problem, it's often because overwatering, cold weather, or perhaps rough handling troubled it. Certain beetles, mites, and other tiny pest insects target certain succulents, but fortunately they're fairly rare. The bigger nibblers also give these plants a pass. In a word, succulents are tough.

Discovering favorite low-growing succulents

Succulents are a fun and practical alternative to lawn or traditional groundcovers. You can fill an area nicely with closely planted succulents, or establish them in a setting of small rocks or mulch. Many different ones answer the call, whether you stuff them into an area shoulder-to-shoulder, or let ones with creeping habits fill in. Here are some excellent candidates, listed by common name first and botanical name second — useful information when you set out to go shopping:

TIP

Which ones are *cold-hardy* (can tolerate cold winter weather) and which ones are not? Determining this can be tricky. They may not be labeled, and it's difficult to discover their hardiness by looking them up online because of a surplus of information, some of it conflicting. If it's important for you to know this, your best bet is to buy your succulents from garden centers with knowledgeable staff, or from succulent specialists who can advise you.

>> **Agaves:** *Agave* species and cultivars. A huge genus of rosette-forming plants. You can fill a whole bed with one selection or mix and match. Color varies, from all shades of green to blue hues. When planted in groups or massed, Perry's agave, *A. parryi*, is a stunner; it's 1 to 3 feet (.3 to .9 m) tall and wide and hardy in Zones 6 to 9.

>> **Blue chalksticks:** *Senecio serpens.* Blue-gray, slow-growing, and handsome, it only gets a foot (.3 m) tall and will spread over time. Only suitable in Zone 9 and warmer.

>> **Echeveria:** *Echeveria.* You probably know these — they're deservedly popular and widely planted. They're mostly small, balled shapes or rosettes; mature size varies, but they aren't as big as the agaves. They come in shades of green, red, pink, purple, and yellow, and some with a mixture. Therefore, when using them as a groundcover, we recommend interplanting different kinds for a colorful carpet. Flowers appear on stalks in the spring; you can remove the stalks if you don't care for how they look and also to help the plants conserve energy. Echeverias make offsets and form colonies. Zones 9 to 12.

>> **Ghost plant:** *Graptopetalum paraguayense.* Little, attractive rosettes grow on ever-lengthening stems that over time ramble and form colonies. They grow a foot tall and 2 to 3 feet wide (.3 m tall and .6 to .9 m wide), which is quite suitable for covering lots of ground. More cold-hardy than most succulents, they can be grown outdoors from Zones 7 to 10.

>> **Hens and chicks:** *Sempervivum* species and cultivars. Size varies, hence the cute common name, with several plants over time expanding to create dense, weed-excluding mats in your landscape. Lots of colors to choose from, including bicolors; some have furry texture. There are literally hundreds, so we encourage you to do some looking and make a truly creative, colorful display. Low-growing plants, no more than 3 to 5 inches (7.6 to 12.7 cm) tall. Hardy to Zone 5 or 6.

>> **Myrtle, or silver, spurge:** *Euphorbia rigida.* Where you need a substantial succulent plant for low-care, poor-soil groundcovering, this plant is a good option. It gets about 2 feet (.6 m) tall and 3 feet (.9 m) wide at maturity, so bear

that size in mind — that is, give small plants room to expand. It has thick upright stems clothed in tough green foliage that takes on red hues in fall. Small green-chartreuse flowers make a flurry in spring. Hardy to Zone 8. Will seed itself around.

» **Resin spurge:** *Euphorbia resinifera.* At first glance, you may mistake this multi-stemmed, mound-former for a cactus. Its ascending pale-green branches are ridged and have short, sharp spines. The flowers are nothing to write home about. Its ability to grow densely, spread out, and fill an area is valuable in dry climates; it can reach 2 feet (.6 m) tall and spread out around 6 feet (1.8 m). Zones 9 to 11.

WARNING

The milky, whitish sap of euphorbia plants helps protect the plants from insect or fungal damage and seals off physical injuries, such as when a stem is snapped. But it's irritating to human eyes and skin — toxicity varies from one species to the next and not everyone reacts badly to it. To be on the safe side, place these plants where they aren't likely to be romped through, and handle them with care when planting and maintaining.

» **Rock purslane:** *Calandrinia spectabilis.* One-foot (.3 m) mounds of gray-green leaves are joined 2- to 3-foot (.6 to .9 m) stalks of magenta flowers that last for months. Planted densely, it looks amazing. Zone 9.

» **Stonecrop:** *Sedum* cultivars. Stonecrops are good, eager-to-please groundcovers. Most people know the overplanted *S. spurium,* but there is a huge array of others, from red-hued jellybean plant (also called "pork and beans") (*S. × rubrotinctum*) to *S. kamtschaticum,* which forms mats of handsome green foliage nearly obscured by scads of starry yellow flowers. Zones 4 to 9.

Creating fun and fabulous vignettes

In horticulture and gardening a *vignette* refers to a smaller composition — something simple and effective that attracts attention and delight, even if it's part of a larger landscape.

Although landscapers often create a vignette when they make compositions of, say, three compatible perennials or a small planting flanking a front door or some such, vignettes seem to be the darling term of succulent fans. Perhaps it's because these plants are so well-behaved as to be almost passive; composing with succulents is about as easy as arranging inanimate objects.

TIP

To create a succulent vignette, follow these simple steps:

1. **Gather together a small but diverse group of succulents.**

   Shoot for three or five. Aim for contrasting textures, sizes, forms, and colors.

2. **Pick a suitable spot or container (or containers).**

   Stay in the same or similar styles and color range, so the containers don't steal the spotlight from the little plants. Make sure the soil mix is suitable (check out the section, "Displaying in containers," later in this chapter for more details).

3. **Create your composition by setting the succulents in place without yet planting.**

   You want the colors to contrast so you can pick out each individual one. Play around with the placement.

4. **After you're satisfied with their placement, go ahead and plant.**

REMEMBER

When you're ready to display your vignette, make sure people can see and enjoy your work. Consider the following when displaying yours:

>> **In the garden, in the ground:** Vignettes benefit from a nondistracting backdrop, such as a fence or wall. Other plants may overshadow the succulents, literally and figuratively. We've admired entire narrow side-yard or walkway-side beds planted to succulent vignettes, or knee-high planters or terraces that bring them closer to the viewer. Such schemes look like an undersea garden or an elfin forest.

>> **In pots and containers:** These smaller venues have a focus and intimacy that really suits succulent vignettes. People can appreciate them at eye level. A windowbox, or boxes mounted on the edge of a porch or balcony, are suitable. Or arrange the composition up several steps — to the side, of course, out of the direct path of foot traffic.

Displaying in containers

When grown in containers, many plants dry out quickly and can wilt or perish if you neglect them (refer to the section, "Examining the Containerized Landscape," later in this chapter). Not so much with succulents! Succulents are durable and drought-resistant, and many are also slow-growing, so life in some sort of pot tends to suit the smaller-size ones just fine.

REMEMBER

Growing these beauties in containers is a good option for gardeners who live in cold-winter climates that would kill the plants if they left them outdoors. Just keep them indoors during the cold months in a nonfreezing spot.

Here are the best types of containers we suggest:

>> **Clay or terra cotta:** These materials look great with many succulents; there is a natural compatibility, it seems, between the reddish hue and these desert

natives or desert descendants. Furthermore, these materials wick moisture away from plant roots, which is often just fine with succulents.

A drawback is that they don't overwinter outdoors well where conditions are wet or freezing. They can crack and flake. Instead use containers (fiberglass or plastic) that are made to look like them.

>> **Windowboxes or planter boxes:** You can arrange succulents the length of a window or planter box, either by planting them directly into the box or by keeping the individual succulents in individual pots and setting them in place (after which you can add planting mix to hide the truth, if you wish; just don't submerge the succulents).

>> **Hanging baskets:** Moss-lined ones hold too much moisture and succulents will struggle. Any other kind of hanging basket is better and allows you to choose some of the plants with trailing stems to hang down.

WARNING

Plastic containers aren't ideal for succulents. Whether classic green or some other color (red, tan, white), the succulents don't tend to look good in them. The pots seem too frail or thin contrasted with the substantial or chubby succulent foliage. Also plastic holds in soil-mix moisture, which isn't a good thing for these sorts of plants, particularly if you happen to overwater.

TIP

Nesting is a clever and useful idea when you're planting succulents. You can tuck a single potted succulent plant into other sorts of containers, where it will be hidden from view but hold the plant in place. We're talking about any sort of other container: old coffee cans, an old teapot or watering can, a worn-out work boot, or even discarded toy trucks. Use your imagination with nesting.

Shopping and planting tips

Most local garden centers, unless you live in a desert or fairly dry climate, have a limited selection of succulents. Another place to look, actually, is at a florist. Some know quite well how beautiful and durable succulents are and make a practice of including them in mixed potted arrangements; they may have some to sell you.

TIP

If you can't find succulents locally that charm you, turn to mail-order suppliers. Look around online for succulent specialists, view their many choices, and/or message them and get their advice and ideas. Buying plants by mail isn't as risky as you may think — the specialty nurseries have packing and shipping down to a science.

Planting your succulents in a container

After you have the succulents you want, it's time to plant. Follow these steps to give them their best chance of survival in a container:

1. **Take each plant out of its pot.**

   That's right! Why? Most nurseries, including the ones that ship mail-order, tend to plant them in overly dense, moisture-retentive soil mix (to boost them through the stresses of their journey to your door). Handle the succulent very gently, teasing off as much of the soil mix as you can without damaging the roots.

   Don't rinse them off with water! Doing so may harm or snap fragile or small roots.

2. **Separate off any pups.**

   Pups refer to the baby plants coming off the main plant. Even on a small succulent plant, they aren't always obvious. When you take the previous step to remove the plant from the pot it arrived in, you may spot little plants coming off the main one. Go ahead and separate them off, carefully. Congratulations — you have a few bonus plants.

3. **Prepare the new home.**

   Use a clean container and, if it has a drainage hole or holes, sift in some small pebbles or cover the hole(s) with a bit of screen or mesh. This prevents the soil mix from falling out. Fill the container with soil intended for succulents (you can purchase bags of cactus and succulent soil mix; a key ingredient, not surprisingly, is sand).

   You can make your own suitable soil mix. Just blend equal parts of regular potting mix and sand, with a bit of perlite or pumice. A good formula for this recipe is 3 cups, 3 cups, 1.5 cups. You don't have to be super-precise; you just want a container that drains well rather than holding in moisture that can cause your arid-land plant roots to rot.

4. **Set the plant or plants in place, gently filling the soil mix carefully around them.**

   Make sure none of the fleshy leaves come into contact with the soil mix, which can lead to rot. If you want, top the pot with decorative pebbles or stones.

Planting your succulents in the ground

To plant succulents in the ground, follow the first two steps from the previous section, and then:

1. **Pick an appropriate outdoor spot.**

   Contrary to popular belief, most succulents don't love being in direct, full-on, full-day sun. The best spot is one that gets some relief from the heat of the sun for at least part of the day. If you garden in a cooler climate, however, more hours of sunlight may be just fine.

2. **Prepare the soil.**

Soil preparation is the same as for any other incoming plants. Clear out an area first, removing weeds and rocks, to a depth of several inches/cm at least. If the soil seems damp, dig in some sand and/or perlite or pumice to lighten the soil and improve drainage.

3. **Set the plants on the site and stand back a moment.**

Do they have space to spread out (some will whereas some grow so slowly you don't need to give them elbow room)? Are they back from the edge of the bed? Do they look good together? Make adjustments to your planting scheme until you're satisfied.

4. **Dig the holes and put in the plants.**

Remember two important points:

- Always make a planting hole at least twice as big as the root system. Doing so is just good practice, so the roots can move out into and prosper in their new home.

- Set the plants in place a little higher than you may think because they'll settle. You don't want the foliage to be in direct contact with soil if you can help it because that can lead to rot.

5. **Top the planting area with pebbles, rocks, or a dry organic mulch such as weed-free straw.**

Doing so provides a neat, finished appearance, but it's also practical. You don't want any weeds trying to take back the territory while your baby plants are trying to get going.

Caring for succulents

Whether you're growing succulents in some sort of container or in the garden proper, they do have some basic needs. Here are a few pointers:

>> **Water your succulents' soil, not their leaves.** Don't use sprays from the hose, watering wands, watering cans, misters, or sprinklers. A low trickle from the hose, a leaky hose, or an inground irrigation system will deliver the minimal water to the best and necessary place, the roots. For pots, try setting them in a tray of water so they can slurp up only what they need — watering from below is easy and effective.

The number one mistake people make when growing succulents is overwatering. Closely related is plunking them in poorly draining soil or a poorly drained container. Their roots can rot and the plants will die. Only water when their soil medium is dry and, even then, lightly and sparingly. Let your plants dry out between waterings. They'll benefit from a touch more water when actively growing and will get by with much less in their off-season. Be attentive to how they're looking and intervene if you notice their foliage has become soft, wrinkled, or puckered, all signs of dehydration.

>> **Groom your plants occasionally.** Even happy succulents exhibit shriveled or past-their-prime leaves and faded flowers. Pinch or snip off spent flowers, stalk and all, if they flower on a stalk. Pests and diseases aren't major problems, but keep an eye out for them. If you spot a potential problem, figure out what it is and what to do (the nursery where you purchased the plants is a good source if you ever need help).

>> **Repot and replant potted succulents every two years or so, mainly to give them fresh soil mix.** Some, such as hens and chicks and aloe, produce offsets that may deplete the mother plant. Repot everything individually; the mother plant may or may not revive, but in any event you'll have new babies. The best time to do this is when growth picks up in the spring months.

Succulents rarely need fertilizing, but if you feed your succulents, use a general formula and feed them only when they're actively growing (summer, for the most part).

Examining the Containerized Landscape

Even if you have a big yard to landscape, and especially if you don't, growing plants in pots is worthwhile and satisfying. We think it's a matter of scale; potted plants are always close at hand and easy to enjoy. We wager the following sections may bring up more ideas or facets than you may have imagined.

Tapping into the joys of container gardening

You may wonder why you'd want to add potted plants to your landscape. Here are a number of persuasive reasons:

>> **You can grow plants in places that don't have soil.** Container plants add character to patios, decks, porches, and windows. They make basically flat places interesting and soften the edginess of hard materials like wood, brick, and concrete. But even more important, if you live in an apartment or small home with very little outdoor space or anywhere with muddy gumbo or hard rock for soil, growing in containers may be your only chance to have plants. Check out the color insert.

>> **You can move plants around.** Containers allow you to show off plants when they're looking their very best. For example, when your potted azalea is in bloom, it goes right on the front porch. When it's out of bloom, it moves out of the way for the next show-off. Plants growing in containers can also be moved to protected areas if bad weather threatens.

>> **Containers can make plants look better**. Lance's wife says that an attractive plant growing in a good-looking container is like a handsome man in the finest uniform. It just can't help but look better. A nice pot can turn even an ordinary plant into a piece of art. We wonder what a uniform could do for Lance?

>> **You can get creative.** A plant doesn't have to go into a store-bought pot. Try repurposing something like a few smaller plants tucked into the bed of an old toy truck, vegetable and herb plants in large tomato cans, or an old colander turned into a hanging basket. Have fun. (Just make sure it has drainage holes.)

Think of your yard as an outdoor room. Potted plants can be your decorations — the items that turn a simple room into a comfortable or stylish home. Container plants help give your landscape personality and a lived-in look.

Almost any plant can be grown in a container. Your local nursery is proof of that. But, of course, larger plants will eventually outgrow their pots, so you need to consider plant size. If you really want to know the possibilities, get yourself a copy of the recent edition of *Container Gardening For Dummies* by Bill Marken, Suzanne DeJohn, and the National Gardening Association (John Wiley & Sons, Inc.). But let us whet your appetite with just a smattering of plants you can grow in pots:

>> **Small trees:** Japanese maples

>> **Shrubs:** Camellias, azaleas, and roses

>> **Fruiting plants:** Dwarf citrus, apples, peaches, and pears

>> **Berries:** Strawberries and blueberries

>> **Annual flowers:** Petunias, marigolds, and impatiens

>> **Flowering perennials:** Salvias, geraniums, and ornamental grasses

>> **Bulbs:** Tulips and daffodils

Heck, try whatever you want!

Picking pots

Make sure pots have drainage holes. Roots are at risk of drowning and rotting otherwise. Most pots have them, but you may have to drill a few in wood pots, half barrels, or offbeat containers like a vintage teapot. If you have a great pot with no drainage holes (and it's not possible or practical to create or drill some), here are two workarounds:

>> Put an inch (2.5 cm) or more of small gravel in the bottom of the pot before adding the soil and plant(s), and then always water carefully. The idea is for excess water to drain down into the stones, so the roots don't sit in muck, and rot.

>> Nest by inserting a smaller pot that does have drainage holes inside the attractive, impractical pot.

When you're selecting pots and arranging them in your yard, you're setting the stage, ready to put on a show. Here are some tricks for getting the best display:

>> **Use some big pots.** Splurge a little and buy a few really sizeable clay pots or urns, or the ones that look like them (often made of resin) but are nowhere near as heavy or expensive. Particularly if you have a big deck or patio, a big potted display will bring it into scale with the rest of the yard as well as with patio or deck furniture.

TIP

Match the size of a plant with the size of the container. Bigger plants are better off in bigger pots, but a small plant can look dwarfish in a large container.

>> **Match pot and plant.** You have a huge choice of container sizes, styles, colors, and materials, so think carefully about how you match plants with pots. A glazed ceramic pot may beautifully accentuate the feel of a Japanese maple, but look a little funny filled with bright yellow marigolds. A dwarf fruit tree matches nicely with the rustic feel of a half whiskey barrel, but more refined plants may look a little campy.

>> **Group different pot sizes and shapes.** Start with one big one and then surround it with smaller pots of varying shapes and sizes. It helps to stick to one style of pot, like clay or wood. Things get pretty busy-looking if you mix too many different kinds of pots.

Potting plants in containers

Get container-grown plants off to the best possible start by following these simple planting steps:

1. **Start with a clean pot.**

If the pot is new, not a problem. If you're reusing a pot, take a few moments to scrub it inside and out. You don't want old dirt or roots clinging to the inside walls because there's a chance they'll pass on a plant disease. Wiping down or scrubbing the outside just makes an older pot look better — plus it's a lot easier to tidy it up now rather than later when it's full.

2. **Add dampened potting mix.**

   Don't pour dry mix into the pot. Instead, pour the dry mix into a bowl or bucket and add water. Take it out by handfuls, squeezing out excess water each time, and tamp it into the pot. Fill to within an inch (2.5 cm) or so of the rim.

TIP

   Buy potting soil mix at your local nursery or garden center. Don't fill pots with regular garden soil because it's too heavy and may even harbor sneaky weed seeds. In other words, it causes nothing but headaches.

3. **Scoop out holes for each incoming plant (see Figure 15-1).**

   You can use your bare hands or wear gloves. Make the holes larger than the incoming root systems so you won't be forcing them into place.

FIGURE 15-1:
Scoop out holes
for each plant.

4. **Gently remove or knock out each plant from the small container or flat it came in.**

TIP

   Handle it by its root system. Don't tug or pull on the young foliage, because you could inadvertently tear the leaves or dislodge them from their roots.

5. **Settle each plant into the waiting spot in the container.**

   Firm it into place, making sure it's upright and at the same level it was in the nursery pot. See Figure 15-2. Add more damp potting mix around it (squeezing excess water out of each handful as before) as needed.

FIGURE 15-2:
Put the plant in
the hole and firm
it into place.

© John Wiley & Sons, Inc.

6. **Gently water at the soil level.**

You won't need much because you pre-dampened the mix. Let the plant rest. Some water may drain out the bottom.

7. **Place the finished project in a semi-shaded, sheltered spot.**

Do so even if it's a sun-lover or bound for a bright, open spot on your patio. It just needs a couple days to adjust to its new life in its new pot.

8. **Move it to its spot.**

Remember to look in on it often to be sure it's doing well. Water regularly, as potted plants dry out surprisingly quickly.

Working with thrillers, fillers, and spillers

The first time we heard "fill a container with a thriller, a filler, and a spiller," a light bulb went on. Of course! Exactly! Flower arrangers have used this idea for a long time, and you can use it just as well with living plants in a pot. Remember the following:

» A *thriller* is a dramatic, upright-growing plant, usually placed right in the center.

» A *filler* takes over the main surface of a pot.

» A *spiller* is a plant that trails or cascades over the side.

TIP

Plant everything a little closer, more tightly together, than you would in the ground. They'll be just fine and the look will be full and dynamic. For example, put an annual salvia or zinnia in the center of a pot and then add a spreading plant like alyssum around it. Finish with some trailing lobelia to spill over the side (see the color insert for an example).

Whether you use this technique or decide to plant single-plant pots or fiddle with other combinations, here are a few more ideas that lead to good-looking results:

>> **Use foliage color and texture.** Flowers will eventually go out of bloom, but if you mix in some foliage plants, like gray-leafed dusty millers, ornamental grasses, or ferns, the display will still look good.

>> **Move the best plants forward.** When a pot is really looking good, move it up front where people can see it.

>> **Rotate.** Plants naturally lean toward the sun, and pot displays can start to look one-sided if you do nothing. During peak growing, intervene every few days or at least once a week and turn each pot a quarter-turn, and your displays will look nicely balanced.

Caring for potted plants

Growing plants in containers is a bit of a different deal than growing them in the ground. In a nutshell, here are the things you need to know:

>> **Water frequently.** Container plants dry out quickly and need to be watered often, especially big plants in small pots. In hot weather, pots may need to be watered *daily,* especially if the plants have been growing in the container for a while. When you water, make several passes, ensuring the entire rootball is getting wet.

>> **Fertilize frequently during active growth.** Frequent watering washes nutrients, especially nitrogen, from the soil mix. Use a water-soluble fertilizer about every two weeks. Follow label instructions.

>> **Transplant when necessary.** Plants that have been in a pot too long get *rootbound,* meaning the pot is full of a mass of tightly woven roots that are very hard to get wet. Your plant is rootbound if water passes through and drains out the bottom of the container entirely too quickly after you've watered the plant. If that happens, move the plant into a larger container, loosening the roots around the outside of the rootball as you do so.

Chapter **16**

Covering Lots of Ground

For most people, some open space devoted to lawn grass or a groundcover in the landscape is both necessary and desirable. The lush color and smooth, uniform look are a practical and attractive way to complement the house and the trees, shrubs, and other plantings.

But these days, finding out what to do and being happy with the results is something of a challenge for many reasons. Chief among them is the fact that a traditional lawn turns out to be a lot of work (constant mowing, watering, fertilizing, and other maintenance). We suggest you not spend those resources/expend that energy . . . and . . . instead spend more time enjoying your home landscape.

Furthermore, in many areas water is precious, making a lush green carpet of lawn impractical. Or perhaps your yard is too shady and grass struggles. Or maybe your yard slopes and maintaining a lawn is a hassle.

You're probably aware of increasing and legitimate environmental-impact concerns about lawns: Fertilizer runoff into the water table isn't good (it burdens the local environment with excess nitrogen). Pollinators need help and mowed grass impoverishes them. Weedkillers (herbicides) can harm more than their intended targets, not just other plants but also the unseen web of life in the soil.

Foot traffic can also be an issue. Whatever you grow, groundcover or lawn grass, needs to be tolerant of people and pets crossing it or playing on it, and yet still look good.

No worries — you have lots of options. We aren't suggesting lawns should be banished altogether. If you want one, by all means, have one. We just help you approach your groundcovering project wisely. This chapter includes useful information about groundcovers . . . and then tackles some savvy advice on lawns. We also tuck in some helpful general information about mulch because mulch comes in handy both when covering cleared ground and after installing plants.

Before we delve into these topics, though, we explain what you need to do if you want to start anew in your yard.

Getting a Fresh Start: Clearing the Way

Whether you're contemplating installing a groundcover or starting fresh with a new lawn, more than likely your old, raggedy, weed-infested lawn is in the way. You have to remove it and prepare the soil for your new groundcover or lawn. Ask a few friends or family members to help and follow these steps to clear your lawn:

1. **Pick a suitable work day (check your forecast and plan ahead).**

   A cool or drizzly day is ideal, so nobody gets overheated or sunburned. Work the day after it's rained, or water the area the night before. Damp ground makes this project so much easier.

2. **Dig up the old growth.**

   Using garden forks, shovels, and/or grubbing hoes, start digging. The object is to strip away not only the surface growth, but their roots. You don't have to dig deep. The root systems of old turf generally don't go deeper than 4 to 6 inches (10 to 15.2 cm). Stab into the ground and peel back old sections, like beat-up carpet. Shake out the excess soil so it can remain on-site.

   You need the exercise! Make sure you have helpers. Many hands make light work. On average, two people can remove and haul away up to 300 square feet (around 30 square meters) in an hour.

TIP

   If you have a big area, tackle it in stages/sections or bring in a tiller or rent a piece of gear called, not surprisingly, a sod-cutter.

WARNING

   Never remove an old lawn or groundcover using weedkillers (herbicides), even if you aren't against garden chemicals. They can ruin the area for planting going forward by adversely affecting beneficial but unseen soil organisms, not to mention the water table.

3. Remove the sod pieces to the disposal area.

Use tarps, wheelbarrows, or wagons to haul away the old turf. Assign at least one person to this part of the project.

Dispose of the pieces in a compost pile or, if the incoming material will overwhelm the compost pile, in its own pile adjacent. After it dries out (weeks from now), you can deliver it in parts to the compost pile. This is true even if it contains weeds; you just want to be sure everything is dead. (An alternative is to bury it all, after fully dried out.)

TIP

Stack discarded sections of old turf plants-side down and roots-and-dirt-side up. Why? Because you don't want it to try to root in wherever you're putting it.

4. Tidy up.

Go back over the cleared area and extract and throw out any large weed roots. Take out rocks. Rake over the site neatly.

5. Cover when done.

REMEMBER

We can't emphasize this enough. Nature abhors a vacuum. Your digging probably stirred up dormant weed seeds (honestly, it can't be avoided), and nearby or bird-deposited weed seeds and bits can invade amazingly fast — in a matter of a couple of days.

So, until you're ready to put in improved soil and plant the area, you must keep it covered. Mulch heavily, several inches/centimeters thick (see the nearby sidebar). Additionally or instead, secure a large tarp or tarps, spread out layers of flattened cardboard and newspapers, or use all of these things, to protect the cleared area until you're ready to plant.

MUCH ADO ABOUT MULCH

This book, like every other landscape and gardening reference, advises that you use mulch. The uses are myriad: covering cleared ground before you plant a lawn or other new addition; protecting the planting area and root systems of newly planted trees, shrubs, flowers, or groundcover plants; blanketing vulnerable plants before winter cold arrives; or even just creating a visual border or strip between one planted area of your garden and another.

The following clarifies what's important:

- **Organic mulch:** This is organic material spread on the surface of the ground. Classic examples include bark products (avoid the red-dyed kind; the color leaches into the soil and groundwater), aged compost, dry pine needles, dried lawn clippings, weed-free straw, chopped-up dry leaves, cocoa hulls, aged sawdust.

(continued)

(continued)

- **Stones as mulch:** You may also use pebbles, gravel, or similar materials. These can serve well as a mulch, so long as they aren't likely to stray from their appointed spot — that is, you don't want water or playing children to move the stones. Only use these if the plants in their area won't mind or will benefit from their ability to hold warmth (thus these inorganic mulches are popular for areas devoted to dry-climate plants like sedums and other succulents; see Chapter 15).

When applied thickly and thoroughly enough, mulch confers helpful benefits. It helps keep in soil moisture and moderates soil-temperature fluctuations. It helps keep weeds at bay. For the organic ones, as they break down over time, their organic content contributes some nutrients and improved texture to the soil. Plus, depending on what you choose and if you're neat, mulch of any kind can look great!

Just remember that all mulch is temporary. Time, water, and weather deplete it, and/or it works its way into the ground. This isn't a problem if you've covered an area with mulch temporarily. Otherwise, replenish it periodically.

Calling Groundcovers to the Rescue

Groundcovers can be true, dependable problem-solvers for you. After they get going, they're generally low-maintenance and suppress most weed growth. After they get going, they look good!

REMEMBER

Groundcovers are low-growing, spreading plants that, when planted close together, can do the same or similar job a lawn does — cover and fill large areas of your yard in a uniform layer of foliage. With some selections, you get the bonus of seasonal flowers or autumn color changes. In any event, after they're installed, they tend to be a lot less work and no mowing.

Plants that qualify as groundcovers range from very low-growing plants that are just a few inches/centimeters high to more shrubby types that are several feet (a meter or so) high. Some of the lowest-growing ones, such as chamomile and creeping thyme, can handle a little foot traffic — you can plant these types between stepping stones, on a flagstone terrace, or in other areas where people occasionally walk.

Groundcover plants have an artistic side, too. If you wish, you can create contrasts with them, mixing in other shrubs, vines, annuals, and perennials for a variety of effects. Foliage textures can range from grassy to tropically bold, and colors can range from subtle shades of gray to vibrant seasonal colors.

Although the number of possible candidates is nearly infinite, the following common ones have proven themselves in a multitude of situations and environments. As usual, we provide the common name first and follow it with the botanical name and some other relevant information.

Top groundcover choices for sun

Some of these groundcovers are great for sun, and some of them also tolerate part-day shade.

REMEMBER

The sun dries out soil and therefore plants; thus you can't utterly neglect an area devoted to one of these plants. During the warm summer months or whenever rain is sparse, we advise you to thread a leaky hose through the area or pay regular visits with a hose or a watering can. Here are our favorites:

>> **African daisies:** *Osteospermum.* A group of spreading, evergreen plants with daisylike flowers. Widely grown as groundcovers in mild-winter climates. Flowers on 1- to 3-foot-high (.3-to-.9 m) plants, available in shades of magenta, white, and pink. Generally hardy into Zone 9 and 10.

>> **Blue fescue:** *Festuca ovina* var. *glauca* or cultivar 'Glauca.' A mounding, grassy groundcover with silver-blue foliage. Grows 4 to 10 inches (10 to 25.4 cm) high and gets by on little water. Plant in full sun, spacing the plants 6 to 12 inches (15.2 to 30.5 cm) apart. Hardy to Zone 5.

>> **Creeping St. John's wort:** *Hypericum calycinum.* Evergreen. These adaptable groundcovers thrive under a variety of conditions. They grow 12 inches (30.5 cm) high and have bright-yellow flowers in summer. The plants spread rapidly and can be invasive. Prefer full sun but will take partial shade. Space the plants 12 to 18 inches (30.5 to 45.7 cm) apart. Hardy to Zone 5.

>> **Gazania:** *Gazania.* With sunny summer flowers in single and multicolored shades of white, red, pink, yellow, and orange borne on 6- to 12-inch (15.2 to high 30.5 cm) clumping or trailing plants. Plant 1 to 2 feet (.3 to .6 m) apart in full sun. Hardy in Zone 8 and south, grow elsewhere as an annual.

>> **Ice plant:** Evergreen. *Drosanthemum floribundum* and *Lampranthus spectabilis.* Many different, trailing, succulent ice plants are useful groundcovers in mild-winter climates, especially arid areas. Two popular blooming types are rosea ice plant, *Drosanthemum floribundum,* which grows about 6 inches (15.2 cm) high and has pink flowers in spring and summer; and trailing ice plant, *Lampranthus spectabilis,* which grows 12 to 15 inches (30.5 to 38 cm) high, covering itself with pink, red, or purple flowers in spring. Plant in full sun, spacing them 12 to 18 inches (30.5 to 45.7 cm) apart. Hardy to Zone 9.

- **Kinnikinnick:** *Arctostaphylus uva-ursi.* Evergreen. Several selections of this hardy, shrubby plant make excellent groundcovers. Features shiny green foliage. The plants' small, urn-shaped, white spring flowers are followed by red berries. 'Point Reyes' and 'Radiant' are two fine choices and generally stay below 12 inches (30.5 cm) high. Plant in full sun about 3 feet (.9 m) apart. Hardy to Zone 2.

- **Spring cinquefoil:** *Potentilla tabernaemontanii (P. verna).* Evergreen. This plant's dark green, divided leaves form a soft-textured cover 3 to 6 inches (7.6 to 15.2 cm) high. Has small clusters of yellow flowers in spring and summer and can take some foot traffic. Plant in full sun to partial shade and space the plants 10 to 12 inches (25.4 to 30.5 cm) apart. Hardy to Zone 4.

- **Star jasmine:** *Trachelospermum jasminoides.* Evergreen. This spreading, vining plant has shiny green foliage and fragrant white flowers in spring. Grows about 18 inches (45.7 cm) high when left to sprawl. Confederate vine, *T. asiaticum,* is similar but grows slightly lower, has dull green leaves, and bears yellowish-white flowers. Plant in full sun and space the plants 2 to 3 feet (.6 to .9 m) apart. Hardy to Zone 8.

- **Woolly yarrow:** *Achillea tomentosa.* Evergreen. A tough, spreading groundcover that reaches 6 to 9 inches (15.2 to 22.8 cm) high. Its ferny, gray-green leaves are topped with small yellow flower clusters in summer. Although woolly yarrow can take some foot traffic, it can also be invasive. Plant 6 to 9 inches 15.2 to 22.8 cm) apart in full sun. Hardy to Zone 3.

WARNING

Don't plant the groundcover bishop's goutweed, *Aegopodium podagraria,* in its modest-looking plain-green-leaves form or in its variegated-leaved form (light green splashed with creamy white). It spreads fast and is a thug, insinuating itself into treasured flowerbeds and overrunning other plants. Getting rid of it is extremely difficult. If you have inherited it in your yard, you may have to dig up and tarp its entire area for several seasons. (For more on battling unwanted plants, see Chapter 17.)

Top groundcover choices for shade

Some of these also tolerate part-day sun, and their leaf coloration may vary depending on how much sun they get. They do best in shade without fading fast or burnt-leaf edges. Here are our choices:

- **Carpet bugle:** *Ajuga reptans.* Evergreen. Forms a low-growing, spreading groundcover with attractive dark green or purplish-green foliage reaching 2 to 6 inches (5 to 15.2 cm) high. Carpet bugle has blue flowers in summer. Plant in partial to full shade (some types with colored foliage can take more sun), 6 to 12 inches (15.2 to 30.5 cm) apart. Hardy to Zone 4.

>> **Epimedium:** *Epimedium* species and cultivars. Evergreen. The low-growing ones stay under a foot (30.5 cm) high and offer handsome foliage (some have red leaves or highlights), joined by delicate little spring flowers (white, yellow, or pink). It grows slowly and steadily. It's low-maintenance and deer-resistant. Hardy to Zone 5.

>> **Japanese spurge:** *Pachysandra terminalis.* Evergreen. Japanese spurge is an attractive spreading, foliage plant for shady, moist conditions. Features rich green leaves on upright 10-inch (25.4 cm) stems, with fragrant white flowers in summer. Plant in partial to full shade and space them 6 to 12 inches (15.2 to 30.5 cm) apart. Hardy to Zone 4.

REMEMBER

Pachysandra does well in dry, rocky soil, where it may have to compete with tree or shrub roots for moisture and nutrients. Grown in loose, fertile, moist soil; however, it grows too rampantly, so choose its site with care.

>> **Mondo grass or lily turf:** *Liriope* or *Ophiopogon.* Evergreen. Mondo grass and lily turf are two similar grasslike plants that make attractive groundcovers in shady situations.

- *Liriope spicata,* creeping lily turf, is one of the most adaptable, growing 6 to 10 inches (15.2 to 25.4 cm) high.

- *L. muscari* grows up to 2 feet (.6 m) high and has blue summer flowers that are partially hidden by the foliage.

  The hardiness of both species varies, but most can be grown into Zone 5.

>> **Spotted nettle:** *Lamium maculatum.* Good-looking, trouble-free foliage is the reason to invite this justly popular groundcover into a shady area in your yard. The rather oval leaves are fresh green, spotted, ribbed, or marked with white, light green, or silver. The most commonly found cultivars — 'White Nancy' and 'Beacon Silver' — have green-rimmed foliage that is otherwise entirely silver. Tiny white or pink flowers appear for several weeks in summer. Zones 4 to 8.

>> **Sweet woodruff:** *Galium odoratum.* This plant is a charmer, from its long, thin, apple-green leaves (which occur in whorls along the slender stems) to its small, dainty white flowers. The name refers to the fact that the entire plant exudes a sweet, spicy scent when dried — like vanilla. Easy-going, spreads over the years. Looks wonderful with other shade-loving plants popping up above its pretty carpet. Zones 3 to 9.

WARNING

Beware of dwarf periwinkle (*Vinca minor*), also called creeping myrtle. This spreading, evergreen groundcover prospers in shady conditions, grows from 6 to 12 inches (15.2 to 30.5 cm) high and has violet-blue flowers in spring and summer. Its domineering ways are fine if you're turning over an entire shady area to it, but otherwise, unfortunately it's invasive. (For more on battling unwanted plants, see Chapter 17.)

Top groundcover choices for slopes

We admit it, we flinch a little recommending some of these, because they can be aggressive growers. But they can also be a godsend for areas that have erosion problems, or you don't want to climb up and down or try to mow. Just make sure they stay in bounds. Refer to the section, "Planting groundcovers," later in this chapter for special instructions on how to plant groundcovers on a slope.

>> **Creeping juniper:** *Juniperus.* Refer to the section, "Shrubby plants to cover the ground," later in this chapter for more information.

>> **Creeping phlox:** *Phlox stolonifera.* Its habit is short (4 to 6 inches, 10 to 15.2 cm, tall) and spreading (about a foot, 30.5 cm) — it expands by runners. Little green leaves, which are overwhelmed in spring when the plants cover themselves generously in lightly scented little flowers (white, blue, pink, purple hues). Impervious to mildew and untroubled by nibbling slugs. Zones 3 to 8.

>> **Creeping St. John's wort:** *Hypericum calycinum.* See the section, "Top ground-cover choices for sun," earlier in this chapter.

>> **Dwarf periwinkle or creeping myrtle:** *Vinca minor.* See the section, "Top groundcover choices for shade," earlier in this chapter.

>> **English ivy:** *Hedera helix.* Evergreen. With its dark green, lobed leaves, English ivy has been a popular groundcover but fallen out of favor due to its rampant, aggressive ways. However, it may be the solution you need a in difficult site like a steep or hard-to-access slope or embankment. It grows well in sun or shade. Many varieties (differing in leaf size, texture, and color) are available. Space plants 12 to 18 inches (30.5 to 45.7 cm) apart. Hardy to Zone 5, although some small-leafed types are less hardy.

WARNING

English ivy can become invasive, climbing into trees and over structures if not kept under control. If you choose to plant it, keep a watchful eye on it and clip it back, anytime, where necessary.

>> **Mondo grass or lily turf:** *Liriope* or *Ophiopogon.* See the section, "Top groundcover choices for shade," earlier in this chapter.

Top groundcover choices for wet areas

Perpetually damp ground doesn't have to be changed nor does it have to be full of weeds or otherwise look terrible. You can install one of these plants and let it take over the area.

REMEMBER

Just be vigilant because some of these plants can get overly enthusiastic. To keep them in bounds, patrol their boundaries and mow or cut back growth that strays.

- **Bunchberry, creeping dogwood:** *Cornus canadensis.* In its native woods, it grows in broad colonies, lighting up the gloom in spring with large (for the plant's size) white dogwood flowers — a sight you can imitate in your garden. Needs acidic soil. Don't transplant from the wild; for best results, start with young seedlings from a reputable nursery. Zones 2 to 6.

- **Chameleon plant:** *Houttuynia cordata.* Heart-shaped leaves, in abundance. You have a choice of plain green, green-and-cream, or the rather splashy multicolored cultivar 'Chameleon' (pink, red, cream, green, on every leaf). Plants get between 6 and 12 inches (15.2 to 30.5 cm) high and spread. Zones 4 to 9.

- **Goldenstar:** *Chrysogonum virginiana.* A low (to 12 inches, 30.5 cm), spreading, but not aggressive plant, this native wildflower blooms like crazy in late spring and summer. The pretty yellow flowers are about 1½ inches (3.8 cm) across. Mass plantings, such as along a woodland walkway or bordering a line of shrubs, always look great and call attention to the vivacious if small flowers. Zones 5 to 9.

- **Japanese sedge:** *Carex morrowii.* Sedges are well-known for prospering in wet conditions, and this one has made its way into garden centers and nurseries. Forms a grasslike clump, up to 2 feet (.6 m) tall. 'Variegata' has white-striped leaves. Zones 5 to 9.

- **Moneywort, golden creeping Jenny:** *Lysimachia nummularia.* This is a tough plant for tough locations. It grows quickly and thickly — common sense counsels against planting such a vigorous plant adjacent to a perennial bed or manicured lawn. But if you have a shady area with damp soil, moneywort will do the trick. Rounded, coin-shaped bright green leaves, bright yellow flowers in spring. Zones 3 to 8.

- **Ostrich fern:** *Matteuccia struthiopteris.* Easy to grow, creates a lush look in a season or two, and lasts for years and years. Partial shade is preferred. Vase-shaped habit, bright green fronds that reminded someone of ostrich feathers. Can get around 4 feet (1.2 m) high and 3 (.9 m) feet wide. Zones 3 to 8.

Top choices between paving stones

Planting groundcover between paving stones is a great look. Not every plant can tolerate the limited space and occasional foot traffic, but the following can. Just remember, when planting, to give them enough loose, good soil between the pavers or stones. No plant, not even these, likes lousy, compacted, shallow soil. Check out these great choices:

- **Blue star creeper:** *Isotoma fluviatilis.* An amazingly tough, durable plant. Flat-growing, bright green foliage. After it's established, it will produce scads of tiny, starry light blue flowers from spring to summer. Zones 6 to 9.

» **Chamomile:** *Chamaemelum nobile.* Evergreen. Chamomile's fine-textured, aromatic foliage can take some foot traffic. Has small yellow flowers in summer. Chamomile stays low and compact in full sun, rarely getting over 6 inches (15.2 cm) high; plants grow taller in partial shade. You can mow chamomile or plant it between stepping stones. Plant in full sun, spacing plants about 6 to 12 inches (15.2 to 30.5 cm) apart. Hardy to Zone 7.

» **Corsican mint:** *Mentha requienii.* Yes, it's really a mint — imagine people walking over it on your terrace or flagstone path and that refreshing scent releasing into the air. Forms a dense, low mat that looks a bit, at a glance, like mint. Like all mints, it does need water or it will dry out. Zones 6 to 9.

» **Creeping thyme:** *Thymus praecox arcticus.* Evergreen. A low-growing, creeping herb that is especially useful between stepping stones. Can take foot traffic and can even be grown as a lawn alternative. Creeping thyme grows 3 to 6 inches (7.6 to 15.2 cm) high and has white-to-pink flowers in summer. Plant in full sun and space the plants 6 to 10 inches (15.2 to 25.4 cm) apart. Hardy to Zone 3.

» **Dymondia:** *Dymondia margaretae.* These spreading little plants naturally grow horizontally and flat. The tiny, slender leaves are green above and silver below, and because they tend to curl a bit, you get an appealing two-tone look. May bloom in spring; tiny yellow daisies. Hardy in Zones 9 to 11.

Shrubby plants to cover the ground

For those sites where you want something taller to cover a broader area, certain shrubs may fill the bill. These plants generally stay low–growing without a lot of intervention or maintenance from you like a good groundcover should.

Ideally your selection naturally grows rather densely after you plant them close together. Here are our top picks for this job:

» **Cotoneaster:** *Cotoneaster.* Deciduous or evergreen. Cotoneasters are a large family of shrubs that includes many dependable groundcovers known for their bright-green foliage, small flowers, and red berries. Favorites include the following:

- The evergreen bearberry cotoneaster, *C. dammeri*, grows only 8 inches (20.3 cm) high and spreads up to 10 feet (3 m).

- The deciduous rock cotoneaster, *C. horizontalis* grows from 2 to 3 feet (.6 to .9 m) high and has orange-to-red autumn color.

- The evergreen rockspray cotoneaster, *C. microphyllus* rarely exceeds 2 to 3 feet (.6 to .9 m) in height.

Hardiness varies, but most cotoneasters can be grown into Zone 5 or 6. Plant at least 3 feet (.9 m) apart in full sun. (Some of the widest-spreading types should be spaced 5 feet, 1.5 m, apart.)

>> **Creeping juniper:** *Juniperus.* Evergreen. Many low, spreading junipers (differing in height and foliage color) are available. Junipers are tough plants that get by with little care but must have well-drained soil. Consider these:

- *J. chinensis* 'San Jose' has grayish-green leaves and grows 2 feet (.6 m) high.

- *J. horizontalis* 'Bar Harbor' grows about a foot (.3 m) high and spreads up to 10 feet (3 m); the gray-green leaves turn bluish in winter.

- *J. horizontalis* 'Wiltonii' is only 6 inches (15.2 cm) high and has silver-blue foliage.

Plant junipers in full sun. Most should be spaced 2 to 5 feet (.6 to 1.5 m) apart, depending on the variety. Most are hardy into Zone 3.

>> **Groundcovering rose:** *Rosa* cultivars. Yes, some roses have been developed for this purpose, so specifically ask or look for groundcovering roses. Plant size, flower color, and hardiness varies.

WARNING

Even if some local nursery is unethical or uneducated enough to sell invasive shrubby plants to the unsuspecting public, don't put in pesky, aggressive winter-creepers (*Euonymus fortunei* and cultivars) or barberry (*Berberis thunbergii* and cultivars) bushes. They make poor groundcovers thanks to their rampant, sprawling ways.

Planting groundcovers

After you have an idea which groundcovering plants you want, it's time to install them. These sections explain what you need to know when planting and how to keep weeds at bay while the groundcovers get established.

Putting the groundcovers in the ground

When you're ready to begin planting groundcovers, keep the following pointers in mind to make sure the process goes smoothly:

>> **Start the project at a low-stress time for baby plants.** For many people, early spring is best. If you live in an area with hot, dry summers and mild winters, wait until fall, when winter rains should get the plants off to a strong start.

>> **As with all plantings, attend to soil needs before introducing your plants to your landscape.** Chapter 17 discusses how.

>> **Plants sold as groundcovers usually come in small containers or in flats, depending on their growth habit.** You may separate those grown in flats into individual sections before planting.

- If you're planting your groundcovers from pots, place the plants into individual holes. To plant small plants from pots or packs, dig a hole just deep enough for the rootball. For larger, container-grown plants, taper the hole outward at the base and create a mound for the rootball. For more information on planting container-grown plants, see Chapter 15.

- If starting from flats, prepare the whole planting area. Planting ground-cover from flats is very much like planting annuals and perennials, which we describe in Chapters 13 and 14.

>> **Be aware of plant spacing.** Spacing is a matter of how much patience and money, you want to invest. Setting baby pachysandra plants, for example, only 6 inches (15.2 cm) apart means buying more plants, but they'll fill in in a season or two. If you're more frugal or trying to cover a larger area, you may decide to set seedlings 12 inches (30.5 cm) apart and wait four years or so (of course, fast-growers like creeping St. John's wort will take less time). Certainly, you can plant groundcover plants more closely than you would if you were just adding an individual or two to a flowerbed.

TIP

When planting on a steep slope, set each plant on its own terrace or flattened spot (with the top of the rootball slightly above the soil level) and create a watering basin behind the plant.

>> **Water plants adequately to help get them established.** After the plants are growing well, many types need only minimal maintenance.

Controlling weeds until the groundcover is established

Plan on controlling weeds between plants until the groundcover is established. You have three options:

>> **On planting day, cover the area.** Use black plastic or *landscape fabric* (a porous material sold in rolls that permits water penetration but retards weeds) and create a hole (or cut an X) for each new plant. Mulch afterward to hide it from view.

>> **Mulch the area.** Mulch several inches/cm thick, after installing the baby plants, and replenish it from time to time. Shredded bark is ideal because it looks nice and yet lets water through, but pine needles or straw (not hay, which contains weed seeds) will also do. If you live in cold climate, the mulch also offers protection from winter's cold and helps prevent *frost-heaving* (rootballs getting pushed up out of the ground by freeze-thaw cycles).

>> **Interplant with annuals.** This tactic is temporary, with the annuals acting as placeholders and prettying up the area while you wait for the (perennial) groundcover plants to get going. If the site is in sun, try marigolds or zinnias; if in shade, plunk in some colorful pansies.

TIP

Many spreading, nonwoody groundcovers (such as English ivy, St. John's wort, and vinca) can be rejuvenated or kept looking fresh by occasional shearing. Cut the plants back to several inches/cm above the ground in spring before perhaps fertilizing them. Within a few weeks, the plants will regrow and look full, clean, and healthy. Yes, some groundcovers can become overly vigorous, but this way you can keep them under control *and* looking good.

Considering How Much Lawn You Need

A lush, well-kept lawn has been considered the pride and joy of many a home landscape over the years. However, people nowadays seem to be busier than ever and also interested in other landscape looks. So the question we ask you to ponder in the following sections is whether you really want a traditional lawn. If you do, we offer some suggestions of lowering the amount of maintenance and reducing the impact on the environment, including, simply, making it smaller.

Recognizing what having a lawn means

Do you really want to spend what leisure time you have constantly mowing (on hot days) and then dealing with the demanding regimen of fertilizer, weedkillers, pesticides, and watering? Lawn care is time-consuming, expensive, and tiring, more so, in fact, than virtually any other garden element.

Nowadays more information and a heightened awareness is available of the impact that a traditional lawn has on the environment. A proportion of the high-nitrogen lawn fertilizer people put on their lawns is inevitably wasted, running off and entering the local water table, and eventually nearby waterways. When this happens, algal blooms follow, killing fish and other aquatic life. Weedkiller applications, too, are hard to get just right (you maykill or harm unintended targets right in your own yard) and runoff is also a problem. And although pesticides may kill your targeted lawn pest, they also adversely impact beneficial soil organisms and threaten good bugs, including some beleaguered pollinators.

Lawns consume a lot of water as well, and often at least some of that water is lost to runoff and evaporation. Water is increasingly a precious resource and not just in the arid West and Southwest.

In addition, lawns are, to be blunt, an ecological desert. That means unlike the rest of the home landscape, not to mention surrounding parks and wilder areas, lawns aren't contributors to the environment or participants in the food chain. Most lawn grasses are nonnative species, sterile, and cut off before they have a chance to form plumes/flowers/seed; they don't sustain wildlife.

Well. All this is pretty sobering. However, the life lawns do support is . . . your own. A lawn allows you to sit, snooze on, or play with friends, family, and pets. A lawn anchors a landscape and gives the eye a rest from your busy flower, shrub, and edible plantings. People can appreciate the inviting repose of a plain horizontal element before looking more closely at the vertical growth of your diverse adjacent plantings. Also, of course, some people enjoy mowing and savor the smell of fresh-cut grass.

REMEMBER

We're just asking you to think twice. If a lawn is impractical due to your lifestyle or climate, refer to the section, "Calling Groundcovers to the Rescue," earlier in this chapter. Or consider putting in a rock garden adorned with succulents; more hardscape, such as a new deck or patio; a water feature — advocates point out that a water feature (after initial filling of the pool) uses less water than the same area devoted to lawn; or installing more flowers and edibles.

Choosing a lower-maintenance, lower-impact lawn

If you still really want a lawn, consider making it smaller and smarter. With planning, you can satisfy your penchant for a lawn without putting too many demands on your leisure time or the environment. Keep these points in mind:

>> If you have a newly built home and you're starting from scratch with the landscaping, think seriously about how much weekend time you want to spend pushing the lawn mower (or sitting on the riding mower) and what's appropriate water use for your part of the country — then size your new lawn area accordingly.

   If you already have a lawn, check out the nearby sidebar about how to easily reseed and keep your yard in top shape.

>> Forget about the idea that your lawn must be square. Check out the photo in the color insert that shows a unique lawn shape.

>> Choose for your lawn one of the many new low-maintenance grass varieties available today.

>> Select a grass that's adapted to your climate to reduce the amount of work and resources required to keep your lawn looking good. Refer to the next section for some ideas.

Putting In a New Lawn

You create a lawn by planting *turfgrasses* — grasses especially bred for this particular use — and you can do it in two main ways:

>> **Spreading grass seed:** The most economical way to plant grass, it requires proper soil preparation and follow-up care. The first week or two after planting, pay constant attention to your newly seeded lawn to make sure the seeds don't dry out. (Weed seeds are likely to germinate during this time as well.)

>> **Laying sod:** The fastest way to put in a new lawn, this method sets large sections of fully grown turf in place on the soil. The idea of an instant lawn certainly has its appeal, but sod is an expensive option, and you still have to prepare the soil as thoroughly and maintain the newly planted area until the sod gets its roots in the ground.

REMEMBER

Keeping weeds out of the bare soil until the lawn fills in is critical.

Before you launch into this project, we have excellent news for you: You have a bounty of interesting and worthwhile choices — so many, in fact, that it may take some study and thought to come to a decision that is right for your home landscape and appropriate for your climate. The following sections guide you through selection.

Choosing grass types

Growing the appropriate variety of grass for your area of the country is critical. Selecting right makes all the difference between a thriving lawn and one that doesn't survive the winter or languishes in the heat of your climate.

Turfgrasses fall into two broad groups: cool-season and warm-season. Each type of grass has its named varieties, many of which have been bred for conditions like drought or shade tolerance or for sheer ruggedness. Your local extension office or garden center can recommend varieties for your area.

Cool-season grasses

Cool-season grasses grow best between 60°F and 75°F (15°C and 24°C) and can withstand cold winters. In general terms, cool-season grasses are grown in Zones 6 and colder.

Try the following cool-season grasses:

>> **Fine fescue:** *Festuca* varieties. Fine-textured turfgrass. Quick to germinate and get established; does well in less-than-ideal growing conditions. The most

shade-tolerant of the cool-season grasses. Drought-tolerant and requires little feeding. Newer varieties offer insect resistance.

>> **Kentucky bluegrass:** *Poa pratensis*. The most common lawn grass for cold-winter regions. Slow to get established, but with its spreading habit, it fills in nicely. Fine texture with a rich green color. A heavy feeder. Very hardy; many disease-resistant varieties are available.

>> **Perennial ryegrass:** *Lolium perenne*. This finely textured grass is one of the quickest types to get established and will grow in up to 60 percent shade, but it doesn't tolerate the temperature extremes of bluegrass or hold up under mowing as well. Newer varieties offer insect- and disease-resistance.

>> **Turf-type tall fescue:** *Festuca arundinaceae*. This coarse-textured grass makes a lush, rugged lawn under difficult conditions. New varieties are resistant to everything: heat, drought, diseases, and insects.

>> **Crested wheat grass:** *Agropyron cristatum*. A native grass of the Rocky Mountains and High Plains; very drought tolerant.

Warm-season grasses

Warm-season grasses, which grow vigorously in temperatures above 80°F, are planted in mild-winter regions. Warm-season grasses are grown in Zones 7 and warmer.

For warmer climates, here are warm-season grasses:

>> **Bahia grass:** *Paspalum notatum*. This low-growing, coarse-textured grass isn't as attractive as some of the other warm-season grasses, but it's low maintenance and grows in partial shade.

>> **Bermuda grass:** *Cynodon dactylon.* The most common lawn grass in mild-winter climates. Texture ranges from coarse to fine, depending on the variety. This rugged, drought-resistant grass spreads quickly and can crowd out weeds. Needs frequent, close mowing. Some varieties offer disease and insect resistance. Common Bermuda grass can be grown from seed; the improved *hybrids* (recently developed varieties) can be planted only as plugs or sod and aren't as weedy because they don't set seed.

>> **Blue grama grass:** *Bouteloua gracilis.* A fine-textured grass with flat, gray-green blades. Native to the U.S. Great Plains; very drought resistant and requires little or no fertilization.

>> **Buffalo grass.** *Bouteloua dactyloides.* Fine texture and curled, gray-green blades. Another heat- and drought-resistant Great Plains native. Requires little mowing and little or no fertilization.

- **Carpet grass:** *Axonopus* varieties. Coarse texture and low-growing, pointed blades. Spreads quickly and does well in sandy soil.

- **Centipede grass:** *Eremochloa ophiuroides.* Coarse to medium texture and flat, blunt blades. A low-maintenance, shade-tolerant grass that does well on soils that are acidic or low in fertility. Some disease resistance.

- **St. Augustine grass:** *Stenotaphrum secundatum.* This coarse-textured grass tolerates partial shade. In general, susceptible to insect and disease problems, although some improved varieties have been introduced in the past few years. Planted from sod or sprigs.

- **Zoysia grass:** *Zoysia* species. A coarse- to fine-textured grass with stiff blades. Slow growing but very tough after it's established. Drought resistant and shade tolerant. Considered invasive in some settings, so ask how it fares in your area before investing. Planted from sod or sprigs.

Seeding your lawn

The first step in preparing the area to be sown is to test your soil to see whether it's fertile and has the proper pH to grow grass. Then you need to add the proper soil amendments, work them into the ground with a rototiller and level the whole area.

The best time to seed a new lawn in cool climates is in the late summer or early autumn and in mild climates, in spring or early summer.

TIP

Your lawn is a landscape feature that you'll have for years to come, so skip the cheap stuff. How to recognize fine quality seed? Look for the following on the label:

- A variety name, such as 'Nugget' Kentucky bluegrass instead of generic Kentucky bluegrass

- Weed and other crop seed content of 0.5 percent or less; the highest-quality seed is free of weed and other undesirable crop seed

- *Germination percentage* (percentage of seeds in your bag that will sprout and begin to grow) of 85 percent or greater for Kentucky bluegrass and above 90 percent for all other grasses

Remember to measure the dimensions of the area that you plan to seed; the label also indicates how large an area the package will cover.

When you're ready to plant, assemble all the tools and equipment that you need: soil amendments, rotary tiller, grass seed, lawn spreader (a device, shown in Figure 16-1 that scatters seed evenly as you roll it over the soil — also called a drop spreader), board scraper (a board that you drag over the soil surface) or rake, lawn roller (a large, heavy drum, shown in Figure 16-1 with a handle that you roll over the scattered seed to press it into the soil; the drum can be filled with water to increase the weight), and mulching material such as straw. You can rent expensive tools for the day.

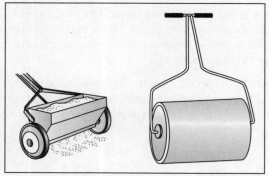

FIGURE 16-1:
One of several types of lawn spreaders (left) and a lawn roller (right).

Then follow these instructions:

1. **If necessary, spread amendments over the soil to correct the pH and apply a complete fertilizer recommended for new lawns in the amount given on the bag.**

   Chapter 17 has more information about soil.

2. **Till the soil 6 to 8 inches (15.2 to 20.3 cm) deep to loosen it.**

   Don't overcultivate — leave small lumps and cracks to catch seed so that the grass sprouts quickly. Remove stones and debris.

3. **Level the soil with a board scraper or rake to eliminate high spots.**

   Without this step, your mower would cut the grass too short as well as depressions where it might miss spots or where water can collect (see Chapter 5 for information on solving drainage problems).

4. **Roll the seedbed with a half-filled roller to firm the soil.**

   Make sure that the soil is dry before you roll; otherwise, it compacts, preventing seeds from sprouting.

5. **Sow the seed with a mechanical spreader or by hand.**

   Don't be tempted to oversow; if you do, the plants won't develop properly.

6. **Rake the surface lightly, barely covering about half the seed and leaving the rest exposed.**

   The seed needs light to germinate.

7. **Roll once more with the half-filled roller to press seeds in contact with the soil.**

8. **Lightly mulch the seedbed.**

   Mulch keeps the soil moist until the seeds germinate. A light mulch — less than ¼-inch (.6 cm) deep — is all you need. If you're planting a large area, ask your nursery associate if you can borrow or rent a cage roller — an easy-to-use device that lays down a thin layer of organic matter. The mulch also keeps the seeds from washing away in a heavy rain.

9. **Give the newly seeded area a thorough initial soaking and then keep it well watered until the grass is established.**

   After the initial soaking, frequent light sprinklings will keep the seed moist. After the seed sprouts, each watering should penetrate the soil to a depth of several inches/cm to promote good root growth.

Installing sod

The best time to lay sod in cold-winter regions is in autumn; in mild-winter regions, the best time is early spring.

TIP

Sod is expensive, so buy from a quality supplier. Look for sections that are ½-inch to 1 inch (.5 to 2.5 cm) thick, with no brown patches or dried-out edges. Have the sod delivered on planting day so that it doesn't sit in a pile and heat up.

When you're ready to lay your new sod, assemble all the tools and equipment that you need: soil amendments, rotary tiller, sharp knife, board scraper or rake, and lawn roller. Prepare the planting area as you would for a lawn from seed (Steps 1 through 4 in the previous section of this chapter).

Then follow these instructions for laying sod:

1. **Roll out a piece of sod (green side up!) and press it into position.**

   Start along a straight edge, such as next to a walkway or driveway. If the lawn is irregularly shaped, stretch twine across the middle to establish a straight line. Fit the next section against it tightly but don't overlap.

2. **Continue laying sections, staggering them slightly, like bricks (see Figure 16-2).**

   Don't let the sod dry out. Lightly sprinkle finished sections as you go. Use a knife to cut sod to fit curved or irregular areas.

3. **Use a half-filled roller over the newly laid turf, going back over it a second time at right angles to the first pass.**

4. **Water the lawn thoroughly and keep the sod moist until roots knit with the soil (try lifting an edge to check).**

In hot weather, you may have to sprinkle the new sod several times a day to keep it moist.

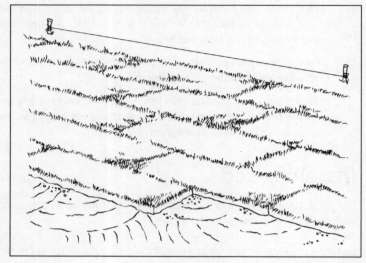

FIGURE 16-2: Stagger the ends of the sod, as if you're laying brick.

© John Wiley & Sons, Inc.

Watering efficiently

Keeping lawn grass lush takes a lot of water, so make sure you water correctly and efficiently to avoid waste, and avoid runoff and puddles.

That said, we recommend that you water deeply, so the roots grow more deeply than they might otherwise. In this way, they'll be better able to manage and keep looking good during dry spells. You won't have to water as often. Also less-frequent, deeper waterings help your lawn resist disease.

TIP

Here are the best times to water:

>> **Morning or evening:** Less will be lost to evaporation. Morning is a little better because watering late in the day means a wet lawn overnight, which may lead to lawn-grass diseases.

>> **On a still day:** Wind definitely is a factor in evaporation and can also blow water beyond the lawn borders. No point in letting that happen.

The best option is to install an in-ground irrigation system. Of course, that's best put in place *before* the lawn goes in, although you can have one installed after the fact and the lawn rehabilitated afterward. For more on in-ground systems, turn to Chapter 5.

TIP

If water is scarce and expensive where you live, we hope you're dealing with a smaller lawn and a grass or grass blend adapted to your climate and known to be drought-tolerant — that goes a long way toward reducing water consumption. If so, consider watering your lawn in this order:

>> Irrigating your lawn and supplementing with *gray water*, which is used water collected in your shower and home (keep a pail handy). A little soap in that water won't do your lawn grass harm. (Read more about gray water in Chapter 5.)

>> Watering with sprinklers, which deliver water lightly over a broad area so it has a chance to soak in.

>> Squirting a lawn with a hose is the least efficient, for you and for the lawn. The water is delivered too fast and too hard to a smaller radius. If your lawn is of manageable size, skip sprinklers and spend 10 or 15 minutes outdoors waving a watering wand (set to fine spray) attached to your hose over it.

Buffering the borders

Defining a border (also called *edging*) between where lawn stops and garden beds, or paths or patio and so forth, begin gives your landscaping a neater look. Lawn grass encroachment damages hardscape, and lawn grass can overtake a flower-bed. Furthermore, borders also prevent runoff; borders should keep lawn water, and fertilizer or weedkillers, if you use them, where they belong. However, be careful how you install borders because you don't want anyone to trip or the mower to repeatedly ding it.

Borders come in various forms and styles. Here are some basic alternatives and how to place them:

>> **Bricks:** Create a long trench along the lawn's edge, about 6 inches (15.2 cm) deep. Sift in some construction sand. Lay bricks in vertically. Tamp down their tops with a rubber mallet until they're flush with the soil surface.

>> **Flagstone:** Create a long trench along the lawn's edge, but wider and shallower (based on the dimensions/thickness of the flagstone pieces). Sift in some construction sand. Lay in the stones, smooth side up. Stand on the stones to see if they shift or rock; if they do, lift them up, add more sand, and try again until all is level and secure.

>> **Metal or plastic edging:** Create a long, narrow trench along the lawn's edge, just deep enough to accommodate the material you've chosen. Wedge in the edging so that the top is barely above the soil level, then backfill the trench with construction sand in order to secure it in place.

Even if you choose plastic edging that looks strong and durable, it does become brittle over time because of exposure to the elements, including water and UV light. Steel edging is much more long-lasting (just don't use flimsy, thin aluminum).

ROLLING IN CLOVER? SPARING DANDELIONS?

We invite you to ease up on the idea that a lawn must be a smooth green carpet. Consider clover . . . all those little white (or pink) flowers. A weed? We've met much worse (crabgrass, for example). Clover is a member of the bean family, which means it has the remarkable ability to *fix* nitrogen in the soil. Plain English translation: Clover takes nitrogen from the air and, with a little help from friendly root bacteria, converts it to a form it can use to live and grow. So can your lawn. What's the main ingredient in lawn fertilizer? That's right. Nitrogen. Leave the clover, fertilize a lot less.

Lawn clover confers other benefits. It stays green all summer. It helps your lawn withstand foot traffic. It co-exists with lawn grass, and it can crowd out broadleaf weeds. It helps prevent soil erosion. It feeds bees. Maybe it's time to let it be.

Speaking of bees, every spring, social media gets jammed with people reminding one another not to kill or yank up dandelions, so the bees can feed. If the bees don't eat, they'll perish, and their honey production or, most importantly, their critical pollinating services will be diminished or lost. The bees we're fretting about here, by the way, are nonnative honeybees. They get out earlier than native bees, as soon as the weather is warm enough for them to fly. They have other options, but dandelions are early bloomers and browsed. Dandelions also provide nectar and pollen to some beetles, butterflies, and moths.

Well, that's a far cry from the eradication fervor of our youth. It has become uncool to poison dandelions out of lawns (weedkillers should be uncool, in our opinion). And it's long since been uncool to offer a neighborhood kid a nickel per plucked dandelion flower.

Here's a compromise position: Let the honeybees and other insects enjoy the yellow flowerheads, but get out and mow the lawn as the flowers start to pass and the white puffballs of seeds begin to form.

4

Outside Factors You Can and Can't Control

Take some simple actions to improve your soil, install your own compost pile, and feed your plants what they need to prosper.

Make changes to your landscaping without breaking the bank.

Recognize ways you can deal with critters and insects so everyone can live in the same ecosystem.

Handle weeds and unwanted plants without inflicting chemicals on your garden.

Use climate zone maps to select plants that will succeed where you live.

Care better for your plants in warm and cold climates and challenging weather conditions.

Chapter **17**

Maintaining Your Landscape

Y ou can design the most beautiful landscape on paper with wonderful plant combinations and eye-catching color, but if the plants don't thrive where they're planted, they won't look good and neither will your yard. In this chapter, we describe ways you can maintain your landscape including preparing your soil, composting, fertilizing, pruning, and making changes.

Bettering Your Soil

The number-one cause of unhappy, struggling plants? Lousy soil! We urge you to attend to your yard's soil early and often — you'll be amazed at how much heart-ache this saves.

REMEMBER

Soil preparation ensures that plant roots have a balance of all of the things they need for healthy growth, namely, air, water, and nutrients. Without any one of these, your plants languish. And with many permanent plantings like flowering perennials, groundcovers, perhaps a hedge, as well as today's smaller lawns, you only get one good crack at soil preparation — prior to planting.

The best time to improve the soil is after any major drainage problems have been fixed (see Chapter 4), features like paths and patios are in (see Chapters 7 and 9), and any leftover junk and debris are out of the way. After that, pause to take a close look at the soil you have, give it a good squeeze, have it tested, amend it, and then work it into shape.

TIP

If the soil around your new home looks and feels more like pavement than dirt, consult with a landscape contractor about fixing it. Bringing it up to an acceptable level will take some work and, probably, heavier equipment. The extra effort is definitely worth it. You may be able to buy and truck in new topsoil, but be careful that what you're bringing in is similar to the original topsoil and not full of weed seeds and other junk. Also make sure that it's properly spread and worked in. The best advice if you're considering this route — get help from a professional.

Here we help you figure out what you already have. Then you can assess and upgrade as needed. Honestly, inheriting wonderful soil is rare, although soil improvement isn't a mysterious process.

NO MATTER WHERE YOU LIVE, YOUR SOIL NEEDS LOVE

Most people aren't fortunate to live on land that is already healthy, as the following demonstrates:

- Modern subdivisions, in particular, need remediation because the topsoil was probably stripped away and/or compacted by heavy construction equipment. In such settings, you must improve the soil or face endless struggles with your landscaping plans.

- Former farmland isn't guaranteed to have a thick layer of organically rich soil; depending on their crops or types of livestock, farmers don't always prioritize soil health. They or someone before them may have applied farm chemicals or other materials that still linger and may adversely affect garden health.

- Inner-city neighborhoods and even many suburban ones have been inhabited for a long time and don't tend to come with good soil either. Even if your present yard was once cultivated by a good gardener, soil gets depleted over time.

This is an opportunity to leave the world better than you found it. Improve your soil!

BREAKING DOWN THE LAYERS OF SOIL

Soil typically is layered. This is a simplification of the basics:

- **Topsoil:** The uppermost layer, that good native soil that was on your property before your house was built. If present, it tends to be darker in color and lighter in texture than what lies below. It's easier to work in and for plants of all kinds to grow in.

  Depending on where you live and how much organic matter, minerals, and moisture exist in the topsoil, it may be light or dark brown, yellowish, or reddish.

- **Subsoil:** The lower lighter-colored layer, subsoil may be quite deep (or it can be shallow, until rock or groundwater is hit). Some plant roots do reach down here, in order to bring up important minerals or access moisture. The subsoil is home to some microorganisms, beetles, earthworms, and the like. Just like your topsoil, it can be aerated and improved.

Cultivating living soil

Nowadays, scientists know more about soil than ever before, although, amazingly, they still have more to learn about how it sustains plant life and about the small creatures that inhabit and contribute to it. To simplify, soil isn't just a substrate to plunk plants into. Soil is alive.

Living soil hosts a community of tiny or unseen players (microbes, fungi, bacteria, and more) and ones you can see (*arthropods*, such as roly-polies, potato bugs, beetles, as well as *invertebrates* like earthworms). Not to mention the decomposing bodies and waste of animals, birds, and insects, large and small. Soil is also made up of inorganic materials, mainly weathered and decomposed rocks and minerals.

You can appreciate just how amazing soil truly is. When you kneel in your yard to put in or move plants or when you take an early-morning walk, examine how your plants are doing. You can see and feel the life. Respect the soil. Don't compact it and don't pollute it. Feed it and nurture it. Work with it.

Identifying the three main types of soil

Soils come in three main types with a lot of variations in between:

>> **Sandy soils:** They're composed of mostly large mineral particles. Water moves through them quickly and takes nutrients with it as it does. Sandy soils are well aerated, quick to dry out, and often lack the nutrients that vegetable plants, especially, need.

>> **Clay soils:** They consist of mostly small particles that cling tightly together and hang on to water. Clay soils are slow to dry out and have poor drainage.

>> **Loam soils:** They're a happy mixture of large and small particles, and they usually contain an abundance of organic matter. Loamy soil is well aerated and drains properly and is able to hold water and nutrients.

You get a pretty good idea of what type of soil you have by grabbing a moist handful and squeezing. When you let go, sandy soil falls apart and doesn't hold together in a ball. Clay soil oozes through your fingers as you squeeze and stays in a slippery wad when you let go. Loamy soil usually stays together after squeezing but falls apart easily when you poke it with your finger.

Adding organic matter to your soil

Your garden probably doesn't have that ideal amount of loam soil. To fix mucky clay or loose sand, you need to add organic matter. *Organic matter* helps loosen and aerate clay soils. Organic matter also improves the water- and nutrient-holding capacity of sandy soils. In other words, organic matter makes soil more loamy and much better for plants.

Author Steven Frowine's definition in *Gardening Basics For Dummies* (John Wiley & Sons, Inc.) is succinct: Organic matter is "once-living material that releases nutrients as it decays."

Here are some good sources of organic matter:

>> Homemade compost (refer to the section, "Composting 101: Making Black Gold," later in this chapter)

>> Bagged aged compost or humus

>> Old sawdust (fresh isn't good for your soil, so let it rot for a while before using it)

>> Shredded or ground-up composted bark

>> Leaf mold (composted, chopped-up fall leaves)

>> Decomposed grass clippings (assuming they don't contain any fertilizer or weedkillers)

>> Bagged dehydrated and aged cow manure

Never use fresh manure, steaming-hot *or* dehydrated. It needs to be composted first (allowed to sit and break down for several months to a year) or it will burn or damage plants.

>> Mushroom soil

>> Bagged Milorganite. This high-nitrogen organic matter can be used in soil improvement as well as a slow-release fertilizer. It's been around for decades and some gardeners swear by it. Its name reflects its origin; it's made by the Milwaukie, Wisconsin Sewerage district. It contains no human feces, however; it's heat-dried microbes that have digested organic matter in the city's wastewater.

>> Cover crops, such as rye, that you sow in autumn and till under the following spring

To add the organic matter of your choice (and you can certainly add more than one kind), stick to these steps:

1. Prep the area beforehand.

Clear out existing plants, especially weeds, hopefully by the roots. Remove rocks and any other debris.

2. Lay down a 1- to 2-inch (2.5 to 5 cm) layer of organic matter on the area where you're planting.

The best way to spread it is with a wheelbarrow and shovel, but if you're landscaping a large area, you may want to rent a small tractor with a front-end scoop to simplify things.

TIP

Lay more in a new garden or if the soil is heavy clay or very sandy. Go for the lower end if you've been gardening there for years or if the soil is pretty good.

You need 3 cubic yards of compost to spread a 1-inch-thick layer over 1,000 square feet (in metric, 2.3 cubic m, 2.5-cm layer, 30.5 m).

3. Work it in to a depth of at least 6 inches (15.2 cm).

Do your best to distribute it evenly. Then rake over the area when done, for neatness.

4. Either cover the improved area, or plant ASAP.

An open area of good soil is an invitation to weeds. If you can't plant the area right away, cover it with a tarp (with the corners anchored).

WARNING

Adding sawdust to your soil robs the soil of nitrogen when it decomposes, so you have to add more fertilizer to compensate. Livestock manure is wonderful because it adds nitrogen to the soil. However, livestock often eat lots of hay that's full of weed seeds, which can end up germinating in your landscape. If you use either of these two materials, make sure it's fully composted — in other words, let it sit around for a year or two until very little of the original material is visible and the salts have leached out.

Putting your soil to the test

You also need to know some things about your soil's chemistry. Don't worry, though, you don't need a lab coat.

Many plants are kind of picky about soil chemistry. Too much of this or too little of that, and you have problems. The only way to see whether your soil will be to your plants' liking is to have it tested. Autumn is a good time to have a soil test done and add recommended amendments because they work slowly in the soil.

Soils tests can be performed in either of two ways:

>> **A do-it-yourself kit:** These tests measure the soil's acidity and alkalinity, and sometimes major nutrient content. This basic *pH* (a number that represents the acidity and alkalinity of your soil) test is really easy to do. Buy the kit at a nursery, follow the instructions, and voilà! — you know what your soil pH is. However, these tests aren't always reliable, and besides, you want to know more than just the soil's pH. These tests are cheap and easy, though.

>> **A soil lab test:** Your local Cooperative Extension office or a private soil lab can conduct a more complete and reliable soil test. (To locate a private lab, search online for "local soil testing" or ask your Cooperative Extension office.) This test gives you not only your soil pH but also its nutrient content.

When you know the nutrient content, you can tell how much and what kind of amendments to use (refer to the section, "Incorporating amendments," later in this chapter). A lab charges quite a bit more to conduct a test.

Besides providing pH and nutrient content, a soil lab test can also help identify local problems. For example, in dry-summer areas, you may have salty soil. A remedy is to add gypsum, a readily available mineral soil additive.

TIP

If the plot you wish to raise plants on is in an area of present or former old homes or commercial buildings, also get your soil checked for lead and heavy metals. Mainly this caution applies to urban areas, but lead paint was once widely used, even in rural areas. You never want to raise edible plants where such toxins linger.

REMEMBER

Changes in pH and most nutrients are gradual. If you're dealing with a significant imbalance, test the soil every year. In which case, a home testing kit may be best. For maintaining soil that's already in good balance, only test every three to five years.

Adjusting soil pH

Soil gets scored on a pH scale with a pH of 1 being most acid and a pH of 14 being most alkaline. Most plants enjoy growing in a slightly acid soil with a pH between

4.5 and 6.5, but certain plants have specific requirements. Azaleas and rhododendrons, for example, must have an acid soil.

If the pH isn't within a suitable range, plants can't take up nutrients like phosphorous and potassium even if they're present in the soil in high amounts. On the other hand, the *solubility* (ability to take up nutrients) of certain minerals such as manganese may increase to toxic levels if the pH is too low.

Generally, soils in areas with high rainfall tend to be acidic. In these areas, you likely have a pH of below 6, and you can add ground limestone to the soil to raise it. Where less rainfall occurs, soils are more alkaline, and you likely have a pH of above 7.5; to lower it, add soil sulfur.

Be advised that nudging your soil's pH up or down can be a slow process. Start in the fall the year before, is our advice. Allow even more time for the additives to have their desired effect if you are aiming for a big change, that is, you may have to do the work in stages over a couple of seasons.

All Cooperative Extension offices, any soil lab, and many lawn and garden centers have charts showing how much lime or sulfur to add to correct your pH balance. Detailed charts and application information are also provided on the additive bags/labels. The scale is based on pounds of material to add per 1,000 square feet/m so you'll have to get a tape measure and determine the square footage of your garden first.

TIP

The best way to apply these materials is with a drop spreader (see Chapter 16). These simple machines don't cost much, and they help you spread the material more evenly. Borrow or rent one. Or, if you're careful and wear gloves, you can spread these materials by hand; just make sure that you work the soil well after spreading.

Incorporating amendments

With various amendments and perhaps some fertilizer (check out the section, "Feeding Your Plants — Which Type of Fertilizer to Use?," later in this chapter) spread over an area, you have to work everything into the soil. *Amendments* are materials you add to the existing soil to improve it.

If the soil is dry, water well, and then let it set for a few days before digging. Don't work soil that's too wet. Soil that's in good condition to work crumbles easily in your hand with a flick of your finger.

TIP

The easiest way to turn the soil, especially on large plots, is with a rototiller. If you're not up for buying one, rent or borrow one. We prefer types with rear tines and power-driven wheels — they let you lean into the machine and use your weight to till deeper.

If you use a rototiller, adjust the tines so that the initial pass over the soil is fairly shallow. As the soil loosens, set the tines deeper with successive passes (criss-crossing at 90-degree angles) until the top 8 to 12 inches (20.3 to 30.5 cm) of soil is loosened. (To loosen the soil in smaller areas by hand, use a straight spade and a digging fork.)

After turning the soil, level the area with a steel rake, breaking up clods and discarding any rocks. Make sure that you maintain any natural contours that promote drainage (see Chapter 4).

Don't leave the space bare after you do all this. Opportunistic weeds will appear. Plant as soon as possible or, if you must wait, anchor a tarp over the site.

REMEMBER

Soil improvement isn't a one-and-done project. Organic matter is always breaking down and being used up and must be replenished from time to time. Even though we are urging you to do major work on an area or bed before planting, bear in mind that you'll continue to improve and maintain your landscape's soil in the future.

DOUBLE-DIGGING: BIG EFFORT, BUT BIG BENEFITS!

We won't lie, double-digging is a lot of sweaty work. *Double-digging* is a time-tested British gardening technique for mixing amendments into lousy soil. Here's how it works:

1. **Dig a trench about 2 feet deep and 2 feet wide (.6 m deep and .6 m wide), remove the topsoil, and set it aside.**

2. **Scoop in organic matter (see the list in the section, "Adding organic matter to your soil," earlier in this chapter).**

3. **Use a garden fork to work some of organic matter a few inches /cm into the subsoil.**

   Doing so benefits whatever you choose to plant in this spot.

4. **Put the topsoil back in the trench and mix everything together (like cake batter).**

5. **Make a new trench adjacent to the completed one.**

   Pile the removed topsoil on top of the first trench while you add amendments to this new trench and then replace and mix. Keep going, trench by trench, until the whole area is done.

Sounds arduous? Yes. But it makes for a great spot for growing beautiful plants.

Gardening with no-till methods

Novice and experienced gardeners and landscapers alike dig. It's perhaps reflexive. After the initial work is done in assessing and improving your soil or if you're fortunate to have inherited good soil, you can consider stopping.

Yes, that's right. No-till gardening means no major digging. The object is to mimic what happens in nature: allow decomposition and avoid disrupting the soil and its natural layers.

Digging and tilling can cause the following problems that no-till gardening doesn't: (Makes sense to get off the tilling treadmill, right?)

>> **Tilling encourages weeds.** Weeds love annual digging and tilling because annual digging brings long-buried weed seeds to the surface where they're only too happy to awaken from their slumber, enjoy some light and air, germinate, and take over your new planting area. Many weeds also can regenerate from bits of roots, rhizomes, and stems, and tilling chops these up and spreads them around — again, encouraging weeds to grow.

>> **Tilling disrupts the soil's natural layering.** Spring digging jump-starts a burst of microbial activity in the soil; you have to wait to plant until it settles down, usually a matter of a couple of weeks. Digging in wet soil leads to compaction, making it harder for plants to grow, not easier.

   Research has even shown that if you abstain from tilling, pores and channels in your soil (created by earthworms, freeze-thaw cycles, and gravity) remain intact and the plant roots in that area are better able to get the water they need in springtime and beyond. Organic matter on the surface can break down and contribute its nutrients and texture to the soil at its own rate.

No big secret or mystery here. Avoid routinely turning over your soil. At season's end, when you clean up the garden, you may still remove spent plants, but instead of yanking them out entirely, you cut them off at soil level and leave the roots to decompose in place.

REMEMBER

With no-till gardening, you can start earlier, planting new plants, sowing seeds, and moving plants around. Your soil will be healthier and reach its own equilibrium in terms of organic matter and water consumption. Just like it does in, say, a forest or wild field. It's easier on you and easier on the land.

TIP

If you have lots of fallen wood, logs, and leaves, look into a method of bed prep called *hugelkultur.* You'll be impressed with its long-term time and money-saving benefits.

DRESSING YOUR PLANTS

Top-dressing your plants means adding something on top. You sprinkle some organic matter on the soil, generally at the beginning or end of the growing season, by handfuls or shovelfuls — up to 6 inches' (15.2 cm) worth. Compost is great for this purpose. It can also temporarily act as a mulch, keeping plant roots cool or less vulnerable to temperature fluctuations and perhaps also keeping encroaching weeds at bay. You may or may not choose to dig some or all of it into the area, based on how you feel about digging and tilling.

Side-dressing is done after the plants are bigger, ordinarily later spring and in the summer months. You just sprinkle and spread some organic matter around individual plants. Consider the delivery a maintenance item or a good snack for hungry, growing plants.

With either top- or side-dressing, the idea is that your watering and/or rainfall will work it in and the plant's roots will ultimately enjoy a nice, beneficial boost.

Composting 101: Making Black Gold

Composting enables yard waste, agricultural waste, wood scraps, and even sludge to decompose into a relatively stable end-product, a crumbly soil–like organic material called *humus.*

This project leads to a long–term supply of good organic matter for your plants. Just mix the compost, sometimes called *black gold*, into planting holes, spread it as mulch, dig it in here and there for soil improvement, sprinkle it on your lawn, and give your shrubs a healthy snack. In the meantime, your outgoing household trash will diminish as you instead deliver kitchen scraps to the compost pile (and, we hear, the wave of the future is that landfills won't accept organic waste).

Composting is so easy we suggest you consider making your own. If you start this spring, chances are good you'll be using it by late summer . . . and for years to come. We break down the steps just ahead.

If you're too busy or don't want to hassle with a compost pile, you can buy compost in bags or have it delivered by the truckload. Many municipalities make compost and give it away or sell it relatively cheaply; if that's your source, do ask if it's okay to use in edible gardens and/or if it contains any contaminants.

Step 1: Locate a suitable spot

We recommend you designate a spot away from your neighbors' and your own back door (because of organic smells, though if you follow these directions, they are never as bad as you feared). Look for some place along a back fence, up against the side of the garage, in a corner. Make sure the spot isn't dark (because warm sunshine speeds decomposition) and difficult to access because you'll be making many trips.

Tucking it out of the way is also an aesthetic decision; we admit a compost pile isn't beautiful, and we've never seen anyone try to decorate one. (You can screen it with plants or hardscape items such as a fence or trellis.)

Step 2: Get a bin

You next need a bin. Research has shown that something around 3 x 3 feet (.9 x .9 m) works best, which is wide and long enough to cook the ingredients from organic waste into black gold. Get one with a fitted lid that is also easy to dislodge when you're making deliveries. Obtain one with one or more hatches at the bottom, so you can easily scoop out the organic matter at the bottom. And yep, these ready-made ones have vents here and there to let in air.

REMEMBER

If you live in a densely populated urban or suburban setting, you and your neighbors may worry about rats, seagulls, or other animals raiding the pile. The solution: Buy an enclosed bin. You can find various designs available, but we find one of those basic black plastic bins sold by garden suppliers or offered by some municipalities works just fine.

Alternatively, you can make your own with wire mesh, snow fencing, or stacked straw bales or cinder blocks. You can also use wooden fencing materials or stacked logs — just make sure you avoid pressure-treated lumber (it's been treated with chemicals you won't want in your compost, particularly if you are raising edible plants). Notice that all these suggestions allow for air and water to enter from above (unless you put on a cover) and from the sides — decomposition does require that a little air get in.

Step 3: Set up your compost pile

After it's erected on the chosen site, get it ready for business. Because compost piles, homemade or store-bought, come bottomless, lay some branches or cut-to-fit dried cornstalks in a layer on the open bottom, right on top of the native soil, to differentiate it from the native soil so air can enter.

You create successful compost by layering, creating alternating layers of green/nitrogen and brown/carbon materials — more on that in the next step. For now, if possible, obtain a bale of straw (not hay, which often contains weed seeds) and set it adjacent. Alternatively, other suitable brown materials include shredded, dried fall leaves, bark, and chopped twigs, which you can either stockpile nearby or bring to the pile as needed.

Step 4: Start making deposits

Put in green organic materials: kitchen scraps, yard waste (make a habit of chopping up or mashing bigger pieces into smaller ones to speed things along), manure, spent crops, and more. Yes, crushed eggshells and coffee grounds are welcome.

WARNING

Avoid adding oil, bones meats, pet waste (dogs and cats are meat-eaters, plus their waste may also contain disease pathogens), plastic, and ashes. These items don't break down quickly if at all and make your pile smelly.

Step 5: Layer

When you layer, put one part green materials to three parts brown materials. For example, always toss in some handfuls from the nearby straw bale or other brown materials after each kitchen delivery.

TIP

Sprinkle in a bucket of garden soil now and then, which introduces worker microorganisms to your pile. Some people invest in compost activators, available at garden suppliers, but we feel they're unnecessary.

Step 6: Stir it up

Getting air into the pile speeds decomposition. We like to use the handle from an old broken hoe; it's long enough and strong enough, but any sturdy stick will do.

If your pile seems a bit dry, just sprinkle it with some water from the hose or a watering can and stir it. It shouldn't be soggy, however; moist texture like a wrung sponge is ideal.

Step 7: Harvest from below

The good compost is in the bottom of the pile, so if you buy a prefabricated composter, make sure you get one with a lower hatch or two. Scoop it out and marvel at how garden and kitchen scraps turned into crumbly black humus, so good for improving the nutrition and texture of the soil everywhere in your garden.

If you hear mention of hot compost and cold compost, the terms refer to the pile's temperature:

>> **Hot compost:** This compost is productive — you can get usable humus in a matter of weeks or months. If you skip stirring and watering, your pile will still make compost, just much more slowly.

>> **Cold compost:** This compost pile may make take a full year to decompose into usable humus.

You should notice warmth, or even steam, rising off your pile at times which is a sign that microbes are at work decomposing your layered deliveries,. In fact, a temperature between 135 and 155°F (57.2 to 68.3°C) is both normal and desirable as the heat kills harmful organisms and pathogens.

Feeding Your Plants — Which Type of Fertilizer to Use?

Why, you may ask, do you need to feed your plants? Don't plants in the wild get by without a human coming by with fertilizer? Isn't there plant nutrition available in the soil, water, and air? No, yes, and yes.

Giving a plant, large or small, a dose of fertilizer delivers it a boost. It will be bigger, produce more flowers, ripen more berries or other fruits, and generally be more robust and healthier. Not instantly, perhaps, but the effect will be at least noticeable and at best, dramatic. Wait two to four weeks to see results.

People sometimes mistakenly think that fertilizer is plant food. It's not. It's soil food. And good soil leads to thriving plants.

Finding out what they need

Plants — principally their leaves, but also their overall look — signal to you that they're hungry or unhappy. If their problem is hunger and not thirst, and not a disease or pest (about which, we discuss in Chapter 18), you may see some of these signs:

>> **No or slow growth:** They may need a dose of a balanced fertilizer.

>> **Yellowing or blueish leaves, starting at the tips, thin stems, small leaves, or leaves dropping (oldest ones first):** These symptoms may indicate a need for nitrogen.

» **Dull, dark-green leaves, perhaps with discolored spots; stunted growth; poor flower and fruit development:** Your plants may need phosphorus.

» **Scorched-looking leaves, curling of leaf tips, yellow leaves, purple spots on leaf undersides, and weak stems:** All are signs of potassium deficiency.

» **Leaves turning yellow between veins, leaves developing brownish to purple patches, followed by leaf dropping:** All indicate a magnesium deficiency.

» **Pale leaves on plants with weak and stunted growth:** Your plants may lack iron.

Most plants aren't highly particular. You don't need to go shopping for the one missing ingredient or a fertilizer especially high or low in something. A balanced fertilizer, applied according to label directions (more isn't better; and apply with water!) should remedy any common deficiency.

Figuring out the finer points of fertilizer

Plant food traditionally offers the three major nutrients most all plants can benefit from:

» **N (nitrogen):** Nitrogen enhances leaf and stem growth (that's why it's the dominant ingredient in lawn fertilizer).

» **P (phosphorus):** Phosphorus aids the production of roots as well as flowers, fruits, and seeds.

» **K (potassium):** Potassium promotes vigor and increases plants' disease-resistance.

Fertilizer may also offer some secondary nutrients such as calcium and magnesium and trace elements such as boron and iron. Test your soil (refer to the section, "Putting your soil to the test," earlier in this chapter) to find out whether you have a deficiency problem in your home landscape.

These sections identify the different types of fertilizer and help you figure out how much to feed your plants.

Recognizing the types of fertilizer

Here are the types of fertilizer used to feed plants:

CHEMICAL OR SYNTHETIC FERTILIZERS

They're man-made and may be synthesized from and/or using petroleum products or derived from minerals treated with chemicals to make them more soluble. They're sold in granular or liquid formulations. Dilute them according to directions.

The pros to using them include the following:

>> Their benefits are readily available to plant roots.

>> They're widely available.

>> They're not expensive.

On the other hand, here are the cons to chemical or synthetic fertilizers:

>> They're made from nonrenewable resources that release harmful methane (also known as *greenhouse gas*).

>> If they come into direct contact with plant roots, they can harm them (burn or scorch them).

>> Long-term use allows soil structure to deteriorate.

>> Excess that runs off pollutes waterways.

ORGANIC FERTILIZERS

They're materials derived from living things, or rocks, that are added to garden soil in their more-or-less natural form. Generally speaking, they supply all the main nutrients, as well as some secondary and trace ones. Soil microorganisms convert the organic compounds into forms that plant roots can absorb.

You can buy these as dry (granular, powdered) or liquid products. We love to use fish and seaweed-based products, but these fertilizers are concentrated and rather intensely, err, scented, so be sure to dilute them with water according to label directions.

The pros to using organic ones include

>> They're considered natural, environmentally friendly, and boost plant health naturally.

>> They don't harm the soil by introducing artificial compounds.

>> They are a positive contributor to soil structure.

>> Organic material feeds soil microbes.

>> They don't harm or burn plant roots.

And the cons are as follows:

>> Results are slower, less dramatic than applications of inorganic ones.

>> Using them perhaps aren't as virtuous or low-impact as you may think. In the case of ones made from farm-animal waste, remember that those farm animals are major methane producers.

>> Excess that runs off pollutes waterways (especially manures).

>> Their cost per pound of actual nutrients can be much higher than synthetic fertilizer.

TECHNICAL STUFF

A *balanced* fertilizer is also sometimes called an all-purpose fertilizer. It contains relatively balanced amounts of the three main nutrients, N (nitrogen), P (phosphorus), and K (potassium). Most plants are don't have special needs and are grateful for a dose or regular doses throughout the growing season.

Formulations include 5-5-5, 5-10-5, 10-10-10; 5-10-5 and 5-10-10 are also considered multi-purpose.

Other fertilizers are variations, some with specialized uses. Both chemical (synthetic) fertilizers and organic ones have some or all of three nutrients and, if store-bought, are so labeled. For example, organic fish meal fertilizer is often 9-7-3; dried cow manure is typically 2-1.5-2; bonemeal, popular for dosing bulb plantings, is 2.5-24-0; a common lawn fertilizer is 26-0-5.

HOMEMADE FERTILIZERS

You can make your own organic liquid plant food. Commonly referred to as *compost tea* or *manure tea*, they're easy to concoct: Put some in a mesh bag, set it a bucket or barrel of water, wait a day or two, and voila! Feed the dark, microbe-rich liquid to your plants.

Here are the pros to using homemade fertilizer:

>> They're mild and easy on plants, generally releasing nutrients of a longer time.

>> They're convenient to use.

>> They're low-impact on the environment/ecosystem (see the section, "Deciding which choice is best: Go natural," later in this chapter).

And the cons are as follows:

>> You need substantial amounts.

>> They smell.

>> Their nutrients aren't immediately available to plants.

Knowing how much and when to apply fertilizer

The amount of fertilizer you use depends on several different factors: the plant, the type of fertilizer, whether a plant is desperate for nutrition, the quality or condition of your soil, and so on. Fertilizing soil that is organically rich is, frankly, optional, especially if you continue to amend it regularly as we recommend in this chapter.

However, if you think fertilizing is needed or would be beneficial, our general advice is always to follow the instructions on the label or package regarding dosage and timing. When in doubt or when using homemade concoctions, try a little a first, wait for results, and adjust the amount in subsequent feedings.

Feed only when your plants are actively growing. You don't need to fertilize them when their growth is naturally slowing down in autumn, or when they're dormant or at low ebb in winter. You'd not only disrupt their normal rhythms, but you'd inspire fresh new growth that can get damaged by cold weather. Many gardeners like to feed their plants at least once in spring when growth begins and perhaps again, every couple of weeks, throughout the growing season.

WARNING

Be careful about overdosing your plants and feeding them too concentrated or too much fertilizer. If you or someone else does, dilute ASAP with the hose or watering can and drench the area. If the plants are damaged or die, remember your lesson — more isn't better!

Deciding which choice is best: Going natural

As far as the plants are concerned, the nutrients are the same whether you use organic/natural fertilizers or chemical/synthetic ones. So the decision to garden organically has more to do with the supply chain, with what you purchase and consume.

If you have or nurture good garden soil, your landscape may not require fertilizers. Plants become addicted or accustomed to plant food, and the gardener becomes lazy, dosing instead of building up and caring for healthy, fertile soil.

Another reason to use homemade fertilizers is pollution. Collateral damage is real — fertilizers run off and enter waterways, leading to algae blooms and fish kills. Although agriculture is a major culprit here, why should gardeners be part of this problem especially when it's possible, indeed easy, to raise plants without these products?

Giving Your Plants a Trim — Pruning 101

Some gardeners misunderstand this common maintenance task, so let us be clear and keep it simple: Don't prune for the sake of pruning. Grab a cutting tool only to prevent or correct a growing problem or to redirect or stimulate growth. Prune for a reason, in other words.

Here are the basic rules of pruning. For more specifics, we refer you to Chapter 11 (trees) and Chapter 12 (shrubs). Keep these tips in mind:

>> **Cut a plant so it can grow attractively.** As we say again and again, you may remove clearly dead, damaged, and disease branches at any time. Take out crossing or rubbing branches, which also lets in air.

>> **Make large cuts, such as removing a tree limb, correctly.** You don't want the branch to start to split when it's only half cut off and tear back into the tree. If you're not up to this project, hire an arborist (see the section, "Calling in a professional," later in this chapter).

>> **Prune at the right time, for the plant's benefit and recovery.** Generally speaking, spring is best — plants are full of energy then and will rebound and generate thick new growth. Don't do this work late in the year (fall or early winter) or the cut parts may get cold-damaged and die. To avoid pruning off flower buds and therefore compromising or eliminating next year's show, prune flowering plants *immediately* after this year's flowering ends, before next year's buds begin to form.

REMEMBER

Pruning is so much less of a chore, so much easier, even pleasurable, when you have the right tool for the job. Don't force a saw or loppers to do something beyond its capacity. Use smaller tools for smaller jobs, and bigger ones for bigger jobs.

We have two other helpful suggestions:

>> **Invest in quality pruning equipment.** They can include hand pruners, loppers, shears, pruning saws.

>> **Keep the tools sharp.** If you're not a tool-sharpening type, pay someone else to do this for you, at least annually.

Editing Your Landscape

In your home landscapes, second thoughts or buyer's remorse can set in, whether it's a hardscape item like a too-big deck, a tree that is shedding fruit all over its immediate area or casting too much shade, or a hedge that drops its leaves every fall, unfortunately exposing your neighbor's junk-car collection for several months until it releafs in spring. The good news: You can take action to fix or change a garden regret.

Landscaping is a living art, and changes are part of it. Some are at the will or whim of nature, some are a result of your own rethinking, and some result of household changes (the kids grow up and it's time to give away the play structure and realize your dream of a big flowerbed or an herb garden). This process of making changes is called editing the landscape. We hereby give you permission to change your mind, change any major or minor element, or find another way. (If you're simply interested in maintenance pruning, see the overview above and then go on to Chapter 11 for trees and Chapter 12 for shrubs.)

The following sections offer suggestions for working with what you have. We cover altering an existing plant's appearance, making and following through with the decision to remove an existing one, and splitting up overgrown plants into multiple new ones. You can consider these sections your heavy-duty maintenance tasks.

Improving rather than replacing a plant

Sometimes your landscape doesn't require a major change, and/or you are unwilling to go shopping. All it really needs is a good haircut or trim for a new look and feel. You can try one or more of the following modifications:

>> **Modify an existing hedge.** If your hedge isn't as effective as you want at blocking a view or minimizing noise and distractions, help it to fulfill this role or to do a better job that it currently does. Lop off the tops or ends of branches to encourage the side branches to grow more thickly. Springtime, when growth is ramping up, is the best time to do this. Repeat for a few seasons, maybe by nudging things along with soil improvement or fertilizing in the area, and you'll be impressed.

>> **Groom to control size and upgrade appearance.** Even the prettiest trees and shrubs benefit from occasional grooming to shape them more attractively. Take out dead, damaged, or diseased wood at any time. Take out branches that rub and cross each other. Trim in spring.

WARNING

We advise against training a shrub into a ball, cone, or some other unnatural shape, unless you're committed to topiary as the look for your landscape. After you train or shear your plants into these shapes, you'll be forced to keep this up every year.

>> **Inspire a good harvest.** This item is for fruit and nut trees you may have in your landscape; proper, targeted care can turn them from ornamental or neglected plants into valuable, attractive food-producers. Thin out most of these in late winter or early spring to let in more light and air. Then check with a tree nursery or look online for suggestions on how to improve their productivity (for example, removing some blooms can help the remaining ones go on to become bigger fruit).

>> **Train a plant into a certain direction or shape.** Doing so is easiest when a plant is young and malleable. You can remove lower limbs, take out skinny, tall-growing limbs, or pinch back lanky branches to encourage thicker growth. You can tie wayward vine stems to train the plant to grow over a fence or trellis.

All this said, repeatedly fussing with a plant to control its size or appearance can become frustrating. If a tree or shrub wants to be bigger or taller, especially if it's crowding your house or garage, heading into the powerlines, or its roots are encroaching on a walkway or patio, you may only be able to work with it for so long before you get tired of the routine. (Seriously consider replacing it with something more suitable, should you decide to remove it; consult the next section for information.)

Knowing when take out a plant

The day comes when you're in your yard, looking out the window, or receive a comment from someone, and you find yourself standing in judgment. Shouldn't you remove that tree, shrub, perennial, vine?

Here are the reasons you may need to remove a plant:

>> It's in poor health or its overall appearance is in decline.

>> It's past its prime. Plants, like people, have life spans. Like people, their life spans may vary or get cut short.

>> It's naturally too large or vigorous for its allotted spot.

>> It has become a safety hazard (think of a bush blocking the line of sight at an intersection).

>> It casts too much shade or litters too much.

>> You want to make way for something you like better.

>> You have plans for a hardscape item such as a deck or patio, and the plant is in the way.

Taking out a plant

To evict a plant, follow these steps (if you're trying to remove an invasive vine, the steps are a bit different — pop over to the instructions in Chapter 18):

1. **Select a time when the work will be easiest.**

Stay away from hot, sunny days. Choose a cooler day or time of year. In fact, spring or fall when the ground is workable is usually good (and it's always easier to pry roots out of damp ground).

TIP

Don appropriate gear (long pants, gloves; if working with a saw or chainsaw, wear steel-toed boots and goggles) and gather sharp tools.

2. **Work in stages.**

1. **Cut the top growth down in sections.**

2. **If you're taking out a shrub or tree, remove as many of the branches as you can before turning your attention to the main trunk or main stems.**

3. **Tackle evicting the whole rootball, so the plant can't resprout.**

   In the case of a tree, bring in a professional and watch them do it.

If you plan to put a new plant in the vacated spot, don't do it immediately.

Instead take the time to improve the soil, which was probably depleted by the previous resident. Wait a few weeks or even a full season, just to make sure you didn't miss some of the old root system, in which case you'll want to do more digging until you get it all.

TIP

Other possible fates for an evicted plant: move it to another part of your landscape; pot it up; give it away.

Calling in a professional

You can probably handle most landscape maintenance and editing on your own or with some helpers — yank out smaller plants, dig out a shrub or rosebush, and such.

However, if you have bigger aspirations like removing large, mature trees, bring in a pro. Removing a tree, or even just taking off some major limbs, isn't easy and can be dangerous to you as well as to anything in the vicinity including your house, your other plants, and even your neighbor's property.

Reputable arborists can come out and give you a free estimate. Be sure to ask for references and their insurance. In addition, ask:

>> How long do they estimate the job will take?

>> If you want the tree entirely removed, can they dig up or grind the stump? (*Stump grinding* is a process whereby a heavy, loud tool that looks like a cross between a circular saw and a lawnmower turns a stump and roots into small pieces, or chips.) You'll be left with a big hole to fill . . . with nice new, organically rich soil.

>> Will they cut the trunk and branches into firewood for you or haul it all away? (In the latter case, how about a discount, because they're taking away something of value?)

If you try to remove trees, you could botch the job or hurt yourself. In which case, you'll need to call in a professional (and a chiropractor).

DIVIDE AND CONQUER

In the case of a perennial plant or ornamental grass that's outgrown its location, instead of digging it out and tossing it on the compost pile or foisting it off on a neighbor, you can divide it. That is, you can separate into *divisions* (smaller sections, each with roots attached).

The best time to do this is spring when active growth will help the plants rebound from surgery. Some perennials may also be divided without trauma in late summer or fall, such as irises, daylilies, and peonies.

If a rootball turns out to be too big and thick to pry into new sections with your bare hands, don't be afraid to bring in heavier artillery. You can hack or chop with a sharp shovel or trowel, two garden forks braced back-to-back, or a sharp, heavy-duty knife. Sure, some bits of roots will be sacrificed in the process but if the root system is robust, the resulting divisions will survive just fine.

Maybe pick one of the pieces to remain in the spot. Replant the rest in other locations or give them away to a neighbor or friend.

An additional nice effect of this operation: Newly replanted sections are revitalized. For example, a sprawling clump of irises that no longer blooms well, once divided, is rebooted and the pieces all bloom the following season. Yay!

Chapter **18**

Dealing with Critters, Weeds, and Other Common Problems

You and your family and friends aren't the only creatures in residence. Observing your yard at different times of day, in different seasons, and even from different vantage points (relaxing in an Adirondack chair with a cocktail, crawling around on the ground yanking out weeds, gazing out the kitchen window) amply shows this. Birds of all kinds, squirrels, bunnies, woodchucks, mice, voles, snakes, woodchucks, skunks, and deer can be regulars. And the small critters: beetles, caterpillars and butterflies, moths, worms, snails, slugs. And the very small critters: soil-dwellers and spiders and other things you can barely see. Your yard is teeming with life.

That's not to say that all creatures great and small are totally welcome. Some cause trouble in the course of their normal activities — munching or otherwise damaging plants, digging up beds, nibbling on roots, eating your veggies or fruits, and so on. Is it possible to co-exist?

If you want to cause no harm — and we counsel that, of course, because maintaining a nice home landscape shouldn't be destructive or depleting — what can you do about problem animals? We have ideas. This chapter explains how to handle those critters, first the smaller critters, and then working up the food chain to large mammals.

REMEMBER

Are you new to landscaping? If you know, or are told, that a certain kind of pest (say, slugs, gophers, or deer) is a major problem in your area, pause. Take a deep breath. Find out and shop for plants they don't favor or seek out varieties specifically marketed as "resistant." Install fences or barriers. You'll save yourself a world of heartache.

In addition to critters, you may have to contend with unwanted plants in your yard, including weeds, which often are difficult to get rid of. They may be well-established, popping up here and there either due to their seeds getting moved around by animals, water, or the wind, or due to impressive, traveling root systems. Deal with them early and often. Many of them thrive in lousy soil, so improving an area can push them out. Take back your real estate.

Discovering Natural Pest Control

If you build it, they will come — bugs, beetles, and other creepy-crawlies always show up in your yard. However, understand that not all are bad guys.

In the past, you may have been advised to attack and eradicate any marauder you spotted. Garden-supply shelves were chock-a-block with sprays, dusts, and granules intended to poison them. Nowadays, gardening experts promote tolerating the bugs' activity and some of the damage they inflict to your plants in exchange for not upsetting the balance of nature — shorthand for respecting and not tampering with natural cycles.

As it happens, your yard (and every other yard) is part of a food web, which you can learn about, nurture, and use to your advantage. The following sections are our top recommendations for dealing with insects.

Avoid using pesticides

Pesticides are toxins. Even though they may harm or kill their intended targets, sometimes the insect pests build up immunities over time and the remedy doesn't work or doesn't work as well as it used to. Meanwhile, there are other downsides. You may have harmed your property's soil or water, as well as unintended targets. We're not saying "never use pesticides," we're arguing caution. They shouldn't be the first thing you reach for, but the last.

Though not the intended targets, bees (and other insects like ants, various butterflies and moths, and more) are harmed or killed by certain garden chemicals, and nowadays humans are keenly aware of how much we depend upon these important pollinators. According to biologists David Grimaldi and Michael Engel, authors of *The Evolution of Insects*, specifically if bees, ants, and termites were eliminated from the planet, "all terrestrial life would collapse."

Bees in particular are the world's most efficient and prolific pollinators and worthy of our forbearance. One of our favorite Internet memes shows two panels: in the first one, a spray can is directed at a flower garden and the bees are flinching in its path; in the second one, a gardener is tenderly holding a bee and inquiring "Oh hello, little one, can I get you anything?"

WARNING

Don't buy seeds or plants that have been treated or embedded with *neonicotinoids,* a pesticide that has been shown to be a major culprit in bee deaths. In most states, nurseries, garden centers, and box stores are required to label plants that contain this poison.

Know thy enemy

When you see a bug or caterpillar nibbling something in your landscape, pluck one or take a phone photo and go find out what it is. Just make sure you never kill or spray willy-nilly.

TIP

To identify a small bug or creature in your yard, go online and try whatsthatbug. com, bugguide.net, or the iNaturalist app. These resources also explain what the bug is doing (nesting? laying eggs?) or eating (specifically what does it favor?) as well as details about its life cycle. With that information, you can determine if it's a significant threat to a valued plant or crop.

For example, you may discover — to your amazement — that that green and yellow parsley worm caterpillar turns into a beautiful swallowtail butterfly. Can you tolerate some nibbled parsley in exchange for allowing that natural metamorphosis to occur? Of course you can!

Be aware of the enemies of your enemy

Yes, many buggy pests have natural enemies, which are generally termed *beneficial insects.* Ladybugs (as larvae and as adults), lacewings, and hoverflies all dine on pest insects. If you're patient, perhaps tolerating some plant damage, and watch, you may be astounded to witness a pest problem resolving itself.

Here's some more important information about these beneficial insects that you can consider for your landscaping:

TIP

>> **Ladybugs:** In particular, ladybugs can consume a huge amount of aphids and scale insects (both may trouble your vegetable garden and fruit plants).

If you decide to add ladybugs to your yard, don't buy ladybugs, even though they're for sale in some outlets because they're collected when they're dormant, which means they arrive not-very-hungry and fly away home. Instead entice them to your yard with some of their favorite plants: German chamomile, a rather small, unobtrusive plant, is an absolute favorite. They also relish flowers like coreopsis, cosmos, and alyssum and herbs with large, flat flowerheads such as dill, cilantro, parsley, and fennel.

>> **Lacewings:** They're as delicately beautiful as their name implies, but they're ferocious killers in a garden, going after many pest insects, including aphids, scale, and whitefly nymphs. You can buy and release them, and they generally will stay and make themselves at home and useful. Among the plants they like are alyssum, asters, coreopsis, cosmos, and daisies.

>> **Hoverflies:** Also called *flower or syrphid flies,* these tiny big eaters are amazing to watch as they zip around the garden, sometimes hovering, reversing, or flying sideways. They're good pollinators and also predators of other insects. Their larvae look like itty-bitty slugs, but don't be fooled; they can eat huge amounts of aphids. Hoverflies favor smaller-flowered plants such as alyssum and small-flowered asters.

Combat with care

If the natural-enemy route doesn't work for you, more often the case in a vegetable patch than in an ornamental garden, you have options. You can try less-objectionable remedies, including insecticidal soaps, milky-spore powder (a bacterium), covering or collaring vulnerable plants, and traps.

Whatever remedy you decide to try, always study the label to see if it is appropriate to the pest, then follow instructions regarding timing and amount to the letter. Here are a couple specific options:

>> **Neem:** Neem is an extract from a tree that grows mainly in India and the African continent, *Azadirachta indica.* Gardeners, especially those who raise vegetables, have come to value it (in oil or granulated forms) as both a fungicide and a pesticide. Buy formulations intended for garden use and follow the directions about dosage and timing to the letter. It can control mildew on many plants as well as many sap-sucking insects, including aphids

and whiteflies, and cabbage worms, corn earworms, and tomato hornworms. However, it's harmful to fish and other aquatic life. Use with care.

>> **Blood meal:** A common and safe organic fertilizer, blood meal can also be deployed as a rabbit deterrent. It's literally dried blood (of cows or other livestock). Be careful — a little goes a long way, that is, it's highly concentrated.

REMEMBER

Timing is important. No matter the remedy you choose, it will be most effective applied on a dry and windless day of moderate temperatures.

Gardening Basics For Dummies, 3rd Edition, by Steven Frowine and the National Gardening Association has thorough discussions by plant type, including how to cope with common pest problems. You can find some additional vegetable-garden troubleshooting and recommended remedies in *Vegetable Gardening For Dummies*, 2nd Edition, by the National Gardening Association and Charlie Nardozzi (both by John Wiley & Sons, Inc.).

Coping with Small Rodents

Many gardeners contend with nibbling, destructive rodents and other smaller mammals: Squirrels, chipmunks, woodchucks (also known as groundhogs), rabbits, skunks, gophers, voles, mice, and shrews. Each in their own special ways relish plants in landscapes, elevating your blood pressure and ire.

REMEMBER

Perhaps the first order of business is, don't tempt them by taking care of the following:

>> Harvest your vegetables and fruit promptly. Don't leave them on the ground to rot.

>> Invest in a self-contained composter with a closeable lid.

>> Seal garbage cans.

>> Clean up under bird feeders.

>> Fence off the vegetable garden. Digging creatures can be deterred when the fencing is sunk into the ground a foot or so; as for fence height, or literally caging the patch, you'll have to find how protective a fortress is needed.

>> Protect young, vulnerable trees with collars designed for this purpose.

WHAT ABOUT RACCOONS?

Though not rodents, raccoons can be quite pesky and persistent, especially in areas where their natural habitat and food sources have been reduced or eliminated. Omnivorous by nature, they'll raid garbage bags and cans that aren't secured, but they aren't great garden pests unless you grow corn (which they adore; they seem to know exactly when it's at perfect ripeness) or have a water garden. Electric fencing is the best deterrent, but you can try noisemakers, motion-sensitive lights, or plastic or wire mesh on the ground near the popular plants.

TIP

>> Leave the dog, or cat, in the yard if you have one. Your pet may not be capable of killing the marauder, but neither one of them may know that! Of course, this tactic isn't always practical. You probably shouldn't leave a dog, tied up or not, outside all day long, and besides, your pests may come around at night and do their damage under cover of darkness. Cats accustomed to outdoor life can be formidable hunters.

Here's a menu of other do's and don'ts to try:

>> **Do plant unappealing plants.** Most small nibbling animals give aromatic plants a pass. Rarely of interest are strongly fragrant herbs (mint and dill) and pungent flowers (marigold and nasturtium) or the stinky spring-flowering bulb fritillaria. A buffering barrier of any or all of these may help keep animals away from plants you're trying to nurture.

>> **Do install bad vibrations.** Some gardeners insert pinwheels at intervals, counting on the noise and vibrations to deter invaders. Even wind chimes, clanging metal garden sculptures, and other noisemakers have been known to work.

>> **Do deploy repellents.** Small animals have sensitive noses, so put them off with stinky repellents. Popular choices include sprays of minced garlic or hot pepper, used coffee grounds, and even fox urine (for sale at home and garden centers — we don't want to know the backstory). Reapply after watering with a sprinkler or a rain.

TIP

Voles can do a lot of damage, particularly to perennial gardens, lawns, and fruit trees. An effective, organic remedy that deters them is a solution of *scented* castor oil mixed with dish detergent and water (in the following proportions: 2 tablespoons of the oil + 1 tablespoon of detergent + 1 gallon of water). Thoroughly soak the soil in the area you wish to protect.

- **Don't use poisons — don't strew mothballs or other pelleted toxins in the garden or stuff such things into burrows.** An animal can crawl off to die, perhaps after a period of agony. If another animal eats the carcass, the poison enters the food chain! Your dog or a neighbor's pet can be harmed or killed if they eat the carcass.

- **Do install barriers.** You can protect an individual plant with netting or wire cones or cloches sold for this purpose. These need to be of ample size, so the pests can't reach through. To protect an entire bed, set up supports and swath the entire thing in netting, anchoring and securing edges with wire or clothespins so you can still get access.

- **Do block or attack their nesting or resting areas.** Low dense bushes, hedges, and areas of taller grasses (along a fence line, for instance) provide shelter for some of these creatures. Clean up, cut back, trim back the ankles (from where the plant emerges from the ground up to about 6 to 12 inches, 15.2 to 30.5 cm) so to speak. Remove dense vegetation. Pruning like this is paramount in springtime, when the critters are hungry and have little ones to feed, but if the pests are still lurking in summer, you'll have to keep up with the pruning.

TIP

Many critters find refuge in the area under a porch, deck, shed, or stoop. They'll hide or nest in crawl spaces, spaces too small for people to get into. You can try sealing off the area with wire. Erect it completely around the perimeter (after first making sure there are no animals hiding in a shadowy corner). Use heavy-duty wire mesh, such as tough galvanized steel — mesh chicken wire is flimsy and rusts after a few seasons. Secure the bottom by burying it several inches/cm to a foot (30.5 cm) deep and then secure the sides and top with galvanized nails or staples.

- **Do bother their little feet.** Wire mesh or netting laid along the ground, believe it or not, is a deterrent because animals dislike having their feet or claws snagged. Even aluminum foil arrayed around the base of plants may work. Be sure to hide these materials from view with a dusting of soil or mulch.

- **Don't use live traps.** Unwanted animals, including unintended or nonharmful targets (for example, maybe a fox, a turtle, or a neighborhood cat), can be lured into a trap and be maimed or killed, depending on the type of trap or how you've set it up. If you fail to check on the trap in a timely fashion for some reason, a trapped animal can suffer from injury or starvation. Also many municipalities ban trap-and-release of live animals on the grounds that relocation isn't humane and trapping just moves the problem around rather than solving it. Plus, even if you succeeded in capturing one animal, there's probably plenty more. It's just not a great solution, in our opinion!

Dealing with Doe, a Deer

As with other wildlife, development has reduced deer's natural habitats. Combine that with a lack of predators and a banquet of tasty, nourishing garden plants, and modern-day deer not only survive — they thrive. The most important thing to understand about fighting deer is that it's easier to prevent damage than to react to it. The following sections offer a range of ways to deal with them, from what you plant to how to keep them out of your yard.

Choosing plants to deter deer

A hungry deer will eat practically anything, but both scientific research and anecdotal evidence have found that some plants are at the bottom of their lists. If you garden in deer country, try growing these:

- Agave
- Ajuga
- Aloe
- Bee balm
- Black locust
- Boxwood
- Butterfly bush
- Clematis
- Columbine
- Daffodil/narcissus
- Ferns
- Foxglove
- Hellebore
- Holly
- Iris
- Lavender
- Lilac
- Marigold
- Mint
- Pine
- Rock rose
- Rosemary
- Russian sage
- Smokebush
- Spruces
- Vinca
- Wax myrtle
- Yarrow
- Yucca
- Zinnia

Trying home remedies

If your deer problem isn't severe, some of these low-tech deterrents, which aren't expensive or time-consuming, may be worth a try. For the smelly and bad-tasting ones, remember that a good rainstorm tends to rinse them away, so you'll have to reapply. Consider trying the following:

- » **Human hair:** Any hair salon should oblige you with bags of its sweepings. Stuff the hair into mesh bags or discarded pantyhose, and then hang them throughout the yard or on or near the deer's favorite plants.

- » **Soap:** Some say Irish Spring, others say Lava. Just pick a bar of soap with a very strong scent. Loop twine or string around the middle and hang bars at intervals — they'll look like eccentric Christmas ornaments, to be honest.

- » **Pepper spray:** Deer are said to dislike hot and spicy flavors. Coat entire plants or leaves in reach. Spray on a dry, windless day and take care not to get any in your eyes.

- » **Radio or smart speaker:** Seal it in a plastic bag if the weather is damp and tune it to talk or loud rock music, which can fool deer into thinking you're in the yard.

- » **Lights:** Choose either motion-activated or constantly blinking lights, and place them as close to the garden area as possible. When deer come under cover of darkness, the lights will spook them.

- » **Water:** Seek out a battery-operated or remote-controlled gadget that detects motion and fires a blast of water.

Considering anti-deer products

Resort to commercial products only after you've tried the homegrown methods in the previous section. These products aren't especially expensive or toxic to the environment, it's just that they're heavier artillery. A great deal of research has gone into developing these repellents. Be sure to read and heed the label directions, for safety's sake, as well as maximum effectiveness. Properly timed applications are key.

Active ingredients include putrescent egg solids, ammonia, garlic, or hot pepper. These products repel by taste and odor.

Fencing them out

If you've exhausted the options in the preceding sections and the deer damage hasn't been reduced to a tolerable level, a barrier is your last resort. In fact, a deer fence is widely acknowledged to be the only thing that truly keeps these pests out of your yard and garden. A deer fence isn't a mere wooden or metal fence. Although it may be made of such materials, it must be substantial, sturdy, and reinforced.

A deer fence must also have two other characteristics:

>> **Height:** Deer are great leapers, and when motivated, they can clear barriers of 6 or more feet (1.8 m) high. Something as high as 10 or 12 feet (3 or 3.6 m) is often warranted. For smaller flowerbeds, shorter fencing can be effective, say, a 5-foot (1.5 m) fence.

>> **Strong wire:** It's a must. Deer hooves can kick in, bend, or make holes in lesser wire. Get advice from neighbors and a good local contractor before making important decisions about material.

Grappling with Weeds

Not all yard and garden pests have four or six legs. For some, weeds are the main nuisance. Here's some straight talk on dealing with annoying, unwanted plants.

Avoiding the biggest mistake

The number one way weeds get into yards is, sorry to put this so bluntly, people invite them. You clear out a new bed or vegetable patch, or dig out an area. You're so proud of yourself when the work is done. You rake it over, and go inside.

And here the weeds come, seemingly overnight, but certainly more with each passing day . . . because you weren't done. Every time you clear out a garden space, you create a golden opportunity for weeds. You've stirred up the soil and brought dormant weeds up to the surface, where with a little light and air, they start growing. You've stirred or chopped up the soil and bits of weed roots and even stems, gain a foothold and start growing. Any weed seeds drifting by on a breeze or carried from one spot to another by rain or hose water find the open ground and start growing.

TIP

No matter what you do, don't leave open space. If you do clear a bed, keep these suggestions in mind to keep the weeds from moving in:

>> **Cover the planting area immediately after the raking step.** Use a tarp, black plastic, an old carpet or remnant, even flattened cardboard boxes. Anchor the cover in place. Don't remove it until you return to plant what *you* want to grow in that spot.

>> **Plant placeholder plants.** For example, in a new flowerbed, you can plant a few plants that you really want, but you haven't yet decided what else. And/or you're not sure how much space your top picks will take up. A good

placeholder plant is one that grows thickly enough to outcompete most weeds, but is easy to yank out when you no longer need its services.

Some of our favorite placeholder plants are any annuals (pansies, million bells, California poppies), lamb's ears, feverfew, and dianthus.

>> **Mulch, but don't till.** Mulch blocks light, air, and even moisture from getting through and encouraging weeds. Put down several inches/cms around and between your desired plants, and replenish when it naturally breaks down or rains wash it away. In time, of course, your desired plants should grow and spread out and cover over open spaces with shading foliage, which further prevents weeds. Chapter 16 lists mulches we recommend.

WARNING

Tilling, digging, or otherwise disrupting the soil can be counterproductive. Weeds regenerate from chopped-up bits, and dormant seeds delivered to light and air burst into growth. A main benefit of turning over soil is to aerate it, but if the soil wasn't highly compacted in the first place, you should probably abstain.

Patrolling, inspecting, and suspecting

There's no substitute for paying attention. Walk around your yard regularly. Keep your eyes open and your nose to the ground. Remove suspicious seedlings the minute you spot them by the roots whenever possible.

Here are a few other helpful ideas to keep on top of weeds from invading your yard:

>> **Mind your borders.** Neighboring properties, whether a nongardening neighbor, conservation land, or a vacant lot can bring in unwanted plants. Look over the fence and past your property line, particularly areas uphill from you (rainwater brings weeds downhill) and upwind (breezes blows seeds and fluff your way). A fence or a better fence maybe in order. See Chapter 6 for information about installing a fence.

>> **Check newcomers.** Weeds often hitchhike in, hiding in the soil or under the foliage of a potted plant from the garden center or a plant sale. Evict those interlopers.

>> **Shop with care and quarantine topsoil, loam, compost, and other such deliveries.** Cheap fill dirt is likely to be full of weeds or weed seeds. Pre-screened compost may be lovely but still harbor invaders. Our advice is to designate a staging area for the delivery and let the pile sit for a week or two before using. Weeds sprout quickly, and they're much easier to evict before the new soil is spread around in your landscape.

Considering alternatives to spraying — Try natural weed control

Roundup (glyphosate) and other weedkillers (also called herbicides) have received a lot of bad press due to alleged and established risks to humans, pets, wildlife, birds, bees and other insects, soil life, and more. Additionally, some weedkillers may be regulated or soon banned, and so you may be interested in alternatives. Here are some other, natural ways to control weedy invaders:

>> **Start early.** You can save yourself a lot of trouble with early intervention. In early spring, yank out weeds by their roots (right after a rain or watering, when the ground is soft and damp). Or drag a sharp hoe across them, which dislodges them, roots and all.

>> **Kill topgrowth.** For larger weeds that are deeply rooted, try an aboveground attack. If you do this repeatedly, the root systems will struggle and eventually die. Use a weed-whacker or lawn mower set low, and scalp them. Smother them with a covering or mulch (there's a list of various mulches in Chapter 16). Scald with hot water — this works best for spot-treating small patches (use oven mitts and wear long pants and good shoes).

MAKE YOUR OWN WEEDKILLER?

Instead of buying weedkiller, you can make your own at home. In a large, clean jug, mix a gallon of white vinegar, a cup of table salt, and a tablespoon of dishwashing soap (for some reason, Dawn is always recommended). Shake well. Vinegar and salt dry out a plant's cell membranes, causing death by dehydration; soap helps the mixture adhere to the plants.

Fill a spray bottle with the mixture and hit aboveground growth on a sunny day — hot sun boosts the vinegar's effectiveness. Repeated applications are often necessary. Protect nearby valued plants with an old towel or upended box. Label and store left-overs out of reach of pets and children.

A few cautions about this tack: This concoction only harms the weed leaves; it isn't conducted down into the root system. So unless the target plant or patch is young or shallow-rooted, just one application may not be sufficient. The ingredients, although familiar, aren't harmless to the environment; however, other nearby plants may be scorched or killed. Also salt's not good for the soil (look at what road salt does to plants near the road). We say give it a try, but other remedies may be more effective.

Considering other ways to fight weeds

If you choose to try one of these, follow the label directions to the letter, for safety and for best results.

>> **Use organic sprays.** Organic herbicide products contain citrus oils or clove oil. They work by stripping leaves of their protective waxy coating, drying them out past the point of no return.

>> **Zap them.** You can scorch the topgrowth of weeds in nonflammable surfaces such as stone terraces and walkways with a propane-fueled flame tool called, aptly, a Mini-Dragon. It incinerates what you can see of the weeds but evidently shrivels up and kills the roots as well.

Handling Disease Problems

The biggest secret of maintaining a beautiful landscape is in plain sight: Healthy, vigorous, well-cared-for plants are far less likely to get sick, to suffer from attacks of diseases like rots, mildews, spots and worse. Here we focus on prevention first. If your plants do get sick, we offer some remedies.

Preventing common diseases

Plant diseases are caused by fungi, viruses, or bacteria. Plants weakened by insect or weather damage are, understandably more vulnerable. The exact cause and diagnosis may be difficult; you may need to seek expert help. Prevention is the best remedy.

Here are some best practices that specifically prevent common diseases:

>> **Choose disease-resistant plants.** Some phlox just succumb to mildew every summer, others carry on in glory. The difference? Some are simply stronger, right in their genes. Reputable seed catalogs and plant nurseries are always happy to point out the ones that are especially resistant. (How will you know which diseases are most problematic where you garden or within your favorite plant types? Ask neighboring gardeners, ask at your local nursery, join a local garden club and discuss with the members.)

>> **Keep your garden tidy.** Clean up debris in the yard and especially at the base of plants; snip out and get rid of marred plant parts.

- » **Dispose of marred plant parts properly.** Send them away with the household garbage. Don't put them in the compost pile or toss them over the back fence.

- » **Keep your tools clean.** Pruners, loppers, and saws can spread disease from one plant to another. We keep a canister of disinfectant wipes (a bit of bleach in them) with the tools and wipe down the blades after every use.

- » **Water plant roots, not leaves.** Yes, the foliage gets wet when it rains, and you can't do anything about that, but watering at ground level is wise.

- » **Give plants elbow room.** Crowded, crammed plants reduce air circulation, and close conditions both encourage and spread plant diseases.

- » **Practice crop rotation.** Certain diseases target certain plant families/related plants and can be thwarted by leaving a trouble spot unplanted for a season or installing totally different plants.

Taking care of sick plants

If your plants get sick, follow these suggestions:

- » **Quickly swoop in and dispose of marred plants or plant parts.** Save one sample to get a diagnosis, either from some Internet sleuthing or by showing it to someone knowledgeable such as a garden-club friend or a garden-center staffer.

    After you know, you can explore treatment options. The funny thing is, you'll find that the treatment options lead you right back to the best practices.

- » **Pay close attention.** One afflicted plant can soon become several faltering or dying plants so keep a vigilant eye on things and act fast.

REMEMBER

Trouble with plant health accelerates. If a plant or group of plants does develop bad signs like marred leaves, pustules on leaf undersides, limp or blackened stems, or deformed flower buds, you may have a disease problem. Or you may have a pest problem. Or the pests may move in on debilitated plants.

Chapter **19**

Coping with Mother Nature and Weather

No matter whether you're brand new to landscaping and gardening or have worked hard and enjoyed your best-laid plans, nature and weather are always going to be wild cards. Everything you work with outdoors is either alive and growing and/or subject to wind, rain, and more, so nothing behaves as expected or desired — it's humbling. Take heart, though. Knowledge is power, as the saying goes, and that's true in landscaping. The more you know, the better you can plan and prepare, and thereby dramatically increase your odds of success.

This chapter explains how to understand and work with your plants as they deal with what may come their way, such as very hot or very cold weather, including an occasional extreme event such as fire or flood.

Peeking at Zone Maps

All the plants in this book (see Part 3) are coded with a hardiness zone that corresponds with a system devised by the United States Department of Agriculture in 1960, and most recently revised in 2012. There's a similar map for Canada. If you live in one of a plant's recommended zones, you have some assurance the plant is hardy enough to survive winter. You can find both maps in the color insert.

The USDA Zone map divides North America and Europe into 20 separate zones. Zones are numbered 1 through 11, but Zones 2 through 10 are subdivided into "a" and "b" regions. Each zone number is 10°F warmer (or colder) in an average winter than the adjacent zone. The greatest virtues of the USDA map are its widespread use and the fact that many plants have been categorized according to its zones.

But the USDA system has shortcomings. Its key problem is the absolute reliance on average winter minimum temperature, which can equate regions of climates that differ in every way but temperature, such as San Diego and Florida. Gardeners in the West have a more accurate, relevant alternative, the Sunset Zones map. Gardeners in the South and Gulf Coast regions may find the American Horticultural Society's innovative Heat Zones map worthwhile. See the nearby sidebars for more about these.

Additionally, because of climate change, we're watching for the USDA to issue an update. *Global warming* is an oversimplification of what is happening; it's more accurate to say that we're in a time of instability and more extreme weather. For now, though, the 2012 United States map remains a decent guideline. The zone numbers themselves won't change, but we anticipate that the details for each zone will.

WEATHERING WESTERN WEATHER

Due to the influence of mountain ranges and proximity to the ocean, the USDA Zones are less useful in the West than in the East. If you live in western North America, we recommend the zone maps featured in the *Sunset Western Garden Book of Landscaping* (2014). The criteria that define the different western zones are winter cold, summer heat, amount and duration of precipitation, humidity, seasonal winds, and number of sunlight hours.

In the low-elevation West, winters are mild. Vancouver, Seattle, Portland, San Francisco, Fresno, Los Angeles, San Diego, Phoenix, and Tucson all experience average winter lows of 30° to 48°F (with all-time lows mostly in the high teens and low 20s). And between 30° and 32°F, plant damage from freezing is comparatively unimportant. In most places, freeze damage is not significant enough to qualify as the single defining climatic factor — but it's the primary criterion for USDA zones.

At the same time, the West gets from a fraction of an inch to maybe 10 to 11 inches of rain each year. That's not enough to grow a lawn, a flower garden, or a vegetable garden without regular irrigation, but it's sufficient to grow western native plants. That's why, in the late 20th century, many western landscapers turned to native plants and highly efficient irrigation systems to provide foliage and flowers in the dry season. (If you live in a wildfire-prone area, even more tactics should be used; refer to the section, "Firescaping," later in this chapter.)

Surviving Hot Summers

Many areas always experience long, hot, dry summers. Others are experiencing more heat than in the past. What can you do to keep your landscape going to avoid losing valued plants during such challenging conditions? The operating strategy is conserving water, which we discuss in Chapter 5.

Here are some of our suggestions. Use the ones that work for you:

>> **Focus on smart plant selections.** Growing drought-tolerant plants, including natives, make sense. A visit to a regional nursery that specializes in these types of plants can open your eyes to what's available. Chat with the staff for recommendations and ideas.

>> **Use a lot of mulch.** Mulch is especially helpful for keeping soil cool and mitigating soil-temperature fluctuations.

EXPLORING THE AHS PLANT HEAT-ZONE MAP

The significance of winter's lowest temperatures decreases as you shift from places where winter freezes may kill many plants to areas where freezes merely mean frost on lawns and windshields. On the other hand, areas with mild winter temperatures often have soaring summer temperatures. Too-cold weather will just kill a plant, while signs of heat stress and damage are more subtle.

In 1997 the American Horticultural Society (AHS) published a zone map that accounts for plant's adaptability to heat. Called the Plant Heat-Zone Map, this 12-zone map of the United States indicates the average number of days each year when given regions experience temperatures of 86°F or higher. Like the USDA one, this map is due for an update, although it remains useful as a general guideline.

According to the AHS, 86°F is the temperature that many common plants begin to suffer physiological damage. The zones range from 1 (one day or less at 86°F or warmer) through 12 (210 days or more per year).

Find the Heat Map online as a downloadable free PDF at http://solanomg.ucanr.edu/files/245158.pdf.

>> **Water wisely.** Watering in the morning or evening hours reduces evaporation. Make sure you water regularly, rather than putting your plants through the stress of dry-soak cycles. Water deeply, low and slow, such as a trickle from the hose at the base of valued shrubs, rosebushes, and trees. Create basins around plants so water soaks in instead of running off.

>> **Help prevent drying out.** Wind is a big culprit in drying out both plants and soil. If you have a windy landscape or even just an exposed area, do what you can to lessen the impact of breezes. For instance, you can install a hedge or plant a windbreak (which takes time to be fully effective, but will be worth it in the long run), install a pergola (see Chapter 10), drape shade cloth over vulnerable plants during midday, or even shelter certain plants with a big umbrella.

Surviving Cold Winters

Even though landscapers are natural-born experimenters, imagine investing a few thousand dollars and your free time in spring and summer planting a new landscape only to watch the plants curl up and die their first winter. To avoid that scenario is exactly why climate zones were invented.

Climate zones are most critical for permanent landscape plants — the type of plants you find in this book. If you want a tree, shrub, vine, or perennial to survive and grow year after year, the plant must tolerate year-round conditions in your area — most often, that means the lowest and highest temperatures. Of course, other factors are important too, namely the amount and distribution of rainfall (or availability of irrigation water) and soil conditions.

Terms such as *cold hardy*, *frost hardy*, and *winter hardy* are used to describe woody plants that can survive freezing temperatures without injury during the winter. Of course, "cold" is a relative term. For plants, it's *cold* in Venice, California (where coauthor Philip Giroux lives), on those rare occasions when the thermometer dips to 30°F. In central New York (home of coauthor Teri Dunn Chace), cold is a lot colder: −10°F isn't unusual.

REMEMBER

The safest course to ensure plant adaptability is to grow only plants that are native to your particular region. Native plants are most likely to have the constitution to survive in your landscape. However, plants don't stay in their regions of origin any more than landscapers do. For instance, plants native to China, Siberia, or Mexico thrive alongside each other in many American landscapes. Furthermore, a landscaper in California may want to grow a plant native to the Great Plains. In these cases, the person selecting plants needs some way to compare the landscape's climate with the climate where the plant is known to grow well. That's when zone maps play a critical role.

Although a down time for the landscape and for you, winter can be stressful and damage and losses can occur. The good news is that you can do plenty of easy and sensible things, which we discuss here.

Maximizing winter hardiness for plants

You can, to some degree, help plants adapt to winter by doing the following:

>> **Reduce nitrogen fertilizer applications after mid-July and stop by late summer.** Plants should enter autumn as healthy as possible, but not rapidly growing, or their acclimation may be affected.

>> **Water soil in mid-to-late autumn before the soil freezes.** Because plants — especially evergreens — often dry out (or *desiccate*) during winter, their soil needs to be irrigated in mid-to-late autumn before the soil freezes. If the landscape where evergreens are located is in a dry site, sandy soil, or under the overhang of a roof, irrigate the soil in midwinter when the temperature is above freezing.

This practice is especially beneficial for plants, such as rhododendrons, which continue growth late into the season and are susceptible to early freeze damage.

Identifying and mitigating winter plant injuries

Winter injury refers to several types of plant damage caused by environmental conditions during late fall, winter, or spring. Damage ranges from a marginal scorching of leaves to complete killing of plants. You may have difficulty differentiating winter injury from disease, insect, or chemical injury. Winter-injured plants often leaf out normally in the spring only to collapse after stored food reserves have been totally used up by the plant. Occasionally, damage doesn't become apparent until one or two years after the injury occurred. These sections take a closer look at some common injuries and offers ways for you to reduce their effects.

Frost injury

Late spring and early autumn frosts injure plants that aren't yet sufficiently dormant and able to withstand cold temperatures. This type of injury can occur on native plants, but more exotic plants usually are more vulnerable. A result of late spring frosts can be the death of expanding flower buds on species such as magnolia or lilac, or the death of young, succulent, actively growing shoots.

TIP

Clip and destroy dead tissues in the spring; cut off dead branches at any time. The plant won't suffer any long-term effects.

Low temperature injury

Cold temperatures damage plants in several ways, most commonly in early autumn or late spring, when there is little or no snow cover. Plants are also likely to be damaged during winters of little snow cover and during periods of prolonged low temperatures. Rapid fluctuations in temperature are dangerous for plants no matter what time of year they occur. Consider the following as well:

>> Plants injured or killed directly by low winter temperatures are those planted in areas colder than their minimum hardiness zone. For instance, if a plant is rated as hardy in USDA Zones 5 through 9 and is planted in Zone 4, it'll likely suffer in an average Zone 4 winter. Such species can't *harden off* (become accustomed and more resistant to cold) at an appropriate rate or to an extent sufficient to withstand prevailing winter temperatures. However, even hardy plants can be injured during unusually cold periods or when temperatures drop rapidly or change frequently.

>> Both too much nitrogen fertilizer in late summer or fall and late summer pruning can promote new growth that doesn't mature and may be damaged by freezing. Flower buds, vegetative buds, branches, stems, crowns, bark, roots, or even whole plants may be injured.

>> Plants in containers are particularly vulnerable to low winter temperatures because their roots aren't protected by being below ground. Roots are much less tolerant of cold than trunks and branches. Roots of even the hardiest shrubs and trees are killed at temperatures between 0 and 10°F. Place container plants in protected areas, sunk into the ground, grouped together, and heavily mulched to avoid low temperature injury to roots.

Winter drought

This problem usually appears in late winter or very early spring on evergreen plants. The injury occurs during sunny and/or windy winter weather when plants lose water from their leaves faster than it can be replaced by roots that are frozen in soil. Broadleaf evergreens, such as rhododendron, exhibit browning or even total death of their leaf margins (leaf scorch) depending on the extent of injury. Narrowleaf evergreens, such as white pine, exhibit browning of needle tips when injury is slight. Extensive injury may result in browning and premature drop of entire needles.

Plants that are properly watered during dry periods in late autumn are better equipped to withstand this type of injury. Mulching around the root zones of susceptible evergreens also helps to minimize the damage. Placing a protective barrier of burlap over or around plants to protect them from winter winds and sun helps to reduce the incidence of this injury. Antidesiccant sprays applied once in late autumn and again in midwinter may also prove helpful.

Soggy ground

In some settings, the problem isn't dry ground but mucky ground, especially in low-lying or downhill areas. Poorly drained soils can lead to winter losses from rotted roots. Anticipate and prevent this by creating drainage channels around prized plants before autumn rains come and/or the ground freezes.

Frost-heaving

This happens when alternating freeze-thaw cycles end up pushing up or ejecting rootballs. New plants, ones that you added to your landscape in the past season, are the most vulnerable because they haven't had enough time to settle in and extend their root systems. When you see this, you can try pushing the plants back into place and hope they'll make it through. But it's so much better to prevent the problem beforehand.

TIP

The best way to protect them is with a thick (6 inches, 15.2 cm, isn't excessive) mulch. Alternatively, some gardeners lay evergreen boughs or other branches over their perennial flowerbeds in winter, which help capture and hold snowfall in place . . . a blanket of snow is also a great insulator. (If you forget or neglect to do either of these protective measures, acting late is better than never.)

Sunscald

This type of injury occurs when the sun heats tree bark during the day and then the bark rapidly cools after sunset. These abrupt fluctuations are most common on south or southwest sides of trunks and branches, and they may kill the inner bark in those areas. Young and/or thin-barked trees are most susceptible to winter sunscald.

TIP

Wrapping trunks of susceptible trees with protective tree wrap is the most effective way to minimize this type of winter injury.

Frost cracks

Frost cracks are splits in bark and wood of a tree that occur when winter sun causes a differential expansion of wood beneath the bark. A loud snap often accompanies the initial crack. In winter, the crack may become wider and narrower during colder or warmer periods. Such frost cracks often close and callus over during the summer, only to open again in subsequent winters. This callusing and recracking may lead to the formation of large *frost ribs* on the side of affected trees. Keep a watchful eye on affected plants; if disease opportunistically moves into the damaged areas, you may lose or have to remove the trees.

TIP

In midautumn, wrap the trunks of young trees with commercial tree wrap paper or burlap to protect against frost cracks. Brace large frost ribs to prevent reopening during the winter and enhance callusing and healing.

Physical damage from snow and ice

Heavy snow or ice on weak limbs or on limbs with foliage (as in the case of evergreens) can result in breakage. Take these steps to prevent problems:

>> Prune trees and shrubs to reduce the amount of snow or ice they collect and/or eliminate those weak branches. Branches with a wide angle to the main stem are generally stronger and can support more snow and ice than can those with a narrow or acute angle.

>> Plant trees and shrubs away from places where snowmelt from roofs drips on them.

>> Build wooden barriers over small shrubs to allow snow and ice to slide off rather than accumulate.

Being proactive with other winter-protection tactics

Take the following steps to decrease the likelihood of winter injury to your plants:

>> **Plant on the north side.** Choose a location for marginally hardy plants with a northern or eastern exposure rather than southern or southwestern. Plants facing the south are more exposed to the sun on warm winter days and thus experience greater daily temperature variation.

>> **Mulch.** Apply a layer at least 2 to 3 inches (5 to 7.6 cm) deep, after the soil freezes to keep the soil cold (rather than to protect the soil from becoming cold). In other words, mulch helps maintain even soil temperatures. It also retains soil moisture. For information on mulch materials, consult Chapter 16.

>> **Tie your plants.** *Multiple leader* (that means *branched*) plants such as arborvitae, juniper, and yew may be damaged by the weight of snow or ice. Prevent plant breakage by fastening heavy twine at the base of the plant and winding it spirally around and upward to the top and back down in a reverse spiral. Use this technique as your plants become larger and begin to open at the top.

>> **Use a burlap screen.** Wrap a section of burlap around four stakes to protect young plants from the south, west, and windward exposures. Don't completely cover the top of the plant because some light is necessary, even in winter.

>> **Use antitranspirants (antidesiccants).** Narrow and broadleaf evergreens lose moisture through leaves in winter. Because the soil moisture may be frozen, plant roots can't absorb what's lost and the foliage *desiccates* (dries out), turns brown, and may drop. This can be serious with evergreen azalea, holly, boxwood, and rhododendron.

REMEMBER

Applying an antitranspirant, also called *antidesiccant,* reduces *transpiration* (loss of water from the leaves) and damage to the foliage from winter drought. At least two applications per season, one in December and another in February, are usually necessary to provide protection all winter.

>> **Prevent animal damage.** Some landscape plants, especially during a time when you have an extended period of snow cover, become a food source for rabbits, mice, or voles. When their normal food supply is covered with ice or snow, rodents turn to the bark and young stems of apple, flowering crabapple, mountain ash, hawthorn, euonymus, and viburnum, among others. Complete *girdling* (removal of the outer bark and transport cells of the plant) of stems by rodents kills the plants and partial girdling weakens the plant and creates wounds for borers and disease organisms to enter.

TIP

Protect stems and trunks of these plants in late autumn with plastic collars cut in a spiral fashion so that they can be slipped around tree trunks. You can also wrap with *hardware cloth* (small mesh wire screen).

Spray or paint trunks, stems, and lower limbs with rodent repellents. Repeat the application at least once if there is a warm period (a January thaw is a common event in some areas with snowy winters). Mixing the repellents with an antitranspirant often results in extended effectiveness. Choose carefully, though, so you get the desired results without poisoning or harming unintended targets.

Gardening in a Warmer World

Those who spend time outdoors, including landscapers and gardeners, are aware that climate change is happening — and plants and animals (including birds, butterflies, and garden insects) are impacted. All landscapers and gardeners need to landscape responsibly, with sensitivity and creativity. The following sections provide actionable ideas you can implement in your yard in order to mitigate or prevent harm from severe weather events.

Firescaping

Your home and landscape can be threatened or consumed by a large and fast-moving fire, but you certainly can take some defensive steps to at least reduce risk and damage by *firescaping* (see Figure 19-1). (Realize, of course, that no plants are completely fireproof.) Local fire districts do try to spread the word, and you can access free public information online or in person to find out the latest preventative information.

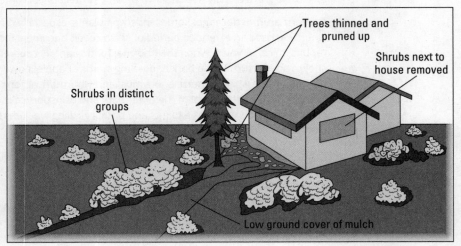

Trees thinned and
pruned up

Shrubs next to
house removed

Shrubs in distinct
groups

Low ground cover of mulch

FIGURE 19-1:
A sample
firescaping
landscape plan.

© John Wiley & Sons, Inc.

That said, here are the basic principles to remember:

>> **Create a buffer zone around your home, garage, shed, or other structures.** Some guidelines recommend as much as 30 feet.

>> **Be tidy.** Always remove dead or dried-out plants, whether they're your own garden plants or encroaching wild plants.

>> **Landscape in islands of plants, with space between them.** Create, for instance, flowerbeds here and there with areas of lawn, mulch, patio, or stones between them.

>> **Prevent a fuel ladder by separating layers of plants.** A *fuel ladder* refers to the proximity of plants (dead or alive) that flames can easily ascend, for example, grasses adjacent to shrubs. You should also not plant shrubs at the base of trees or site a flower garden adjacent to a hedge or windbreak of trees. Instead, give them separate areas.

Anticipating and recovering from flooding

Unfortunately, extreme weather events that bring heavy rain are becoming more common, which means finding landscaping solutions is urgent. Floodwaters do more than damage or wash away precious soil. Water removes oxygen from soil, slowing down root growth and halting the growth of beneficial bacteria and fungi, which causes plants to falter or die. At the same time, harmful bacteria that don't need oxygen are activated, removing nutrients and adding toxins to the surviving soil. Disease organisms flourish and invade some plant tissues.

Being proactive is better than reacting, so here are some strategies you can implement now that will help if a deluge comes:

>> **Install raised beds.** Because they're above the ground surface by several inches or feet cm/m, they may not get inundated, and in any event, will drain faster than garden ground.

>> **Create berms to route or reroute the flow of water.** Work with where the water wants to go — downhill.

>> **Make swales.** *Swales* essentially are homemade dry streams that take on the excess water and route it away from the rest of the yard.

TIP

As for recovering from a flooding event, your response is a matter of triaging. Our recommendations, in order, are to follow these steps:

1. **Wait until the bulk of the water runs off.**

2. **Before walking or taking a wheelbarrow over wet soil or a saturated lawn, lay down planks to evenly distribute your weight and prevent more soil damage.**

3. **Pick up and get rid of large debris.**

4. **Stake leaning trees.**

5. **Rake off debris, gently loosening sediment, and avoid disturbing any exposed roots.**

6. **Order a soil test and follow the recommendations for soil repair.**

TIP

Don't rush to declare plants dead. Some will die quickly, and some will take a season to do so because their roots have been damaged. Others are resilient and will come back to life, given time. Remove obviously dead and damaged growth and watch for signs of new life.

Preparing for new plant choices and challenges

Climate change is affecting plants as well as the pests (all creatures from insects to mammals) that impact them, often in ways that scientists can't predict or quite understand as yet. You have to be attentive and nimble as well as good stewards — gardeners and homeowners who enjoy their yards ought to be the last people who contribute to environmental damage.

We overheard a longtime gardener in Massachusetts remark, "Climate change means I may be able to grow citrus or avocadoes here!" Perhaps. That attitude seems a bit opportunistic, but there's a grain of truth, too: Plant choices are changing. Some plants won't do as well as they used to (lacking necessary cold), whereas others may be brought in (because of milder conditions). However, unfamiliar insect pests and more extreme weather can also arrive.

For now, here is our advice for coping in this volatile situation:

>> **Watch carefully for changes**. Look out for anything welcome and unwelcome, strange or worrisome, and then share the information with others in your neighborhood or gardening community.

>> **Plant a tree or trees.** Not only do they take in carbon and give back oxygen, but trees also provide shade and a home and food for many creatures, including birds and insects. Such a major landscape element also has the ability to regulate moisture and temperature right in your own backyards. Native trees are best (see Chapter 11).

>> **Manage differently to protect and nurture the food web.** The *food web* is made up of all the creatures, seen and unseen, large and microscopic, that live in interdependence; for example, decimate a bird's favorite insects and your landscape's bird population will plummet. We urge you to have a smaller lawn, to grow plants that are favored by pollinators and to use pesticides and weedkillers sparingly if at all.

>> **Encourage diversity.** A diverse ecosystem is a strong ecosystem. Grow lots of different kinds of plants.

>> **Choose or transition to lower-maintenance plants.** They'll consume less water, won't succumb to pests and diseases, need less or no fertilizer, and so on. They're less work for you, too!

5

Time to Add Flair to Your Landscape

Jump-start your thinking for your landscape plan by balancing the pragmatic and the pretty so your garden works for you.

Examine specific situations or settings that may present a challenge or opportunity in your yard.

Find inspiration with different, easy-to-install themed gardens.

Chapter **20**

Contemplating Plans for Special Situations

This chapter helps you plan the parts of your landscape that demand special treatment. In addressing sections of a landscape by themselves, we don't intend to contradict other chapters in this book that encourage you to integrate your whole property into a grand garden scheme. We just know that some situations require special attention. Or, perhaps you may be doing your landscaping one section at a time — nothing wrong with that. But try to keep in mind how each part fits into your overall scheme.

Our idea here is to get you started. You'll probably have to adapt our suggestions for your own garden conditions and slot in plants appropriate to your area. For alternatives, check the plant lists that we give with each plan and consult Part 3.

Planting for Privacy

The challenge in landscaping is to provide privacy while creating an enjoyable and useable space. For this plan, we suggest you use both plants and fencing for privacy. When carefully selected and placed, plants can help screen neighbors, muffle noise, and create interest and beauty of their own. Bear in mind that plants eventually can grow much taller (and of course wider) than a fence.

Consider the following as you're incorporating privacy into your yard:

REMEMBER

TIP

>> **Use fencing for privacy.** If you want a high degree of privacy, use solid stockade fencing. Otherwise, use an open type of fencing, and adorn it with vines. Chapter 6 discusses fences; Chapter 12 explores vines.

Typically you don't need a building permit or permission to erect a fence that's between 6 and 8 feet tall (1.8 to 2.4 m), but do check with your municipality.

>> **Create a private patio.** A free-form patio gives an informal look. You can surface it with flagstone, brick, concrete pavers, pea gravel, or even mulch. Chapter 9 can help you build a patio. Take a look at some of the smaller patios in the color insert.

>> **Use a mix of plants for privacy.** Evergreens are mixed with deciduous plants for screening (more on trees in Chapter 11). Evergreens provide year-round privacy, but the foliage of deciduous plants blocks views during spring and summer when you're most apt to use the space.

Keep in mind the eventual heights of the plants you choose. The taller plants generally reach 5 to 8 feet (1.5 to 2.4 m). For higher screening, consider plants in the section "Deciduous plants for screening," later in this chapter. Also find out and bear in mind the eventual width of the plants you choose; if you set them too close together, eventually they'll crowd one another and your garden area. Lastly, be advised that even though fencing height is often regulated, plant height isn't; therefore, if you desire particularly tall privacy, plants are your answer.

>> **Pay attention to the shape of plants.** The rounded, enveloping shape of the planting creates a feeling of being wrapped in plants — like you're getting extra privacy. It takes time, of course, but they do fill in/broaden as well as grow taller.

>> **Create overhead privacy.** You may be wanting to block anyone looking down from above, from the second floor of your house or a neighboring one, from any taller building for that matter, or even from a nearby bridge or elevated walkway. Lush plants certainly help, as would a pergola, perhaps planted with a climbing plant or vines (see Chapter 12).

When planting for privacy, you may consider evergreen plants or deciduous ones. Even though evergreen plants provide year-round coverage and those that drop their leaves each autumn don't, consider that you may not be outdoors a lot in winter. In other words, pick plants that suit your needs as well as your taste.

Deciduous plants for screening

Consider using the following plants for tall screens or hedges (see Chapters 11 and 12 for more detailed information):

>> Hornbeam *(Carpinus caroliniana)*

>> Hydrangea (*Hydrangea* species and cultivars)

>> Inkberry *(Ilex glabra)*

>> Lilac *(Syringa vulgaris)*

>> Red-twig dogwood *(Cornus sericea)*

>> Viburnum (*Viburnum* species and cultivars)

Evergreen plants for screening

Try the following evergreens for extra privacy (see Chapters 11 and 12 for more detailed information):

>> Arborvitae (*Thuja occidentalis*)

>> Eastern red cedar (*Juniperus virginiana*)

>> False cypress (*Chamaecyparis*)

>> Holly (*Ilex*)

>> Incense cedar (*Calocedrus decurrens*)

>> Juniper (*Juniperus*)

>> Leyland cypress (*Cupressus × leylandii*)

>> Photinia (*Photinia*)

Adding a Low-Water Garden

If you live in an area where water conservation is a priority — like much of the western U.S. — you may want at least part of your landscape to thrive without irrigation after it's established. (Keep in mind that almost anything you plant needs regular watering to get it started and for the first year or two.)

A low-water plan works in most climates with the plants that are hardy in Zones 3 to 8 or 9 (see Chapter 19 for more). In Western climates that are milder, you can choose from an additional palette of plants. Just because the planting has low-water requirements doesn't equate to boring.

Special features of a low-water plan include the following:

» **Layered plants:** Plant low plants up front, tall ones at the back. Low plants grow underneath the window so not to obstruct the view. (Chapter 2 discusses layering in more detail.)

» **Plenty of colors:** Aim for a mix of plant colors, not just flowers but also foliage. Seasonal flowers can add their colorful punctuation.

» **Drought-tolerant larger plants:** Plan for the long term by putting in trees and shrubs that get by on less water once established. These will be anchors; choose based on size as well as the looks you like.

Trees that require less water

You can find many low-water trees to choose from, depending on your climate. Check the adaptability of the following in Chapter 11: (Note that many larger types of trees are available in smaller mature-growth cultivars.)

» Arborvitae (*Thuja occidentalis*)

» Chinese pistache (*Pistacia chinensis*)

» Crape myrtle (*Lagerstroemia indica*)

» Italian stone pine (*Pinus pinea*)

» Leyland cypress (*Cupressus × leylandii*)

» Maidenhair tree (*Ginkgo biloba*)

» Oak (*Quercus* species)

» Olive (*Olea europaea*)

» Palo verde (*Parkinsonia*)

Shrubby plants that require less water

Be sure to include bushy plants like the following that offer the ornamental qualities you seek (such as flowers or colorful foliage) but are also adapted to your climate: Chapter 12 offers more information and advice on shrubs.

- ≫ California lilac (*Ceanothus*)
- ≫ Cape plumbago (*Plumbago auriculata*)
- ≫ Euryops (*Euryops*)
- ≫ Flannel bush (*Fremontodendron*)
- ≫ Flowering quince (*Chaenomeles*)
- ≫ Lemon bottlebrush (*Callistemon citrinus*)
- ≫ New Zealand tea tree (*Leptospermum*)
- ≫ Oleander (*Nerium oleander*)
- ≫ Pride of Madeira (*Echium candicans*)
- ≫ Rockrose (*Cistus*)
- ≫ Rosemary (*Rosmarinus officinalis*)
- ≫ Sage (*Salvia greggii, Salvia leucantha*)
- ≫ Smoke tree (*Cotinus coggygria*)
- ≫ Toyon (*Heteromeles arbutifolia*)

Drought-tolerant flowers

A surprising number of flowering plants — annuals and perennials — are able to prosper in low-water growing conditions. There's no need to worry about lack of color in a dry garden! Here are some of our favorites (consult Chapters 13 and 14 for more information).

- ≫ California poppy (*Eschscholzia californica*)
- ≫ Catmint (*Nepeta*; warning, some cultivars spread!)
- ≫ Coneflower (*Echinacea*)
- ≫ Hummingbird Mint (*Agastache* species and cultivars)
- ≫ Lantana (*Lantana*)
- ≫ Lavender (*Lavandula*)
- ≫ Lavender cotton (*Santolina*)
- ≫ Penstemon (*Penstemon* species and cultivars)
- ≫ Russian sage (*Perovskia/Salvia yangii* cultivars)
- ≫ Scarlet sage (*Salvia splendens*)

>> Silver mound (*Artemisia schmidtiana*)

>> Yarrow (*Achillea* species and cultivars)

Getting Ready for a Dip — around a Pool

Landscaping around a pool first involves choosing the kind of look you want — tropical, natural, sleek, and so on. Keep the following practical considerations in mind when making your plans and selecting your plants:

>> **Don't create shade.** Plants shouldn't cast shade where you don't want it. Choose low-growing or dwarf-type plants. Palms are different — even big ones may not cast too much shade.

>> **Stay away from mess-makers.** Avoid leaf, blossom, and berry shedders that drop debris into your pool.

>> **If bees are a problem, either don't plant flowering plants, or plant ones that flower before pool season is in full swing.** Anticipating this issue will make lounging poolside, and swimming, more pleasant.

>> **Choose low-maintenance plants.** If you're like most people, you want to use your poolside areas for relaxing and not for heavy-duty gardening.

Heed the following features of a good pool landscape:

>> **Stick with low-maintenance materials.** We find your best bet is durable, long-lasting, economical Kool Deck (a trademarked name); it's a topping applied over your concrete base around an inground pool while the concrete is still curing. It's worthwhile because it dramatically lowers the surface temperature so bare feet can stand or walk around the pool area in comfort. Kool Deck also resists stains, mold, and mildew. Your pool-installation contractor will have full information.

>> **Use fencing around the pool.** Check with your municipality or HOA for restrictions and regulations regarding pool fencing. Then consider utilizing an informal post and rail fence or more formal aluminum with the look of wrought iron. If you need a solid fence, break up the monotony by growing vines on it.

>> **Utilize plants for privacy.** Evergreens such as holly and conifers provide a privacy screen plus interesting changes in texture.

>> **Keep grass to a minimum.** Don't plant any lawn inside the fenced area. The idea is to keep maintenance requirements low.

>> **Reduce plant maintenance.** Choose compact, low-maintenance types.

>> **Choose a few stunning plants for color.** Look at vines that bloom in the summer when the pool is used the most. (If you grow thorny roses, make sure that they don't grow close to foot traffic because thorns may scratch skin or clothing.)

   For additional color, plant annual flowers and bulbs as a front border.

REMEMBER

When choosing flowering plants for the poolside, don't forget to consider whether they attract lots of bees that may trouble you and your guests.

Here are few suggestions for other plants to use around a pool (Chapter 12 has more on shrubs and Chapter 16 discusses groundcovers in greater detail):

>> **Low shrubs and groundcovers:** Lily of the Nile (*Agapanthus*), juniper (*Juniperus*), Cape tulips (*Moraea*), rosemary (*Rosemarinus*)

>> **Medium to large shrubs:** Holly (*Ilex*), Japanese black pine (*Pinus thunbergii*), Pittosporum (*Tobira*)

Designing a Hillside Rock Garden

Instead of viewing a slope as a landscape liability, consider it a great opportunity — a place to display a rock garden. Rock garden plants are quite beautiful, and growing them on a slope near a walkway gives you the opportunity to view them up close. A rock garden can work in the backyard at the edge of a lawn or in front, right off of a sidewalk. It combines plants, steps, and boulders.

REMEMBER

Keep the following in mind for creating a rock garden:

>> **The steps are stones.** Use stones of different lengths for a more natural look. Choose stones with a smooth, flat surface, and put them in place firmly. Create planting pockets on the steps. Chapter 7 can help you build walkways and steps.

>> **Rocks help the soil.** Rocks and stones of varying size stacked randomly are an economical way to help retain soil on the slope — the steeper the hillside, the closer together they should be to stabilize the soil effectively. Make planting pockets between them to soften their harshness.

>> **Boulders add a natural touch.** Keep them in scale, not too big or too small for the site.

>> **Color and texture come alive.** Typical rock garden plants are small and slow-growing, offering a variety of textures that are best viewed close up. For color, include blooming perennials like lavender, coreopsis, and salvia. See the color section of this book for more ideas about using color in your landscape.

When it's time to choose plants for your rock garden, there are a range of attractive and appropriate choices. The following lists are some tried-and-true, smaller-size types that look great in such a setting.

Small trees for a rock garden

You can find many potential rock garden trees for your own landscape (see Chapter 11 for more on trees):

>> Dwarf Albert spruce (*Picea glauca*)

>> Dwarf arborvitae (*Thuja occidentalis*)

>> Dwarf hemlock (*Tsuga canadensis*)

>> Dwarf hinoki cypress (*Chamaecyparis obtusa*)

>> Dwarf sand plum (*Prunus pumila*)

>> Japanese maple (*Acer palmatum*)

>> Mugho pine (*Pinus mugo*)

Dwarf shrubs for a rock garden

Try these shrubs for your rock garden (Chapter 12 has more details):

>> Bog rosemary (*Andromeda polifolia* 'Nana')

>> Dwarf heath (*Erica*)

>> Dwarf Japanese holly (*Ilex crenata*)

>> Dwarf junipers (*Juniperus*)

>> Dwarf Scotch heather (*Calluna vulgaris*)

Small perennials for a rock garden

The following perennials brings bursts of color to a simple rock garden: (Don't forget succulents; flip to Chapter 15.)

>> Basket of gold (*Aurinia saxatalis*)

>> Bellflower (*Campanula*)

>> Candytuft (*Iberis sempervirens*)

>> Columbine (*Aquilegia*)

>> Cranesbill (*Geranium*)

>> Creeping Phlox (*Phlox subulata*)

>> Creeping Thyme (*Thymus serpyllum*)

>> Dwarf Coreopsis (*Coreopsis auriculata* 'Nana')

>> Dwarf Iris (*Iris reticulata*)

>> Pasque Flower (*Pulsatilla vulgaris*)

>> Primrose (*Primula*)

>> Snow-in-summer (*Cerastium tomentosum*)

>> Thrift (*Armeria*)

>> Yarrow (*Achillea*)

Considering Shade When Gardening

Plants have different sun requirements — some like a lot, some like a little. Plant them in the wrong place and you have problems — shade lovers turn yellow, fry and die in the sun, sun lovers get leggy, won't bloom, and often become diseased in the shade. We can give you an easy tip on where to put plants that like a lot of sun: Plant them in a sunny spot.

Things are a little trickier with plants that grow in shade. That's because not all shade is the same. Here are the three types:

>> **Partial shade:** This is the sunny in the morning, shady in the afternoon, and the vice-versa scenario. Many plants thrive in cool morning sun and afternoon shade. In fact, in very hot climates, partial shade is often the ideal situation.

REMEMBER

Shade in the morning and sun in the afternoon is a different story altogether. In the afternoon, the sun is hotter, further stressing plants that would rather have shade. In such situations, you're better off planting sun-loving plants.

>> **Dappled or filtered shade:** This is the kind of shade you get from tall trees. As long as the canopy isn't too dense, dappled or filtered shade is a great situation for shade lovers (including you on a hot summer day!). There is, however, one caveat: Large trees often have very greedy roots. Tree roots suck up water and nutrients quickly, making it difficult for new planting to get established. If you're planting under existing trees, be ready to watch the plants carefully and water more often than usual. Depending on how plants are positioned or how big the trees are, dappled shade can be more like partial shade if plants get direct sun early in the morning or late in the afternoon.

>> **Full shade:** This is where it's shady all day. It may be in a woodsy area under a large canopy of trees, on the north side of your house, or in any substantial woodsy area in your home landscape.

TIP

If you plant small trees in your landscape, they won't cast much shade until they get bigger. You're probably better off planting sun lovers (or ones that can grow in partial shade) that will grow well initially. The truth is that as a landscape matures, you often have to make changes. But if a plant is described as "growing well in sun or partial shade," it's probably a good choice for such a situation.

Shade isn't a liability. You have many plants to choose from and ways to combine them into handsome shady scenes. The following sections examine.

Shade-loving plants

How well certain plants will grow in those various types of shades depends on how hot a climate you live in. Here we give you lists of different kinds of plants that grow in some type of shade. Read more about their descriptions in Part 3. Chances are that if a plant is described as suitable for full sun or part shade, it's better for areas with brighter light. If, however, a plant is clearly labeled as a shade plant, likely it will do okay in full shade and possibly in very heavy shade. In either case, you can't really find any hard-and-fast rules.

TIP

Check out your neighborhood to see which plants are growing well in shady conditions similar to yours. Even with that information, you may have a failure or two before you find a group of plants that all thrive.

TIP

From a design standpoint, plants with big leaves, white flowers, or variegated white foliage put on the best show in shady landscapes. In fact, planting anything with light-hued flowers is a good way to light up a shady area. See color insert.

Trees for shady landscapes

The following are mostly smaller-statured *understory* trees (a forestry term that simply means they naturally prosper under the canopy of taller trees): Turn to Chapter 11 to learn more specifics about these trees.

- American hornbeam *(Carpinus caroliniana)*
- Blackhaw viburnum *(Viburnum prunifolium)*
- California buckeye *(Aesculus californica)*
- Dwarf magnolia (*Magnolia* Little Girl series)
- Flowering dogwood *(Cornus florida, Cornus kousa, Cornus nuttallii)*
- Japanese maple *(Acer japonicum)*
- Katsura *(Katsura)*
- Red Horse Chestnut *(Aesculus carnea)*
- Redbud *(Cercis)*
- Serviceberry *(Amelanchier)*
- Silverbell *(Halesia)*

Shrubs for shade

Here are some shrubs that do just fine in shady conditions (for complete descriptions of shrubs, see Chapter 12):

- Azaleas and rhododendrons *(Rhododendron)*
- Boxwood *(Buxus)*
- Camellia *(Camellia)*
- Fothergilla *(Fothergilla)*
- Gardenia *(Gardenia)*
- Hydrangea *(Hydrangea)*
- Inkberry Holly *(Ilex glabra)*
- Japanese pieris *(Pieris japonica)*
- Leucothoe *(Leucothoe)*
- Mountain Laurel *(Kalmia latifolia)*
- Oregon Grape Holly *(Mahonia)*

>> Pittosporum *(Tobira)*

>> Viburnum *(Viburnum)*

>> Witch Hazel *(Hammamelis)*

Vines for shade

These vines are good choices to train on a shady wall or trellis (refer to Chapter 12 for information):

>> Creeping fig (*Ficus pumila*)

>> Chinese or star jasmine (*Trachelospermum jasminoides*)

>> Virginia creeper (*Parthenocissus quinquefolia*)

Annual flowers for shade

We break down these annuals according to cool season and warm season plants, depending on whether they grow best in the cool months of spring and fall or the hot months of summer (for additional information, see Chapter 13):

Try the following cool-season annuals:

>> Chinese forget-me-not (*Cynoglossum amabile*)

>> Geranium (*Pelargonium*)

>> Larkspur (*Consolida*)

>> Nasturtium (*Nasturtium*)

>> Primrose (*Primula*)

>> Pansy and viola (*Viola*)

>> Stock (*Matthiola*)

>> Sweet alyssum (*Lobularia maritima*)

Check out the following warm-season annuals:

>> Bacopa (*Sutera*)

>> Bedding begonia (*Begonia*)

>> Coleus (*Coleus*)

- » Flowering tobacco (*Nicotiana*)
- » Fuchsia (*Fuchsia*)
- » Impatiens (*Impatiens*)
- » Lobelia (*Lobelia*)
- » Madagascar periwinkle (*Catharanthus roseus*)
- » Torenia (*Torenia*)

Flowering perennials for shade

Many other perennials can grow in partial shade, but they'll produce fewer flowers. Here are our recommendations (for more information, see Chapter 14):

- » Astilbe (*Astilbe*)
- » Bellflower (*Campanula*)
- » Bergenia (*Bergenia*)
- » Bleeding Heart (*Dicentra*)
- » Brunnera (*Brunnera*)
- » Columbine (*Aquilegia*)
- » Coralbells (*Heuchera*)
- » Crested Iris (*Iris cristata*)
- » Dead Nettle (*Lamium*)
- » Dianthus (*Dianthus*)
- » Foamflower (*Tiarella*)
- » Hosta (*Hosta*)
- » Japanese anemone (*Anemone japonica*)
- » Lungwort (*Pulmonaria*)
- » Primrose (*Primula*)
- » Roof Iris (*Iris tectorum*)
- » Toad Lily (*Tricyrtis*)
- » Trout Lily (*Erythronium americanum*)
- » Woodland Phlox (*Phlox divaricata*)

Flowering bulbs for shade

Many of these — plants that emerge from bulbs, tubers, and thick rhizomes — can be grown in the shade of deciduous trees. They'll bloom before the canopy of tree foliage overhead fills in and becomes too dense (or more details on bulbs, flip to Chapter 14):

>> Calla lily (*Zantedeschia*)

>> Crocus (*Crocus*)

>> Daffodil (*Narcissus*)

>> Fancy caladium (*Caladium*)

>> Glory-of-the-snow (*Chionodoxa*)

>> Grape Hyacinth (*Muscari*)

>> Grecian Windflower (*Anemone blanda*)

>> Hyacinth (*Hyacinthus*)

>> Iris (*Iris*)

>> Snowdrops (*Galanthus*)

>> Spanish bluebells (*Scilla*)

Lawns and groundcovers for shade

Most lawn grasses don't grow well in shade. The most shade-tolerant are fine fescues and St. Augustine grass, but you'll be better off planting a shade-tolerant groundcover. For more information, turn to Chapter 16. Here are our suggestions:

>> Barren Strawberry (*Waldsteinia fragarioides*)

>> Bunchberry (*Cornus canadensis*)

>> Carpet Bugle (*Ajuga*)

>> Crested Iris (*Iris cristata*)

>> Epimedium (*Epimedium*)

>> Japanese Spurge (*Pachysandra terminalis*)

>> Mondo Grass (*Ophiopogon japonicus*)

>> Pennsylvania Sedge (*Carex pensylvanica*)

>> Spring Cinquefoil (*Potentilla neumanniana*)

>> Star Jasmine (*Trachelospermum jasminoides*)

>> Sweet Woodruff (*Galium odoratum*)

>> Wild Ginger *(Asarum)*

DON'T FORGET FERNS

No discussion on shade landscapes is complete without mentioning ferns. Their arching, feathery leaf (fern leaves are actually called *fronds*) patterns are as at home in the shade as are hammocks.

You can find many ferns to choose from. Tree ferns, such as the Tasmanian tree fern (*Dicksonia antarctica*) and the Australian tree fern (*Cyathea cooperi*), have long arching fronds and tall stalks that can reach higher than 15 feet (4.6 m) under ideal, moist conditions. They're not very hardy, though, and can't be grown in areas colder than Zone 9.

Some hardier native ferns include the following:

- Autumn fern, *Dryopteris erythrosora*, which can be grown into Zone 5. This fern is interesting because its 2-foot (.6 m) long leaves are pinkish when they unfold and turn rust-brown in autumn.

- Alaskan or soft shield fern, *Polystichum setiferum*, is also hardy into Zone 5; it has lacy, flattened fronds that can grow up to 4 feet (1.2 m) high. It's easy to grow.

- Sword fern, *P. munitum*, produces upright fronds on a spreading plant. In its native western United States, it's a tough plant that can get weedy if given too much water. It is hardy into Zone 7.

- Ostrich fern, *Matteuccia struthiopteris*, is justly popular in Zones 3 to 7 because it remains lush and handsome from spring to autumn.

- Christmas fern, *Polystichum acrostichoides,* does well in Zones 3 to 9 and remains evergreen over the winter.

- Japanese painted fern, *Athyrium nipponicum* 'Pictum,' does best in Zones 4 to 7. Its fronds are silvery with a tinge of red if they get some sun. Plants stay under 18 inches (45.7 cm), making them good citizens in a shade border. (The Perennial Plant Association named this fern Plant of the Year in 2004.)

Check your local nurseries or shop online for much more.

Chapter **21**

Considering Theme Landscapes

This chapter offers theme gardens — admittedly, somewhat of a catch-all category. These gardens have specific purposes, and you don't usually create them out of necessity, because you may have a landscape that provides privacy or prevents erosion on a slope. You mostly create theme gardens for pleasure — they make your yard more interesting, fun, and useful.

These theme gardens range widely in complexity from simple wildlife garden ideas to a fairly intricate formal herb garden. Get professional help and advice as needed.

Pay attention to your climate zone when selecting plants. Dealing with climate zones (see Chapter 19) isn't that vital when the plans call for annual flowers and vegetables. The most important factor for these types of plants is when your planting season begins (last killing frost) and ends (first killing frost). Plant selection also depends on other climate variables, such as summer heat or autumn coolness. Consult the plant lists and descriptions provided in Part 3.

Attracting and Nurturing Wild Creatures

Nothing brings a garden to life more than living things — *desirable* living things, that is — not competitors like gophers, voles, and deer. The sight and sound of birds is particularly appealing and easy to arrange. But you can also invite butterflies and beneficial insects (check out Chapter 18) to your landscape. What brings most creatures into a garden are plants, and certain plants bring certain creatures.

Following are a few general points to keep in mind when you want your garden to attract different types of life:

>> **Garden organically.** Pesticides and herbicides (weedkillers) are toxic not only to their intended targets but also to many other insects and small creatures, including those in the critical *food web* (made up of all the creatures, seen and unseen, large and microscopic, that live in interdependence in the soil) and those who eat them (such as birds). Wean yourself and your landscape off these products. Tolerate some nibbled plants; grow extra plants so there's enough for you and enough for wildlife visitors. Interestingly, you may observe that nibbled plants tend to respond not by dying off but by putting out new growth.

If you stay the course, you'll discover that ultimately many pest insects are controlled by their natural predators.

REMEMBER

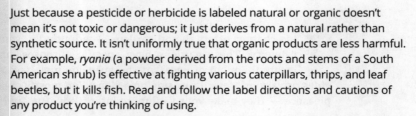

Just because a pesticide or herbicide is labeled natural or organic doesn't mean it's not toxic or dangerous; it just derives from a natural rather than synthetic source. It isn't uniformly true that organic products are less harmful. For example, *ryania* (a powder derived from the roots and stems of a South American shrub) is effective at fighting various caterpillars, thrips, and leaf beetles, but it kills fish. Read and follow the label directions and cautions of any product you're thinking of using.

>> **Strive for diversity in your plant selection.** Even though this concept may conflict with a designer's approach to unity of planting fewer plants like we discuss in Chapter 2, the more different types of plants you have, the greater the chances of attracting a variety of wild creatures.

>> **Provide water.** A water source can be a pond, fountain, or a birdbath.

>> **Grow plants that are native to your region.** Plants should be familiar and attractive to your local creatures. True, non-natives can also draw them, but ultimately they tend not to sustain wildlife in the same way as native plants.

The plan for attracting wildlife includes a mix of plants designed to attract birds (including hummingbirds), butterflies, chipmunks, and insects. It also includes enough attractive plants to please humans as well. Other features that contribute to its appeal are the following:

>> A post-and-rail fencing has a rustic look that fits in nicely and supports a berry-producing shrub.

>> Crabapple *(Malus),* cranberry bush *(Viburnum trilobum),* cotoneaster *(Cotoneaster),* blueberry *(Vaccinium),* winterberry *(Ilex verticillata),* and service-berry *(Amelanchier)* all have berries that draw a variety of birds and animals.

Use upright or vase-shaped trees (like redbud, *Cercis,* or dogwood, *Cornus*) so that other plants can grow underneath.

>> Milkweed and butterfly weed *(Asclepias* species and cultivars*)* are traditional butterfly lures.

>> Tubular-shaped red or pink flowers generally attract hummingbirds. *Weigela* (not native) and bee balm *(Monarda)* do the job here.

>> You can find many other bird-attracting plants. Exactly which to choose depends on your climate and garden conditions. Here are a few favorites: serviceberry *(Amelanchier)*, Eastern red cedar *(Juniperus virginiana)*, hawthorn *(Crataegus)*, mulberry *(Morus)*, holly *(Ilex)*, rowan *(Sorbus)*, and other juniper *(Juniperus)* species.

DO EVEN MORE TO BE WELCOMING

If you're earnestly interested in making some or all of your home landscape appealing to wild creatures, here are some additional steps you can take:

- **For the birds:** Don't just concentrate on providing food and shelter. They'll appreciate and use laddering landscaping — plants that give them the opportunity to land in a tall tree and hop down to lower perches on your shrubs and other plants. Also put in a birdbath to provide both drinking and bathing water. Keep it full and clean.

- **For the butterflies:** Welcome them from the caterpillar stage forward. In addition to the milkweed and butterfly weed, you can try fennel *(Foeniculum vulgare)*, parsley *(Petroselinum)*, Dutchman's pipe vine *(Aristilochia)*, spicebush *(Lindera benzoin)*, paw paw *(Asimina triloba)*, and rue *(Ruta graveolens)*. Adults especially favor nectar-rich flowers like bee balm *(Monarda)*, butterfly bush *(Buddleia)*, and Russian sage *(Perovskia atriplicifolia,* also called *Salvia yangii)*.

(continued)

(continued)

- **For the pollinators:** Pollinating insects and flowering plants co-evolved, so offer their favorite pollen-laden flowers, and they'll come. Your best bets are plants in the aster, parsley, mint, mustard, and rose families. Additionally, annual (self-sowing) native wildflowers are always a good idea.

For even more recommendations, look online (start with the Audubon Society for birds and the Xerces Society for butterflies).

Providing a Garden Space for Kids

What do kids want in a landscape? Better not ask them, or they'll say a mudhole full of earthworms. As grown-ups, you want to turn kids on to the beauty, fun, and educational value of gardening and the great outdoors. Kids just focus on the fun.

WARNING

Always be cautious when selecting plants for your child's garden. If you have any questions, research poisonous plants online and/or check with the Poison Control Center (www.poison.org/articles/plant). Ask again when buying.

We suggest a square area with a clock design and plants flanking a central sandbox. Feel free to change its scale (the minimum space is 10 by 10 feet; 3 by 3 m) or, instead of a clock, make it into a sun, a daisy — whatever suits your needs. An additional possible option is a low wall or boulders to jump off or leapfrog among, popular with elementary-school-age kids.

Here are some features to include — modify as you wish:

>> **A sandbox is at the center.** We recommend that you cover it with a tarp or piece of plywood when it's not in use to keep the sand cooler and to discourage neighborhood cats from considering it a nice outdoor litter box.

>> **The brick clock garden is a real eye-catcher.** Strawberry and blueberry plants alternate in cutouts between numbers or spaces left blank. You can make numbers in the brick work (although doing so won't be easy) by cutting bricks and leaving space for cut bricks of contrasting color or sand or gravel.

>> **The plants don't just sit there.** Various training devices get them off the ground and make them more interesting — trellises for cucumbers, cages for tomatoes, and so on. A section of fence can be used to train the apple tree into a flat *espalier* (plant that grows flat along a fence — consult Chapter 11 for more about this technique).

» **The plants are fun.** In addition to the berries, other edibles include pumpkins, figs, and grapes. Sunflowers are big and striking — and irresistible to kids. Sensory plants, such as prickly coneflower seedheads, fragrant herbs, or rustling grasses, help children explore in different ways. Refer to the nearby sidebar for more ideas.

Putting in a Kitchen Garden

A fresh take on the traditional vegetable garden, kitchen gardens are actually nothing new — British and European gardeners, especially those with limited space, have been doing them for ages. North American gardeners seem to be late to the concept that a food garden can be pretty.

TIP

Your kitchen garden can be as big or small as you like, though we recommend keeping it a manageable size (say, 12 by 12 feet, 3.6 m by 3.6 m, or 10 by 16 feet, 3 by 4.9 m). Use raised beds if your soil isn't up to snuff, if you have nibbling rabbits in the neighborhood, and/or if you wish to spare your back/minimize bending for tending.

For inspiration, check out the photo in the color insert. Also visit the websites or thumb through the catalogs of specialty seed catalogs, trawl Pinterest and Instagram, or do a general online images search with the term "kitchen garden" and feast your eyes.

TIP

Plant vegetables and herbs your family really eats. If they hate zucchini, eggplant, or cilantro, you'll just be giving away your harvests.

Follow these basic principles when creating your own kitchen garden:

>> **Locate it near your kitchen.** The idea is that you can pop outside with a basket and clippers and harvest a few ingredients for tonight's salad, dip, soup, or other recipe on a moment's notice because it's right there!

>> **Make your kitchen garden easy to care for by putting it close to the water source/hose.** Other practical needs include a good, sunny spot (most vegetables and herbs thrive in six to eight hours of sun), and of course good, fertile, well-drained soil.

>> **Include everything.** Veggies, herbs, and edible flowers. The more variety, the better it looks (and the more pollinators that come by).

>> **Maximize the use of space.** Add trellises and teepees to support upward-growing crops like pole beans, cucumbers, decorative gourds, and more. Include plants growing in containers and intersperse them where they won't interfere with the growth of in-ground plants, of course, but also so you can move them out when they've produced and are past their prime.

>> **Select colorful plants.** Plant not just edible nasturtiums and annual bachelor buttons, but also 'Rainbow' Swiss chard, colorful lettuce varieties, purple-podded beans, yellow cherry tomatoes, and more.

>> **Add fruit.** Include strawberry plants, an espaliered fruit tree (see Chapter 11), a container-grown fig tree, a dwarf blueberry, or currant bush (where permitted).

>> **Protect the plants.** Raise or fence your kitchen garden if there are bunnies, voles, gophers, or deer in the vicinity (see Chapter 18 for more information). Interplant colorful marigolds as a natural repellent.

>> **Add ornaments.** Tuck in colorful statuettes, flags, a gazing ball, decorative little birdhouses, and so on. Create a scene that's appealing at all times, regardless of which crops are producing.

Incorporating an Herb Garden

If you want to focus just on herbs, you can consider adding an herb garden to your landscape design. You can find all sorts of reasons to grow herbs somewhere in your garden — use them fresh or dried in cooking, breathe in their aromatic fragrances as you brush past them, or rely on their color and beauty to add life to your garden. Many also attract beneficial insects.

Use the following tips when creating your own herb garden:

>> **Establish a focal point.** Consider something man-made such as a sundial, birdbath, gazing ball, or outdoor sculpture.

>> **Establish pathways.** Use brick for traditional, formal pathways. More informal alternatives include stepping stones, bluestone, mulch, or *pea gravel* (small stones with smaller aggregate mixed in so it can be packed down). For more on path-building, refer to Chapter 7.

>> **Keep herbs separate.** Define and separate the herb plantings with buried edging, which can be brick, metal, or wood. Doing so is important to control the spreading tendencies of mint and spearmint *(Mentha)*. If you'd rather not worry about mints, substitute a more docile herb.

>> **Create herb hedges.** Lavender *(Lavandula),* lavender cotton *(Santolina),* rosemary *(Rosmarinus),* germander *(Teucrium),* or dusty miller *(Senecio)* around the outside can be shaped into hedges for a formal look. If your climate allows, *dwarf* boxwood *(Buxus)* edging is a traditional choice.

>> **Maintain, maintain, maintain.** Any formal herb garden needs regular maintenance — mostly pruning and trimming to keep plants confined to their spaces. For bushy growth, pinch and trim plants while they're small and tender-stemmed — don't wait until they get too tall and woody.

TIP

Trimming and pruning may be a chore in other parts of your landscape, but in your herb garden, we like to call it harvesting. Bring along a basket and collect the sprigs for use indoors, in recipes, potpourris, dried bouquets, and other craft projects.

Invite friends over for a harvesting party. Serve them homemade herbal iced tea or drinks garnished with fresh herbs and biscuits made with herbs from your garden.

As a general rule, most herbs need similar care, such as the following:

>> Provide a spot in full sun.

>> Don't worry about having rich soil high in organic matter. Most herbs don't require it.

   For instance, lavender, unlike many other herbs, prefers soil on the alkaline or limey side. Simply tuck a piece of ordinary chalk into the root area of each lavender plant.

>> Keep the soil well drained and keep plants on the dry side. A few herbs, such as parsley and chives, need more water than others, so keep an eye on them.

Winter performance depends on your climate. In mild climates, many herbs stay evergreen all year. In colder areas, you can dig them up in autumn and overwinter pots in a cool spot indoors.

TIP

Even if you don't create a formal herb garden, you can still grow herbs in a variety of ways:

>> Mix herbs in with other plants — rosemary and lavender are versatile landscape plants, but are also herbs.

>> Grow them in containers so that you can snip parsley right out your back door.

>> Combine them with perennials because they're attractive and because many herbs and perennial flowers thrive under similar conditions.

Establishing a Meadow Garden

A trend in lawn alternatives is to use native grasses and other low-growing, prairie-type plants. These create meadowlike landscapes that can be beautiful year-round. Certain wildflower mixes composed of low-growing plants can also be used for meadowlike lawns. Meadow lawns are less formal-looking than most grass lawns and can be walked on or played on and have a wild beauty all their own.

Before proceeding, check with your local municipality and/or homeowner's association to make sure what you have in mind is allowed.

WARNING

Be wary of "meadow in a can" (or sack) products. You get what you pay for when you buy any wildflower seed mix. A cheap mix may not only germinate poorly or unevenly, but it may contain weed and grass seeds as well as seeds of non-native or not-adapted-to-your-region plants. They'll end up outcompeting/overwhelming the native plants . . . not a recipe for success or beauty. If you try this route, we urge you to look up the ingredients on the label, or at the very least purchase a curated blend from a regional seed company.

To find native plants, look online. Every state has a website with native plant lists, as do universities with agriculture or horticulture departments. Just search for "native meadow (or, prairies) plants [your area]." Search also for mail-order nurseries that sell seeds or flats with plants selected for different regions.

Note the following features of a meadow garden:

>> **The plants behave wildly.** Some are actual wildflowers, but all of them have the ability to reseed themselves as many wildflowers do.

>> **The space can be enlarged.** Simply repeat the pattern for greater length and width.

>> **You can adapt the plan for constant blooms.** Take into account the blooming dates of various plants in your region and spread them around in the design so that you always have something blooming.

>> **The look is natural.** If you need a fence, a natural-looking style is best. For more on fences, see Chapter 6.

WILDFLOWER GARDENS THAT COME BACK FROM SEED

For another kind of natural garden, consider sowing seeds of annual wildflowers — the kind that come back from seed year after year. The flowers and the planting times vary widely from region to region. In cold climates, spring is the main planting season, whereas in mild, winter-rain climates such as California, autumn is the chief planting season.

In addition to giving over a larger area to this project, you can try it in your curb strip (where allowed — check with your local municipality) or as a narrow or wide border elsewhere in your yard.

Here are some annuals that you can grow like wildflowers (that is, you sow seeds once and then let them reseed themselves). Those that are North American natives are so flagged:

- African daisy *(Osteospermum)*
- Baby blue eyes *(Nemophila menziesii),* native
- Black-eyed Susan *(Rudbeckia hirta),* native

(continued)

(continued)

- Blanket Flower *(Gaillardia)*, native

- Butterfly Weed *(Asclepias tuberosa)*, native

- California poppy *(Eschscholzia californica)*, native

- Clarkia *(Clarkia)*, native

- Columbine *(Aquilegia)*, native

- Cornflower *(Centaurea)*, one is native *(C. americana)*

- Cosmos *(Cosmos)*

- Flax *(Linum)*, one is native *(L. lewisii)*

- Forget-me-not *(Myosotis sylvatica)*

- Lupine *(Lupinus)*, many natives

- Shirley poppy *(Papaver rhoeas)*

Composing a Cottage Garden

Trends come and go in the world of garden design, but plants keep on doing what they will. Too much time spent poring over images that promote highly manicured landscapes, or too many hours spent gaping at gardens that permit tours may blind you to the simple reality that plants just love to grow. This very quality may account for the enduring, homespun popularity of the cottage garden.

A cottage garden doesn't require you to have a cottage. Generally speaking, a *cottage garden* is a smallish space that isn't rigidly designed. Plants are well-tended, but they're also allowed to express their natural exuberance. If the sweet peas smother the fence, so be it; if the old-fashioned rosebush swoons over the herb garden, no matter; if the foxgloves self-sow all over the place, nobody yanks them out. The cottage garden is allowed to evolve and eventually can become a bit overgrown, all while being lush and generous.

TECHNICAL STUFF

What makes a cottage garden different from, say, a wildflower meadow, has to do with the selection of plants (you're not restricted to natives), but also with the garden's structure. Plants are placed intentionally, usually in larger swathes or groupings, and structure is provided by fencing, paths, trellises. Also, whimsical attractive décor is incorporated among the plants — unlike, say, a formal herb garden where décor is set apart or placed as a focal point.

Such a garden doesn't just happen, however. The most enchanting cottage gardens involve thoughtful choices. Start with the foundations:

TIP

» **Establish boundaries.** A fence defines the area like a picture frame (while keeping out any marauding animals). Flowering vines eventually may drape over it, shrubs may lean against it, but the bounds are evident nonetheless. An entrance arch or gate is nice.

» **Lay out paths.** Paths and walkways running to and from the house intersect a cottage garden and carry you to every corner. Ideally they're straight and sensible, but if you want a curve, provide a reason for it, such as a rosebush or garden sculpture to go around. (Refer to Chapter 7 for information about your path options — for a cottage garden, you'll want more informal materials, such as weathered bricks, irregular flagstones, or even crushed shells.)

Because, ultimately, you want your cottage-garden plants to feel free to wander, trail, and spill, make paths wide enough to allow this and still be passable. About 3 feet (.9 m) wide should work.

» **Offer seating.** A cottage garden is meant to be enjoyed, indeed savored. Put in comfortable, practical seating that will get used, whether benches or weathered or colorful Adirondack chairs or even a petite French bistro table-and-chairs set where you can sit and enjoy a hot or cold beverage.

When it's time to plant, follow these principles:

» **Select plants with relaxed profiles.** Old-fashioned and heirloom varieties of favorite flowers and shrubs are especially suitable.

» **Put in lots of fragrant plants, from roses to herbs.**

» **Aim for a mix of all types of plants.**

» **Furnish with informal, somewhat rustic-looking ornaments.**

Finding Your Meditation Area with a Retreat Garden

Ideally, an outdoor retreat space is separated from the hectic world and is a place where you (and garden visitors) can relax and gather your thoughts in peace and quiet. The best way to create it is to keep it simple. Here are our recommendations:

>> **Select an area or corner of your garden isolated and away from buildings.** Under shade trees or near a fence is fine.

>> **Prioritize privacy and protection.** This can be done with dense screening plants, in the ground or in pots, with vine-covered trellises, or even with hardscape-style screening (read about privacy screens in Chapter 6). The idea is to block out sights and sounds.

>> **Add a water feature.** A small circulating fountain or bubbler is a great addition to a retreat area. You may even be able to find a nice solar- or battery-powered one, or just flip the switch when you're out there. Running water offers a gentle noise barrier; it's inherently soothing as it blocks out or distracts from neighborhood sounds.

>> **Pare down plant choices.** Otherwise the temptation to jump up and attend to garden chores like pruning or removing spent flowers defeats the purpose. A variety of green foliage plants suits, or keeping the flower colors to one or two soothing hues is wise. You want beauty, not a riot of color.

>> **Install comfortable seating to encourage rest and repose.** A hammock, free-standing on a support or strung between trees, is wonderful, as is a chaise lounge or two. Alternatively, furnish an ample bench or put in wide chairs with arms for perching a mug of coffee or a glass of wine.

>> **Decorate with care.** Stick to the theme and include simple ornaments that have meaning. Choose one item to be a focal point like a stone (or stonelike) Japanese lantern, Buddha, Aquarius, animal, or other statue, delicate (not noisy) windchimes hung from a branch, an urn (with or without plants), or a vintage bell.

Making an Enchanting Evening Garden

When you're away at work or school all day and finally get back home, you want to be able relax in your yard. Unfortunately, the light may be fading. Good news — we have some good ideas for a garden that shines at dusk. In fact, you'll enjoy pleasures that aren't center stage and only dimly imagined in daytime. Try some or all of the following:

>> **Install lighting, both practical and decorative.** Turn to Chapter 10 for a round-up of options and ways to use them.

>> **Plant plenty of white flowers.** Some great choices include shrubs, roses, perennials, and annuals (notably stock, flowering tobacco, and moonflower vines). Many of these naturally bloom later in the day and well into the

evening, enticing pollinators — particularly moths — that are drawn to their beacon brightness and sweet scents. See the color insert.

» **Use containers, pots, hanging baskets, planter boxes, and so forth.** In this way, you can easily move or elevate the plants you want to see into view. Using them also allows you to make sure the show is at eye level, important if you and others are relaxing in seating.

» **Favor white bloomers in clusters or drifts so they stand out better.** Seek out fragrant ones. Good choices include annual flowering tobacco *(Nicotiana)*, fragrant vines of jasmine or honeysuckle, and shrubs such as gardenia or sweet pepperbush *(Clethra alnifolia)*.

» **Choose white or light hues for non-plant items**. You can paint them white yourself; consider including furniture and their cushions to trellises, arbors, fences, gates, statuary, and other garden décor.

» **Don't forget wind chimes.** We prefer the lightweight, tinkling ones that move slightly in an evening breeze, adding to the relaxed mood. If there's no good place to install a hook, you can suspend them from the branch of a tree or shrub near your sitting area.

6

The Part of Tens

Create something unique about your landscape design that makes your garden stand out above all others.

Discover ten ways you can make your garden more environmentally friendly and your neighbors green with envy.

Chapter **22**

Ten Ways to Make Your Surroundings Unique

Suppose that last night you came home from work feeling pretty tired. You pulled into your neighborhood filled with similar houses and you couldn't quite remember which one was yours. Thank goodness for numbered addresses!

Or suppose after walking your dog around the neighborhood and observing some landscapes that inspired you and some that bored you, you remarked to the dog, "I feel we can do better!" And the dog agreed.

After all, character and uniqueness are what make a house a home. You certainly can make some changes, so that at least you'll find your way home at night or you and dog can return from a stroll with a glow of pride.

This chapter has some ideas — besides painting your house purple.

Work on Your Front Yard

Here are some easy ways to improve your front yard:

>> Lay a brick or stone walkway from the street. Try a herringbone pattern with cobbled edges (see Chapter 7).

>> Add unique lawn edging, using concrete or brick. Add an edging of decorative stone in a runnel adjacent to your walkway.

>> Plant a single, beautiful, accent tree (like a Japanese maple) or a cluster of matching trees (like weeping birch, small magnolias, or redbuds) near the entrance. Flip to Chapter 11 for more on trees.

>> Include garden lighting (see Chapter 10) — path lights, uplights on trees, or lights around major shrub plantings.

>> Make part of the front yard a semi-enclosed courtyard, furnished with attractive garden furniture and accented with containers. If the area faces east, it can be a shady retreat in the summer months.

>> Take out most or all your lawn and replace it with enlarged flowerbeds, shrub borders, fruit trees, an array of interesting dwarf evergreens, a rock garden, or raised beds of vegetables, herbs, and flowers.

TIP

Sidestep neighborhood critics by making your yard formal in outline and appearance and/or taking extra-good care of your landscaping choices so nobody can accuse you of sloppiness or neglect.

Reflect the Architecture of Your Home

Look at the architecture of your house. What style is it? Colonial, Tudor, Spanish mission, Victorian, Craftsman bungalow, something else? Design your landscape to reflect your home's architecture.

TIP

Stand back (across the street) and take a good, hard look. Focus on highlighting the best features of your home with lighting. You may also be able to accent certain features with certain plants. Standing back can also help you discover plants that aren't working well. Replace or completely remove those that detract from or hide the unique style of your home.

Perhaps you decide that a Tudor home isn't complete without neat little boxwood hedges. Or that your Spanish-style home looks better with Mediterranean plants.

Bungalows go from ordinary to charming when you add interesting, in-scale plants, ornaments, and decorative lighting. And if you can't get a statue of Paul Revere for the front of your colonial home, try adding a new brick walkway up to the front door.

Go Native

Take cues from the plants that grow naturally in your area. After all, these plants are superbly adapted to your climate and are probably the easiest to care for, demanding less water and having far fewer pest and disease issues.

To find out more, visit a native-plant nursery or a nearby botanic garden with a good collection of native plants, and explore some of the most beautiful plants around. You can also join a local native-plant society or at least attend one of their plant sales or speaker presentations. Your nursery or local botanic garden should be able to put you in touch with one.

You can discover more about the qualities and virtues of native plants in Part 3. The more you know, the more you'll want them.

Coordinate with Neighbors

What if there were no fences or other boundaries between yards, or several friendly neighbors agreed to take down fences, and the neighborhood had a casual flow to it with children moving around like a school of fish and adults lingering and chatting?

What if everyone adopted a similar project — a front-yard rock garden, native flower beds, or fruit-bearing bushes and trees — and the area began to gain a community continuity? What if everyone fixed up their front porch and steps, with potted plants and hanging baskets and little strings of lights and colorful lounging furniture? What if . . .?

A neighborhood becomes a community in appearance as well as in spirit. You can start a trend, a planting scheme, or an outdoor-decorating idea, and then show it off to your neighbors, sharing your plant choices or shopping sources. You can then stand in the street, and discuss and brainstorm with your neighbors.

TIP

Share not only plants, but tools and compost bins and other resources. Certainly several neighbors can pitch in to buy large deliveries of loam, mulch, or pea gravel and split the cost. You can also split the raising of food — someone has a grapevine, someone else can raise bell peppers, and someone has pumpkins — and then share or trade the harvest.

Design a Secret Garden

Inspired by the classic children's book *A Secret Garden* by Frances Hodgson Burnett, you can create a spot that is set apart from the rest of your landscape, walled or fenced off, visible and accessible only through a gate or door. Share it with special garden visitors.

Wherever you place it, it doesn't have to be very big; in fact, it'll be easier to maintain if you keep it small. Lavish it with some of your most-favorite flowers with at least one star performer for each season.

Then add a chair or bench, perhaps a little décor (a small statue, delicate windchimes, or a petite French bistro table and chairs), and sneak in there to relax and enjoy.

TIP

If you have a long, narrow yard, instead of putting a lawn or patio in the middle and flowerbeds along the sides, divide the space in half (or thirds), with the space nearest your access door as a small garden, backed by fencing, a privacy screen, or screening plants. You and your visitors have to pass through that area and beyond that barrier in order to emerge into a second, larger garden area. It will be open and hopefully sunny, perhaps offering seating or a table for outdoor dining. This design gives the impression of stumbling upon a secret spot.

Bring the Inside Out

If you can afford it, consider buying some attractive, stylist outdoor furniture, but an alternative tactic is to just bring indoor tables and seating outside (protecting them from the elements as needed and hauling them back indoors when the season is over). Be inventive — remember not just the table you serve a meal upon, but also a side table or two for a bar or a buffet table.

You can inject style into your outdoor living space. For dining and entertaining, use a colorful tablecloth and napkins, candles or a candelabra, vases (with homegrown bouquets), and real dishes and glasses (instead of paper and plastic). For the seating, use colorful cushions, pillows, and throws or blankets as accents.

Have Fun with Accessories

Put in stuff — birdbaths, sundials, statues, antique garden tools and farm equipment, garden art, wall ornaments, big rocks (our favorite), fountains, whirligigs — you name it. Make compositions. Watch out, though — you can get addicted to collecting.

Materials such as stone or faux-stone ornaments can bring style or even a touch of formality to an area or corner. Decorative flags or painted birdhouses keep things bright during those times when flowering is at a lull. The results don't have to be kitschy (though we have nothing against kitsch, it's a hoot!). Colors can coordinate with adjacent blooming flowers or shrubs.

Pick a Color Theme and Go For It!

Put in some flowers — a lot of flowers. Start by choosing a color theme (you can find a get-you-started list in Chapter 2). Masses of flowers in similar tones *always* work.

Choose flowering shrubs, perennials, annuals, bulbs, some of them in pots if you'd like. Take into account blooming times and plan to sustain the show over the full growing season. Refer to our many lists and suggestions in Part 3. Plant in every open space that you can find.

Mix Ornamentals and Edibles

Rules are meant to be broken! You don't have to put vegetables in a rectangular patch with flowerbeds along the edges and fruit trees out back and ornamental flowering trees placed in the front.

Take a renewed look at your home landscape and put plants in unexpected places: a pear tree in the front yard, blueberry bushes next to the rose bushes, kale and Swiss chard in the flowerbed alongside the coneflowers and coreopsis (purple and yellow do look good together).

As long as a plant is getting the sun, soil, and care it needs, it will thrive, no matter where you put it. Refer to Chapter 13 for more ideas about foodscaping. Be adventurous, have fun, have it all in your yard — food *and* beauty!

Add the Element of Sound

How wonderful it is when a garden that is already lovely to look at also awakens your other senses, particularly hearing, in two ways:

>> Sound inspires curiosity in a visitor. "Where is that coming from?" they ask themselves as they enter your yard.

>> Sound can also mask or block out the outside world, creating a comforting, enveloping feeling of intimacy and retreat.

Sound can come from a variety of sources: birds at a feeder, in your shrubs, or cavorting at a birdbath; windchimes hanging from a branch or hook; a tinkling fountain tucked into a secluded corner; the breeze sifting through leaves; a bright-sounding bell on the garden gate or shed door.

Chapter 23

Tens Ways to a Greener Landscape

In our view, who but gardeners can help nature in these uncertain times? Gardeners like you are already fans of the great outdoors and its many plants and creatures. Gardeners are keen observers. We have dirt under our fingernails, and we care about the landscapes we shape and tend. Ultimately, caring for a home landscape is about stewardship. No matter how big or small yours is, you can examine its ways, help heal its problems, and nurture its residents.

Here are ten ways to tend your home landscape wisely and with sensitivity. Some of these ideas can also save you time and money and conserve precious resources. Try some or all of the following suggestions, then — pass them on.

Plant Trees for Shade

Trees absorb carbon and give back oxygen — something the whole planet certainly needs more of, but planting trees has even more benefits.

Shade trees are insulators. They shield your landscape and home from buffeting winds, snow, and rain. In summer, they not only lower temperatures by providing cooling shade, but they also literally absorb heat. Trees also absorb pollution and improve air quality, which is especially critical in urban settings, but it's also true in suburbs, small towns, and rural areas. Trees are a necessity, not a luxury.

TIP

Plant trees in your yard for you and your family's health, for the health of your neighborhood, town, or city, and for the environment in general. Plant trees that are in scale and do well in your climate and soil. Expand the benefits by choosing ones with beautiful flowers or edible fruit. You can find plenty of information for this important choice in Chapter 11.

Compost

Composting is easy and fun, and your soil will improve as you spread free organic matter over your garden and dig it into new beds, your vegetable patch, and individual planting holes for new additions. As you continue to use your compost, your compost pile will continue to produce more, so get in the habit, and you'll never turn back. To get started, flip to Chapter 17, where we explain more about composting and help start you on your way.

REMEMBER

When you compost, you'll notice your outgoing household trash will be greatly reduced, and less stinky. (That said, don't add oil, meat scraps, or bones.) One day in the not-too-distant future landfills may no longer accept organic waste, so get on the compost wagon now.

Wean from Garden Pesticides and Herbicides

For at least a couple of generations, gardeners have indulged in the sad irony of altering and poisoning their landscapes and the creatures that inhabit them in service of the goal of an attractive landscape. Yes, you surely can have lush flowerbeds, big crops of edibles, and a good-looking yard without pouring on expeditious but harmful pesticides and herbicides.

No product will fix everything, and ultimately, these pesticides and herbicides often do more harm than good to the environment: to the insect life, seen and unseen, as well as to larger landscape residents from birds to amphibians. Discover how you can wean from using these chemicals and care for your yard and garden, which are in fact part of a complex *food web* (the complex of interdependent creatures in the environment, large and small).

Even using synthetic fertilizers has undesirable impacts and deserves a fresh look, for reasons you may not suspect. Chapter 17 provides additional information and sensible alternatives.

Use Solar Lighting

Doing so is a no-brainer. Although you or a hired, licensed electrician can wire your landscape in order to illuminate it at night, for reasons both practical and aesthetic, solar lighting has come a long way in recent years and deserves your consideration; plus, no cords! The lights can be just as bright, the cost is reasonable, and installation is easy. Check out Chapter 10.

Conserve Water

Your home landscape can consume less water — from the plants you choose to the way you water. When talking water, you obviously want to avoid runoff, and you don't always have to use tap water.

TIP

You even may be able to reuse water. You can redirect so-called *gray water* (used water from your laundry, tub, shower, or any of your sinks) to garden plants.

A simple way to conserve is to install a rain barrel and use its contents as needed. Consult Chapter 5, which discusses this and other water issues and ideas in greater detail.

Match Plant Choices to Climate and Soil

The trouble and heartache you can avoid if you simply install plants that are appropriate to your site and region. You won't have to alter the soil, or pamper them and fret about them once they are in place, or to lose them to pests and diseases.

Many native plants (including horticulturally improved versions, such as ones that grow more compactly or bloom more generously than their wild counterparts) abound. Shop at native-plant nurseries for an eye-opening experience. Refer to Part 3 for more information about native plants.

Welcome/Tolerate Wildlife

If you have the impression or have come to believe that having an attractive landscape is a constant battle against wild creatures, relax. There can be enough for everyone, and — as a side benefit — your yard won't be a fortress or a dead zone.

We're not recommending outright surrender, but rather landscaping in ways that are compatible with the existing ecosystem. (We concede, you should consider fencing or getting a watchdog if you're contending with marauding deer or woodchucks.) Details are in Chapter 18.

Reduce or Eliminate Your Lawn

The great North American trophy lawn — bright green, lush, and constantly cut to a certain height — comes at a great cost to the environment. For most gardeners, lawns are high-maintenance resource sucks, to be blunt. You can steal space away from your lawn to put in more flowers or edible plants, you can put in a pretty patio, courtyard, or deck on the site for a former lawn, or you can consider lush-growing, weed-inhibiting groundcovers, all that are better for the environment and don't require the care that a lawn does. (Note that some communities and homeowner's associations require lawns, so if you decide to get rid of yours, make sure you have permission.)

You have many options when you decide to get off the lawn-care treadmill. Chapter 16 has lots of useful information and advice.

Use Tools That Don't Require Fossil Fuel

Consider using tools that don't require fossil fuels. The rewards are less air pollution *and* less noise pollution. For your lawn, use an old-fashioned, properly sharpened reel mower to mow your yard. Mowers, weed-whackers, chainsaws, and more such occasional-use tools also come in electric versions.

Stay Away from Sphagnum Moss

Many gardeners buy *sphagnum moss,* the product a result of thousands of years of organic processes, in large or small bales; and it's also a major ingredient in pre-mixed potting soil. We suggest you give it a pass the next time you see it in your lawn and garden store.

Sphagnum moss is traditionally harvested from sphagnum bogs in northern areas (the Canadian province of New Brunswick is a major source), and the harvesting process is a major enterprise. Taking the moss from the land destroys a habitat and impacts groundwater, air, and creatures large and small. It's also sobering to realize that these bogs don't renew quickly.

Suitable substitutes for garden-soil improvement include compost, leaf mold, *coconut coir* (a by-product of coconut processing that would otherwise be wasted), good old-fashioned composted manure, and more.

Appendix A
Landscaping Resources

Whether you're creating your own landscape or thinking of making a career out of landscaping for others, you can find a deep and rich vein of information to mine. Although you may be first inclined to dig around online and explore social media, that approach may also yield an overwhelming amount of information. That approach is similar to taking a drink from a firehose! In this appendix, we help you navigate through everything and bookmark our favorite resources to help you start. More than likely, you'll find them to be a bit of an eclectic mix — but, we hope, useful.

Reading for Ideas and Knowledge

We know this sounds old-school, but we believe that actually sitting down with printed matter and pondering (rather than scrolling on a screen) is an important part of the creative process of reckoning with and envisioning your landscape.

TIP

Visit a large, well-stocked, bricks-and-mortar bookstore or your public library. Browse the gardening, landscaping, design, nature, and home-improvement sections. Try also home-improvement stores and the curated book selections at some garden centers and the gift shops attached to botanic gardens and arboretums. In any case, treat yourself to (or check out) a few useful and inspirational books, bring them home, and sit down with them.

You may also benefit from thumbing through colorful magazines. Buy a single issue from a newsstand or bookstore, send away for a sample issue, visit their websites, and perhaps even commit to a subscription. A couple of good ones are

>> *Better Homes & Gardens* www.bhg.com

>> *Birds & Blooms* www.birdsandblooms.com

>> *Fine Gardening* www.finegardening.com

>> *Garden Design* www.gardendesign.com

>> *Southern Living* www.southernliving.com

>> *Sunset Magazine* www.sunset.com

>> *The English Garden* www.theenglishgarden.co.uk

Finding Specific Help

Focused searching online can direct you to local and regional landscape resources. You not only can find places to purchase specific materials (for example, search for "fieldstone," "privacy panels," "untreated mulch," "native trees and shrubs"). You can also navigate to qualified helpers in designing, installing, and planting.

TECHNICAL STUFF

We need to clarify between the professionals you may work with and consult when creating a landscape design. They are as follows:

>> **Landscape designers:** Also referred to as *garden designers,* these professionals are suited to smaller and residential planning and planting jobs.

>> **Landscape architects:** They go through a more intensive education (a bachelor's and/or master's degree) and licensing (by state; includes passing the Landscape Architect Registration Examination). This process qualifies them for bigger and commercial projects and/or ones that involve some engineering work (including significant hardscaping installations and major landscape renovations, upgrades, and makeovers).

>> **Landscape contractors:** They may be a third type of necessary helper. These folks do heavier physical work, such as excavating; installing a patio, deck, pergola, water feature, or irrigation system; and planting trees, hedges, and more.

Take a look at how these businesses or individuals market themselves, read reviews, and ask around to find recommendations you're inclined to trust. When you get close to hiring somebody, ask about insurance (liability and worker's compensation), check references, request estimates, and sign a contract agreement.

Check with the following professional groups before embarking on a landscape project, including getting a referral to one of their members near you:

» **Association of Professional Landscape Designers (APLD):** Website: www. apld.org. Use the "Find a Designer" function on the website to find a member near you.

» **American Society of Landscape Architects (ASLA):** Website: www.asla.org. They can connect you with a regional or state chapter where you can find a member to consult with or hire.

» **Canadian Nursery Landscape Association (CNLA):** Website: http://cnla. ca. The preeminent Canadian resource for accredited professionals and those who seek them; various provincial associations are also under their umbrella.

» **Ecological Landscape Alliance (ELA):** Website: www.ecolandscaping.org. Its membership is diverse, ranging from garden coaches, arborists, and ecologists to landscape designers and landscape architects. You can find more about an array of workshops, newsletters, conferences, and referrals.

» **National Association of Landscape Professionals (NALP):** Website: www. landscapeprofessionals.org. You can choose "Find a Member" on the main page's dropdown menu to locate ones near you.

Exploring Learning Opportunities

We urge you to branch out as you gather information and ideas like we discuss here. You and your landscape will always grow from this process. Remember the famous Thomas Jefferson quote, "Though I am an old man, I am but a young gardener."

Classes, lectures, presentations

You can find out a lot about landscaping and gardening by tapping into resources, some local and some online. They include the following:

» **Public gardens, botanical gardens, and arboretums:** You can sign up, pay for, and attend classes, presentations, and lecture series — entirely online.

Doing so brings the offerings of, say, Brooklyn Botanic Garden (New York), The Native Plant Trust (Massachusetts), Denver Botanic (Colorado), or the Huntington (California) in range no matter where you live. Other programs are in-person.

>> **Local public and private colleges and universities:** You may be surprised to find helpful, interesting continuing-education classes, workshops, or lectures that you can attend, either for free or for a reasonable fee.

For hands-on learning, look to a community college that offers trades instruction and can also direct students to area internships and job opportunities.

>> **YouTube:** If you're simply needing visual, narrated directions for something specific, instructional videos abound on YouTube. Quality certainly varies — watch several on your topic and choose wisely.

>> **Master Gardener Programs:** Typically offered through universities in the United States and Canada, offering intensive horticultural training to individuals. Once certified, Master Gardeners volunteer in their communities, offering events (presentations, plant sales, and more) and advice (creating gardens, participating in research, assisting new gardeners, and more).

>> **The Cooperative Extension Service:** A federal program (in partnership with the USDA) with offices in most counties, charged with "bridging the gap between a state's Land Grant University and its people by translating research into education and action." A great source for practical information, educational materials, and referrals.

Going to school for landscaping

You're having so much fun creating your own home landscape that you want to try it professionally. If so, you can start at the **Council of Educators in Landscape Architecture,** commonly referred to as CELA. Virtually every U.S. school with a landscape architecture program is a member and is linked from their site: www. thecela.org.

Alternatively, look for certificate and degree programs in landscape design. A simply online search will lead you to many good ones, which you can apply to and attend either online or in person (if near you).

Blogs, podcasts, websites

You can broaden your views and kick-start ideas with these diverse voices of experience. Visit, follow, subscribe, support, listen, and learn! Our favorites include the following:

» ***A Way to Garden:*** Hosted by Margaret Roach, it offers fascinating, insightful interviews with experts, seasoned advice, and much more. Website: `https://awaytogarden.com/`

» ***Cultivating Place: Conversations on Natural History & The Human Impulse to Garden:*** Hosted by Jennifer Jewell, it offers thoughtful interviews with leading innovators in gardening, horticulture, landscaping, and more. Website: `www.cultivatingplace.com`

» ***Dirt Simple:*** It's the long-running blog of Michigan landscape designer Deborah Silver. Practical and inspiring. Website: `https://deborahsilver.com/`

» ***Gardenista:*** It demystifies outdoor design. Website: `www.gardenista.com`

» ***Gardenzine:*** Chocked with information, advice, and great ideas. Yes, it's British, but North American gardeners will find loads to enjoy and use. Website: `https://gardenzine.co.uk/`

» ***Garden photographer and garden coach Karen Bussolini's blog offers garden news, musings, and insights.*** Website: `https://karenbussolini.com`

» ***The Herb Cottage Blog:*** Full of help, ideas, and tips. Website: `www.theherbcottage.com`

» ***Small Town Gardener:*** Mid-Atlantic garden writer Marianne Willburn's website and blog, full of variety, nifty ideas, solid advice, and plentiful photos. Website: `https://smalltowngardener.com`

» ***The Spruce:*** You wouldn't know it from the name (a coniferous tree), but this excellent website is dedicated to offering ideas and providing plenty of how-to's, including plants and landscaping. Website: `www.thespruce.com`

For general information and a wealth of resources, we suggest you check out and explore these two big, active websites:

» **American Horticultural Society:** They offer a magazine, webinars, education opportunities, and much more. Website: `https://ahsgardening.org`

» **American Community Gardening Association:** This online community links more than 2,000 gardens across the United States and Canada. Website: `www.communitygarden.org`

Viewing Other Gardens and Landscapes

When you want to see, smell, touch, and walk through a garden or landscape, get your walking shoes on and go. Check out our following suggestions.

Garden tours, near and far

Check out garden tours particularly in your own town, city, or region for ideas and plants most applicable to your own aspirations. Tours are also a great way to meet other gardeners and exchange information.

Another great resource is your local garden club. Their meetings, newsletters, websites, and social media can lead you to their garden tours, open houses, and plant sales/exchanges. Just search online, ask other local gardeners, or check with your favorite garden center or nursery.

You can also find garden tours offered by public gardens, botanical gardens, and arboretums. When traveling, make time to visit such places on your own.

Guided tours are also an inspiring experience. You can take a curated tour of English countryside gardens or visit the private gardens of California's wine country. Browse specialized travel companies such as the following:

>> www.brightwaterholidays.com

>> www.holbrooktravel.com

>> www.sisley.co.uk

Flower and garden shows

For what will feel like an intense one-day garden tour, attend one of the big open-to-the-public landscape or flower-and-garden shows. They're often held in the spring, in big spaces (convention centers) in major cities, such as Boston, Philadelphia, and Seattle (in the U.S.) and Toronto (Canada).

TIP

When you go, take pictures, jot down notes, and grab brochures so you can study and be inspired at home. Resist impulse-buying overpriced plants and garden décor!

GARDENING INFORMATION FROM THE AUTHORS

The National Gardening Association is the largest association of gardeners in the world and is coauthor of this book. Their website — https://garden.org — includes searchable articles, active discussion forums, and a large database of plants. Anyone can ask any kind of gardening question and get an answer fast, usually within a few hours.

Appendix B
English-Metric Conversion Tables

All the measurements in this book are in English measures and weights, and we realize that much of the world's gardeners use the metric system so we include this conversion to help you convert the most common weights and measures that you'll encounter in the garden. Many field guides to plants, insects, and other creatures use the metric system, as do scientific references. Most U.S. seed and nursery websites and catalogs use inches.

ENGLISH TO METRIC	METRIC TO ENGLISH

LENGTH (APPROXIMATE)

ENGLISH TO METRIC	METRIC TO ENGLISH
1 inch (in) = 2.5 centimeters (cm)	1 millimeter (mm) = 0.04 inch (in)
1 foot (ft) = 30 centimeters (cm)	1 centimeter (cm) = 0.4 inch (in)
1 yard (yd) = 0.9 meter (m)	1 meter (m) = 3.3 feet (ft)
1 mile (mi) = 1.6 kilometers (km)	1 meter (m) = 1.1 yards (yd)
	1 kilometer (km) = 0.6 mile (mi)

AREA (APPROXIMATE)

ENGLISH TO METRIC	METRIC TO ENGLISH
1 square inch (sq in, in^2) = 6.5 square centimeters (cm^2)	1 square centimeter (cm^2) = 0.16 square inch (sq in, in^2)
1 square foot (sq ft, ft^2) = 0.09 square meter (m^2)	1 square meter (m^2) = 1.2 square yards (sq yd, yd^2)
1 square yard (sq yd, yd^2) = 0.8 square meter (m^2)	1 square kilometer (km^2) = 0.4 square mile (sq mi, mi^2)
1 square mile (sq mi, mi^2) = 2.6 square kilometers (km^2)	10,000 square meters (m^2) = 1 hectare (ha) = 2.5 acres
1 acre = 0.4 hectare (he) = 4,000 square meters (m^2)	

MASS - WEIGHT (APPROXIMATE)

ENGLISH TO METRIC	METRIC TO ENGLISH
1 ounce (oz) = 28 grams (gm)	1 gram (gm) = 0.036 ounce (oz)
1 pound (lb) = 0.45 kilogram (kg)	1 kilogram (kg) = 2.2 pounds (lb)
1 short ton = 2,000 pounds (lb) = 0.9 tonne (t)	1 tonne (t) = 1,000 kilograms (kg)
	= 1.1 short tons

VOLUME (APPROXIMATE)

ENGLISH TO METRIC	METRIC TO ENGLISH
1 teaspoon (tsp) = 5 milliliters (ml)	1 milliliter (ml) = 0.03 fluid ounce (fl oz)
1 tablespoon (tbsp) = 15 milliliters (ml)	1 liter (l) = 2.1 pints (pt)
1 fluid ounce (fl oz) = 30 milliliters (ml)	1 liter (l) = 1.06 quarts (qt)
1 cup (c) = 0.24 liter (l)	1 liter (l) = 0.26 gallon (gal)
1 pint (pt) = 0.47 liter (l)	
1 quart (qt) = 0.96 liter (l)	
1 gallon (gal) = 3.8 liters (l)	
1 cubic foot (cu ft, ft^3) = 0.03 cubic meter (m^3)	1 cubic meter (m^3) = 36 cubic feet (cu ft, ft^3)
1 cubic yard (cu yd, yd^3) = 0.76 cubic meter (m^3)	1 cubic meter (m^3) = 1.3 cubic yards (cu yd, yd^3)

TEMPERATURE (EXACT)

ENGLISH TO METRIC	METRIC TO ENGLISH
$[(x-32)(5/9)]$ °F = y °C	$[(9/5)y + 32]$ °C = x °F

Index

bedding plants, 226
bee balm, 326
bees, 321, 352
bellflower (*Campanula*), 243, 355, 359
benches, 162–165
bender boards, 114
beneficial insects, 321–322
bergenia (*Bergenia*), 359
Bermuda grass (*Cynodon dactylon*), 288
Better Homes & Gardens, 11, 392
bindweed (*Convolvulus arvensis*), 224
bins, storage, 16
birds, 365
Birds & Blooms, 11, 392
bishop's goutweed (*Aegopodium podagraria*), 278
bittersweet (*Celastrus orbiculatus*), 224
black locust, 326
black walnut (*Juglans nigra*), 194
black-eyed Susan (*Rudbeckia*), 243, 371
black-eyed Susan vine (*Thunbergia alata*), 221
Blackhaw viburnum (*Viburnum prunifolium*), 357
blanketflower (*Gaillardia grandiflora*), 243, 372
bleeding heart (*Dicentra*), 359
blogs, 394–395
blood meal, 323
blue, 28
blue chalksticks (*Senecio serpens*), 261
blue fescue (*Festuca ovina* var. *glauca*), 277
blue grama grass (*Bouteloua gracilis*), 288
blue oat grass (*Helictotrichon sempervirens*), 248
blue star creeper (*Isotoma fluviatilis*), 281
blueberry (*Vaccinium*), 214

boards, decking, 138–139
bog rosemary (*Andromeda polifolia* 'Nana'), 354
boltonia (*Boltonia asteroides*), 246
bonemeal, 258
borders, 149, 240–241, 293–294
botanical gardens, 10, 393–394
bougainvillea (*Bougainvillea*), 220
boxwood (*Buxus*), 204, 326, 357
Bradford pear (*Pyrus calleryana*), 194
brick ties, 106
bricks
    benches, 165
    borders, 294
    combining with concrete, 49
    outdoor ovens, 169
    paths with, 114–116
    patio surfaces, 148, 151–154
    planters, 166
    walls, 104–107
broadleaf evergreens, 182, 193
Brooklyn Botanic Garden, 394
broomed finishes, 147, 157
brunnera (*Brunnera*), 359
bubbler attachments, 83
buffalo grass (*Bouteloua dactyloides*), 288
bulbs, 250–258
    buying, 255
    digging and storing, 257
    examples of, 252–254
    fertilizing, 258overview, 250–251
    planting, 256–257
    for shade, 360
bunchberry (*Cornus canadensis*), 281, 360
Bussolini, Karen, 395
butterflies, 365
butterfly weed (*Asclepias tuberosa*), 372
buttering, 106

C

caladium (*Caladium*), 231, 252, 360
calculators, 47, 80, 149, 175
California buckeye (*Aesculus californica*), 357
California lilac (*Ceanothus*), 213, 351
California poppy (*Eschscholzia californica*), 227, 351, 372
calla lily (*Zantedeschia*), 252, 360
camellias (*Camellia*), 204–205, 357
camphor (*Cinnamomum camphora*), 193
Canadian Nursery Landscape Association (CNLA), 393
candytuft (*Iberis sempervirens*), 242, 355
canna (*Canna*), 255
canopies, 175
cape plumbago (*Plumbago auriculata*), 351
carpenter's levels, 63
carpet bugle (*Ajuga reptans*), 278, 360
carpet grass (*Axonopus*), 289
cascades, 178
catmint (*Nepeta*), 243, 351
cedar (*Cedrus*), 213
CELA (Council of Educators in Landscape Architecture), 394
centipede grass (*Eremochloa ophiuroides*), 289
chalkline, 41, 62
chameleon plant (*Houttuynia cordata*), 281
chamomile (*Chamaemelum nobile*), 282
cheat sheet, 4
chemical fertilizers, 311
children
    gardens for, 366–367
    safety, 13–14

creeping thyme (*Thymus praecox arcticus*), 282, 355

crested iris (*Iris cristata*), 359, 360

crested wheat grass (*Agropyron cristatum*), 288

crocus (*Crocus*), 360

crushed stone paths, 113–114

crusher run stone, 113

cultivars, 185, 203, 246

Cultivating Place podcast, 395

Cupressina (*Picea abies*), 194

curing, 257

cypress (*Chamaecyparis*), 213

D

daffodil (*Narcissus*), 252, 326, 360

dahlia (*Dahlia*), 252–253

dangled shade, 356

Dave's Garden, 249

daylily (*Hemerocallis*), 244

dead nettle (*Lamium*), 359

deadheading, 237, 253

deadmen, 70, 71

debris, 60

deciduous plants, 184–185
  hedges, 217–218
  for screening, 182, 349

decking boards, 128, 130

decks, 127–144
  components of, 128–129
  finishing, 143–144
  footings and piers, 134–136
  joists, 137–138
  laying decking boards, 138–139
  ledger board, 132–134
  materials, 131
  planning and preparation, 129–131
  posts and beams, 136

railings, 141–143
  stairs, 139–141

decorative lighting, 172–173

deer, 326–328
  anti-deer products, 327
  fencing out, 327–328
  home remedies, 326–327
  plants to deter, 326

Degroot's Spire (*Thuja occidentalis*), 194

Denver Botanic, 394

design, 7–24, 25–34, 35–54
  achieving unity, 26
  adding décor, 30–31
  base map, 36–38
  color, 28–29
  creating final plan, 43–44
  decks, 130–131
  details, 32
  Goldilocks Theory, 32–33
  hardscape, 31
  layering, 33–34
  low-maintenance landscape, 24
  paths and walkways, 112
  with practical issues, 12–16
  preparation, 50–52
  professional help, 52–54
  repetition in, 27
  rhythm with, 29–30
  shopping list, 44–50
  site analysis, 16–23
  test-driving, 41–43
  wish list, 8–12

details, 32

dianthus (*Dianthus*), 244, 359

digging
  bulbs, 257
  double-digging, 304
  surface growth, 274–275
  tools for, 62

utilities and, 51
  weeds and, 328–329

dimensions
  calculating step, 121
  paths, 112
  ramps, 124–125

Dirt Simple blog, 395

diseases, 184, 331–332

divisions, 253, 318

dogwood (*Cornus florida*), 188, 190, 214, 357

dosage, fertilizer, 313

double-digging, 304

drainage, 58, 75–80
  holes in planters, 166
  installing subsurface drainage, 77–78
  rain gardens, 78–80
  site analysis, 18
  surface drainage, 76–77

drawing
  base map, 36–38
  site analysis, 17–19

drought, winter, 338–339

drought-tolerant shrubs, 212–213

dry wells, 77

duplex nails, 94

dusty miller (*Centaurea cineraria*), 232

dwarf Albert spruce (*Picea glauca*), 354

dwarf arborvitae (*Thuja occidentalis*), 354

dwarf conifers, 191

dwarf Coreopsis (*Coreopsis auriculata* 'Nana'), 355

dwarf heath (*Erica*), 354

dwarf hemlock (*Tsuga canadensis*), 354

dwarf hinoki cypress (*Chamaecyparis obtusa*), 354

dwarf iris (*Iris reticulata*), 355

maps
  base map, 36–40
  tax maps, 13
  zone maps, 333–334
marigold (*Tagetes*), 230, 326
masonry benches, 165
masonry planters, 166
Master Gardeners, 11, 54, 394
meadow gardens, 370–371
measurements
  for base map, 37–38
  converting, 397–398
  fence height guidelines, 88
  for planting bulbs, 259
metal
  edging, 299
  fences, 90–91
metric system, 397–398
microclimates, 19
micro-irrigation,
  aboveground, 84
microsprinklers, 84
million bells (*Callibrachoa*), 230
mimosa (*Albizia julibrissin*), 195
Mini-Dragon, 331
mint, 326
misters, 84
miter joints, 162
moderate weathering (MW)
  bricks, 148
mondo grass (*Ophiopogon*), 283,
  284, 360
moneywort (*Lysimachia
  nummularia*), 281
monuments, 12
morning glory (*Ipomoea*), 174,
  221–222
Morpholio Trace app, 40–41
mortar, 49, 105
mortared stone walls, 103–104
mortises, 94
moss, sphagnum, 389
motion-sensing lights, 170

mountain laurel (*Kalmia latifolia*),
  207, 357
mugho pine (*Pinus mugo*), 354
mulberry (*Morus alba*), 195
mulch, 49, 275–276, 329
multipurpose landscaping, 23
mum (*Chrysanthemum* and
  Dendranthema), 246
MW (moderate weathering)
  bricks, 148
myrtle spurge (*Euphorbia rigida*),
  261–262

N

nasturtium (*Tropaeolum majus*),
  228, 358
National Association of
  Landscape Professionals
  (NALP), 393
National Gardening
  Association, 396
Native Plant Trust, The, 394
native plants
  exploring, 381
  perennials, 247
  shrubs, 201–203
  trees, 185
natural fencing, 91
natural pest control, 320–323
  beneficial insects, 321–322
  identifying pests, 321
  options of, 322–323
  pesticides, 320–321
natural settling, 58
naturalizers, 254
Nature's Best Hope (Tallamy), 201
neem, 322–323
neighborhood, 10, 89
neighbors, 20–21, 381–382
neonicotinoids, 321
nesting, 264
New Guinea impatiens
  (*Impatiens hawkeri*), 230

New Zealand tea tree
  (*Leptospermum*), 351
ninebark (*Physocarpus
  opulifolius*), 207–208, 212
nitrogen, 310, 343, 344
no weathering (NW) bricks, 148
noise, 18
nondurable woods, 61
Norway maple (*Acer
  platanoides*), 195
nosings, 121, 139
no-till gardening, 305
nurseries, 9–10, 184
nut trees, 183
nutrients, fertilizer, 310
NW (no weathering) bricks, 148

O

oak (*Quercus*), 187, 193, 350
offsetting, 66
oleander (*Nerium oleander*),
  208, 351
olive (*Olea europaea*), 350
online references
  Accessible Gardens, 11
  blogs and podcasts, 394–395
  bug identification, 321
  calculators, 47, 80, 149
  cheat sheet for this book, 4
  Council of Educators in
    Landscape Architecture
    (CELA), 394
  Dave's Garden, 249
  Heat-Zone Map, 335
  magazines, 392
  National Gardening
    Association, 396
  professional groups, 393
  software programs, 41
orange, 28
Oregon grape holly
  (*Mahonia*), 357
organic fertilizers, 311–312

sweet alyssum (*Lobularia maritima*), 228, 358

sweet autumn clematis (*Clematis terniflora*), 224

sweet peas (*Lathyrus odoratus*), 222, 228

sweet pepperbush (*Clethra alnifolia*), 210

sweet potato vine (*Ipomoea batatus*), 232

sweet woodruff (*Galium odoratum*), 279, 361

sweetfern (*Comptonia peregrina*), 210

sweetshrub (*Calycanthus floridus*), 211

synthetic fertilizers, 311

syrphid flies, 322

T

tacks, 66–67

tall fescue (*Festuca arundinaceae*), 288

tamping machine, 70

tapestry hedge, 217

tax maps, 13

temperature
  converting, 398
  low temperature injury, 338

terra cotta containers, 263–264

terracing, 69

test-driving, 41–43
  filling in remaining items, 42–43
  large elements, 42

testing soil, 302

texture, 146

thatch, 291

theme gardens, 363–375
  attracting and nurturing wild creatures, 364–366
  cottage gardens, 372–373
  evening gardens, 374–375
  herb gardens, 369–370

for kids, 366–367
  kitchen gardens, 367–368
  meadow gardens, 370–371
  retreat gardens, 373–374

thornless honey locust (*Gleditsia triacanthos f. inermis*), 187–188

thorny plants, 14

thrift (*Armeria*), 355

thrillers, 271–272

timber retaining wall, 72–74

timing, fertilizer, 313

toad lily (*Tricyrtis*), 359

tobira (*Pittosporum tobira*), 211, 212

toenailing, 98, 137

tools
  construction, 62–63
  not requiring fossil fuels, 388
  shopping list, 48
  storing, 15–16

top-dressing, 306

topsoil, 299

torenia (*Torenia*), 359

torque, 94

Torx drive screws, 71

total rise, 121

tours, 396

toyon (*Heteromeles arbutifolia*), 213, 351

training vines, 223

transplanting seedlings, 233–236

tread, 121

tree of heaven (*Ailanthus altissima*), 195

trees, 181–198
  to avoid, 194–195
  evergreen trees, 193–194
  finding healthy trees, 184
  flowering trees, 188–190
  fruit trees, 192–193

green landscaping and, 385–386
  for low-water gardens, 349–350
  native trees, 185
  overview, 182–183
  planting, 197–198
  for rock gardens, 354
  for shade, 186–188, 357
  shopping for, 196–197
  for small spaces, 190–191

trellises, 173–174

Trex, 61, 90

trout lily (*Erythronium americanum*), 359

trumpet creeper (*Campsis radicans*), 221

tubing, 84

tulip (*Tulipa*), 254

tupelo (*Nyssa sylvatica*), 188

turfgrasses, 287

U

undersides, deck, 143–144

understory trees, 357

unity, 26, 200–201

unstable soils, 58

uplighting, 170

utilities, 51

V

valve box, 86

valves, 84

Vegetable Gardening For Dummies (Nardozzi), 323

vegetables, 240. *See also* foodscaping

verbena (*Verbena hybrida*), 231

viburnum (*Viburnum*), 211, 212, 214, 349, 358

views, 18, 19

vignettes, 262–263

About the Authors

Teri Dunn Chace is an author, editor, and speaker on horticulture, gardening, and natural history. Among her nearly 40 titles are *Seeing Flowers: Discover the Hidden Life of Flowers* and *Seeing Seeds: A Journey into the World of Seedheads, Pods, and Fruit* (the latter won a prestigious American Horticultural Society Book of the Year award), *How to Eradicate Invasive Plants, The Anxious Gardener's Book of Answers, Beautiful Roses Made Easy, Water Gardening,* and *Potting Places.* She's also written and edited for major consumer gardening/outdoor-living publications (*Horticulture, North American Gardener, Backyard Living,* and *Birds and Blooms*) and is presently the garden-and-nature columnist for the award-winning "Bottom Line Personal" newsletter.

Raised in Santa Barbara, California and educated at Bard College in New York, she currently resides in a small village in the heart of central New York's farm country; she and her husband also have a second home on a small island off the southwest coast of Nova Scotia. The most intriguing job she's ever held? Monitoring rare turtles for The Nature Conservancy. Or. . . raising teenage boys. More information at www.terichacewriter.com.

Philip Giroux is a second-generation Californian who developed his desire for planting and his love of gardens watching his father, an avid gardener, and graduated from the University of Arizona with a degree in landscape architecture and ornamental horticulture. He established his landscape designing and building firm in 1978, specializing in custom residential installations, including the estates of Rupert Murdock and Henry Mudd. Philip is responsible for numerous large-scale commercial projects, such as the Los Angeles County Museum of Arts Sculpture and Japanese Pavilion Garden. His garden column in the *Manhattan Beach Reporter* is both a practical guide for weekend gardeners and a garden travelogue from such faraway places as Japan, France, England, Canada, and Israel. Philip has served as L.A. chapter president for the California Landscape Contractors Association and is a member of the Royal Horticulture Society.

Bob Beckstrom is a licensed general contractor, living in northern California. He enjoys building things, spending time outdoors, and sharing what he's learned with other people. His first building experience was as a VISTA volunteer in 1968, as the coordinator of a self-help housing project in rural Alaska. He taught elementary school for ten years; has taught adult courses in house building and remodeling at The Owner Builder Center in Berkeley, California; and has written and edited extensively on home-improvement topics.

Lance Walheim has been gardening most of his life. He started when his father forced him to turn the soil and plant tomatoes in the family vegetable garden as punishment for a deed he can't recall. Funny thing was, he found that he enjoyed working in the soil and has been doing it ever since. In 1975, he graduated from the University of California, Berkeley, with a degree in botany. Shortly after, he started writing and researching books on gardening and since has written or contributed to more than 40 gardening books on subject ranging from citrus to roses. He has also written extensively about lawns and lawn care. He also has served as a writer for *Sunset* and *National Gardening* magazines and is part owner of California Citrus Specialties, marketers of specialty citrus fruit. But his true loves are family and gardening, the "composts" that enrich his heart and soul.

Dedication

Teri Dunn Chace dedicates this book to the memory of keen gardener and dear friend Harry "Heru" Hall.

Author's Acknowledgements

For their expert help and advice, **Teri Dunn Chace** would especially like to thank Barbara Hall Popolow of Yard and a Half Landscape Design and William Lucas, seasoned contractor and trades instructor. Additional thanks to land surveyor and chief cheerleader Alan Chace; carpentry and masonry expert Ricardo Rosero; deck-builder extraordinaire Jaime Pohleven; and Susie Nacco of Sirius Landscapes, Inc. Also thanks to Andy Moir and the FCDA for printing and deliveries.

Also grateful thanks to Chad Sievers and Steve Frowine for their expertise and encouragement. Inspiration was an indirect but important factor in the work on this book, so a bow goes out to the following folks: Doug Tallamy, Roger B. Swain, Duron Chavis, Virginia Johnson, Robin Wall Kimmerer, Frédérique Lavoipierre, Jayne Ritz, Amy Ray, and Rhiannon Giddens. Last but not least, apologies to Kagan, our red golden; while Mom typed, typed, typed, he waited patiently to go out for walks.

Publisher's Acknowledgments

Acquisitions Editor: Kelsey Baird

Project Editor: Chad R. Sievers

Technical Editors: Steven A. Frowine and Kim Benton

Production Editor: Mohammed Zafar Ali

Cover Image: © Jacky Parker Photography/ Getty Images